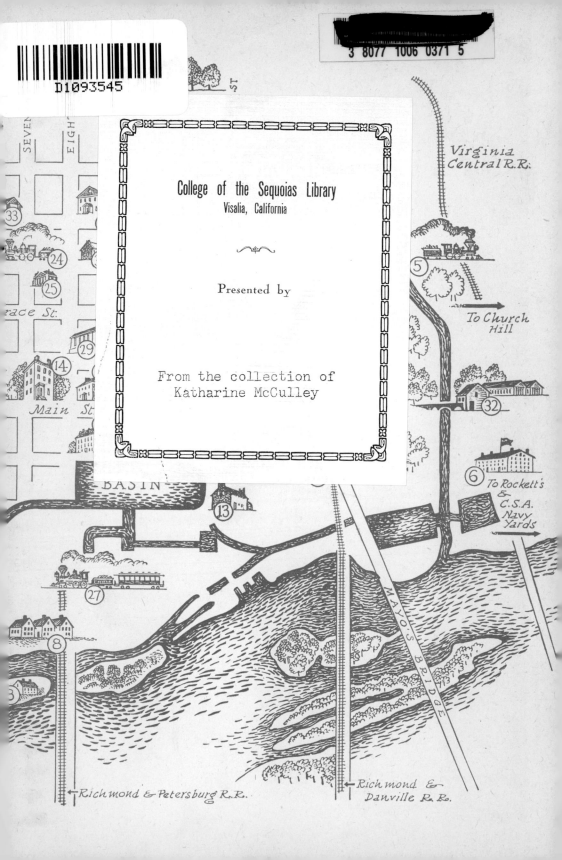

EXPERIMENT IN REBELLION

EXPERIMENT IN REBELLION

BY

Clifford Dowdey

DOUBLEDAY & COMPANY, INC.

Garden City, New York

1946

For Frances

Contents

CONTENTS

[viii]

Illustrations

The Nature of the Experiment

YOU SEE them in the fixed poses of statues, always of that age, that rank, the action of that hour, and from the perspective of today's convictions. The heroes, lending themselves to America's pageantried interpretation of its past, assumed the pose of their historic moment. They were deeply aware of posterity. "As history shall judge us" runs like a refrain through their letters. Though there was inevitable rhetoric and posturing, most men were only acting as their own Shakespeares in recording the convictions by which they wished to be known.

In their country's hour of division, in 1861, the framework of the nation had not been built in its final form. Molds had not yet hardened, and men were caught in the flux and pressure of movements which demanded decision then and there, once and for all. Many were not ready. They were not sure, the alternatives were too drastic, perhaps there could be some temporizing. After all, the choice involved tremendous personal consequences—fortune, life, and, what was dearer to some, honor. Only, in the crisis, each could not always be certain which was the honorable course.

These men who played at being giants would not wish it known that decisions were caused by fright or anger, by chance or self-interest or inability to get off a limb. They rationalized in assuming the pose, for better or worse, in which you find them.

Their poses form the characters in the morality plays which pass, loosely among the populace, for America's history. In this way they fulfill the American desire for simplification. We need not study the elements of which evolutionary conflicts are compounded. An episode (black and white) need not be interrelated in the totality of events. The heroes serve as symbols. Liberty. Democracy. Freedom.

You see Lincoln the Great Emancipator—the demigod and not the troubled man trying to compromise, reassuring the Southerners in his inaugural, "I have no intention of interfering with slavery where it now exists . . . nor believe I have any right to do so."

You see Lee the Rebel—the demigod of the defeated and not a tortured man choosing between the country, whose armies he had served for nearly forty years, and his own people in a cause for which he had no heart.

You see Farragut, opening the Mississippi at Vicksburg (as at Mobile, "Damn the torpedoes; full speed ahead"); you do not see the Tennessee boy going to New Orleans to join the Navy, and then choosing that service against his own people. You see Pemberton, Defender of Vicksburg, stiff and soldierly in the statue on the hill overlooking the Mississippi; you do not see the Philadelphia boy going to West Point, and then leaving the Army to follow his sympathies with the South—only to be disclaimed by the South as the Yankee who surrendered, and disowned by his family for joining the Confederate Army.

You see George Thomas, forever grimly immovable as the "Rock of Chickamauga," saving the Union Army; not as the young Virginian who in his moment of tragic decision was counseled by a brother officer, Fitzjohn Porter—himself later court-martialed for alleged failure in action in Thomas's state. In the battles outside Richmond, Jeb Stuart was not the singing Cavalier, but a 29-year-old husband fighting his father-in-law, another Virginian, who led a cavalry charge in the assault on the city where his daughter lived.

Winfield Scott, the first commander in chief of the Union armies, was a Virginian regarded as a Benedict Arnold in Richmond, where he had been a social favorite; and Farragut's executive officer, an Ashley of the leading secessionist state of South Carolina, fought his own kin.

Within the Confederacy, the adjutant general was from the Hudson River country; the ordnance genius, Gorgas, was a Pennsylvanian; three of their four best representatives abroad were an ex-New Yorker, a Connecticut Yankee, and a Swiss, and practically every nationality of Europe was represented in their armies.

You see the individual element most dramatically in border states, like Kentucky, where brother literally fought brother and father fought son. But even in South Carolina, during the struggle for Port Royal, the opposing commanders were brothers fighting for the island on which stood the home where they had been raised.

These lives refuse to fit the group symbols in the historical pageant with which America dramatizes its tradition of making the world safe for generalities.

They interpose a doubt in the comfortable concept of one political entity solidly committed to a conscious and articulated ideal which another entity is solidly and consciously committed to oppose.

The group pose of the South was represented by the plantation master. Though this class was dominant, no more reason exists for suspecting every Southerner to be a slaveholding planter than for suspecting every American, during the period of corporation dominance, of being a Morgan partner—or every Northerner of marching in a crusading phalanx singing, "We are coming, Father Abraham."

The rise of what was to become the dominant group in America was obviously effected by a merger of ill-assorted interests, composing the Republican party, with Lincoln as a safe-and-sane compromise candidate. When the political party of these new industrial-financial powers gained national control, the politicians of the dominant Southern power seceded from (what was to them) a compact, in preference to continuing as a subservient minority. In their formation of a separate political entity the palpable interests only *appeared* less assorted. The static South more completely subscribed to its dominant system (plantation) whether or not the individual was bound to it economically. They also carefully chose a compromise candidate in Jefferson Davis.

Nevertheless the division in the nation made strange bedfellows in the South as well as in the North. Economically Virginia shared more in common with New York than, say with Mississippi, and Ohio more with Mississippi than with New York. The independent farmers of the West aligned with Eastern capital, and the independent farmers of the South aligned with slave capital. Actually the dispossessed of the country aligned with the privileged of each section in the power fight between Northern Hamiltonian capitalism and Southern Jeffersonian landownership.

The difference was that the financial powers, controlling destinies by wages, shouted "democracy," while the planter class, owning their workers outright, came out flatly for caste. Virginia's John Randolph said it. "I'm an aristocrat; I love liberty; I hate equality." The aristocrats fought two wars for that belief, one for liberty and one for inequality—not of the white man over the black, but of their ruling class over the North's.

The European peasant migrating to America had as his natural ally the poor farmer everywhere. They all shared the same toil and insecurity and underprivilege. But the Northern mills needed him, and he was soothed there with the concept of "the land of the free." The big plantations did not need him and made no concessions to concepts.

King Carter of Virginia, when the Protestants came with religion for his people, said, "Damn their souls, let them plant tobacco."

He was not less democratic than an industrialist; in his system he could afford to be more honest. Every Northern mill town had (and does today) its version of "slave quarters" and its big houses on the hill. However, the political system of the North provided a technical opportunity for the emergence of *individuals* from the fluid exploited group, largely immigrants, though not for *class* emergence. The political system of the South did not provide this for its static exploited group, the Negro, and the ante-bellum rulers displayed the same unified resistance to change affecting *caste* as their Northern counterparts to change affecting class.

In this resistance the real plantocracy, less than one twentieth of one per cent of the population, achieved sectional unity because the Southern whites did not function as an exploited class. Poor they might be and without privilege, but they belonged finally to the ruling caste and, hence, existed without class consciousness as a motivating factor. Born in the self-sufficiency of a frontier-agricultural life, knowing the kinship of a homogeneous people and stable neighborhoods, their own pride was enhanced by the community glory of the plantation master. Fief to no man, they could express the sectional hedonism in their highly personal world as well as the lord in his.

The soil was rich for money crops, such as cotton and tobacco, easy for garden crops and staples and stock. Summers were long and winters mild. Outdoor life was pleasant and cheap and provided lazily obtained sustenance. The farmer with a few shells for his shotgun and one hound dawg enjoyed sport equally (and more profitably) with the Master of Hounds leading his pink-coated horsemen on the formalized chase of the fox. He chased his rabbit and ate him too. Fish were in the streams for everybody.

A gregarious people, their love of social groups was satisfied without regard to pocketbooks. Churchgoing and camp meeting and political barbecues cost only what one had—if nothing. One deck of cards would serve a lot of players and one bottle of busthead would go a long way. You could dance all night with one fiddler, and a corn pone with a little chitling would serve as a midnight supper as well as caviar —to which, in any case, they preferred the roe of their own freely caught shad.

This way of life developed a civilization based primarily upon the field rather than the study. The self-expression of these people naturally became oratory. The orator's role became dramatist and actor. He held up to the people their romanticized self-image, caused each man to feel that he was a hell of a fellow, and united their emotions by primitive place appeals. When these orators became spokesmen for the ruling planter class, it was easy to direct the group emotions toward a common love of region against aliens.

2

For one hundred years an economic-psychological division had been growing between the North and the South. Just as earlier the frontier molded British settlers into the new ethnographical group of Americans, so divergent geography continued the process in the hot and cold regions, with all of the methods of money-making and money-spending and the resultant *mores* implied by hot and cold. The progressive North was like a cocoon, always becoming and never being, while the archaic South was like a butterfly, bright and gay and complete in that moment.

Its physical contentment produced its easygoing economic system. Fat with raw material, the natives squandered it mostly on cash crops with inefficient and wasteful labor, while the United States—with all its industry—perfected an intelligent agricultural pattern. It formed a part of the whole balanced economy. But the South, possessing an adequate agricultural potential despite its cash-crop concentration, failed to develop it.

Also, even with its agrarianism, its philosophic opposition to manufacture, its lack of fluid capital and skilled labor, industrial needs had been met in spots, such as Richmond; Pratt in Alabama and Gregg in South Carolina had made real advances in textiles; and half a dozen Southern states mined about one tenth of the coal in the country. But agriculture and industry were not employed with relation to the total requirements because the South, in thrall to the planter ideal, lacked adaptiveness and resourcefulness.

While the North was practical and dynamic, the South was personal and self-indulgent. The people just did not like indoor work in plants and factories. The figures tell you: while 1 of 8 people in New England worked in manufacturing, 1 of 15 in the Middle States, in the South there was 1 of 82. There were 110,000 industrial workers in the South, compared with 1,300,000 in the North; 18,000 manufacturing establishments in the South to 110,000 in the North—the North had as many establishments as the South had workers.

The South manufactured only 2 per cent of the country's wool, 6 per cent of boots and shoes; 27,000 tons of pig iron was smelted (mainly in Tennessee and Virginia) to 850,000 in the North; 24,000 tons of bar and rolled iron (chiefly in Richmond) to 382,000 in the North. Despite the large flour manufacturing in Richmond, the South had only about one seventh of the nation's. Only in tobacco manufacturing did it stand up, where Virginia alone produced half of the nation's.

However, with all the indifference to manufacturing, the South grew less corn per inhabitant than the Western states, much less wheat and Irish potatoes. It was ahead only on sweet potatoes, hogs, and cattle—but as much of the cattle were west of the Mississippi, the use of them only gave the Confederate commissary another problem, which it was not destined to solve.

Nor was lack of supremacy in its chosen field explained entirely by the system of slave labor. There were more slaveless farms than slave-operated, and the preponderance of farms that used slaves were not truly in the slave-labor plantation system. Slave labor was wasteful almost everywhere; the land was worn out and so were the methods; but chiefly it was a lack of dynamism in the people.

The competitive drive simply turned flaccid by the end of a Southern summer, and when the long open fall came it called to the outdoors and pleasure, not to the office and factory. This culture produced a relative indifference to cash, which is one reason why the people allowed their economic system to suffer from the high tariff walls protective to Northern industry. That deal was made by their leaders in Washington, in exchange for protection of the slave system.

But the new Republican party coming into Washington possessed a power that did not need to make deals with the Southern leaders. Here again the simple hedonists of the South followed their leaders. These spokesmen for the plantocracy convinced their people that the old sociological division between the sections must become political. In urging this ultimate break they found ample constitutional sanction.

New England had started it at the Hartford Secession Convention, when it disapproved of the War of 1812. State sovereignty had been stressed at the Connecticut ratification convention and in the New York convention by Hamilton. Later, in 1839, John Quincy Adams said that when "the magnetism of conciliated interests and kindly sympathies" is gone, it is better for "the disunited states to part in friendship" and, as in the first formation of the Union, "to leave the separated parts to be reunited by the laws of political gravitation to the center."

Jefferson had come out unequivocally against the assumption of undelegated power by the government, and said "this government . . . was not made the exclusive or final judge of the powers delegated to itself; since that would have made *its* discretion, and *not the Constitution,* the measure of its powers."

Following this line, the Southerners claimed that Lincoln was the government, not the Constitution, and Virginia's Hunter said, "we are sworn to support, not the Union, but the Constitution."

Only two years before, in 1859, Wisconsin actively asserted the right of the state to judge the government's administering of the Constitution. This was over the Fugitive Slave Laws, which the state wished not to enforce, and this stand was applauded by Ohio's Ben Wade, who said that other states "will fall into the wake of noble Wisconsin."

Clearly then interpretations of the Constitution depended on whose toe the shoe was pinching. If the South's version, in supporting what they wanted to do, was like Henry VIII's legalizing divorce, Northern states did the same thing.

As the position of the Southern leaders was postulated on an anachronistic institution—slavery—they had grown adept at abstract logic and at maintaining the *status quo* in all phases of the region's life. The *status quo* was more simply maintained among a homogeneous people with less than negligible influx, with naturally perpetuated customs, and with a passionate, personal, and immediate love of and identification with their own place—their state.

When the political leaders wished to arouse this state consciousness against outside hostility, they used first the Northerner's differences— his acquisitiveness, his urge to get on in the world, to make money, all depending on a certain shrewdness which the Southerner distrusted. He was closemouthed, harsh-voiced, bad-mannered (to the Southerner), a thoroughly unpleasant character out to do his fellows.

With this premise it was easy to use actions of certain Northerners to convince the provincial Southerner that *he* was the one the Yankee was out to do. Though the abolitionist carried negligible influence in the North, he provided a handy symbol for Yankee methods.

As of their day, slavery was a law, and stealing slaves was stealing the one property of a man on which his livelihood depended. Like the horse thief in the West, a man who would steal slaves was regarded as being capable of anything. To prove this assumption, abolitionists exhorted slaves to kill their masters, causing even the more thoughtful Southerner to believe (as about some utterances today) that the Northerner was less sympathetic to the Negro than hostile to the whites. Two years after David Walker, a freed Negro in Boston, published a pam-

[xvii]

phlet urging slaves to murder, Nat Turner in Virginia led such a rebellion against the whites. This was followed by a deluge of incendiary literature from the North urging the Negro to further insurrection.

A Southern white did not have to be a slaveholder to resent an outsider, in the safety of New England, inciting black men to kill him. All this was topped by the apotheosis of John Brown. For all the marching songs about his moldering body, he was a paranoiac bent on murdering innocent people. Like so many, before and since, he was pretty all-inclusive about the Southerner's guilt.

John Brown, like his deifiers, had been taken in by the South's romanticized version of itself. They cannot be blamed for this credence when Southerners, even today, so accept the legend that virtually the whole people will proudly claim, "Befoh de wah we had plenty of slaves." Actually one person in thirteen owned any at all, and those who owned "plenty" held about the same percentage in the total population as the percentage of great concentrated wealth and political power in any society.

3

Of the more than 5,000,000 whites in the South, only 385,000 owned any slaves at all. Of these, 77,000 owned only one slave, and 110,000 owned between two and five. Many of these Negroes were house servants, and those who worked on farms would occupy the place of hired hands, in either case bringing their owners into no practical relation to the slave-labor system. As 90,000 owners had more than five but less than ten, roughly three fourths even of slaveholders belonged to the small-planter class. As 61,000 had more than ten but less than twenty, then nearly 90 per cent were still outside the class of the grandees—the Old Massas of the symbol.

Where the owners' slaves approached twenty, those planters belonged at the top of the middle-class economically—whatever their social pretensions, habits of life, or coats of arms—and beyond them, in the upper middle-class, 44,000 owned more than twenty and less than one hundred. They were getting pretty big by then, but, in current values, they were a prosperous local concern compared with Standard Oil.

The real Bourbons, the true plantation-system masters with over one hundred slaves, numbered only 2,300 in thirteen Southern states— less than one twentieth of one per cent of the population.

Their fabled ante-bellum mansions decorate the legends, but few white men in the South had ever set foot in one. In the one hundred miles of the tobacco-rich Peninsula of Virginia, where the plantocracy was founded, there were less than twenty great houses of plantation masters. Even the names of the families are so few that reverent past-worshipers can recite them in their own saying of the beads.

Finally, 500,000 farms were operated by non-slaveholders as compared to 306,000 by owners of any slaves at all, whether or not or however they were used in farming.

Among the non-slaveholding population (some of whom had freed their slaves in disbelief in the institution) many anti-slavery societies had been active until the attitude of Northern extremists made abolition, at the least, unpopular.

However, much underground work in freeing Negroes continued in the South, though it was less voluble than in the North. In fact the real heroes of the abolition movement were the unsung Southerners who risked their lives to send slaves on their northward flight, and they have been neglected in the folklore because they do not fit the concepts.

Aside from active Southern abolitionists, a large percentage of the non-slaveholding population was theoretically opposed to the institution. This group, including a small but articulate German population in Richmond, was one the Secessionists won over through the indiscriminate Northern attacks that included the whole South.

On them such uninformed indictments as *Uncle Tom's Cabin* did not sit too well. For their part they were aware of the foul child-labor situation in the North, where, in New York, newspaper ads specified that a child must be ten years old. The freed Negroes there fared even worse than they do today. Instead of a Harlem they had the infamous Old Brewery, jammed with a thousand whites and blacks, in filth, depravity, and hunger, where at least one murder a day was committed. "Their eyes had seen the glory . . ."

But, with all the resentment stirred up against the North, the South was not solidified, even when Lincoln was elected and caricatured as the archabolitionist. It is one of the paradoxes of our folklore that the Great Emancipator assumed his role in history partly on the propaganda of his opponents. The body of the South was less convinced of their own extremists' scare stories of Lincoln's abolitionism than the rest of the country has been ever since.

When, on Lincoln's election, the Southern plantocracy believed its interests could best be served outside the compact of union, their politicians were able to carry out only seven states of the lower South. Six other Southern states—including Virginia, which was to be the battleground—did not leave the Union until after the war began.

Even then, the South was not the solid entity of legend. Unionist societies were active against the South in nearly every Southern state; the Union Army pension rolls included veterans from every Southern state; and Tennessee furnished men to the United States armies in comparative numbers to some New England states.

In the North there was similar opposition, such as the Copperheads, and no assured backing of the Lincoln administration at all until the fighting itself.

The Confederacy solidified the Union—against danger.

As in our wars since, *men were forced to fight* (in North and South) frequently for what they did not believe in—because of their country's danger.

4

As the diverse interests in the South were not always apparent, neither were the personal conflicts of individuals forced to their decisions. Members of the armed forces who went with their states all form the group figure of "Rebel."

But, having no stake in the institution of slavery or planter politics, as Raphael Semmes said:

It must be admitted indeed that there was some little nerve required for an officer . . . to go with his state. His profession was his only fortune; he depended upon it for the means of subsisting himself and family. If he remained where he was, a competency for life, and promotions, and honors, probably, awaited him; if he went with the South, a dark, uncertain future was before him; he could not possibly better his condition, and, if the South failed, he would have thrown away the labor of a lifetime.

Among Regular Army officers from Virginia, more men of field and general ranks stayed with the Union than resigned. Among the younger men, lieutenants and captains, forty-seven went with their states and sixteen remained in the Army. All over the Confederacy more men stayed in the Navy than followed their states. This would indicate the pull of the loyalties in the armed forces, especially in the Navy, where they spent long periods at sea, and among the older men who had spent their lives in a service.

The words of two other men here will indicate the motivations of personal decision. Lee said:

Every brave people who considered their rights attacked and their constitutional liberties invaded would have done as we did. Our conduct was not caused by any insurrectionary spirit nor can it be termed rebellion, for our construction of the Constitution under which we lived and acted was the same from its adoption, and for eighty years we had been taught and educated by the founders of the republic and their written words which controlled our conduct.

When Lee said founders, he was speaking of his own father who had fought in another war of independence with the same clarity of conscience that his son brought to this one.

Then, quite simple are the words of an obscure young Regular Army captain on resigning:

Some of those cross-stitched mottoes . . . such as, "He who provides not for his own household is worse than an infidel," made a lasting impression upon me; and while I love my neighbor, i.e., my country, I love my household, i.e., my State, more; and I could not be an infidel and lift my sword against my own kith and kin, even though I do believe . . . that the measure of American greatness can be achieved only under one flag. . . .

Gettysburg was more than two years away when George Pickett wrote this letter to the girl he married.

Among others who were forced to make this tragic decision were a former United States President, a Vice-President, cabinet members, and members of Congress, army and naval officers who had risked their lives in the country's wars—believing then what they did now. To them it was not abstract states' rights. It was young Pickett's "kith and kin."

In a land not then the continental entity it is today, it was not that they loved the whole less but their native place more.

The British correspondent Russell, in speaking of North and South from the vantage point of an observer, said, "They are all Americans."

EXPERIMENT IN REBELLION

CHAPTER ONE

The Amateur Gentleman

THEY had waited for their leader so long in Richmond that, when his train approached from the South, the moment was like the tenor's entrance in opera. "Here comes the Prince! Here comes the Prince!"

The bands tuned up, the gunners prepared their pieces for the salute, and young girls arranged their bonnets and ribands again. Everyone in the crowd waiting at the depot was dressed as for Sunday. Miles of silk billowed in the bright flowing dresses of the ladies, and tall hats gave stature to the frock-coated gentlemen. Little girls readied their bunches of flowers and, outside the small depot near the river, liveried coachmen sat erect on the carriages drawn each by four white horses.

It was an indolent morning in late May of 1861. Wistaria was in its brief dramatic bloom against iron-grille balconies, and rambler roses budded along the red-brick walls of gardens. New Confederate flags flew from the windows of the slope-roofed Queen Anne and Georgian houses.

From the train crossing the bridge over the James, the President's party could see the old city rising from the river, with Jefferson's white-pillared Capitol bold in the center. The chief clerk of the new Treasury Department recorded his first impression:

At the wharves could have been seen the flags of all nationalities float-ing from the masts of vessels whose tonnage ranged from the famous clipper and ocean steamship to the schooner and sloop of the inland and coast trade. Main and Cary streets, from the "Rocketts" to the famous basin of the James River Canal, a distance of at least one mile, was a busy scene from morn to night of all that makes the active life of the merchant or the manufacturer.

As distinct from all this . . . [was] that part of the city about the beauti-ful park that surrounded the Grecian capitol building . . . the secluded retreats furnished by the clubrooms or the snug offices and elegant homes of men whose culture and goodness had been transmitted from the early colonial days, with the treasure of a history and the lore of traditions. . . .

This spirit rested upon the whole city in these golden days; it made every man and woman who dwelt there, whether white or black, bond or free, rich or poor, more or less a gentleman or a gentle-lady.

A Virginia gentleman of the old school may not have been produced alone in Richmond. Far be it from me to locate the virtues of the old Commonwealth exclusively at this place, but I do say that they were to be found in this glorious old city in 1861, in the fullest expressions of the highest type of civilization America has ever seen.

Jefferson Davis was more interested in the last part of the observation —the nature of Virginia gentlemen—than in the physical beauty of the city to which he was coming as Chief Executive of a new nation. Of all the men of his day who acted for the ages, none lived more by concepts than he. And of his concepts, none was held dearer than that of being a gentleman in a caste society. But at Richmond he was a frontier neo-aristocrat coming to the real thing.

As he stepped down from the train, an erect and graceful figure, he was little impressed by the crowd. He had been facing those all over the South for four months. He was tired of them, and he was tired. The journey in the train coach had taken forever, with countless changes from one depot to another in nameless towns, and it had been hot all the way. He wanted to get to whatever place the city had prepared for him to rest. He missed his wife. But this was the citadel of the aristocrat, and he needed to make a good impression.

While his mind was turned inward to the concept of himself at this hour, his arrival was being recorded by reporters, foreign visitors, and enemy spies.

They all agreed on one thing. In a first impression of him the iron will of determination stood out over all else. It hollowed his cheeks, sharpening the fine modeling of his features. It set his mobile mouth and gave firmness to his chin and jaw, underscored with a thin line of whiskers. His whole expression seemed molded in pride, with little warmth, but not without appeal. He had distinction, he had style.

His hair was still dark, parted on one side and swirled across his forehead, falling loosely over his ears and worn long in the back. His eyes were gray and so bright that few realized one was blind. Jefferson Davis would wish no one to know of any infirmity. At this time he was just past fifty, and he carried himself like a warrior. His self-image included the military leader. He could well be vain of his soldier's past, and there was enough romance in his life for the hero of a picaresque novel.

In his youth, as a lieutenant in the Indian country, he had incurred the wrath of the commanding officer, Zachary Taylor, by aspiring to that general's daughter. She loved Jefferson Davis enough to go against her father—a future President of the United States—and he loved her enough to resign from the Army for which he had prepared at West Point. Together they retired to an idyllic lover's land on an island in the Mississippi—and there she died.

Byronically, the young Davis turned recluse in the lush retreat provided by his hugely successful older brother, Joseph. Their father had been an unsuccessful, itinerant farmer who moved down into the bayou country from the backwoods of Kentucky. Joseph, much the older, was more paternal than filial in his feelings toward Jefferson, and wanted his intelligent and appealing younger brother to enjoy all the advantages which he had lacked.

When the solitary widower turned scholar, all his needs were attended to by slaves, and in the long slumberous days he devoted himself to books and blooded horses. He was a superb rider. A young belle (called by a Northern writer "the Rose of Mississippi") saw him on a horse when he was thirty-seven and she not yet twenty. Though Davis made a powerful impression on Varina Howell, there was nothing in their first meeting to indicate a fated love.

Her parents were friends of Joseph Davis, whom she knew intimately, and Varina thought she would never like Jefferson as well as she did his brother. Yet, in her letters to her mother, Jefferson Davis's name kept cropping up. To the young girl he poured out all the political theories absorbed in his solitary studies, and she was baffled by the man and his ideas.

Varina Howell's grandfather had been governor of New Jersey, her mother's people from Virginia, and she held all the scorn of the Whig for the revolutionary rabble of Democrats. Yet here was this elegant gentleman (as she wrote her mother) showing good manners even though he was a Democrat. So the impressionable young woman became interested in Democrats.

She was by no means swept off her feet by his ideas, as she brought to their talks an alert, informed intelligence of her own. In a land where physical beauty is much esteemed, she was a striking young woman—dark, full-bodied and vital—but she had never passed on her looks alone. She possessed a natively good mind, curiosity, and had the fortune to be tutored by an amiable old scholar from Salem, Massachusetts. She had long studied the theories of governments (she read the *National Intelligencer* as a child), and she attacked Davis's fiercely one-sided arguments.

[3]

She said, "He impresses me as a remarkable man, of intense temper, and has a way of taking for granted that everybody agrees with him when expressing an opinion, which offends me." Apparently Varina Howell did not observe the reason for this.

None of Davis's ideas had grown out of the stresses of living. Competition and insecurity, hardship and turmoil, compromise and decision, none of these had molded his thoughts. Deep in the scented, shaded land of magnolia and cypress, he read other men's thoughts and used for his own those which buttressed his concept of an aristocratic society free of compromise with the commercial North.

As their association progressed, Varina found, along with the intense temper, a sweetness of nature and a mental habit that kept companionship stimulating. Also, along with his rigid convictions, she discovered an integrity of character, and, as he knew nothing of the necessity of compromise, he did not admit its possibility. He possessed the standard virtues of his day and region—high physical courage and sense of personal honor—and he shared her religious devoutness.

Slowly her early reservations vanished and the power of his first impression grew, until the romantic girl was absorbed, then obsessed, by her love of Jefferson Davis.

They married as lovers and they never ceased being lovers. She said that just the thought of being his wife made her "a proud young creature." She was never interested in another man, and from the moment he knew her, Varina was the one woman in Davis's life.

2

When they married, he emerged from his shadows and entered the political life at Washington. Through the power of his brother and his associates, it was relatively simple for Davis to become congressman from Mississippi. When the Mexican War started, it was also simple for him to become a colonel of Mississippi volunteers.

At Buena Vista he became a hero.

Arriving at a critical moment in support of a battery, he fought under the eyes of the commanding general, Zachary Taylor, his former father-in-law. His old enemy recommended him for "gallantry and coolness" entitling him "to the particular notice of the government." When Colonel Davis returned home on crutches (he was wounded in the foot), he was feted the whole length of his journey—through New Orleans, Natchez, Vicksburg, and to the plantation house deep in its

[4]

magnolia world. Before this heady wine had worn off he returned to Washington as senator.

This was fast going for a man not yet forty, who never once in his life had known the frustrations and mutations of earning his own living. Today it is fashionable among some men of fixed position to champion the so-called common man, but in Davis's day the wealth was too new for him to feel assured of his superiority. In the first rapture of privilege he was enchanted by its power and glory. He loved the wearing of the purple to which he had not been born.

Jefferson Davis was a product of the new semitropic grandeur that blossomed in the flush times of the lower South. In Mississippi it was a day of new fortunes, where the slave population had increased from 65,000 in 1830 to 437,000 in 1860. Life was a high gamble, of vivid color and ostentatious pride, and the winners wore their arrogance with a new assertive power. They built huge colonnaded mansions as monuments to their vanity as well as for comfort, for these neo-Bourbons were not always linear descendants of the rulers of the old South. Though many of the gamblers in this El Dorado came from the traditional upper South, most of the new powers were such men as Quitman of New York, Prentiss of Maine, Walker of Pennsylvania, and Jefferson Davis's tough-fibered brother from the Kentucky backwoods.

Successful in this feudalism, they adopted a pattern of feudal nobility modeled on the original Virginia design of aristocracy. As Virginia's early plantocracy had invented the legend, the whole ruling class of the South became a figment of its own collective imagination.

From Virginia's earliest beginnings, no sooner had ruthless men of ambition achieved power than they assumed the pattern of British landed gentry. Their descendants devoted their energies to living as if they hadn't the faintest notion where money came from.

When the new bloods of the lower South joined the Virginians in living this fantasy, they made it a personal reality. They would actually lose their money just so long as they were accepted as "gentlemen" and could look down upon those uncouth persons who soiled their hands with cash. One reason for the preponderance of Southerners in the Regular Army was that this offered about the only honored profession that could be followed with gallant debts as a heritage.

However, it can scarcely be denied that, in its self-made archaic world of chivalry, the South created a beguiling legend so convincingly that even today pioneers are considered only those trekkers West in the covered wagons. No one ever thinks that Virginians were the first Indian fighters on this continent.

Yet, when the later pioneers trekked, Virginians had been at it for two centuries, pushing back the frontier and sending forth adventurers to chart the way the covered wagons were to take.

You forget they were tough a long time because when they fought Indians everybody fought them. It was commonplace, and nothing was made of it. The interesting thing was to be a gentleman.

George Washington achieved it most spectacularly. He was a professional Indian fighter, but you remember him for Mount Vernon and —in pursuing the exercise common to his place and time—for fox hunting. That was the pattern of the South. They did not want to talk about their Indian-fighting days any more than the new squire's lady wishes to be reminded of her days on the other side of the tracks.

It is also true that the self-made patricians brought to their role much grace of living and some fine native traits. They kept the faith in physical courage as a virtue, and whatever side they took they were willing to support with more than words. Though this was unfortunately expressed at times with violence (and the formalized violence of dueling), still it had a tendency to restrain those showy generalities tossed out with no regard to truth or ultimate consequences.

Dignity was given concepts when men were expected to live or die by them and not use them as ideological springboards for exhibitionism. It gave validity to the personal honor of men and women. That kind of honor is old-fashioned now, a little quaint, but in those days it constituted the most real value an individual could claim. No one lived more by this honor than Jefferson Davis, and no one more devoutly accepted the whole system.

3

Davis's idol, Calhoun, in evolving his aggressive states' rights stand for the South, perceived that state independence provided the South with its only protection against Northern financial domination. Davis, in embracing Calhoun, did not evolve the broader economic reasons for the position. To him the question was the aristocrat or the mob. To insure the aristocratic rule, the South must maintain national political equality or withdraw. Far from making any defense of slavery, he said it "superseded the necessity for an order of nobility."

With this concept Davis naturally became a spokesman for the cotton princes. He believed in their rule as sincerely as the Stuarts believed in the divine right of kings. There was one difference. The Stuarts were born to their belief; Davis learned his. The point about this tautly honorable man is that he learned everything.

Because what he learned, in seclusion, constituted his only civil achievement, his intellectual gifts formed the center of his vanity. Men who have succeeded in the world enjoy the use of their minds; with Davis it was his only success. He was as touchy about his opinions as a reformed madam about her respectability, and to attack his opinion was to attack him.

After they were married his wife said, "If anyone disagrees with Mr. Davis, he resents it and ascribes the difference to the perversity of his opponent." And Davis, in making an apology, once said, "I have an infirmity of which I am heartily ashamed: when I am aroused in a matter, I lose control of my feelings and become personal."

This blindness to the merits of the other side, with his unquestioning faith in the rights of the Southern plantocracy, strengthened his position among the extremists. Though he never went all the way with the radicals, he did call compromisers and moderate Southerners "recreants," and he was called, in a toast, "the gamecock of the South." The point was that to deny the full privilege and complete validity of his master-class South was to deny the master class—and hence himself. With this personal identification his approach grew austere and imperious as his own ego grew threatened.

Even when the alignments within the government became irreconcilable, Jefferson Davis engaged in no rabble rousing. He disclaimed any disunionism, and that was true—so long as the South had its way. He wanted the way of the planter South unchallenged and uncontrolled within the Union. When the new political party was elected and he knew his South's position was no longer safe, that marked the end of the compact of union. It was very simple and very clear—but the reality of separation was something else again.

It is even possible that, when the moment came, Davis regretted the course from which there was no turning back. Certainly Mrs. Davis left Washington in sorrow. And certainly her husband showed not the least inclination to assume any active part in the government of the group of seceded states. He retired with his wife to their island retreat and offered his services to the military forces of Mississippi.

At that time only seven states of the lower South had seceded, and each acted as an independent republic. Though it was obvious that a confederation between them was necessary, Jefferson Davis restricted his interests to the Mississippi state troops whose command had been given him. He was major general. If the secession came to armed conflict, he wanted to be in the field, the place of the true glory.

Here Davis personified the medieval concept of the knight leading his people to battle. He would never have risen from the ranks, and even at West Point his record was mediocre. It was not soldiering he loved, but the heroics of war and the privilege of command. Happily then he readied himself for battle while the men of words gathered in Montgomery, Alabama, to erect a new nation on earth out of the seven seceded states.

It was February (1861), but spring comes early in the Deep South, and Jefferson and Varina Davis were paring rosebushes in their garden when a telegram from Montgomery was delivered. "When reading the telegram," his wife said, "he looked so grieved that I feared some evil had befallen our family. After a few minutes' painful silence he told me, as a man might speak of the sentence of death." He told her he had been summoned to lead the Confederacy, not in the field, but as its President.

His wife was as stunned as he. In the garden of their slumberous private world they faced each other in depressed silence.

There was no possibility of refusing. He had gone too far in his theories of the rule of the plantocracy—in or out of the Union. His words had caught up with him.

4

The South loved action and loved talk, but action was not necessarily an implementation of words. Action and ideas could be quite separate things. In this Jefferson Davis typified the experiment he reluctantly led.

As spokesman for the Southern rule he lived in a world of ideas; when the decision came he abandoned ideas for the heroic world of war. When suddenly he was placed in the position of implementing his ideas *in terms of civil action,* the essential duality of the man was revealed.

He assumed leadership with this division of character. Now, in the gamble against destiny, he abandoned the bold tone of Washington. He proclaimed the rights of the Southern states to independence; he affirmed their determination to defend those rights by arms if necessary; but he breathed no defiance:

There can be but little rivalry between ours and any manufacturing or navigating community, such as the northeastern states of the American Union. It must follow, therefore, that a mutual interest would invite good and kind offices.

If, however, passion or the lust of dominion should cloud the judgment of those states . . . and the integrity of our territory and jurisdiction be assailed, it will but remain for us, with firm resolve, to appeal to arms and invoke the blessings of Providence on a just cause. . . .

These temperate words caused extremists to fear he had lived too long among the Yankees. Other observers found him sad and worried and strained. The burden of creating an actuality out of a concept was beginning to be felt.

With his self-awareness of the aristocrat, personally and now nationally, he came to Richmond—a city of the generic Southern aristocracy.

The ladies and gentlemen who waited to greet him on that spring morning were long past learning the codes by which he lived. As one of his fellow Southerners said, "The Virginian . . . particularly when he boasted a high Colonial descent, was still the nearest counterpart to the landed gentry of the motherland of any American so ever. . . ."

Jefferson Davis was aware of this when he came to the capital of the Old Dominion—first explored by Captain John Smith in 1607, then a trading post under the great Byrd, a frontier rival of classic Williamsburg, then the Revolutionary capital under Governor Thomas Jefferson (who designed the building now to be used by the Confederacy). Here Washington brought his army after Benedict Arnold had burned the town, Lafayette danced, and the Lees visited. The lordly planters of Tidewater built their winter houses here and the tobacco men their mansions. Thackeray (whom he did not read) found the hospitality charming, and Poe (whose poetry was not on his list) had roamed its streets. Near the Capitol, Henry Clay had learned his law and John Marshall the lawgiver had built his red-brick house.

Here he was, the son of an itinerant farmer from the backwoods, leading a Deep South rebellion which these proud people had joined —reluctantly. Their reluctance was important too, involved with the new empire's chances for success, and it went a long way back.

CHAPTER TWO

"The Man and the Hour Have Met"

WHEN Davis's nation was first set up in Alabama, Virginia was one of six states of the upper South which had not seceded. Geographically above the Deep South, in a solid block from the Atlantic to west of the Mississippi, they were Kentucky, west of Virginia; North Carolina, and Tennessee west of her; Missouri and Arkansas across the Mississippi. As long as they remained neutral, forming a buffer territory between the seceded states and the Union, war would be difficult to wage.

While slaveholding states, they had a more balanced economy and stable society than the seceded group and depended less on the slave-operated plantation system. Even if Lincoln had been the abolitionist of the propaganda, this gave them no reason to secede. But with the majority accepting the states' right to secession, neither did they believe in coercing sister states back into the Union. They waited, and the two separated sections waited on them.

In this group Virginia was the pivotal state. Both sides watched to see which way the cat would jump there, and down in Montgomery they handled that rich old relative with care.

Nice little courtesies were exchanged. When the first Confederate flag—with its seven stars in a wreath on a field of red in one corner of a white banner—was raised over the first Provisional Congress, the honor went to the granddaughter of John Tyler, the ex-President who lived in the planters' paradise below Richmond. They were patient even when Virginia sent her own commissioners to Washington to try to effectuate a compromise.

The men of the infant nation knew that all compromise was past. Having sent their own commissioners to Lincoln's government in Washington, they knew that the new majority party felt its power and was determined on a showdown. Not even courtesy was extended the amiable gestures of the Confederacy, nor interest shown in its obviously peaceful intent.

This had its pathos, for never was a government set up in more orderly or traditional style. In fact the Union government was now run by new powers; the Confederacy was stocked with old powers from the Union.

As it was the administration of the Constitution to which the Secessionists objected, they modeled their Constitution on the original, with changes designed to save it from politics. Oddly for these romantic people, Southerners had always hated national extravagance and been extremely watchful of public expenditures. As they believed corporations contributed to political parties in exchange for later legislative protection, their Constitution forbade Congress and the Treasury to promote any branch of industry and strictly limited congressional power in finance.

To control expenses, the President was to be mindful of receipts and expenditures and to make known his suggestions through cabinet members appearing in Congress. Primarily for this reason cabinet members were permitted in the House to defend their departments, and only at department suggestions could Congress appropriate money. Congress was specifically enjoined from appropriations for internal improvements—regarded as another political party expedient—and even navigation maintenance must be paid out of navigation duties.

As a final check on politicking, the President could not succeed himself. He was elected for one term only, of six years. Showing that these constitutional designers were soured on the cloakroom deals in government, the President could veto a rider on a bill without vetoing the whole bill.

The one distinctly Southern note was in the preamble: "We, the people of the Confederate States, each acting in its sovereign and independent character . . ." Of course the citizens could keep and bear arms.

Right off, the Confederacy showed its conservatism by giving the brush-off to the radical Secessionists. The founding fathers of states' rights, South Carolina's Rhett and Barnwell, with Alabama's silver-tongued Yancey, were given no important part in forming the new confederation. Georgia's three big men, in effect, counterbalanced each other and caused what some have claimed a mistake in the delegates' election of President.

Toombs, Stephens, and Cobb had all originally been nationalists in the Washington government. Burly Bob Toombs, fiery and undisciplined, called the Danton of the rebellion, had turned against the

Union during the past decade, and his revolutionary passion had helped drive his state from the Union.

Alexander Stephens, undersized and emaciated constitutional pedant, had never turned against the Union, only following his state with deep misgivings into the new movement.

Howell Cobb, the powerful planter of legend, had turned away with moderation after a Unionist record which made him important enemies in the Deep South. As his anti-Calhoun position caused him to be distrusted by the ardent states'-righters, the delegates elected Jefferson Davis in fear that Georgia would advance Cobb. Except for this mistake, some believe the presidency would have gone to Robert Toombs.

Apparently the chief virtue of Davis, to the electors, was his fulfillment of their requirement that a candidate be unanimously elected. He had not taken part in the politicking. He had been drafted from military leadership for the highest honor. When he came to Montgomery on a wave of popular acclaim, he could be introduced by Yancey with the phrase, "The man and the hour have met."

The man did not see the hour as did Yancey and the fire-eaters. Though events had swept his idealistic concept into practical application, Davis still saw the situation in terms of abstract right rather than in terms of meeting new needs as they arose. While Lincoln, with an established nation, broke the Constitution when expedient and appealed to people with heart-warming generalities, Davis from the beginning acted as if his were the established country which must, for posterity, observe every legality. Far from appealing to his people with the generalities that could stir their emotions, he gave them the cold logic of the justice of their position.

In his inaugural speech in February he said:

Our present condition . . . illustrates the American idea that governments rest upon the consent of the governed. . . . The declared purpose of the compact of union from which we have withdrawn was "to establish justice, insure domestic tranquillity, provide for the common defense, promote the general welfare, and secure the blessings of liberty to ourselves and posterity"; and when, in the judgment of the sovereign states now composing this Confederacy, it had been perverted from the purposes for which it was ordained, and had ceased to answer the ends for which it was established, a peaceful appeal to the ballot box declared that, so far as they were concerned, the government created by that compact should cease to exist. . . .

Actuated solely by the desire to preserve our own rights and promote our own welfare, the separation of the Confederate States has been marked by no aggression upon others, and followed by no domestic convulsion. . . . The cultivation of our fields has progressed as heretofore. . . .

Should the Northern government not be guided by reason,

a terrible responsibility will rest upon it, and the sufferings of millions will bear testimony to the folly and wickedness of our aggressors. . . .
We have entered upon the career of independence.

If those words lacked fire, they expressed his real feelings. Davis was not confident of the South's ability to defend itself if the United States tried suppression by force of arms.

He wrote his wife that beyond the "smiles, plaudits and flowers" which showered upon his "weary heart," he "saw troubles and thorns innumerable. We are without machinery, without means, and threatened by powerful opposition; but I do not despond, and will not shrink from the task imposed upon me."

Even with the weight of his burdens and the harassment of countless details, Davis's wife and family were always in his thoughts. He wrote Varina of his triumphal trip to Montgomery, saying, "I thought it would have gratified you to have witnessed it, and have been a memory to our children. Thus I constantly wished to have you all with me. . . . As soon as an hour is my own I will look for a house and write you more fully."

There was no executive mansion in the new country, and the Cabinet met in a room off the parlor of the Exchange Hotel.

2

This Cabinet was selected by Davis as if his country were not only established but flourishing in fat, peaceful days. He followed in every detail the traditional course of regional selections, like an old political hack paying off party obligations. As Davis owed no political debts, his choices revealed that in his change from ideas to execution, from theories to practice, he failed to perceive the nature of the movement or estimate the threat from the Union.

However just they all considered their cause, it was revolution. Revolutions must succeed by force or fail. They have no *status quo* in which to exist. But Jefferson Davis, believing in the divine right of the South, according to the King Cotton version of the Bible, expected his independence *to exist* and not to be won. On that he acted in erecting the government.

To begin with, for Vice-President he inherited Alexander Stephens, who enjoyed the unique distinction of being a leader of a rebellion he was known to oppose, and who already was privately declaring himself in distrust of the whole thing and the people in it. Apparently to keep Stephens company, Davis appointed another anti-Secessionist, Stephen Mallory of Florida, Secretary of the non-existent Navy.

The Secessionists (though former Unionists) were Christopher Memminger, German-born, orphanage-raised Charleston lawyer, and Texas' rugged John Reagan, heading respectively the equally non-existent departments of Treasury and Post Office. From Louisiana, Davis selected the Attorney-General, Judah Benjamin. Born in the British West Indies of Jewish parents, a nationally known lawyer and state-machine senator, this suave enigma was a shrewd and erudite opportunist.

To Alabama went the Secretaryship of War, Leroy Pope Walker, a lawyer who so disbelieved in the possibility of warfare that he promised his constituents to wipe up with his handkerchief every drop of blood spilled.

As something had to be done with Toombs, a financial expert, and South Carolina had received the sop of the Treasury Department, Toombs was placed in the one slot where his intemperate language and general violence could not possibly fit—the State Department.

Here were a President who wanted to be a soldier, a Vice-President who disbelieved in the whole thing, a finance-minded revolutionary in the State Department, and, in a country swarming with trained soldiers, a lawyer in the War Department.

The new Rebel government, anything but rebellious, was thoroughly unrepresentative of the fabled plantocracy. Not one depended directly on the institution of slavery for his livelihood, and each of them, except Davis, had risen by his own efforts in careers that could have been just as successful in another region—three coming up from the bottom like Alger heroes.

Half of them had opposed secession, two until their own states seceded, and all of them had at one time been Unionists. Three of them were foreign-born first-generation Americans—or first-generation Southerners to those to whom the South is not in the Union—one was a Catholic and one a Jew. This was the setup of the "Solid South."

3

Had this ill-assorted group been allowed to build their nation in peace, Virginia and the bloc of border states would be less important. But Davis and the Cabinet were growing apprehensive of Lincoln's intentions. They received no satisfaction from him on the evacuation of the two United States forts still held by the Union in Southern territory. Also his eloquent words indicated to them a design to place the onus of any aggression on the South.

He said:

In your hands, my disaffected fellow countrymen, and not in mine, is the momentous issue of civil war. The government will not assail you. You can have no conflict without being yourselves the aggressors. You have no oath registered in heaven to destroy the government, while I shall have the most solemn one "to preserve, protect and defend it."

This, the Constitution-minded Southerners knew to be untrue. Lincoln's oath was, "I do solemnly swear that I will faithfully . . . defend the *Constitution* . . ." This clearly did not say "government." As they saw the possibility of Lincoln's forcing them to make the issue over the forts, the new rulers needed Virginia to lead the other border states into commitment. But the old Old Dominion was not to be hurried.

In Richmond the state set up a convention to talk things over calmly. While the nation divided north and south of her, the members of the Secession Convention went on debating every day until they seemed like a permanent part of the city's life.

Richmond's three delegates, chosen in open election, were fairly typical of the state's position. Two were conservative Unionists and one the least radical of the Secessionists; the candidate who finished last in the voting was a Unionist who considered secession as rebellion.

From the state, ex-President Tyler, ill and old before his time, was there as a conservative Secessionist, and Henry Wise, governor during the John Brown insurrection, represented fire-eating Secessionists. One of the most rabid anti-Secessionists was a profane tobacco-chewing Western Virginian, Jubal Early, destined to lead a division at Gettysburg.

The middle-ground majority kept both factions hog-tied. Feelings ran high. Squabbles and fights were frequent, and some of the extreme Unionists (called "submissionists") said they were scared to go out on the streets at night.

But to Jefferson Davis and the little group of men who held the fate of the cotton empire down at Montgomery, this was not the kind of fighting they wanted from Virginia—and Virginia must be seen as they saw her then.

Only one generation from the period of her greatness under the Virginia dynasty, the state held vast prestige, considerable physical power, and was much larger with the forty western counties now forming West Virginia.

Omitting that section west of the Alleghenies, Virginia lay in three sections: mountain, piedmont, and tidewater. The fertile and beautiful Shenandoah Valley, between the Alleghenies and the Blue Ridge, was rich with grain and cattle, and its sturdy and self-reliant people were largely non-slaveholding.

East of the Blue Ridge, where the piedmont rolls, there were wheat and corn and fruit, tobacco and fine horses, and fast shallow streams for gristmills and sawmills.

East of that, the flatland tilting to the Chesapeake Bay was tidewater. Many rivers and streams, running southeasterly, formed channels of trade for land producing wheat, corn, oats, staple crops, and the big-money crop, tobacco.

Here the plantation system originated, and here, along the great rivers—Potomac and Rappahannock, York and James—strutted the original grandees of the South and the fire-eaters of another revolution, Patrick Henry and Thomas Jefferson and the Lees. Robert Lee's father, the Revolutionary hero, Light Horse Harry Lee, had come for his bride at Shirley, and George Washington had come for his rich wife near Williamsburg.

Richmond was the planters' city and powerful for its size of thirty-eight thousand. Tobacco manufacturing was the backbone. From the counties, planters "carried 'baccer down" by canal boat and wagons, and the finished products were shipped everywhere. Shipping itself was important. Trade with their west went on the Kanawha Canal, which terminated in the great Basin in the center of the manufacturing district. At the city docks, where the river was being dredged for larger navigation, freight handled was on the increase.

In came coal and iron, hay and oats, fish and guano, rosin and tar, coffee from Brazil and plaster from Nova Scotia ground for agricultural use. Out went primarily flour and tobacco and corn meal, all over the world, and the world's largest flour mill (the Gallego) was in Richmond.

There were many manufacturers of machinery and farm implements and ironworks, topped by the Tredegar, which made boilers for U.S. frigates and heavy guns for the U. S. Navy, locomotives and boilers, and iron pipes for the city water.

Everything for railroads was manufactured in the city except rubber car springs, and a new company was starting to make "vulcanized indiarubber" springs which hoped to rival the Goodyear patent. There were also a new sugar refinery, a woolen mill, and a shipyard. There were makers of brick, brush, cabinets, caps, carriages, dresses, guns and pistols, instruments, regalia, sails, and wigs.

There were grocers and wholesale merchants by the score, commission merchants of agricultural products and livestock, insurance companies and flourishing banks. In its conservative, leisured, provincial self-sufficiency, Richmond was the antithesis of the sleepy Southern town where the slumberous silence was broken only by Old Massa calling for his whip and julep.

Other Virginia cities also were active in flour and corn-meal mills (as the state produced one ninth of the flour and corn in America in 1860), and they sold livestock and slaughtered stock, wool and buckwheat, garden and orchard products to the North and the South. With this type of agriculture, and a more balanced economy resulting through progressive cities, the large-plantation system was on the decline in Virginia. While 5 per cent of Deep South landowners held more than fifty slaves, in Virginia only 1.6 per cent owned so many.

Negroes were on the decrease. The colored population had remained static for thirty years, going from 40 per cent of the total population in 1790 to 30 per cent in 1860. The white population grew slowly, as the worn-out soil caused many families to move south and west. When it is realized that the dust bowls and the wastelands of the cattle West occurred after two generations, Virginia showed a certain resourcefulness in still going after more than two centuries.

Some of the more resourceful natives worked to improve soil conditions, and the planter Edmund Ruffin increased the farm production of his whole section around Richmond by the introduction of marl. Also many planters could stake themselves to other businesses or shift to another type of farming by selling their slaves south.

Richmond was a large slave market. Its Lumpkin's Bottom section was so famous that Negroes today will say of some ill-favored member of their race, "I'll bet they got him from Lumpkin's Bottom." (Not all planters who discontinued the use of slave labor sold them. Sixty per cent of free Negroes in U.S. lived in Virginia and Maryland.)

This slave market gave Virginia planters an economic tie to the South, and her planters were as politically powerful as the bayou barons. Also the cities were based upon the plantation system. Even the poor farmers had economic ties with the South, selling there cattle, hogs, mules, and the hot white liquor made from corn. But none of that was as strong as the homogeneity of the peoples of Virginia and the South, and that is what the little band of new rulers down at Montgomery were counting on. Blood is thicker . . .

A couple of Virginians were encouraging the Confederacy. One was Yankee-hating white-haired old Edmund Ruffin, the discoverer of marl. Aware of his contribution to his state, he now turned against her because she would not heed his advice. He left Richmond for Charleston, renouncing his citizenship in a state that would submit to the rule of a hostile party. He wore the South Carolina cockade, paraded with the kids from military schools, and believed he was living the heritage of the Old Dominion.

In Charleston also young Roger Pryor, fire-eating Virginia congressman and duelist, advised the South Carolinians in a speech. Referring to his native state, he said, "Give the old lady time, don't press her too hard, she is a little slow and rheumatic. . . . But if you would bring in Virginia in one hour by the Shewsbury clock, strike a blow—spill some blood in her face."

4

Down in the charming little town of Montgomery, Davis's Cabinet pondered those words. They did not want war. They did not expect war, though they were trying to prepare.

Davis had dispatched an agent to England with a few thousand pounds credit with which to buy muskets. This agent, Caleb Huse, aged thirty, was a Connecticut Yankee, self-described as of "Puritan stock." For the year previous he had been on leave from the Regular Army, installing a military system at an Alabama university. Having no part of the secession movement, he threw in his lot out of sympathy only and went about his unheroic duties with a skill and energy displayed by few secessionists.

When he arrived in New York the letters through which he was to obtain credit had not reached the bank. This bank, already under suspicion, hastily gave him $500 in gold, probably to get rid of him. He went to Portland by way of Canada, arriving there just before his ship sailed. When he reached London he found the United States there ahead of him, buying up everything in sight. There seemed little to hope for from the Confederates' Yankee friend.

For armament and equipment, the states received offers from all over the East—Dupont in Wilmington, Horstman in Philadelphia, McKnight in New York, Eli Whitney in New Haven, Goodyear for tents, and Tryon to alter muskets at two dollars a piece. Tredegar in Richmond was making cannon for Southern states, and other factories in Richmond turned to percussion caps and equipment.

For powder and munitions the little group of men tried New York direct. In the South virtually no powder was manufactured, only negligible amounts were stored there, and not one foundry in the seceded states could produce cannons. To purchase such supplies, Davis sent Raphael Semmes, U. S. Navy, retired. When he returned on the regular run of the New York-Savannah line—flying the U.S. flag at one end and the Confederate at the other—he reported many New Yorkers sympathetic and willing to help. Actual hostilities would block that.

From Genesee, New York, came an offer to bring ten thousand men, all of whom had armed themselves by selling property and lacked only $11,000 to complete their equipment and make the trip. For that amount in gold, all they asked was "a home in the new Confederacy." Though this proposition showed the Southerner he was regarded as a soft touch, it also indicated that at least certain Northerners regarded the South as gone for good.

With more high spirits than cold purpose, militia companies drilled (very elegantly) and states tried with little success to arm and equip them. There was no hurry, no real threat of war. The United States Post Office still operated throughout the seceded states—thus solving the new Postmaster's problem of the absence of stamps or any way to make them.

When Reagan sent out advertisements for bids for stamps, he received more from the North than from the South—though the South's samples were prettier, with charming water-color scenes from New Orleans firms. When he selected a Richmond engraver, the Postmaster continued to keep all accounts in good order against a peaceful return to the Union.

The first real sour note came from the Confederate commission in Washington trying to discover Lincoln's intentions. Not only were Lincoln's actions lacking in reassurance, but his seemingly devious manner of dealing was wholly unsatisfactory.

The three commissioners had been stalled for a month, trying to obtain an interview with Secretary of State Seward. Finally Judge Campbell, a Southerner on the Supreme Court, speaking for Seward and presumably the government, assured the Confederates of the pacific attitude of the new administration and of the probable evacuation of the two United States forts in the South—principally Sumter in Charleston Harbor.

Suddenly the commissioners learned that, contrary to Campbell's assurances, a relief ship had already started for Fort Sumter.

They felt betrayed. Judge Campbell was outraged at being used as a tool of duplicity; and the men in Montgomery felt angrily that Lincoln's administration was untrustworthy and hostile.

It certainly was hostile. Sending that relief ship to Sumter was a slap where it would cause the quickest resentment—in the face of Jefferson Davis's honor. As honor was of the essence of the aristocrat, so was it of the aristocrat's nation. Practicality, the broader view, ultimate consequences, all vanished. The Union had insulted the dignity of the Confederacy. There must be public retaliation. That relief ship must not reinforce Fort Sumter.

So far as is known, with the exception of Toombs, Davis's advisers either agreed or remained silent. In keeping with the paradoxes, the one voice of caution came from the one revolutionary. In cautioning, Toombs lost none of his violence. His voice came in a rush, a blast. It "was like a trumpet, but without sweetness, and his enunciation was thick."

With all his famed passion he told them that they were doing what the Lincoln government wanted. That administration, lacking the solid backing of the Union, had played a waiting game. Without an overt act from the seceded states they could not get support for war. Lincoln was maneuvering them into an act of violence by reprovisioning Fort Sumter. If the Confederacy resisted with arms, they would strike the first blow and become the aggressors.

Davis was not impressed. Here, in the first critical decision, he acted in the medieval pattern of knighthood: as the South's leader he accepted the Washington maneuver as a challenge to the field of honor. He simply would not sit supinely by while forts within his territory remained the property of a foreign power. His position was highminded and logical—only, as Toombs pointed out, it was not practical.

He said, "This will inaugurate a civil war greater than any the world has ever seen. It will lose us every friend in the North. It puts us in the wrong. It is fatal."

No one supported Toombs, not even Union-loving Stephens, whose

Bible was the Constitution and who was racked already by even this much of a rupture. But Stephens was uneasy among these men and was probably composing in his mind the letters he wrote his brother. "My apprehension and distrust arise from the want of high integrity, loyalty to principle, and pure, disinterested patriotism in the men at the head of the movement. . . . What is to become of us I do not know."

Into the midst of this discussion suddenly was thrust the need for immediate decision. Secretary of War Walker received a telegram:

An authorized messenger from President Lincoln just informed Governor Pickens [of South Carolina] and myself that provisions will be sent to Fort Sumter peaceably, or otherwise by force.

G. T. Beauregard

This name, Beauregard, was little known then. A New Orleans Creole, of the Regular Army, he was a picture soldier with a flair for the fanfare of military doings, and he was pleasing to the militia he commanded at Charleston Harbor. His telegram brought the talk to a head.

Toombs went down fighting before the Cabinet's conviction that, *even* if this did mean war, the United States would have to invade, and they could never conquer a free people. And there was Virginia and the other border states she could influence. . . .

It is not recorded what each thought, or what went unsaid. The record is the War Secretary's telegram, dictated by Jefferson Davis:

If you have no doubt of the authorized character of the agent who communicated to you the intention of the Washington government to supply Fort Sumter by force, you will at once demand its evacuation, and, if this is refused, proceed in such a manner as you may determine to reduce it. Answer.

The answer came immediately:

The demand will be made tomorrow at twelve o'clock.

CHAPTER THREE

To Protect the Commonwealth

WHEN the news of Sumter's fall came to Richmond, "it was like a volcano bursting forth in the center of" the city, according to an Englishwoman, a schoolteacher, caught there by the hostilities. A convulsion seized the public mind. Old Man Ruffin, the venerable expatriate, had ended all Virginia's debating when he fired the first shot that struck the ramparts where the United States flag flew. Lincoln did the rest.

He immediately demanded seventy-five thousand troops to invade the seceded states—"to suppress a combination too powerful for normal procedure," he said—and called on Virginia for her quota of eight thousand. Governor Letcher, anti-slaveryite and anti-Secessionist from western Virginia, would have no part of invading sister states. "You have chosen to inaugurate civil war," he said.

As the new rulers in Montgomery had hoped, the other border states took the same stand. North Carolina and Arkansas, Missouri and Tennessee, all of whom had previously voted against secession, went with the Southern states against coercion. "Tennessee will not furnish a single man for coercion," Governor Isham said, "but fifty thousand if necessary for the defense of her rights or those of our Southern brothers." Claiborne Jackson, of Missouri, went further, calling Lincoln's demand "inhuman and diabolical . . . illegal, unconstitutional and revolutionary in its object."

With the people everywhere making spontaneous "declarations of independence," the voting of the Virginia Secession Convention became a mere formality. The citizens had already possessed the streets. Their voices and bands made carnival, and their torches lit the April sky. Militia batteries fired from the square in front of Thomas Jefferson's Capitol, and cannons roared at the foot of Gamble's Hill, where the buildings of the great Tredegar Iron Works sprawled along the canal. A band played Marseillaise while a Confederate flag was raised over the main building, and the crowd cheered at the announcement that Fort Sumter had been breached by a columbiad cast here.

Everyone who had ever been known to make a speech was exhorted to make one now. From windows and doorways suddenly appeared Confederate flags which ladies had been making in secret, and the palmetto of South Carolina waved in the red flare of the torches. There was a wildness in the excitement, a hysteria in the mass release from indecision. This was action in the direct terms of their heritage.

The legend of aristocracy had originated so long before in Virginia that some of the more violent Southrons of the newer states were wont to sneer at "the darlings of British princes" who had come to Tidewater in their silk stockings and fancy manners (apparently to the delighted admiration of the Indians who had built the river mansions for them and provided rousing housewarmings). Though fifty-seven distinguished Virginia families had been listed when the lower South was still a wilderness, many of those families derived from the "early adventurers" who had carved the first frontier on the American continent, when they won the foothold at Jamestown.

From there they had launched the first American rebellion against a British king, a hundred years before the successful revolution, and across the old plateau of Church Hill in Richmond they still called the ravine where Nathaniel Bacon had fought "Bloody Run Gully."

Though time had elapsed for the creation of a traditional social structure, and the original legend of aristocracy had flavored the whole culture, the Virginians were not far removed from the elemental violence of frontier individualists. Thousands of families who were not "distinguished" had perpetuated the spirit and even actuality of the frontier pattern while embracing certain values and customs and manners evolved of the plantocracy. The self-sufficient world of all plantations—small and large—strengthened the individual will of a people whose limitless prerogatives had never been even touched by an opposing force. Long accustomed to asserting their freedom from molds, their personal liberty and even whims, when a crisis came they reverted to forthright action in proud denial of any will imposed from without.

In their secession marches, in solid mass they swung past the white-frame church of St. John's where Patrick Henry had said, "Give me liberty or give me death." That personal liberty, extended to their state, meant the same to them as it had eighty years before in the other revolution.

2

There were still those who had tried to act by reason. The actual count of the convention's vote went 85 for secession and 55 against.

Though nearly half of those against secession came from the western counties—soon to be a separate state—the rest of the state stood at three to one. Of those represented by the minority, some refused to follow the state—and some of those became spies and Union agents. Some gave only lip service, while others, once committed, went whole-heartedly—however unhappily.

John Wilkinson, of Norfolk, a naval officer and a son of a U.S.N. commodore, was typical. At the age of forty he had never voted and, needless to say, owned no slaves. Speaking for his fellow Virginians, he said, "They were compelled to choose whether they would aid in subjugating their state, or in defending it against invasion. . . . But yielding as they did to necessity, it was nevertheless a painful act."

The fact that, in the first impact, it was equally painful for Northern naval officers to act caused the great navy yard at Norfolk to tumble into Virginia's lap. Before the firing on Sumter both the hotheads in Virginia and U. S. Secretary of the Navy Welles had prepared for action; but Welles's efforts boomeranged.

His official biographer states that Welles said "it was very important that the rebels strike the first blow in the conflict." To this end he sent orders to the Navy at Norfolk which, if obeyed, would have shown evidence of hostility and forced Virginia's hand. However, the naval officers could not bring themselves to move against friends and fellow citizens over what was to them, at the time, a political difference regarding the rights of secession. Between orders and con-science, they stewed themselves into a state of agitation. When Virginia suddenly took the initiative the naval officers—not knowing how to make war on a state—were demoralized.

What Virginia did mainly was make a great show of force. Billy Mahone, V.M.I. graduate and young president of the Norfolk & Petersburg Railroad, filled up cars with civilians a few miles out of Norfolk and ran them in with whoops and yells of the passengers. This was repeated over and over, while militia units demanded surrender. Instead, the Navy evacuated the yards. They burned and scuttled such ships as were not ready to sail, set fire to everything else, and steamed out the personnel on the available ships remaining.

The Virginians salvaged some of the ships (one named *Merrimac*) and some of the machinery. They also came off with hundreds of can-nons intact, including over fifty new nine-inch rifled Dahlgrens, shells, and more powder than the whole Confederacy possessed.

At the same time another group of Virginians from the Valley seized the government arsenal at Harper's Ferry. They salvaged $2,000,000 worth of machinery from the fires of hasty evacuation and several thousand rifles—some of which were brought to equip the old militia companies in Richmond.

For volunteer companies the Richmond Council voted $50,000 for arms and equipment, and Governor Letcher issued the call to arms, in which he aimed an indirect appeal to the state's sons in the armed forces. Ordinance Number 9 gave orders "to repel invasion . . . see that in all things the commonwealth suffers no detriment. . . . All officers, civil and military, and the people generally of this state . . . are hereby released from any and all oaths which they may have taken to support the Constitution of the late Confederacy known as the United States of America. . . ."

Volunteering started all over the state, and units began pouring into Richmond. Just outside the city a lady, hearing music unexpectedly below her hilltop garden, walked out on the bluff from where she could see the James River and the canal to the west. Canal boats, of sweet association, were jammed with men, some with firearms, and their band was playing an unfamiliar song, strangely catchy. It was "Dixie."

3

In the city bands played "Dixie" and "The Bonnie Blue Flag" at all hours, and poems went the rounds celebrating Beauregard, the hero of Fort Sumter:

> With Mortar, Paix han and Petard,
> We tender Old Abe our Beauregard.

Never mind that Virginia was not in the Confederacy yet—they were back where they had started, the independent commonwealth. For that matter the Convention's ordinance to secede had not even been passed by the people. But the state had seized the United States Customs House on Main Street and, whatever their exact status, "the sentiment of the people is that they are engaged in a just and righteous war for independence and the defense of their homes and firesides." This was Frederick Aikien, secretary of National Democratic Executive Committee from Massachusetts, in the South at that time.

Others were too frantic to get out of the South to be making observations. The Richmond office of British consul Cridland was packed from morning until night. Men vied with ladies in telling the most piteous tales. The railroad stations looked like camp meetings. Returning natives had to push through the mobs, and their turn for confusion came when they tried to get lodging.

They had suffered their share of hazards in escaping from the North. Families had been separated. Some men had come first to volunteer for the fighting, others had been arrested and held behind. Two ladies arriving in New York from Europe had reached Richmond by way of Kansas. Refugees had arrived in carts and carriages and on foot, on trains with only hand luggage, and now a new trek for a new home began on the hilly, uneven brick sidewalks of the overflowing city.

To the fortunates coming from the countryside and other cities, especially Washington, with homes of friends or kin to go to, there was an exciting sense of reunion, of recapture of some precious and wonderful quality that had almost escaped them in life.

Many of these ladies were wives and daughters of recent United States officials, and with them came the mood of a new destiny. They were establishing an aristocracy solely of their own, without compromise or irritation with the North. Their own land was to be free that they might live in it their own chosen way. "Some of them seemed going south to a kind of empire."

There were no sabled kings, but the whole freshly born empire was a cotton kingdom with its own nobility. Weep no more, my lady, it's good-by to log-cabin presidents. . . .

Vice-President Stephens, whose nobility was strictly of the mind, joined the rush to Richmond in April. He came, as the Confederates' representative, to form a military alliance with Virginia. There was the usual serenade by Smith's "celebrated brass band," the little man made a speech from the balcony of the Exchange Hotel, and the next day he met the Virginia solons, headed by ex-President Tyler. In solemn convention the state's forces were placed "under the chief control and direction of the President" down in Montgomery.

These vain Virginians, aware of their importance, did not relish the situation of being the outpost of a Deep South capital. When they threw in their fate with the new nation, they included an invitation to shift the capital to Richmond. They seemed indifferent to the fact that this honor would also make their city the point of concentration for the armed forces of the United States.

4

Only a few grimly prophetic newspaper editorials took the war threat seriously. Most people expected some sort of armed invasion for the purpose of forcing Virginia back where she didn't intend to go, but anybody knew a Southerner was worth half a dozen Yankees in any sort of fighting. Though they were boastful enough in their confidence, they were eager to support it and deadly sure of right on their side. If their certainty was somewhat naïve and tactless, they did not lose their graciousness.

Richmond social life was never gayer. For the untitled nobility there were dances and dinners in the large-roomed houses, and for the plain people there were feasts and wassail, with plentiful use of their native products of tobacco and corn. British correspondent Russell said they were "Americanizing Bacchus into Bourbon."

They took simple pleasure and pride in everything of their own new country—even to the new small-denominational money issued in Richmond. These two-dollar, one-dollar, and fifty-cent bills, rather handsomely engraved on pink, showed the determined face of Governor Letcher, his high forehead balding, rimless glasses over his steady eyes.

These bills, marked "Corporation of Richmond," had appeared two days after secession, along with dollar bills from the Southern Rights Bank. No matter where the rights fell, sectionalism was in their hearts, and their hearts were light.

They were given a bad scare on the first Sunday after they seceded when the Yankee gunboat *Pawnee* was rumored to be coming up the James. Even then they had not run away. They had gone toward the place of danger, to look. Now they laughed about the whole thing. "Pawnee Sunday," they called it.

Even Lincoln's dire proclamations failed to disturb them. He had declared a blockade on the Southern ports, and now he came out again, specifically named the recalcitrants as "persons claiming to act under the authorities of the states of Virginia and North Carolina."

Davis answered, proclaiming a state of war between the C.S.A. and the U.S. and, in the old Revolutionary tradition, issued letters of marque to privateers. He gave fine constitutional reasons for it all, but the people were already at war as far as they were concerned, and they preferred to talk of their hero.

Beau sabreur, beau soldat, Beauregard!

There were their own soldiers too, coming home to their native state. They were not then names of legend and glory; some had not earned the name by which history would call them. The V.M.I. cadets had come to Richmond to drill the volunteers at the Fair Grounds, and their instructor, Major T. J..Jackson, was then called "Fool Tom" for his eccentricities.

A twenty-nine-year-old lieutenant, completing a hard trip from a Western cavalry post, had been known by the name of "Beauty," inversely because of his receding chin and the shortness of the stocky legs that supported his powerful torso. He was to become known by a name formed from the initials that became familiar. On his trip to Richmond, he had left a note to his colonel:

From a sense of duty to my native state [Virginia], I hereby resign my position in the Army of the United States.

J. E. B. STUART

At this point, with a luxuriant beard to cover his unworthy chin, he was concerned about a salary for the support of his family—having abandoned his savings in his flight from the West—and about the name of his youngest child. Lieutenant Stuart and his wife had intended naming him for Flora Stuart's father, but the old man had stayed in the Union Army. Now the shamed Stuart was writing his brother-in-law (who had come with Virginia) that they must put on a brave face to the world before the dishonor brought on them by Philip St. George Cooke, the old dragoon commander of the Mormon trail.

Already famous were two middle-aged men. Matthew Fontaine Maury, mild-mannered and renowned Navy oceanographer, had worked quietly in his Washington Observatory to the last minute, hoping against a break which he felt was needless. Like young Stuart, he was worried about money for his family. Joe Johnston, fiery, gray-goateed bantam, had been brigadier general in the old army, highest rank of any Confederate. It was in the quartermaster corps, which did not carry equivalent rank in command of troops, but Johnston was a stickler for the letter. He wanted no commission in Virginia's Provisional Army, which the governor told officers frankly might not hold in the Confederate Army. In the enthusiasm no one apparently thought much about his worry over rank at that time.

There were too many others, too many welcoming parties, too many bands. There were young George Pickett, with his romantic mustache and perfumed curled hair; John Magruder, called "Prince John" for his magnificence, was put to drilling artillery at the Richmond College grounds; Powell Hill, slight and courteous, attractive to women and married to the lovely sister of John Morgan: he was little more than a year from the battle where it would be said of him "and then A. P.

Hill came up." Later the two gods of the Confederate armies were to call for him in their dying delirium.

One of those two was Fool Tom Jackson, and the other had just arrived to take command of Virginia's forces and defense. He wore civilian clothes, a black suit, and a black silk hat when he rode in the carriage from the depot to the new fashionable Spotswood Hotel. He was a strongly built man, 54 years old, with dark mustache and dark hair turning gray. He registered at the hotel, "R. E. Lee," and walked over to the Governor's Mansion to confer on Virginia's defenses.

First he had to be sworn in by the convention, and he was ceremoniously conducted to the House of Delegates. As seen then he was stately and symmetrical; "with no gaiety or abandon, yet with no affectation of dignity; the gentleness was marked, but it did not conceal an iron will." He was a handsome and impressive man in the classic style.

In the Capitol, convention president Janney, veteran of the long debate on secession, did not miss his moment. He referred to Lee's father, General Light Horse Harry Lee, who had made the "first in war" remark about Washington. Then Janney said that Robert E. Lee was first in war among living Virginians, they prayed he would be first in peace, and that he would earn the distinction of being first in the hearts of his countrymen.

Obviously moved, the newly appointed state major general did not attempt to match words. He spoke briefly—three sentences—and finished with, "Trusting in Almighty God, an approving conscience, and the aid of my fellow citizens, I devote myself to the service of my native state, in whose behalf alone I will ever draw my sword."

It was the last speech he ever made. Leaving the vainglory to the paraders, he settled down methodically to the task of preparing an unarmed state to defend itself against a nation.

Lee had been a colonel in the old army, thought by many to be its finest soldier, and at the outbreak of hostilities he had received an unofficial offer to command it. He was superbly qualified for his task, and in his lifetime he had acquired the patience of Job. He needed it.

He had to begin with fitting up a makeshift office in the Mechanics' Hall, across from the Capitol Square, on Ninth Street, and in organizing a staff. Having served nearly forty years in the Regular Army, he suffered no delusions as to the number of Yankees one Southerner could lick. He appreciated that an outdoorsman who had spent years hunting and shooting would likely be a finer physical specimen than a city clerk; but he also appreciated that they were not fighting with fists, nor under the code duello of man for man—and the South was one to four in man power.

Also, he perceived the four main military doorways into the state, as inviting as if the welcome mat were out. He must improvise some kind of defense before the enemy struck.

But defense was not what the hotspurs from the lower South wanted.

Already they damned Virginia leaders for timid inactivity in not attacking the whole United States at once. Knighthood had reflowered, and chivalry wanted its day in the field. Even Davis, in reviewing troops, proclaimed, "When the last line of bayonets is leveled, I'll be with you."

The spirit of Sir Walter Scott champed at this pusillanimous making of maps, dividing the state into avenues it offered the enemy, when gallant action would sweep everything before it. Toombs denounced Lee and Governor Letcher for not throwing a force across the western Potomac above the Shenandoah Valley (presumably armed with rocks), but the state staff went on quietly planning such expedients as could be prepared for checking the gathering forces of the invader.

5

While the papers began to call for Davis, "a tower of strength,"—to come to Richmond—for with him "the victory would be certain," the city had the thrill of feting its first minor hero. From Baltimore, Richard Thomas, a wealthy Marylander, had boarded the steamer *St. Nicholas* as a passenger and in the bay had taken her over with a boldness that no one called piracy.

Using the ship as a privateer, he captured other vessels with cargoes of coffee, coal, ice, cement, and such. When he came on to Richmond, the gratified governor commissioned him a colonel of Virginia Volunteers and the populace hoped mightily for him.

However, carried away by his glory and against all advice, he returned to Baltimore to repeat his exploit. The "pitcher and the well" adage held, and he ended up in jail.

The other activity in Baltimore—the street riots of Southern sympathizers at the passage of United States troops—had also quieted down, and, though individual Marylanders came over as volunteers, hope was lost for the state.

But Richmond seemed confidently unaffected at finding Virginia separated from the enemy only by the Potomac, and there was a good deal of "business as usual." Boat trips to New York (with meals and stateroom included in the ten-dollar cost) were still advertised as leaving Richmond twice weekly. The American ship *Argo* was expected at City Point, a few miles below Richmond, to load for Bremen, and a ship arrived at the city dock loaded with salt, guano, logwood, and fish from Halifax and coal from the North. Northern firearms manufacturers advertised in the local papers, along with the boarding school at Lausanne, and a Main Street bookseller was pushing the fifth volume of Macaulay's *England*.

Rewards were posted for runaway slaves, and a new auction house for the sale of Negroes was advertised on Franklin Street, in the general neighborhood where livery stables and the less fashionable saloons enjoyed a boom business. Nor was there a decrease in the trade of Duquesne's hairdressing establishment and Pizzini's confectionery, where ladies partook of their specialties of ice cream and frappés. The clothiers and haberdashers interspersed their old-line goods with cadet-gray cloth, and the uniforms appearing on the street were styled on personal taste and means in a land to which Government Issue was unknown.

For the ladies, Miss Rebecca Semon returned with new spring styles of Paris fashion, including Arabian mantles, and for boys Spanish suits and Prince Albert aprons. The Virginia Episcopal Convention met in Richmond, and the usual old toper was jailed for failing to give bond not to get drunk and encumber sidewalks. As Richmonders were always giving money to something, it seemed only a new charity when individuals donated sums for the benefit of volunteers' families, and the German Hebrew Congregation contributed $1,230.

Little enthusiasm could be generated even for the fortifications which had to be built around the city against a quick thrust. Some citizens contributed tools and wheelbarrows, making a great show of their patriotism, and slaveholders lent Negroes, but white and black alike faded away before the strengthening sun.

Professional engineers kept the effort going. The penitentiary supplied some workmen, and finally freed Negroes were organized into groups and marched out and back with flags flying and drums beating. They built earthen forts, partly armed by the inexhaustible supply of Norfolk guns.

But this, like everything else, only opened new problems. The job of fortifying a state in a few weeks against an organized nation seemed to make every accomplishment reveal two new needs. When the fortifications were erected at all menaced points, and skeletal units stood everywhere, the men had to be armed.

Half the volunteers had reported unarmed, and most of what the other half brought were outmoded flintlocks. The state armory worked desperately to alter these for percussion fire, but when the cavalry reported with only pistols and a few sabers they were advised to use shotguns or buy privately what they could. For the altered percussion muskets, the harassed agents scraped the bottom of the barrel for an issue of caps and balls, with nothing in reserve.

By herculean efforts, the militia got horses and harness, caissons and equipment, for twenty four-gun field batteries, though some of the caissons were wagons. Getting proper carriages was also the problem with using the heavy guns from Norfolk, but the Virginia "Navy" mounted at least some at all their forts and sent three hundred pieces to other Southern states.

Ordinary wagons for transportation was a shortage that nobody solved, and the problem of Virginia roads was insoluble.

The dirt roads were bottomless pits in the rainy season, and the plank roads were hazards any time. What they lacked in quality they made up for in quantity, and counties were crisscrossed with dusty relics of turnpike companies' follies.

Complete maps were non-existent. The defending forces had no fear of such maps as there were falling into the enemy's hands, for they were sure to be wrong. Even natives felt uneasy ten miles from home, and—with neither intelligence system nor military maps—the natives were to serve as the guides of the Army.

All these clammy facts were regarded as ignoble reasons for a disgraceful timidity by the hotbloods whose urge to the fray was as the bridegroom's to the couch. "Give us Davis," they cried. "Bring President Davis to Richmond and we'll have some action."

6

Among the citizens not concerned with defense problems, the chief excitement was brought by the Confederate troops pouring into Richmond to defend the borderland of the South. With these allies, the glamour of their new land reached its full flower.

First, at six in the afternoon early in May, when the spring twilight was a blue mist and the chimneys stood like rows of flowerpots against the saffron sky, came the First and Second South Carolinians. They were a superb body of men led by Bourbons Maxey Gregg and Bonham, dark and sunburnt from recent exposure.

Later from South Carolina came the aristocratic Hampton Legion, the pride of the massive Wade Hampton, one of the South's great sportsmen and richest planters. The legion set up a luxurious camp. The privates brought trunks, were attended by body servants, and their dress parades were as fashionable as a race meet. They might seem to bear out the *Harper's* cartoon of a puny Southerner staggering to battle under an umbrella, with his Negro coming behind with cocktails. But the South was no one thing.

The opposite of the Hampton Legion were the small, tough, hot-eyed bully boys of the Louisiana Zouaves. The reputation of their rioting in Montgomery had come before them, and they tried to live up to it by stealing, refusing to pay bar bills, and making the streets unsafe for ladies. They were commanded by Dick Taylor—a literate gentleman and son of President Taylor—and by Bob Wheat, a professional revolutionary of manners so soft and courteous the ladies could not believe he, or the well-liked Dick Taylor, was associated with such ruffians.

Still another slice were the Texans who bore out General Taylor's description of them in the Mexican War that "they were anything but gentlemen or cowards." As hardy as the Texans were the tall, rail-hard Red River men from southern Arkansas and northern Louisiana, who looked like a race of warriors. They all had their own flags —the lone star of Texas, the magnolia of Mississippi, the pelican of Louisiana; their own uniforms—the full-skirted butternut of Georgians, the smartly cut blue of Alabamians; and their own names— Guards and Dragoons, Grenadiers and Lancers, and all variations of "Yankee-catchers."

Richmond's own troops had formed the First Virginia Regiment of nine companies and a number of companies for other regiments— Richmond Light Infantry Blues, the Grays, the Rifles, the Sharpshooters, the Zouaves and Guards of all kinds—the Old Dominion, Virginia, Young, Virginia Life, the Montgomery and Emmett Guards of Irishmen, and the elite who with inverted snobbery were simply Company F. They had a full battalion of artillery, the Howitzers, who were to make a magnificent war record, and several other batteries— the Fayette, Otis, Purcell, Hampden, Thomas, Peyton's—and the Governor's Mounted Guard.

Many of the local troops left for points of danger as their formerly quiet home city was turned into an armed camp and carnival. The woods around Richmond became tented villages. Nights were wakeful with revelers and new arrivals. Days were one continuous parade, where bayonets were festooned with flowers and ladies tirelessly waved handkerchiefs from balconies and doorways.

That there was a stiffening among some natives at the way the soldiers took over was natural, but it was surprisingly infrequent. The clearest indication of disapproval at familiarity was given by a very young lady, aged eight. When she was caressed by a handsomely outfitted soldier she turned to her aunt and said haughtily, "Any man that wears a stripe on his pantaloons thinks he can speak to any lady."

In the main the ladies took wine and cakes to the camps, sewed on uniforms and haversacks and many sweet little articles of dubious usefulness, all happily unaware of the problems of divided command these out-of-state troops brought Virginia. Sometimes Confederate troops came into Virginia without Governor Letcher's knowledge, and one outfit in Richmond, whom he ordered to Harper's Ferry, refused to go on the grounds that he had no authority. A technical solution of the dual command was effected in early May, when Lee was commissioned brigadier general in the Confederate Army to straighten out the tangle, but he still bore the burden of Virginia's own problem.

His staff looked at the beckoning highways into the state, listened to the accounts of massing Unions (the uncensored newspapers were the best spies for both sides, and the New York *Herald* was delivered regularly to the Richmond war office), and knew they were not ready.

Even the outfitting of the state's fifty thousand volunteers was woefully far from completion. Such a simple item as clothing them became a well-nigh hopeless task. Except for a few counties where women made serviceable uniforms for their volunteers, the state had to fall back on clothing allowances for the men to supply themselves as best they could.

Such things as knapsacks and cartridge boxes were bought largely at first by the more well-to-do militia outfits. Any volunteer with cash scoured the newspapers for ads, and the heavy demand kept gunsmiths and firearm shops open on Sunday, with prices soaring.

To join the cavalry the simple requirement was possession of a horse. The state, or the Confederacy later, never furnished one.

The patriots ignored these complications and saw the bright variegated uniforms only as symbols of their new independence and saw the Virginia leaders as spiritless fusspots. The cry for Davis became a clamor. He, the long leader of the Southerners, understood action for independence. Even out in Cleveland the *Plain Dealer* called him "a genuine son of Mars."

As it had been said of him, "the man and the hour have met," let the man and the hour meet the place. Richmond was the citadel; he must come to Richmond.

7

Down in Montgomery the new rulers had debated this move. Though the charming little Alabama town was too small, many opposed moving the capital. In fact war clerk Jones heard talk to the effect that, if it weren't for war, the new Confederacy would not even want the Border States.

The chief argument in favor of the change was that Davis, literally commander in chief, should be near the fighting. By the Constitution, civil government could not be delegated to Alexander Stephens—who probably wouldn't have known what to do with it anyway.

To put the President practically in the field sounds like a quaint idea now, but to a people committed to gallantry, their leader led in battle.

For another argument, Howell Cobb, now Georgia's senator, said the move to Richmond was for the purpose of being near the soldiers at the advance posts, so, "when the hour of danger comes, we may lay aside the robes of legislature, buckle on the armor of the soldier. . . ." These words were echoed by other government powers who saw "buckling on the armor" as a way to the military glory that would always be dearer to Southern hearts than statesmanship. In this vainglory and sincerity, powerful men brought pressure for the move.

Finally there was the prestige of Virginia, and her man power and resources that needed a little stimulation—or so they thought. In any event, with misgivings of some, they voted to make the shift to Richmond as the capital of the new Confederacy.

No sooner was the news received in Virginia than the people went to the polls and voted secession, ratifying the ordinance.

The next day the state was invaded.

Bright and early of a morning in late May, old Winfield Scott, Union commander, directed the armies in four drives into his native state.

East from the Ohio River, through the disaffected western counties, McClellan drove confidently toward his rendezvous with destiny. North from the Potomac, at Harper's Ferry, Patterson pushed toward the great valley. From Washington, McDowell (who was to have no luck) occupied Alexandria (long the town of the Lees) and Arlington Heights, including Lee's home. It came to Lee through his wife, a Custis and descendant of Martha Washington, and Mrs. Lee wrote

McDowell asking that the historic ancestral home be spared. The outside was.

Last, straight toward Richmond up the narrow peninsula from Fort Monroe, moved Butler. Already known for subduing the civilians of Baltimore, he was to make warfare on the unarmed his specialty and to fare always much less well when the other side had guns too.

Also starting to Richmond from the Deep South was the tall thin man, as straight as an Indian and as severe as the face on a coin, in the vanguard of the men of desperate fortune who were to make Richmond their capital in their bid for a new country. . . .

CHAPTER FOUR

The Heroes Come

WHEN the rather sweetly stuffy old-liners of Richmond learned that the new government was setting up shop there, "a surprise that was not all pleasurable thrilled to the finger tips of Richmond society." According to DeLeon, the Lucius Beebe of his day, "Its exponents felt much as the Roman patricians might have felt at the impending advent of the leading families of the Goths."

There might have been some apprehensive curiosity among all the excitement in the crowd that stood, early in the May morning, and watched the train from the south cross the bridge over the James River, but none of this was manifest in the enthusiasm which greeted the man of the hour as he arrived at the place of destiny. The cheering was a spontaneous swell. Guns boomed. Bells rang. The official committee swarmed over the erect, tired man from Mississippi and he was assisted by countless hands into the carriage behind the four white horses.

Mrs. Wigfall, wife of the Texas senator, rode beside him. Her husband, now colonel, functioned on the President's staff. Joseph Davis, a nephew, acted as an aide, and also with them was burly Bob Toombs, the revolutionary Georgian and tobacco chewer extraordinary. The band played "Dixie" as the presidential party drove through the crowd-lined streets to the new Spotswood Hotel.

On the way a little girl threw a corsage to Davis's carriage, and it fell short a few feet. The President warmed the hearts of all by stopping the carriage, stepping down, and placing the fallen corsage on the lap of Mrs. Wigfall. That was the gesture the Virginians wanted. It made gallantry complete. Only the most confirmed croakers failed to respond to the magnetism of the stately leader. All now lacking was the sound of his voice. They wanted to hear him.

A path had to be forced through the jam in the hotel entrance, but as he went up to his room the cry for his words became insistent. He was very tired then, and he had been making speeches since February.

He was not a strong man, for all his straight, graceful carriage. Nerves were his problem. Living by the books, by learning the thing to do, he lived under tension. When the strain grew too intense it reflected in neuralgic pains and in upset stomach. Dyspepsia, they called it. His wife said, "He was a nervous dyspeptic by habit."

But he knew his duty. No man could ever accuse him of shirking that. He went to the window above the admiring crowd.

A few blocks up Main Street hill he could see some of the great houses of Richmond—predominantly Georgian and red-brick, with double balconies overlooking walled gardens and servants' quarters. Everywhere he saw that mellowed red brick of Tidewater. Down Main Street the hill dipped more steeply, past the stores and banks, the hotels and commission houses, and the U. S. Customs House which was to be his office. He was a stranger a long way from his stamping ground, among people who had not chosen him—and who now acclaimed him.

He spoke to them briefly, of their rights, of the constitutional ground on which they stood. He had said the same things in every state in the South, and he never tired of these assertions of their non-aggressive sanctity. "All we ask is to be let alone."

The crowd was satisfied. He had dignity and presence. He was a true symbol of gentlefolk.

Official groups formed to pay their respects, and Davis submitted briefly to receptions.

His wife had not yet joined him, and she was the socializer. Varina was considered an excellent conversationalist, of vivacity and humor, and groups stimulated rather than tired her. But her husband felt that such gatherings siphoned off the energy he needed for his business of conducting the war. Without her, Davis left the citizens to go on with their holiday while he conferred with the military men.

2

From the first the President approved Virginia's defensive policy, which allowed the new nation some little time to prepare. He feared that the Union's efforts to subdue the insurrectionists would not cease with one skirmish. A fight could settle down to real war.

He asked for three-year enlistments when the Congress asked for three-months, and they compromised on one-year. Too many people had believed Davis's own optimistic statements, but Davis had not. As a leader he must cheer his own people and put on a bold front to the enemy. Yet, in talking privately to Mrs. Chesnut, one of the Davises' closest friends, "his tone was not sanguine. There was a sad refrain running through it all."

However, he showed only confidence to General Lee, who turned over to him the state military establishment he had built in two months. Forty thousand men—outfitted, armed, and with at least a modicum of ammunition and equipment—guarded the entrances to the state, and naval guns guarded rivers from behind fortifications.

Lee turned over 46,000 guns to be stamped "C.S.A." That the United States in that first year of 1861 was to issue 1,230,000 more than that was a problem to meet as they came to it. For now, the President must grasp the details of Lee's defenses for the state obviously destined to be the battleground.

As the national capital had seemed more apprehensive for its own safety than interested in invading Virginia, Lee had first risked the puniest nucleus of a force on those beckoning plains rolling from Washington south through Manassas—a railroad junction. This small and poorly armed force stayed alerted there while they received their primary training and gradual reinforcements.

West of them ran the Blue Ridge, beyond which spread the Shenandoah Valley. Not only rich in itself, the valley gave a hallway along the Secessionist side of the state and close to the Unionists. At its northern doorway on the Potomac, another force was trained by a hated and merciless drillmaster, Colonel Fool Tom Jackson. He was guarded against surprise by the cavalry of restless young Major J. E. B. Stuart, who had been at Harper's Ferry before—as the arresting officer of John Brown.

Too early for superiors to recognize the genius of Jackson's grim eccentricities, he was supplanted by Joe Johnston when that rank-conscious general was ready to serve. Johnston, gentleman by act of God as well as Congress, who was to prove as ungenerously sensitive about his dignity as about rank, was welcomed as one of the greats of the new army.

At fifty-four, Johnston was a thoroughly trained professional soldier, soundly analytical and defense-minded in his approach, and accustomed to the abundance and discipline of the old army. He instantly retreated to a less exposed position up the valley, complained of the paucity of material for war and of the rawness of the big-boned recruits whom Jackson had found to his liking.

With his training-camp defense line facing a thrust from the north, Joe Johnston apprehensively eyed the unsettled country to his west.

[39]

Beyond the Alleghenies, where the population was soon to secede from Virginia (and, in a war against secession, be accepted into the Union), the third scratch force had assembled to guard against McClellan's advance from the Ohio.

The fourth force, under the resplendent "Prince John" Magruder, was much closer home. On the billiard-table flatland of the Virginia

Peninsula, between the York and James rivers, Magruder formed a force of militia and volunteers near Yorktown. From there he watched for movement from Fortress Monroe, at the tip of the Peninsula on Chesapeake Bay. This was a danger spot for Richmond and all eastern Virginia.

Across Hampton Roads from Norfolk, the fort's guns gave cover to ships of war which could assail Norfolk and land troops in the rear, cutting off the city. Also the fort offered a base for naval action, in

VARINA DAVIS AS FIRST LADY

From a photograph. Courtesy of Confederate Museum, Richmond, Virginia.

JEFFERSON DAVIS

As he first appeared in Richmond, 1861, at the age of fifty-three. From a photograph. Courtesy of Confederate Museum, Richmond, Virginia.

support of ground troops, along the fine waterways that served Virginia's trade so well.

While Richmond, like a staid old lady under the impact of three cocktails, gave little thought to the consequences of its secession party, naval guns were laboriously moved from the captured Norfolk navy yard and mounted along the rivers that approached the city.

Finally there was the Potomac, curving northward from Chesapeake Bay, with its head of navigation at Alexandria, close enough to Washington to be a suburb today. But then it was the first Virginia city in line of a drive south, and there had rushed a "force" under a lieutenant colonel.

Apparently Washington suffered a bad scare before United States troops arrived, but as fearful as was the capital, these valiants were more so—and with good reason. They were two companies of raw recruits, aggregating 150 privates, with 1818 flintlocks, and the Mount Vernon Guard, of 86, with new muskets and little ammunition. Of the group, 52 were without accouterments and 15 without anything.

While they certainly showed that their vaunted valor was more than words, they were judged by their own side as useless for defense and only provocative of attack. As provocation was what Lee had striven to avoid, this punitive expedition retired, and another force erected a battery farther south on the Potomac at Aquia Creek.

This little estuary of the great river was important. Boats from Washington connected there with the terminus of the Richmond, Fredericksburg & Potomac Railroad, which ran thirteen miles from Aquia Creek to Fredericksburg and then fifty-odd miles into Richmond. Here was fought one of the early naval actions of the war, largely unrecorded except in memoirs, but indicative of the first fighting of Americans against each other.

The battery—in charge of the Virginia "Navy"—consisted of a scattering of militia and farmers commanded by several officers recently resigned from the U. S. Navy. They had fought off a landing party, exchanged shots with Union gunboats and armed steamers, and one "engagement" lasted five hours, where the damage done—in addition to that caused by flying splinters on the ships and dirt on the shore—was the loss of the life of the Potomac Flotilla commander, through a gun accident, and on the shore the loss of a finger and several chickens. As the New York *Herald* proclaimed this a victory, the natives were outraged at an enemy who made war on fowls and contemptuous of an enemy who counted such casualties as a triumph, when it was clear the battery grew stronger every day.

[41]

Davis approved of these dispositions, as he looked ahead to sustaining Southern independence against unconstitutional aggression until recognition from Europe established the Confederacy as a nation. Since he believed its movement was not revolution, it followed that the world would come to the same belief and recognize his country.

His wife said, "He sincerely thought all he said, and, moreover, could not understand any other man coming to a different conclusion after his premises were stated. It was this sincerity of opinion which sometimes gave him the manner to which his opponents objected as domineering."

At that time only one official, Bob Toombs, showed resentment of Davis's attitude. The grievances of this unstable man seemed unimportant in those halcyon days when offices of the new government were being set up in Richmond and the President was becoming a familiar and popular figure.

Davis walked every morning the two blocks to his office with no formal staff or bodyguard, like a planter at home in a country town. Richmond was, for all its manufacturing and shipping, rather like a very large village. It lacked the complexity associated with cities, the change wrought by the constant influx of new blood—immigrants and adventurers, bright-eyed country youth and Alger wistfuls. Physically it grew out of fields and woods and farm land, with no clear line between countryside and town. Even at its center it was like an oversize town square.

Technically built on seven hills, the city did not give that impression. Bounded on the south by the James River, the city rose from the river in a sequence of promontories, between the largest of which was the valley of Shockoe Creek emptying into the river. Originally fur and tobacco from the West had been brought along this creek to the trading post out of which the city grew.

To the east of the valley rose the old section of Church Hill, a broad plateau with wide shaded streets and Queen Anne houses. To the west, unevenly and very steeply, both from the river and Shockoe Valley, the newer city climbed to another broad plateau. Both of these plains were sliced by lesser valleys cutting toward the river, and these formed projecting hills—Gamble's, Chimborazo, Libby—and there were minor rolls and pitches between them.

In the center of the rise from the river and Shockoe Valley was Capitol Square, where the pillared Capitol building on the crest dominated the whole scene. Around the green hill of the square were homes and churches, the city hall and state library, the bell tower for the weapons of the city guard, the buildings used for the war office and the chief government bureaus. Streets for residence, for shopping, and for the more garish night life spread from this center like spokes from a hub. Bank Street, along the southern border, was separated only by the depth of one building from Main Street—just like its name.

When President Davis left the new Spotswood Hotel at Eighth, and walked downhill along Main, he passed banks, bookstores, boarding-houses of the better class, wholesale and retail merchants, and office buildings. At the corner intersections, looking south, to his right, he could see the crowded Basin of the canal, the river beyond, and the tall brick buildings of tobacco warehouses and flour mills.

At Tenth Street he would swing north, to his left, climbing a steep short block into Bank Street. As he turned into Bank, on one side the green hill of Capitol Square climbed steeply to the Capitol. On his side of the street rose the granite structure, formerly the U. S. Customs House, now used as the C. S. A. Treasury building.

The Treasury Department occupied the first floor, the President and State Department the second, and Davis climbed the first stairs on the right to the upper floor. Upstairs, he entered the second door on his left, across the hall from his aides. His private secretary's office adjoined his.

He worked until late in the afternoon and then almost invariably rode out to one of the camps. There was no reason for him to go there, and problems of co-ordinating his departments were being neglected. He simply could not resist the call of the bugle. He usually rode out with friends—senators or cabinet members—and people on the street noted with satisfaction his grace on a horse.

To a people wanting a personal leader, he made a fine appearance. He was always neat about his person—*soigné,* his wife said—and sufficiently conscious of clothes to be very observant of the dress of others.

As the British correspondent Russell saw him, "He is like a gentleman—has a slight, light figure, little exceeding middle height, and holds himself erect and straight."

His height varies anywhere from Russell's description of it to six feet two. His tailor's measurement was $33\frac{1}{2}$ inches for the inside leg length. As his trousers were worn long and his torso was average, this would indicate that his height approached but was under six feet. His relative slenderness would be indicated by the other measurements—breast, $37\frac{1}{2}$; waist, $35\frac{1}{2}$; hips, 39.

[43]

Russell found his manner

plain, and rather reserved and drastic; his head is well formed, with a fine full forehead, square and high, covered with innumerable fine lines and wrinkles, features regular, though the cheekbones are too high and the jaws too hollow to be handsome; the lips are thin, flexible, and curved, the chin square, well defined; the nose very regular, with wide nostrils; and his eyes deep-set, full and large. . . .

The expression of his face is anxious, he has a very haggard, careworn, and pained drawn look, though no traces of anything but the utmost confidence and the greatest decision could be detected in his conversation. . . .

The strain the Englishman observed resulted from Jefferson Davis's first efforts to effectuate in the details of a forming government the fixed concepts which previously had been limited to theories, to speeches, and to the procedure of personal intercourse.

Now, in action, he concentrated on the Confederacy's physical defense, and the separate departments were set up in little or no relation to one another. They were like six separate new enterprises, where authority must be delegated and duties defined, men and methods tried. Co-ordination depended on central control, the President. As he had evolved no central plan nor discovered the means of delegating authority, the problems of the unco-ordinated departments kept arising to be met separately. It was a tiring way to work.

At nights he retired to his hot hotel room in the strange city and wrote his wife, hoping she could soon come on with the children. Their letters were cherished when they were separated, and Varina carried his in her bodice.

3

By the time Davis was familiar with Virginia's defenses, a new hero arrived in Richmond—*The* Hero of Fort Sumter.

When Beauregard came, that Manassas line across the northern plains of Virginia was obviously the danger point. Though reinforcements had moved steadily to the first little force alerted there, the position stood in the path of the advance which occupied Alexandria —in what was clearly a drive to Richmond itself. If that center did not hold, all the other carefully placed defenders would be as nought. This vital post waited for the first knight of the Confederacy—*Beau sabreur,* Beauregard.

[44]

The South loved hero worship at least as well as the rest of America, and while today it lacks the equipment for spectacular welcomes, when Old Bory came to town the city had its carriage and four white horses, its bands and flags, and its ever ebullient crowds.

But *soldat* Beauregard had his way of meeting destiny's hour. He asked for a simpler carriage for himself and two of his staff and made it plain that he was a man of action, not words. He did not appear at his window at the Spotswood, let the crowd clamor though it would. And this in its way also seemed fitting: Richmond knew their conqueror had come to fight and not to talk.

Beauregard went to join President Davis with General Lee, and there the two men of destiny faced each other across the quiet gentleman who had done all the work. The defensive plans which Lee had executed, Davis was to operate; the men Lee had organized and equipped, Beauregard was to lead. The Hero was bothered by not the slightest doubt of his right or his ability.

He had graduated at West Point second in the class that included McDowell, the general he was to face across the Manassas line. He had so distinguished himself in the Mexican War that, when later he thought of resigning, he was urged to remain in the Army by Winfield Scott, the commander of the invading armies. Several months before, he had been appointed superintendent of West Point, but after being there only a few days he had resigned to go with his state, Louisiana. Then to this gorgeous Creole came the fame of Fort Sumter, and he accepted with reassuring simplicity the laurels heaped upon him and the acclaims of his genius. Had he not studied the military all his life, known only the single dream of *la gloire?*

Beauregard was forty-three then, slightly below the middle height, wiry in build. His sallow French face, with cropped mustache and bordered with graying hair, was a romantic mixture of melancholy and dramatic self-confidence.

Apparently he was little impressed with Lee—in the anomalous position of military adviser on the defense of Virginia—or aware of his accomplishments and difficulties in preparing the state. Going off to Manassas (to the cheers of the South Carolinians he had commanded at Charleston), the Hero ignored Lee and wrote directly to Davis—his equal.

Beauregard complained at once of the small force that had been so painstakingly collected there. Unless he had reinforcements, he said he must retire at the approach of the enemy or advance to meet him at the fords, there "to sell our lives as dearly as practicable."

Toward this end of reinforcements he went direct to the people in a proclamation exhorting them "to rally to the standard" and "expel the invaders from your land." This was fine rhetoric, befitting the "Conqueror of Fort Sumter," but it neglected the detail of who was going to arm the valiants once they flocked to his call.

4

His fellow hero, Jefferson Davis, was the one to settle down to such details. It had been thought before the President came to Richmond that he might take the field himself. Now in the capital, at the hub of the fighting fronts, he approximated field leadership by interpreting his title, "commander in chief," to mean literally that. As of World War II, he would combine the offices of General Eisenhower (supreme commander), General Marshall (chief of staff), and Stimson (Secretary of War).

Not only was the soldier paramount in his self-image, but his four happiest years in Washington had been spent as the Secretary of War. Through the resumption of this beloved work, as the commander, Davis fulfilled his immediate purpose on secession—to jump from abstracts to military action.

His preoccupation with this field naturally reduced his War Secretary to a subordinate position. The Secretary actually became the executive officer of the commander, relegated to performing all the grimy details of physically maintaining armies in the field and in operating a new office—which happened to be the center of all interest in the South.

Leroy Pope Walker, the Alabama lawyer, was inexperienced both in military affairs and in running a political office. Sickly to begin with, the Secretary was soon swamped in the waves of paper work and the importunities of place seekers.

According to Jones, a clerk in the war office, the Secretary's successful law career was no training for government routine, and Walker knew nothing of avoiding detail work. Also, being "fastidiously tenacious of what is due a gentleman," Walker used much time in exacting the niceties proper to his position, in ceremonious exchanges with brother officials, and in passing full courtesies with the callers who constantly besieged his office.

As the Secretary disliked writing letters as much as he liked socializing, unanswered mail made his office look like disordered archives; and as he procrastinated on final action, work of all kind constantly piled up. The confusion in which he worked and the poorly directed energy he poured into his endless and insoluble details, offending petitioners by not answering their letters or giving them appointments, all kept him feeling bad and frequently away from the office.

As British correspondent Russell saw him, Walker was a tall, angular man of impulsive eye and manner. He was an impulsive speaker too, and frequently came out with fire-breathing threats and boasts that did nothing to help any reputation for brains. He was one of the first members of the Cabinet to come in for public attack, and that sharp-tongued diarist, Mrs. Chesnut, called him a "slow-coach" who wouldn't give Napoleon a commission if he applied tomorrow.

He was definitely unsuited temperamentally to his work. Jones said he was "too finely strung for the official treadmill," and Walker himself, in a fit of frustration, once said to Jones that such office work was no work for a gentleman.

This type of remark was not likely to make him popular with Jones, a most unique character of far more interest than the harassed Secretary. A native of Baltimore who had married a Virginian, Jones had, at fifty-one, twenty years of moderate success as a writer and editor behind him, when he came to Richmond with the avowed purpose of keeping a day-by-day diary of the war.

In the war office he was placed at the clearinghouse of important correspondence and conferences, where his busy eyes and ears missed nothing. Though he was spiteful, jealous, and small-minded, he was a shrewd observer, and if his biases occasionally warped his judgments, they usually shaded him from the glare of heroes and sharpened his gaze on the pretentious. Whatever his personal feelings, he had sound reasons as a conscientious worker (he was a most fervent patriot) for shaking his head at the Secretary.

When the city lived in daily fear of invasion and time was of the essence, when the office had to sift through endless petitions and make urgent appointments, Walker felt it was discourteous to write a letter of less than three pages to any claimant. Not only did this chore overwork the clerks, but it created ill feeling among them.

Colonel Bledsoe, a West Point classmate of Davis and a personal appointee, had a real gift for short letters, which he could rarely pass under the Secretary's signature. When he did he was praised by Scott, the letter-book copier, and when he didn't he was abused by Scott along with everyone else who wrote long letters. In addition, portly poor Colonel Bledsoe was loathed for his connections by Jones, who viciously reported his martyred smiles, his endless groans, and that he

[47]

sweated so heavily he removed his coat. It was anything but a smoothly organized office when pressing and complicated demands would have taxed the best.

Walker came along at the time when in the first burst of enthusiasm Southerners were enlisting in droves, and many of them, loving the word "gentleman" as dearly as did he, clamored for commissions commensurate with their blood. On the other hand, many qualified men— like classes from the University of Virginia, Company F of Richmond, and practically whole regiments of South Carolina's natural leaders —insisted on going in as privates.

Beyond the problem of selection came that of arming. Over half a million men volunteered in those first glowing months, and one third of them had to be turned away. The whole South had started with 15,000 rifles (4,000 in Richmond armories) and 120,000 muskets, most of which had to be altered to percussion fire. Davis estimated only 150,000 serviceable arms, with a few sabers and artillery swords, holster pistols but no revolvers, no equipment of any kind. For battle there were 250,000 percussion caps, less than 1,000,000 cartridges and no lead, and a small store of powder which was chiefly that seized at Norfolk.

Not only was the matériel of war less than would be required for a lusty sham battle, but the means of supplying it immediately were not heartening in a country of few factories and skilled workers, and anything that could come in from abroad seemed fearfully slow with those blue-clad people massing along the entrances into Virginia.

That Walker accomplished anything is remarkable—and he did, by driving himself to industry no matter how disorganized, and by a high patriotism that kept him going in the face of the nervous illnesses and psychic disorders caused by trying to do a job for which nature had not fitted him, and for which he had been chosen—in the policy of regional appointments—by the accident of being born in Alabama.

For the policy of war he made no contribution—though then there was none, except to defend against the movement directed at Richmond. All the decisions involved with that, even the appointment of officers, rested with Davis.

This did not bother Walker, who had enough troubles of his own. But Davis's preoccupation with the armed forces failed to promote cooperation of the other departments toward any interrelated action.

The immediate ends of defense were being met; the ultimate ends —the normal operations of bureaus in an established country at peace —were acted upon *as if they now existed in fact.*

These two levels were unconnected by any dynamic political philosophy because the leader, the theorist of the plantocracy, denied that his experiment constituted rebellion. To prove that it was legal, he refused to act or even to think in the practical terms of successfully establishing his nation against outside opposition.

To him it was enough that the Confederacy discouraged the attempt to suppress its movement by force, and then assume its honored position among the nations. Of the historic forces in conflict, the lean, worried idealist showed no awareness in the sense of pressures—of going with or avoiding. Truly he belonged to the legend where honor was might.

CHAPTER FIVE

One-Man Show

THE members of the Cabinet were cast together by the same sort of chance as survivors in a lifeboat. But their common plight in no sense made them shipmates with a common plan.

As the President advanced no over-all plan for the interrelation of physical defense with the means to support it and the diplomatic end of foreign help, his cabinet members went their separate ways, charting department policy and organizing routine, happily or unhappily, according to their natures and capacities.

Enchanted with their dream of a patrician empire, and no more conscious of rebellion than Davis, they possessed no politics of the nature of which warfare is said to be the ultimate expression. Like their flowers, they merely wanted to bloom in the sun.

As their late political confederates were bent on physically preventing this flowering, their President was gathering an army where the enemy was coming. As foreign recognition was important to an established country, they sent expressions of high-minded idealism (to Europe!) and put their practical faith in the magic of their cotton. This magic was not in the use of cotton as wealth, of which it constituted their greatest source, but as a threat to Europe of *its not being sold*.

For wealth, with a lovely impracticality, these leaders assumed the manner of a dollar-rich power and relied on the one thing they had nothing of—money!

With no coins or mint, no bills or engravers to print them, with scarcely office furniture in a building recently belonging to the United States, Davis's financial policy played lofty politics with the vast riches in cotton bins and adopted the gold standard for the dollar. Gallantry could go no further to prove itself.

To maintain the traditional pattern in all things, the Treasury Department was headed by a conventional, conservative financier who knew all the rules—of what could not be done. As a Secretary, Christopher Memminger was humorless and oppressively earnest, possessing neither the will nor the gifts to put over even his bookkeeping measures by personal force or diplomacy. He stood firm on his upright character, which was small asset in a section where codes of honor came a dime a dozen.

His face reflected the seared man of method, who lived by rules and principles as unmalleable as Davis's. The two understood each other well, though they had arrived at the same point by different approaches.

Memminger had been born too far from the fabled plantations to have cotton in his blood. This offering from Calhoun's South Carolina, far from bearing one of the renowned Secessionist names, was a native of Württemberg, Germany. He was the son of a quartermaster in the Prince Elector's Battalions of Foot Jägers.

Brought to Charleston at an early age, after his parents had died and his grandparents moved North, he was placed in an orphanage. At eleven he was adopted and at thirteen, grave and serious-minded, he was sent to the University of South Carolina. He entered law, became a Charleston alderman, a Unionist against nullification, and went to Congress as an anti-Secessionist.

He had nothing in common with a great slaveholder like Wade Hampton except South Carolina. But the land worked a spell on all who had known its long sweet springs and slow-moving autumns, and the grim worker as well as the grandee went with his state.

Down in Montgomery he showed them at once he meant business. He published in the local paper the location of his office and the hours —9 to 3—and the employees could be called back to the office. He said, "The world must know at once that we are at work, and that we are in earnest." If he had used "I" for "we" he would have written his own motto. Coming on to Richmond, he showed them that his department was no moonlight-and-roses affair for pampered darlings.

The office force was well organized when it arrived and set up on the first floor of the former U. S. Customs House, now the Treasury Building, beneath the President and Secretary of State. The assistant officers—chief clerk, comptroller, auditors, and so on—appointed their own clerks with the approval of the Secretary, and each newcomer was advised that socializing was to be done outside office hours. Even to the First Assistant Secretary, who assumed that the rule did not apply to him, it was made plain that the department would be just as happy if he saw his friends elsewhere. He left in a huff, and the Administration gained an enemy—not an important one, just one of the nucleus of a chorus. They weren't even aware of him in the press of affairs.

First off, a traditional country had to have folding money. Lacking all means of making such, the Confederacy had the first bills printed in New York, by the National Bank Note Company and the American Bank Note Company—though marked "Southern Bank Note Company." All very pretty, they depicted Negroes in cotton fields, train crossing bridge, cattle in brook, liberty and goddess of agriculture, and one $1,000 beauty—green and black—which with rare and unconscious humor displayed Andrew Jackson and John C. Calhoun.

There were not many of this interest-bearing issue, and these were not intended for circulation, as nothing below a fifty was issued. The Treasury Department got down to pocket money with their own engravers—Hoyer & Ludwig in Richmond. This firm of card-and-poster lithographers brought in assistants from Baltimore, from where they also smuggled paper through the land blockade. They made crude notes, black on white with plain backs, which with their decorative pictures were rather sad-looking. These notes were payable in three years, non-interest-bearing.

This solved the problem of the physical medium of exchange, but placed no actual wealth in the basement vaults. For that, as a beginner, the department acquired a few million from U.S. mints in their territory, some specie from their own banks, and a successfully floated $15,000,000 loan in 8 per cent bonds, the principal and interest to be paid from an export levy of one eighth of a cent a pound on cotton.

Memminger quickly perceived that such loans would never meet the needs of purchases abroad, but the basal Confederate policy on cotton prevented him from using that as a source of wealth. This devious cotton policy was an immaculate conception to the extent that no one ever claimed credit for it. After all the counts were in, many claimed they had been against it, and the Administration defended it. But at the beginning, there it was and Memminger accepted it.

The reasoning behind the plan was simple. By withholding cotton from England and France, the threat of a cotton famine to their mills would force their governments to break Lincoln's blockade and lead to a recognition of the Confederacy.

At this time the blockade existed only on paper, as the U. S. Navy had less than fifty steam-run ships of war to patrol thirty-five hundred miles from the Potomac to the Rio Grande, with a double line of coast most of the way, nearly two hundred rivers, bays, and inlets, and eight main harbors. But Davis welcomed this blockade because for a blockade to be legal it must be effective. Its ineffectiveness would provide a legal handle for foreign intervention.

At the same time the motive to intervene would be provided by a withholding of cotton as if the blockade did affect shipping. To this end the Administration encouraged talk about legislation of a cotton embargo. Though no such law was passed by the government, the curtailment of cotton shipping to Europe existed as a law in fact.

Committees of Public Safety did the actual enforcing at the ports, and the government waited hopefully for England and France to holler "Uncle," disregard the blockade, and come and get the cotton.

Committed to this use of potential wealth for political pressure, Davis and Memminger were deaf to the cries of those who wanted to ship cotton while they could and get the money. This plan for immediate use of cotton, championed by some newspapers, was discredited partly because Vice-President Stephens's summary of it sounded even more fantastic than the Administration's policy. This emaciated pedant planned to sell 4,000,000 bales abroad, use the money for building fifty ironclads to keep the coast clear for future operations, and pocket $800,000,000 for buying supplies.

Obviously the details of his plan would not hold up, and Memminger attacked the details. There were no ships; planters wouldn't accept government notes on cotton; and other defenders then and since claimed there was not even that much cotton. There must have been approximately. The Southern states shipped over 3,000,000 bales to England alone in 1860, and nearly 4,000,000 in 1859.

As for the ships and the planters' reluctance to accept government notes, there could have been ways if Memminger had been working to make the plan practical in detail instead of looking for objections with which to defeat it. The plan worked consistently in Texas; later planters accepted millions of government bonds, and scores of ships ran the blockade regularly; from the first, the Ordnance Department— where the great Gorgas worked independently of Memminger—chartered and bought ships for its own purpose. The point was that Memminger did not want to do it.

Stephens, the theorist, with his details all visionary, had for that one time the right idea about policy. He said that cotton's "power is financial and commercial, not political."

The Administration's politico-financial policy was put through by Memminger, though it is doubtful if he originated it. Apparently he favored shipping out some cotton to establish early credit abroad, but he never fought for his idea. There is no mention of it in his fiscal plan, and what he did do later was to explain away with statistics the impossibility of any other plan except the one used.

The actual dealing of Memminger's department with finance started when an officer delivered to Chief Clerk Capers a requisition, signed by the President, for rations and blankets for one hundred volunteers. At that moment the capital of the C.S.A. was exactly ten dollars—in personal cash in clerk Capers's pocket. To fill the requisition he borrowed money from the bank, on his personal security, and the Confederate Treasury never got effectively beyond this manner of financing the nation at war.

Memminger did come up with a thoroughly sound plan—for a sound country. He wanted a direct war tax, a 12½ per cent tariff, foreign and domestic bond loans, and the issue of treasury notes for the purpose of stabilizing currency. Also, to move government bonds, the Treasury accepted produce for some, and realized 400,000 bales of cotton, tobacco, and other stuff to be used directly abroad for credit; wheat and corn, oats and beef for the commissary; and much else. This part was all right, but the actual bonds moved for cash (largely the government's own treasury notes returning) totaled only a million dollars.

This put the matter of raising money squarely up to taxation and tariff, and there Congress went to work on the plan. They howled down high tariff as anathema to everything the states seceded for, and made taxes so light as to be picayune. The Southerners were fighting for independence, and heavy taxation opposed their notion of freedom. Congressmen, in their desire to please, had not changed with their change of capitals. They seized upon the one phase of Memminger's plan which insured their popularity—the issuance of treasury notes. Hurting the feelings of no constituent, the printing presses opened their carnival with $20,000,000 of three-year non-interest-bearing notes right from their own plant. The people took to them.

Never a provident folk and indifferent to accumulations against a rainy day, they spent their cash on immediate needs or pleasures and let the government bonds go. There were no stunts in those days to make bond loans attractive and, anyway, there were some pessimists who suspected that the C.S.A. had no future—or, at least, they were willing to wait and see.

When little Memminger beheld the results of his plan, after going through the wringer of Congress, he retreated to the security of his well-run office. There his bookkeeping would simulate a world of order and he could balance figures to his heart's content, while overhead the President and Secretary of State went their separate ways making war and diplomacy with no regard to him and no awareness of each other.

2

The Secretary of State's office was only down the hall from Davis's, but it is not likely they saw much of each other. Robert Toombs spent less and less time in his office, and in leaving he used different stairs from those the President used. Walker and Memminger might be long-suffering and patient, but the large and natural ego of the Georgian reacted violently against the one-man government.

While Walker was the first cabinet member against whom the public turned, Toombs was the first to turn against the President.

Of course he was vain and ambitious. They all were. But he had stood out among the best for a long time. He was about fifty, a powerful rough-hewn man gone fleshy about the middle, where the added heft seemed only to give weight to his personal force. A blade of chin whiskers jutted from a heavy, hard-living face, his brown hair was unruly and his clothes disheveled, his shirt usually spattered with tobacco juice.

Mrs. Davis said, "His eyes were magnificent, dark and flashing, and they had a certain lawless way of ranging about that was indicative of his character." In brief he looked what he was—an undisciplined extravert charged with energy.

He had been a successful lawyer at thirty, a member of Congress at thirty-four, and when, at forty, he entered the Senate, he was already known for his speeches, his power in debate, his intemperate but pointed language. Some said his violence was a bluster that obscured any real thoughtfulness or originality, but none said he was a chicken-brain.

Like other Southerners who originally believed in Union, when he turned he went as violently against it as he had been for it. In his farewell speech in the Senate he abandoned the balanced reasoning of the days when he defended the Constitution and denounced the new administration in unrestrained vituperation. If the North tried to keep the South in the union of black Republicans, "Come and do it! . . . We are as ready to fight now as we ever shall be. Treason? Bah!"

Then he stormed through Georgia, raging up rebellion. He never called it anything else. He didn't care what you called it. He helped get his state out of the hated Union, helped form the new Confederacy,

[55]

and missed being its President by an accident which from the beginning could not have predisposed him to Davis.

They were also antithetical as men. While Davis had little interest in creative writing, Mrs. Davis said Toombs

loved books of the imagination, travels, anything that would help him (as the English ambassador said of him once) "to utter some of his brilliant paradoxes." During the time of the highest excitement over the compromise measures, when Mr. Toombs was on his feet some twenty times a day, he arose at daylight, took French lessons with his daughters, and became a good French scholar so far as reading the language went. He would sit with his hands full of the reporter's notes on his speeches for correction, with *Le Medecin Malgré Lui* in the other hand, roaring over the play.

I once said to him, "I do not see how you can enjoy that so much."

He answered, "Whatever the Lord Almighty lets his geniuses create, He makes someone to enjoy; these plays take all the soreness out of me."

Jefferson Davis never had anything to take the soreness out of him. This was only one reason why Mrs. Davis could say that the President and the self-indulgent Toombs "were never congenial in their tastes; their habits and their manners were entirely diverse; but we all went on amiably enough, and he [Davis] was very fond of Mrs. Toombs, who was a pleasant, kindly woman, and cheerful like her husband."

Though the amiability between the two men was only surface in Richmond, their conflict was not chiefly a personal thing. Rather, that was an exacerbation of the basic trouble.

In the first place the misguided political appointments which kept Toombs out of the Treasury Department placed him where his talent for extemporaneous floor debate was likewise useless. Then, once the nation was launched on its troublous way, he was, like other revolutionaries, unconstructive—but not silently so. He was not one to hide his light under a basket, especially Mr. Davis's.

In his own State Department what little there was to do he accomplished well enough. There is much talk about what he wanted to do, but on the record he sent sound instructions to the first Confederate commissioners to England and France. What Toombs and the whole Cabinet wanted was recognition from these foreign powers. What apparently all of them subscribed to was the belief that King Cotton would bring it. Thus Toombs sent abroad a clear case for secession, with assurances that the two American countries would never be one again; a generous offer on trade; and a reminder of England's dependence on cotton—all tacitly suggesting the right and practicality of recognition.

What they got from England and France, almost immediately, was the rights of belligerents. Toombs had nothing to do with this. Lincoln did it, when he blockaded the Southern ports.

The United States squawked to high heaven, but England held that the United States could lawfully interrupt trade between the South and foreign powers only on the grounds that a state of war existed. England claimed that the United States, in assuming the belligerent's right to blockade, recognized the Southern states as belligerents—otherwise the United States had no right to stop a single British ship. The United States persisted throughout in claiming that no war existed, but the British stuck to the facts of their acts. The United States could not have its blockade and eat it too.

While Toombs's battle was fought out between the British and the United States, there was nowhere in his own department for him to use his turbulent vitality. Besides, he was a gregarious soul. He liked free talk with the boys, to be where the wine was flowing, and his offices were a lonely spot. To someone who asked about his department, he took off his hat and pointed into it. "My department is in there," he bellowed.

Perceiving that fighting the enemy was all that counted in a government where one man ran everything, he turned the force of his voice, but not his brains, to the problems of war. He was no longer thinking clearly. From being the lone advocate of avoiding the fight at Fort Sumter, he now became (except for the wild outbursts of Walker) the lone urger for instant invasion.

With a blustering disregard for the problems of arming and equipping troops, he excoriated the government for not accepting five hundred thousand men for the Southern armies at once. Having formed the habit of attacking the United States government, he now knew nothing except destructive criticism.

A less autocratic man than Davis would have resented this kind of advice. The President, standing firmly upon the "authority invested in me by the Constitution," was allergic to all advice not tactfully offered —and to some that was.

Caleb Huse, now busily buying up Enfield rifles in England and Austrian artillery, had discovered this weakness in the early days of Montgomery. According to Huse, he went to Davis's office for instructions, at a time when the President was receiving callers. He asked Huse to wait until they were all gone, as he got ideas between calls while catching up on his mail. During one interval he read a four-page letter from a friend. When Davis finished it, he stood up "with a show of irritation" and, tearing the letter in two, said, "I wish people would not write me advice."

Even if Toombs had been aware of that episode, he had too much braggadocio to heed it. He went on talking in cabinet meetings until finally even he realized the war was going on in the President's way, regardless of his own verbal powers that had been so effective in parliamentary debate. Then the real discontent set in.

By late June, when the enemy's storm was gathering, Toombs roamed restlessly the crowded streets of Richmond, saying that Davis would never allow him personal distinction. By then any hope of his usefulness was over. With the chips down he became a frustrated blowhard spreading dissension. He said he would not be Davis's chief clerk, and that was all that was possible for him.

Unfortunately there was some truth in what he said. Davis not only took being commander in chief literally. He also made it read commander *and* chief of the whole works. "Supreme authority" meant exactly that. It could be no other way with Davis.

He brought to the office, as to his life, a rigid concept, and the office became identical with the man. In his acquired concept of the Southern chivalrous character, he judged his fellow men by codes untempered by tolerance for their human motives. Self-molded in the South's romanticized image, he attributed substance to abstract logic, and on neither men nor principles was there any give in him.

Toombs was wrong and that was an end to it. In Davis's conception of the experiment he needed neither passionately loyal followers nor the ruthlessness to cause opponents to disappear. In a gentleman's world ruled by honor, if his own rightness and the nobility of the cause would not suffice for a malcontent like Toombs, then the malcontent could become his enemy.

Toombs became such, and a dangerous one. He could still talk. There was nothing else to do—and there was that germ of truth . . .

3

In that ill-assorted group there was one man who could have helped co-ordination between the bureaus and through Congress, and one who should have. The one who could have, Judah P. Benjamin, was not in the proper position for it. The one who should have, Vice-President Stephens, was beginning a private sulk.

This tormented little man, without a wife or hope óf one, had but two loves—Georgia and the American Constitution. Neither included the Confederacy.

It would seem that Alexander Stephens accepted position in the new government only to gratify personal ambition. His long melancholy, caused partly by his dwarflike appearance and lack of energy, made ambition his only possible gratification.

He had nothing in common with the fabled goateed planter except love of place, and his state attachment was excessive even in a land of provincials. For the rest, he had been born very far on the wrong side of the tracks, in a mean little house on his father's slaveless farm, where he had first worked as a corn dropper.

To get an education, he taught school and received charity, and no New Englander observed more rigidly the copybook maxims for a dutiful life than did this diminutive sickling in his rise to the U. S. Congress. No scholar anywhere surpassed him in the doggedness of his pedantry. His academic knowledge of the Constitution was his refuge from the slights and sufferings inflicted upon him his whole life long by his robust fellow Southerners. Typical of his humiliations was the time on a train when another man, observing his beardless face, said, "Sonny, why don't you get up and give the lady your seat?"

When Georgia seceded, against his efforts to prevent it, he was still strongly allied with the Georgia powers, and much heed was paid him in the early days at Montgomery. Once the new government began to function in Richmond under the control of Davis, Stephens received scant attention, and he grew jealous of the President. It followed that he then turned closer to his old Georgia friend, Bob Toombs.

Their political *rapprochement* developed out of what originally was an attraction of opposites. Dick Taylor said of Stephens, in using the description of another person, "His mind is in a state of indecent exposure." Stephens probably felt protected by the robust and full-living Toombs, who admired Stephens's academic precisions. Their new alliance held seeds of danger to the Confederacy.

Even in that first summer Stephens was in the early processes of forming the opposition to his own administration, while one hundred miles away the enemy capital, possessing everything his own country lacked, prepared to invade.

That enemy capital was the symbol of an actually established nation, with all departments organized and operating, with its known sources of wealth flowing and its credit boundless, with no foolishness about states "acting in independent character." They were a solid working concern, of 22,000,000 people. The Southern states had 9,000,000, of whom 4,000,000 were Negroes, and many of the whites were Unionists.

All of that was beside the point of Stephens's abstractions. In his day, less than eighty years from the founding of the United States, Southerners assumed that the Constitution was the final authority.

As Stephens had been forced by his fellows to leave the United States over an interpretation of the Constitution, he was determined, come hell or Yankee, that the Confederacy would be operated according to the strictest, literal interpretation of *its* Constitution. He had been the main drafter of it, and he established himself as the guardian to watch that each of its *i*'s was dotted and each *t* crossed.

In the books of the Union this sickly pedant became Rebel Number Two, even as he prepared for the role that made him worth incomparably more to the North out of it than in it.

In Richmond he did not even look for a permanent home.

4

The man who could have helped in co-ordination, Judah Benjamin, was as flexibly opportunistic as Stephens was monomaniacal. In the lowly held Attorney-General's office, however, he was not consulted in those early days. But, unlike Toombs, he did not make trouble for himself or others. Benjamin blandly waited his turn at a likelier spot, and, while waiting, he found ways to advise the President—as Davis liked advice. He *had* come to Richmond to stay.

A citizen of the world, Benjamin would seem more at home among international bankers than with this group of rather naïve regionalists, but for now his lot was one with theirs. He had made his own fortune in their world, bought his own slaves in their system, paid for his extravagances in the best of their taste, and not one of them was more class-conscious than he or less in love with equality.

If Lee is a symbol of the Confederacy, Benjamin is the antithesis. A vastly successful lawyer and politician, a many-sided worldling of varied talents, cultivated tastes, and true erudition, he used his shrewd, supple, realistic intelligence primarily for the well-being of Judah Benjamin. In that he had the relaxation of a champion, and whether he was trying a case or trying for independence, when he left the office he shut the door.

He had size, and he always knew which side of the toast the caviar was on. There is nothing to indicate any passion. When fortune placed him in the Confederacy he gave it everything he had—up to the final giving of self. As loyal as any man to it, he was not of it. He was not of any such thing: he was a citizen of the world.

His history started him in that direction. Born in the British West Indies, raised in Charleston, he attended Yale, started the practice of law in New Orleans, and married a Frenchwoman. His political rise was helped by association with John Slidell, the wily New Yorker who founded a local Tammany in Louisiana, and under whose guidance Benjamin was never defeated for a major office. At the time of the war he was a U.S. senator.

A practical machine politician, he believed Louisiana should be controlled by the planter-businessman class, and it followed he was a proslavery man with no use for poor white people. He liked the big money and had a talent for getting it.

As a lawyer, his arguments in a California mining dispute against the United States placed him at the very top where he could command the highest fees. He had worked for the bill to dispossess settlers in the Houmas Indian country, in favor of powerful claimants like Slidell, and he had worked actively in the project of building a railroad in Mexico, holding over $100,000 in stocks and bonds in the development. At secession he stood to make a killing—and took a heavy loss.

Always a states'-righter, he did not hold with secession save as a last resort, but when he turned, like so many others, he went whole-hog. In his farewell Senate speech he said, "You may carry desolation into our peaceful land, and with torch and fire you may set our cities in flames —but you can never subjugate us. . . ."

This would make a good impression on the radical Secessionists, but there is no way of knowing whether it expressed conviction or political opportunism, or both. There is so much about Benjamin that there is no way of knowing. Seemingly haunted by a fear of a biography or revelations concerning his past, he destroyed all letters and papers.

When he first appeared in the Cabinet, a Northern newspaper carried a letter from a former classmate at Yale, accusing Benjamin of leaving the college as a thief under pressure from his fellow students. Benjamin never denied the accusation and refused to permit defense of him by others. The story may not be true, but the record shows that he was forced to leave either by the college authorities or classmates or both (though not the reason why), and when he applied for readmission the Yale president ignored his letter.

His marriage was even more mysterious. When he first went to New Orleans after his Yale experience, very poor, he learned French by giving English lessons to a young girl of considerable beauty and drawing-room charm. From tutor he became husband, but she was not wife very long except in name. Loving everything bright and gay, all the lighter side of society, she found his serious discussions (though interlaced with humor) heavy going. She was extremely extravagant and wrote him (in the only words of hers on record), "Don't talk to me about economy. It is so fatiguing."

This languorous pleasure-loving Creole took her five-year-old daughter to Paris and there remained, indifferent to her husband's achievements and learning, and everything else about him save the fat allowance he regularly sent. From Washington, New Orleans, and Richmond he supported his belle of the boulevards and seemed just as content to live with her brother (as he did in Richmond) and a couple of friends.

This was certainly the acme of equanimity—a quality much needed by the high-strung President, already working under tension in the sticky city summer.

Davis's friendship with Benjamin went back to their Senate days in Washington, though it grew out of a challenge to a duel. Significantly, two of the elements most pronounced in Davis as a President were active in the cause of the argument: physical pain from strained nerves and vanity at his military knowledge.

Senator Benjamin's questioning of the sick man on military affairs snapped his temper, and Davis gave a couple of short answers. Benjamin found his fellow senator at fault and said, "His manner is not agreeable at all."

"If the Senator happens to find it disagreeable," Davis retorted, "I hope he will keep it to himself."

"When directed to me, I will not keep it to myself; I will repel it instanter."

"You have got it, sir."

"That is enough, sir," Benjamin answered, and shortly afterward his second presented Davis with the note of challenge.

Davis had high physical courage and felt no need to prove it, nor did the situation demand that he prove himself right. He said to Benjamin's second, "I have been wholly wrong," and the next day in the Senate offered a generous apology. When Benjamin's acceptance was equally generous, their mutual respect developed into pleasant association, in which Mrs. Davis wholeheartedly joined. She grew very fond of the subtle-minded sybarite with his engaging conversation and social grace.

Everyone mentioned his "perpetual smile," his deferential manners and easy charm, but with his inferiors he was neither charming nor considerate. When he disliked a person who could be of no use to him, he took no pains to hide it, and—as the Davises had discovered—when his pride was offended he showed a lot of iron.

The point of Benjamin was that he adopted none of the historic roles of his day. In a posterity-conscious generation he operated with beautiful simplicity on the pleasure principle. He could have invented the adage, "You catch more flies with honey than with vinegar." Any psychologist could study with profit his instinctual use of diversion and variety as renewals for the main drive.

In Richmond his plump, well-groomed figure, moving like a cat, was soon familiar in sections wholly different from Davis's two blocks of Main Street. He was making his own quiet explorations into the quarters which offered the most relaxing pleasures.

He was adapting himself to the society of a city which, DeLeon said,

was not cosmopolitan in her habits and ideas . . . there was, in some quarters, a vague, lingering suspicion as to the result of the [Confederate] experiment; but the society felt that the government was its guest, and as such was to be honored. The city itself was a small one, the society was general and provincial; and there was in it a sort of brotherly love that struck a stranger, at first, as very curious. This was, in a great measure, attributable to the fact that the social circle had been for years a constant quantity, and everybody in it had known everybody else since childhood.

Benjamin, however, had spent his life as the outlander in established societies, and he set up social shop right in the center of the old-liners and in a style typical of theirs.

In downtown Richmond, around the hub of Capitol Square, no divisions of commercial and residential districts existed, and cheek by jowl stood mansions and all manner of business establishments and elegant boardinghouses. The boardinghouses bore little resemblance to those of the present. There were no apartments then, and people who did not occupy houses lived in rooms. Being unsuspicious and gregarious, the occupants enjoyed gathering at the common table, and talk was frequently at a high level.

Judah Benjamin would not risk his cultivated palate at a table beyond his control, and his love of socializing was highly selective. With his brother-in-law and a friend, he rented a house. The pleasant, typical red-brick city house—on Main Street, near Foushee—was more

[63]

than half a mile from the downtown center and in the more exclusively residential section.

Near by was the solidly built, Doric-columned home of the manufacturer Davenport (later Ellen Glasgow's), and all through that neighborhood were smaller houses, like Benjamin's, with charming simple façades, slanting dormer roofs, and wide hallways for the Richmond summers.

One block away on fashionable Franklin Street were the great colonnaded houses of Taylor, the banker, and Anderson, the Tredegar owner; the beautifully iron-grilled portico on the house of Kent, the dry-goods tycoon; the square house of commission-merchant Dunlop, with its columned double balconies exposed to the south.

Between First and Second was a group of three-and-a-half-story red-brick Greek Revival houses called Linden Row. Though the houses were similar there was no monotony, but with the lindens and magnolias the group gave rather a total impression of distinction and graciousness. Mrs. Pegram's famous girls' school was there, and also Dr. Powell's Southern Female Institute. On Franklin at Sixth were the fine simple lines of the three-storied Archer house, with a huge sycamore growing out of the adjoining brick sidewalk. Another block over, on Grace, was the handsome large-roomed home of Mrs. Stanard, social leader on the literary side, whose salon was the city's most brilliant.

Where Benjamin walked to his office down Main Street, he passed the handsome red-brick Crozet house; the Royster house, where Poe's sweetheart Elmira had lived; off Main, Moldavia, the mansion of John Allan, Poe's foster father, where Poe himself had lived; the octagonal Caskie house and the spacious red-brick Nolting house, with the double balconies toward the river; and down at Cary, the Barret house, with the inevitable but enchanting double balconies overlooking its garden and house-servants' quarters. These parallel streets—Grace, Franklin, Main, and Cary—ran east and west, so the houses benefited by the river breeze from the south.

Along the side streets, and from the straight alleys that bisected nearly every block, the uneven projection of the houses toward their gardens gave an impression of intimate seclusion in contrast with the formal façades. Especially in the misty blue of evening, the smaller rear rooms, shadowed by vines and trees and walls, seemed cozy and secret.

The numbered streets, intersecting the avenues, sloped steeply towards the river, except broad Third Street, which ran along the ridge of one of the sharp valleys. Walking this homey tree-lined street, Benjamin would reach Gamble's Hill. Here, where breezes came on even the hottest nights, the land dropped in a sheer cliff, and from the hill he would have a magnificent view of the James River Valley.

Almost directly below, the buildings of the Tredegar Iron Works sprawled along the canal. Farther down, between the canal and the river, spread the wide, arched state armory. Idle for some years before the war, it was very active now under the able guidance of the Yankee Gorgas.

He saw other little islands near by, crowded now with the busy buildings of arsenal, laboratories, and workshops. Farther up, under Gamble's Hill, the river was dotted with rocks and islets, over which the water rippled. To the westward, paralleling the river, ran the canal, the towpath of which made a favorite strolling place for couples. The whole scene held an unpretentious grandeur, pleasant and friendly.

This was the world that Benjamin made his own, becoming a guest at the choicest dinner tables and in the drawing rooms where the influential members of the government gathered. The ladies were joining their husbands in Richmond, and Benjamin was well aware of their importance in political life, especially Southern.

These ladies brought from Washington their habits of collaboration with their husbands. There was a duality in their ambitions for advancement, for not only the husband advanced in his career, but the wife also in her sphere of power. This developed more interesting relationships and more interesting women, as the drawing room as well as the cloakroom became the arena for behind-the-scenes power deals.

In Washington, Benjamin had been friendly without being an intimate of the Davises. In Richmond, that was going to change. As it did, Benjamin bided his time, making himself charming where he should and useful where he could, in the knowledge that cabinets changed too.

CHAPTER SIX

The *Citadel*

WITH the coming of the wives and daughters, especially of the minor figures, Richmond got its first look at the true representatives of the Deep South plantocracy—who in turn got their first look at Virginians. Most of these ladies of the lower South had lived for years in Washington. It was their second home, and they formed its official society. To them Richmond was the strange city.

There the ladies of the Rebel rulers found themselves on trial in a new society. They were all, in Richmond, "the new girl."

It was a curious position for Mrs. Davis, as First Lady, to have to prove herself like a debutante at a first party. It must have gone against her passionate nature and pride to feel her way through this wary welcome. She thought the Virginia ladies felt the Confederate wives were an inundation of people "of doubtful standards and, at best, of different methods, and reserved judgment whilst they offered a large hospitality." But the people of the Old Dominion were good at social hospitality, and Varina Davis was "impressed by the sincerity and simplicity of their manners, their beauty and absence of the gloze acquired by association in merely fashionable society."

Some of Mrs. Davis's coterie were less favorably impressed with the reserve of their civic hosts. At least one *grande dame* (naturally of South Carolina) resented the Virginians' assumption of superiority. "They thought of themselves," said Mrs. Davis's biographer, "as an exclusive, almost peculiar people, wholly unlike the North and not altogether like the rest of the South."

One element in their peculiarity would be more pleasing to the President's wife than to her ladies in waiting. Virginia Bourbons had started patterning their formal society on England before they drove the frontier back fifty miles. Their first manorial plantation houses on the James River were built while they were fighting off Indians. It was because the mother country would not give them sufficient protection against the Indians, so that they might perfect their pattern of the landed gentry, that they rebelled a hundred years before the successful American Revolution. They went it alone against England in a fight of the bloody bitterness of a family feud.

Unlike the rest of America, they fought not because they wanted to be different from, but similar to, the British upper classes—only in their own Tidewater terms. It was a larger life than England's, freer and more fluid, but for the essence of the social design they looked back to England's system of nobility and monarchy. Now here, in Varina Davis, they had the nearest to a queen they ever hoped to have on this earth—a First LADY!

The log-cabin-to-White-House theme had no appeal for them. Their presidents stepped down from Monticello and Mount Vernon to grace the publicly supported home in Washington. These new rulers had the concept and the bearing of aristocrats, even if they were from the West.

Mississippi was Western to Virginians then, as today, say, Pittsburgh is Middle Western to a Bostonian. Elegant Mrs. Joe Johnston, wife of the peppery little general guarding the Valley, complimented Mrs. Davis as "a Western belle." But belle she was on a grand scale, and not at all humble about it.

Varina made no objection to the royal court the Virginians formed, did not find the homage at all amiss, and gave herself some understandable airs. She was not overimpressed with the importance of her position; she accepted that. Rather she was pleasantly aware of it, and her husband (as autocratic as a minor prince concerning that which was due position) encouraged her by word and example to act always as befitted her place in the world.

The point about Varina was that Jefferson Davis, to her, was greatness and romance and the center of her life. What she valued above all else was his good opinion. What she strove hardest for was his approbation. She said she feared displeasing him more than anything on earth.

Her responses were determined by what affected him, and her thoughts and energies were directed toward his well-being. Her role as a wife was as clearly defined as his as a historic figure. She wanted to be the needed woman—mistress and good companion, sage confidante and courageous sharer of burdens. She was superbly qualified to fulfill this role.

Winnie (as he called her) was anything but the languid belle of Southern legend, drawling drivel and relying on a brief gamut of tricks to attract all men and capture one. She would have scorned the whole idea. There was too much pride and size. There could never have been any "don't worry your pretty little head" from her husband.

On the other hand, she could have known no worries about losing her husband. In his own neurotic fashion an integrated man, Davis needed no cheap parlor conquests to buttress his ego. Though he enjoyed the company of women, he disliked coquetry and was once seen to scowl at the flirtatiousness of some unnamed belle. When Varina gave everything of herself, she got everything of the man in return.

This could not have contributed to her humility, and she must have been hard to take for many women, especially empty-heads. For that smug male who regards women as decorative inferiors to make themselves scarce while the important things are discussed, she was disturbing to his ego. Such a man was apt to be rocked on his heels by the force of her mind, and if he got ugly about it she could trade punches. She could be rude too to the inflated fool who felt that ignoring a woman, as if she had no mind, was a sure-fire weapon.

None of this is meant to indicate that she was looking for trouble or was not ordinarily affable. She possessed her share of surface amiability and adeptness at social situations. To serve her husband's purposes she could put up with a good deal, and she must have suffered many bores and much smiling nastiness with a cheerful front. But her patience wore extremely thin where it came to putting boors and spoiled darlings in a good humor, or to smoothing the feathers of ruffled egos.

With top-flight personalities, she was usually attractive and had the capacities to inspire and give fine friendships. Her stanchest friend and supporter was Mrs. James Chesnut, wife of a South Carolina senator. Shrewd-seeing and tough-minded, in her late thirties, Mrs. Chesnut kept a diary which revealed the most interesting mind of any woman writing in her day. Her malicious wit is as fresh and as pointed as when she wrote, and her pages hold the flavor of a contemporary journal. She was a good woman to have on your side, and it is no coincidence that her favorite was Varina Davis.

They came to Richmond about the same time and lived at the same hotel, and Mrs. Chesnut helped her younger friend over many adjustments. In those days Mrs. Davis was forced to use tact (of which she possessed a full measure) often in defiance of her nature, for she was not of a diplomatic temperament. Frequently she protested to her husband that she "would rather die" than follow some course. But he could persuade her, to almost anything short of flattery, to act for the cause and not for her personal feelings.

This she did so well that she probably never made him an enemy—certainly not one that he wouldn't have had anyway. But the reason for this was not the Cause. He was her cause. The Confederate cause became hers because it was his.

2

Through Davis's forms of the traditional government patterned on the U.S., official society of necessity followed the Washington life they had recently left. To the ladies around Mrs. Davis, however, there was one enormous difference between the two worlds. Washington had been a stable society, where they had their friends and associations, where the cliques had formed and the lines hardened. In Richmond everything was new and unsettled and tentative—even their home life.

Almost everybody was living at hotels, and fashion centered at the Spotswood. This was more like a pleasure resort than the residence of the President and much of the new government.

Not only were the ladies excited by the dramatic change in their lives (with the gamble against destiny), and by the excitement of the new movement in which one people formed their own homogeneous country, but they were suddenly freed of all responsibility of home. There were no servants to look after, no meals to arrange, no house to run—and for some no husband.

The staid routine was all kicked over, and husbands who had been as familiar as old shoes were away, not too far, in glamorous uniforms. Instead of looking after their husbands' laundry, they now looked at the calendar—for they had dates again when the heroes got to Richmond for quick romantic interludes. Mrs. John Preston (daughter of Wade Hampton) and Varina Davis's close friend, Mrs. Chesnut (daughter of a South Carolina governor) had husbands serving on the the staff of the great Beauregard himself.

These men were of the avowed Secessionist type, those who did not get into the conservative government, and James Chesnut's father was a cut-out for the old Southern colonel (which he was, literally). Words were high-flown and emotions ran hot when the boys came back to the Spotswood, and all the time at all the hotels life for the ladies was like a week-end in town for a bunch of girls out of a strict school.

Nobody talked war, and gossip had a field day with all the new personalities and old ones in new alignments to rake over. Any tidbit from Washington was hungrily pounced upon, and especially savored were those about Mrs. Lincoln—whom, uncharitably, they found amusing. All day and all night there were scurryings about the corridors of hotels and whisperings and gigglings behind closed doors. There was no hour when somebody wasn't giving a tea or a dinner or a dance, and they vied at pointing out celebrities like autograph hunters at a *première*.

Outside the hotels the whole life was carnival. Play "Dixie," wave a kerchief, sing a song, throw a kiss, "There goes President Davis, the best rider of them all," "There's beautiful Mrs. Mallory," "There's a flag made from Connie's dress," "Meet me tonight at the Spotswood," "Drink a toast . . ."

Football, race meeting, opening night, hero's day, state fair, New Year's Eve, roll them all together in the birth of a nation to cakewalk time. I dream of Jeanie at the Camptown races 'way down upon the Swanee River. Batter bread and fried chicken, hot biscuits and Smithfield ham, yassa boss, howdo theh honey, there's watermelon growin' on the vine. The bourbon flows and they look on the wine when it is red in the long levee held at the Spotswood Hotel, corner of Eighth and Main, newest hotel in Richmond, finest hotel in the South.

It's the White House of the South right now, but like no official residence in this country ever before or since.

3

In this Stork Club executive mansion the husbands of the ladies brooded over reports which showed the imminence of the "On to Richmond" drive. As the danger approached, Jefferson Davis acted more as he had in his Washington War Secretary days when the other departments were long established and operated under a central control.

As it was, they mainly shifted for themselves, and the less interest he felt in any particular bureau the less he had to do with it. Of all things in which an old Secretary of War felt no interest, it was the Navy.

Though his home was on the Mississippi River; though he had spent years on the Potomac and his present capital was on the James; though the Ohio bordered his new nation and the Tennessee cut down into it; though its whole south coast was on the Gulf and east coast on the Atlantic, where the land was honeycombed with rivers and creeks and inlets and bays; though, in a loose manner, the country was a gigantic island with a separated western territory also sliced by rivers; with all this, Davis showed no awareness of the amphibious nature his defense must of necessity be.

The Navy Department was allowed to go its separate way under the guidance of a Secretary who, not believing in secession, revealed more than any man then in the Cabinet a sense of the measures necessary for successfully establishing a new nation in physical opposition to its parent body. Throughout his service, men without political convictions, who had gone with their states, all approached their tasks with a realism and resourcefulness frequently lacking in the more articulate Secessionists.

Like most of the other cabinet members, Stephen Mallory was the opposite of the legendary Southern princeling born to the chant of the faithful darkies singing, "Little new massa's done come." Probably the first Negroes Mallory heard were the dock wallopers in Trinidad, where he was born of a Connecticut father and Irish mother. His father died when he was a child, and his mother supported the family by running a boardinghouse for sailors in Key West. His only formal education was a few years in the Moravian School in Pennsylvania.

With clear-purposed ambition and industry, he advanced through law to the Senate, and at the time of the war, in his late forties, Mallory was chairman of the Senate Naval Committee and a prominent Floridian.

Having been a lifelong lover and student of boats, he was one cabinet member qualified for his post—except, as a pronounced Unionist who opposed secession even more strongly than did Vice-President Stephens, he had been suspected of betraying the South even before the war opened.

That was at Pensacola's Fort Pickens, the other United States fort held within the territory of the seceded states, and Mallory never denied that he did all in his power to prevent the South from firing on it. He claimed this was to prevent war, if possible. Others thought differently.

Two members of his own state's delegation voted against his confirmation, and it was true he never associated with any secession movement, state or national, and said, "I dreaded the perils of secession..." and "... I never could regard it as but another name for revolution, and to be justified only as a last resort from intolerable oppression." About the only thing he did not say was that *Uncle Tom's Cabin* was his favorite novel, and he did come out in the Senate against John Brown.

Despite the suspicions of the fire-eaters, his actions probably sprang less from political consciousness than from good nature and a complete lack of anything in common with the slaveholding planter alignment.

He came in only because of Florida, and then reluctantly. He hated going against the Union; he could not go against his state.

With his genial nature he loved good living, and his talent for it was shared by his beautiful Spanish wife, Angela Moreno, like him a Roman Catholic. He had a round, robust, unhandsome face framed in jaw-line whiskers and was a complete combination of a Connecticut Yankee and the County Waterford, by way of Florida into the capital of Virginia.

He and his wife were much liked, and the new society liked to attend their dinners. Like his fellow winetaster, Benjamin, Mallory did not make trouble for himself. As the Navy Secretary, he adopted his course to the government's policy of using Lincoln's paper blockade for diplomatic ends. As the Union Navy could be depended upon to make that blockade much more than a gesture, and as rivers and inlets already invited their destructive gunboats, Mallory made his physical plans to fit the government design.

Though some old navy men, like Matthew Fontaine Maury, objected to the policy, Mallory's nature kept him with phlegmatic clearheadedness concentrated on the tasks at hand. Those tasks were admirably suited to his temperament, as there was nothing to worry about. His department did not exist even on paper.

He had not a single ship of war, for resigning officers could not bring their ships with them, or any fleet of merchant vessels in ports. Nor did they have seamen to man the non-existent ships, as the South was not a seafaring region. No enlisted men followed officers out of the U. S. Navy, and to draft men from the Army caused private wars.

As most of the South was devoted to money-crop economy, and its shipping as well as its manufacturing had been done by the North, there were no shipyards, and the only two naval yards, at Norfolk and Pensacola, were menaced by the enemy. Thus, with no papers to play with, his office free of petitioners and advisers, Mallory went to the basic elements of his problem with imagination and daring. Perceiving that it was impossible to compete ship for ship and man for man, Mallory turned to original plans and mechanical methods. He would outsmart size.

Mallory entered immediately into contracts with any kind of firm, from Norfolk to Memphis to New Orleans, who would quickly undertake to get afloat gunboats, floating batteries, and varieties of vessels of war the like of which had never before appeared on any water. Accepting the limitations of experience and resource, he went after designs that used the material at hand and suited his bold means.

VIEW FROM GAMBLE'S HILL

South end of Third Street, showing Tredegar Iron Works immediately below and the State Armory to the left. Lithograph from Beyer's *Album of Virginia*. Courtesy of Valentine Museum, Richmond, Virginia.

VIEW FROM CHURCH HILL

The original section when the city was designed in 1737. Two adjoining houses on the right indicate the use of outbuildings—kitchen and servants' quarters—in even relatively modest houses. Lithograph, E. Sachse & Co. Courtesy of Valentine Museum, Richmond, Virginia.

Regardless of size or shape of vessel, of what devices caused them to move, he wanted them protected—with cotton bales or oak logs and, wherever possible, with iron, even if worn-out old rails. Many were designed to ram, and the fire power on others was terrific. Fitting into no class or nomenclature on earth, they were like an assembling horde of killers—almost as dangerous to their own crews as to the enemy.

Beyond ships, he had laboratories set up in a quickly forming Bureau of Ordnance and Hydrography, staffed by regular navy men such as Matthew Fontaine Maury. They began research on lethal experiments like torpedoes—floating and stationary, primitive and complex electrical—and torpedo-launching boats ranging from rowboats to a non-rising submarine. The pleasant waters of the James became roiled by these strange objects experimenting below the city docks.

Before any of these could be in production, Mallory had to meet the immediate menace of invasion along the countless Southern rivers. On seceding, the states grabbed off a dozen or so oddments of small sailing vessels—revenue cutters, coastal-survey boats, lighthouse tenders, and the like—and a couple of dozen coastal and river steamers were seized and/or bought on the Atlantic and at New Orleans, where both Louisiana and private citizens made up purses. Armed with popguns and manned by literally motley crews, they were used as a temporary makeshift in conjunction with shore batteries.

For the long-range problem of the blockade, including the danger to the South's own navy yards, Mallory had two solutions. One was to build, buy, and have built a fleet of raiders which, by preying on Northern shipping, would so boost marine insurance rates that blockaders would be drawn off to protect U.S. merchant shipping.

The first of these raiders, the *Sumter,* commanded by Raphael Semmes, late of the U. S. Navy, sailed out from New Orleans in early June. The *Sumter* was the best of the screw steamers they had bought, and she had been fitted out, armed, and manned by Commander Semmes.

At the same time in Europe agents dickered for other ships and for something much more important—which involved part two of his plan. These were ironclads, to be used directly on the blockading fleet and the ships of war making free with Southern harbors.

The United States had no ironclads. After a study of the ironclads of France and England, Mallory said, "Inequality of numbers may be compensated by invulnerability. . . ." Regardless of first cost, the possession of such a ship must be hurried, as it "at this time could traverse the entire coast of the U.S., prevent all blockades, and encounter, with a fair prospect of success, their entire navy."

To this end he dispatched to Europe Captain Bulloch, Georgia aristocrat, who was not at the time distinguished for having in New York City a three-year-old nephew named Theodore Roosevelt. Bulloch met with no success in buying a ship of the class of France's *Gloire,* the most powerful ironclad in the world, but he started negotiations with shipbuilders for ironclads and ships to be used as raiders —and started at the same time a shotless war with United States state officials, agents, and spies, which was just as relentless as any fighting on any battlefield and brimming over with the stuff of international thrillers.

But in Richmond, Mallory was not waiting on the possible purchase of such a ship, or on the building either abroad or in the South, where he was already starting native construction of ironclads. He had his eye on the good frigate *Merrimac,* scuttled at Norfolk when the U. S. Navy evacuated.

At a cost of $60,000 he had her raised, and experts estimated that for $450,000 she could be placed in her former condition and shielded "completely with three-inch iron, placed at such angles as to render her ball-proof . . . to arm her with the heaviest ordnance and to send her at once against the enemy's fleet. It is believed that thus prepared she will be able to drive them [enemy's ships] from Hampton Roads and the ports of Virginia." This report he made in secret session in July in asking Congress to appropriate the money, including $170,000 for her armament. He was off to a fast start on sound and resourceful planning.

Even the U. S. Navy, with all the technological resources and Yankee ingenuity to draw on, displayed no more originality than this affable politician. Of all the Confederates none saw his problem more clearly and realistically in its totality and in its details than Stephen Mallory—in his limited sphere.

Many of his fellows expected a short war, and Davis expected foreign intervention to prove decisive. Mallory, the reluctant rebel, planned to defeat the enemy. Starting with necessary expedients, he worked ahead with inventions and buildings (all part of a design) that would take anywhere from months to years to reach fruition. But his department worked not only in no relation to the others, not only on parallel lines and frequently at cross purposes with the Army, but much of Mallory's boldness and energy was nullified by the total planlessness.

Mallory uttered no complaints of this. In the every-man-for-himself atmosphere he did his separate best and ignored the others as they ignored him. If an army failure proved disastrous to navy construction, it did not upset his appetite or dull his palate for wine, and he took the same pleasure in his wife's charming presence at dinner.

In meetings for the discussion of Confederate affairs Mallory usually took little part, but his wife became an early fixture of Mrs. Davis's coterie at the Spotswood, where the ladies enjoyed being on the inside of the momentous events.

4

For Varina Davis, then thirty-four years old, it was exciting to arrange meetings, act as page to her great husband, as hostess at the envied President's table in the dining room, and at receptions in the hotel parlor (number 83) for the wives of the new men of destiny.

In addition to the lovely Mrs. Mallory there was Mrs. Toombs (whom Mrs. Davis found more agreeable than Mr. Davis found hard-drinking Toombs); there were Mrs. Chesnut and Mrs. Preston, the friends, Mrs. Wigfall, wife of the Texan now with the Army, and Mrs. Joe Johnston, wife of Beauregard's closest rival in Virginia, where husband and wife had no worries of social acceptance. (Mrs. Johnston was the daughter of a governor of Delaware.)

There is no mention of the family of grimly earnest Memminger, though Richmond remembered his daughter as "elegant and accomplished" and as a lady who had "graced our society with her presence in the winter of 1859." Of course these gatherings were not attended by the rustic Reagans, who were satisfied that their presence was socially ignored. Mrs. Davis's group was as selective as a bridge party and much more exciting. They were playing against the gods.

The only event which shook them was the whisper that spread through the Spotswood to the effect that someone in the dining room had said Mrs. Davis's "ladies" were not young and not pretty and looked "back-country in their red frocks and flats on their heads."

Their reaction was like that of a self-satisfied group of debutantes who, fancying themselves the admired and envied center of all eyes, learned they had been ridiculed as small-town and tacky. However, Mrs. Davis's ladies ran the rumor down to a woman they considered frumpish and dismissed her comments as spiteful jealousy.

When they had recovered from this blow to their equanimity the only problem confronting them was the humid, incredibly oppressive summer heat closing down on Richmond. Some thought they would go away to the famed Virginia Springs, and some combined more seemly climes with nearness to their lords. Mrs. Chesnut got a letter from her husband saying, "If you and Mrs. Preston can make up your minds to leave Richmond, and can come up to a nice little house near Orange Court House, we could come to see you frequently while the army is stationed here." Mrs. Chesnut comments, "So we go to Orange Court House."

For those who could not make up their minds to leave Richmond, the carnival continued. For all the damp, engulfing heat, the city was attractive in the summer. Streets lined with shade trees, front lawns and deep-walled gardens, vines and ivy on red-brick walls and iron grillwork all gave color and softness and a leisured atmosphere. The slow changing sky at dusk was restful. The slant-roofed houses cut patterns against the saffron in the west, and then the colors faded, and in the mist all outlines blurred and the city seemed cozy and gentle.

The people knew how to move in the hot hours, and they took their ease after dinner when the city baked. Houses were darkened from morning until dusk. Pallets were laid on the floor and in the cool wide halls. Then, in the late afternoons, when the sun was going down and the breeze came up from the river and from the fresh farm land to the south, the ladies drove out to the camps for the daily review. This was the big event of the day.

Mrs. Davis and her favored ladies went in a landau, behind matched bays, and she was one of the features of the review. Varina Davis was a young woman and good-looking in a full-blown fashion, full of the pulse of life and always beautifully dressed. She had to be to stand a chance against the gorgeous uniforms on display.

Camps were not then a grim business in anonymity. They were the pageant field of knights preparing to go off with a lady's rose, and the knights were very individualistic ones. Any sort of indoctrination would have been ridiculous. They were there because they had long since been indoctrinated by the feel of the soil they trod on, the air they breathed, and the look of their cherished land. Any sort of regimentation was resented, for they were there because of the rights of each man to choose his way.

They weren't kidding around when they said states' rights. A state was a big place to them. They started first in their own county or town, and right in the center of everything was the individual. "They were wholly unaccustomed to acting on any other than their own notion," said Eggleston, "and were not disposed to obey anybody except for good and sufficient reason given."

Any business of, "Do it because you're in the Army," had no meaning whatsoever to them. They were not in anything: they *were* the Army. Nor could there have been a single cartoon about the hard-boiled sergeant. One insulting word to some hot-blooded scion of the plantation nobility and you had a duel on your hands. They were gentlemen and to be addressed as such. They would obey only when it was clearly explained that, as in case of a drill, obedience was "necessary to the successful issue of a pretty performance in which they were interested."

In camp routine itself nothing would do but high-minded appeals, and sometimes not even that. A young blood assigned to picket-rope post, finding the guarding of horses a dull and unworthy affair, turned the whole matter over to his body servant. Another princeling, not feeling up to roll call, was so outraged when his lieutenant put him on double guard duty as a punishment that he demanded—and got— a public apology.

In those early exuberant days the men were not creatures of the officers. The officers were elected by the men, as in a club, and if their behavior was not satisfactory, another election would be held. As the officers enjoyed the conspicuousness of their positions on parades and the showier uniforms—epaulets and sword-belt sashes glistened everywhere—they naturally tried to please their constituents. Most of them also tried to learn their business.

Hardee's *Infantry Tactics* became a Bible, and the officers had to find some time to themselves to read up on the drills they would call for. Without the cadets from V.M.I. and the handful of Regular Army men, order would never have come out of the chaos of erecting hasty camps in fairgrounds and college grounds, fields and woods. The swords-and-roses patriots had to be brought water and food and clothes, arms and ammunition and equipment, where few or none ever existed before. Units had to be merged out of divergent and conflicting sectional groups and, worst of all, the antagonisms of different social brackets.

Nowhere was the line so marked between quality and plain people as in Virginia. A gentleman could not respect his social inferior, and his equal was not always efficient. Arguments from jealousies and offended honor were equaled only by arguments over place rivalries.

That all these groups from all over the South got to Richmond, trained and subsisted and went on to lines of defense as any sort of units, was finally because of the singing enthusiasm of the volunteers that gave them, with all the comic-opera aspects, a single shared purpose to meet the enemy and drive him out of Virginia.

5

Those ominous Yankee moves into the state began to get down to business as the summer wore into July. Up on the Northern plains at Manassas, Beauregard, the *beau sabreur* of the Southern knights, grew more rhetorical in his call for reinforcements. Across from him his old West Point classmate McDowell was obviously gathering his forces for the "On to Richmond" push demanded by the Washington politicians.

Down on the Peninsula, east of Richmond, Butler, the terror of civilians, set the precedent for his future behavior against soldiers. Advancing out of his fort, he ran into a little force under Prince John Magruder, the leading-man type among the Virginians from the old army, and scurried back in disorder to safety. The papers made much of this action—Big Bethel, it was called—where the Richmond Howitzers fired the first field-battery shot of the war at a hostile field target.

Out in the western counties things did not go so well. George Mc-Clellan, the rising star of the Union, the first rival of Beauregard, defeated the forces under Pegram and Garnett and secured that territory for the United States. Virginian Garnett, of the old army, was the first general officer killed in the war.

Further west, beyond Virginia, things were going even worse. Kentucky, of whom much had been hoped, was behaving the most typically American of any state: she was straddling. The governor said, "Kentucky will not sever her connection with national government, nor take up arms for either belligerent party; but arm herself for the preservation of peace within her borders."

Lincoln, having brought Virginia and four other states in by insisting that they furnish troops to invade the South, played it cozy with Kentucky and became Davis's rival suitor for her favors. When blustering Fremont made a proclamation of emancipation in Missouri, Lincoln hastily repudiated him in fear of offending Kentucky's slaveholding powers.

Neutrality agreements were made with the governor of Tennessee. The Confederates, strictly honorable, kept on their side of the line, but the Northern forces inched forward, awaiting an opportune moment to pounce. Unionists organized a "home guard" in opposition to the state militia under Buckner, father of the general killed at Okinawa. Citizens volunteered on both sides (more to the Union than to the South), and families became divided.

Tennessee perceived that her protection by the buffer of Kentucky was obviously temporary. To get her forces together, President Davis picked a bishop, Leonidas Polk. A former classmate of Davis at West Point, he came to Richmond to offer himself as a chaplain—and went back as a general. Polk at least was physically impressive. Britisher Fremantle found him having "all the manners and affability of a grand seigneur," and war clerk Jones said he was "a large, well-proportioned gentleman with florid complexion and intellectual face."

Across the Mississippi, Missouri was more divided than Kentucky, only the fighting had already begun—and very badly for the pro-Southerners. Alert, vigorous Union action had scattered the Secessionist militia and government, including the governor, before they could rightly get started. The governor and his loyal legislature were driven down into the hilly country in the southwest corner of the state, where they started to organize in true rebel style. They were commanded by Sterling Price, a lawyer originally from Virginia and a Unionist until these highhanded methods, including a street massacre of Southern sympathizers by German militia in St. Louis.

With all these goings on beginning to resemble a powder keg with the fuse burning, the war office itself jerked and stumbled along with its private feuds and disorders. Jones found the unhappy Colonel Bledsoe giving up writing any letters, but groaning as much as ever, and becoming very conscious of his honor. He almost came to a dueling with a Georgia general who asked him if the Secretary was in. Colonel Bledsoe thought this implied his position was that of a doorkeeper.

Poor Jones himself was pulled away from work every afternoon by Secretary Walker, who wanted company in his daily house hunting. Somehow they found time to commission foreign volunteers—French Prince Polignac, a social favorite, and the great-nephew of Kosciusko—and when the Secretary was out sick, Bledsoe proudly rushed through a mass of appointments and then returned to the dignified idleness of being chief of the bureau.

In spite of the office staff, food and ammunition were getting to Manassas, and Beauregard's flowery calls for reinforcements got a working arrangement with Joe Johnston, in the Valley, to slip away from Yankee Patterson and come to Beauregard's rescue. If Patterson was sharp, this was risky business, opening that Valley highway, but it could not be helped. McDowell was clearly worked up to the point of making his drive, and he had the men to make it stick. This "On to Richmond" began to have an apprehensive sound to the people in the overcrowded city.

Government workers sent their families away. Work grew more frantic on the defenses around the city. In boardinghouses and hotels and homes the tone of talk changed. Suddenly the people faced the realization that the buildings in which they lived might be destroyed. The women who had so gaily waved their gallants good-by suddenly realized where the men had gone, and why. From the Queen Anne houses on old Church Hill to the new mansions on Franklin, from Mrs. Muller's Lager Beer Saloon to the Spotswood Bar, they saw the end of the holiday phase of preparation, almost as if for something they never expected to happen.

Now the living reality came upon them, of what it meant to try to set up a nation on earth. An enemy was planning to destroy their beloved city. The invading armies were now poised to drive toward these old shaded streets, these cool retreats in the sweet, long, familiar summer.

Distant news of the whole lost meaning. Only their own danger was emphasized, even by such outraging news as that of the captured *Savannah's* crew being imprisoned in New York as felons, under Lincoln's piracy act.

In Charleston two members of the Vigilant Rifles got the idea for the ship that was to cause the trouble. The captain was a Philadelphian, Harrison Baker, a florid powerful man of thirty-seven, with some sailing experience. His lieutenant was John Harleston, a 28-year-old Texas rancher. For the crew they had three Irishmen, two Scots, one German, a Filipino steward, and a Chinese cook, and a nineteen-year-old reporter from the Charleston *Mercury*.

These Southern Rebels sailed gaily out at dusk and captured a prize, but when the landsmen saw the seven guns on a Union ship and looked at their one, they surrendered and landed in the Tombs in New York.

Whatever the citizens felt, Jefferson Davis was deeply aroused. This legal violation offended all the principles by which he honestly lived, and the indignity to his people hurt him. He quickly stated the whole position of the rights of the men with irrefutable logic. In 1776 and in 1812 the United States commissioned privateers. In the Paris Convention of 1856 the United States refused to enter a pact outlawing privateers. Clearly, then, the crew of the *Savannah* was acting on the lines set forth by the United States.

The Northern answer was that the Southern states were not a recognized country, nor was there a recognized war.

But Judge Daly of New York pointed out, on the South's side, that "if privateersmen were not acting under the authority of a sovereign and independent state, neither are soldiers." The South, standing on this, claimed that if the Union did not expect the welcome mat out when their soldiers came invading by land, why should they expect the Confederacy to lie down and play dead when hostile ships invaded their harbors for the purpose of cutting off their life supplies with the rest of the world?

The son of a former President set forth all this to Lincoln, but he did not receive even the courtesy of an answer. By this token alone the Confederacy could know the difference of an established nation and the new alignment of seceded states in a bid for independence. Not even courtesy between nations had to be extended them. No dignity was allowed them. By victory in the field alone could they hope to survive as a separate people.

Victory now meant stopping McDowell at Manassas, where the first skirmish had already occurred along the fords of the high-banked creek, called Bull Run. . . .

At any day the full battle would be joined. All that could be done in a little over three months had been done. Joe Johnston, abandoning the Valley, was moving to support Beauregard. They held the fate of the new nation now—a Creole glory hunter and a quartermaster general who started his Confederate career by squabbling over rank.

In Richmond they could only wait. With no radio, no extras, but by word of mouth originating at the telegraph office, the distracted war office, and the secret sources of rumor, the people on the street learned on a Sunday morning that the "On to Richmond" was here. The battle for their existence was joined. . . .

CHAPTER SEVEN

The Champion Goes Down

THE first actual battle between the two civilizations—traditional and progressive—in what the U. S. Secretary of State had termed an "irrepressible conflict," was waged literally by armed mobs. All that made it a contest was the American unpreparedness shared equally by both sides. The technological potential of the United States lacked time to be fully realized, and the battle was fought between individual men with relatively similar weapons in their hands.

Though the commands of both "armies" were sprinkled with West Pointers, the majority of these had been lieutenants and captains a few months before, most of whom had little or no actual fighting experience. The volunteer officers, coming from prominence in civil life, had only recently learned their drilling and organization from manuals. There was nothing to show what they would do in battle.

Now many of them are historic figures, whose names on printed pages are symbols of army units. "So-and-so's *Brigade* moved to attack by the right flank." The unit is a solid thing, like a man in checkers. The symbolic name *decides* to move the unit. It is moved.

On that hot July day these symbolic leaders, and many more now lost in anonymity, were excited men who had just left their homes, fumbled through the unfamiliarity of community camp life, and in new strange uniforms suffered the exposure of their individual nerve systems, character motivations, and emotional patterns.

"Decision" was often a generous euphemism for reaction to shock —in which some men were paralyzed and some acted in the blind, purposeless violence that might result in disaster or what was called heroism. "By the right flank" could mean by the ravine in which shaken men had gotten lost, and out of which they stumbled into a confused mass of the enemy.

Even Old Bory, Victor of Fort Sumter, had become the Confederate Hero by directing the fire of shore batteries on an ill-prepared fort in what, after all, was a very small action. Four months before, the droopy-eyed picture soldier had been a major. Now, along the creek called Bull Run, where the enemy poured across the fords, nothing was going along the classic lines of the campaigns he had studied with colored maps and names that were symbols to him.

Beauregard had planned to attack the enemy's left. Instead of that, the enemy attacked his left! In fact, except for the adrenalin which danger kicked up in a few obscure individuals, the attack would have swallowed up Beauregard's flank before he knew what was happening. As it was, the successful attack was being contained a long way from Old Bory by a group of Virginians under a screwball professor. Standing on ground he had selected with help from no one, and without Beauregard's knowledge, Fool Tom Jackson was to win there the "Stonewall" by which the printed page knows him.

Of all men on that field, on either side, Jackson showed native genius for the murderous business at hand. Of him it could truly be said, "He decided." He had a heart for killing, as well as the head. In his fiercely Presbyterian soul he believed in the God of Vengeance, and that he was that God's armed fist on earth.

At thirty-seven he was an ambitious man, but few knew it. He came from the mountain-region middle class, was proud of his sturdy stock, agonizingly shy, and had been forced to do everything the hard way. Put all that together in a secretive nature, where a stern non-communicativeness hid all that could be hidden, and the character becomes an eccentric. In all the confusion of that battle the big names could be excused for not recognizing what lay under his simple brusque exterior, and they could be forgiven for not recognizing the size of his accomplishment.

Of course Jackson got help when he needed it badly, once from a twenty-nine-year-old Virginian whose name was beginning to show on pages by his initials—J. E. B. Stuart. Then more desperately needed help came from some Deep South troops who charged with a strange yelling, like cowboys, and the Rebel Yell was born there in the swirling dusk.

But finally it was the men themselves who won or lost. Impelled by group response, they were less inhibited than the officers and acted more naturally. Some ran shamelessly and some just rocked back in revulsion, skulking away. Some fought to no purpose and some stood in solid lines, firing with aim. Some charged like stampeded horses and some fought coolly, creeping forward like Indians. One of these, a turkey hunter, heard his companion's feet crashing through brush and whispered, "Sh-h, step light or we won't get a shot."

These men were not supposed to know anything beyond what happened right before them. The great leaders, the heroes, trying to see what went on everywhere, knew less than the turkey hunter. Beauregard was striving to come up with phrases that would resound through posterity, but he could not tell them back in the war office what was going on.

2

In that gloomy office, where the tensely depressed men of the Cabinet huddled, Secretary Walker strode up and down, damning his office and the fate that placed him there. Howell Cobb, one who did own hundreds of slaves, came, studied the reports, and announced he thought it was a drawn battle. Colonel Bledsoe denounced him for saying so. Tempers were short and faces were long. They had everything at stake, and other men held the dice. They could only wait together in the clammy comfort of numbers, and guess like any citizen.

Their President was missing. He had rushed off to the battle himself. Judah Benjamin left them too. He had joined the ladies in the Spotswood, correctly figuring that Davis would first notify his wife.

In the hotel the little groups, formed now of the closest ties of friendship and oldest ties of association, clustered in rooms throughout the halls. Some had their doors closed, some open, some ajar. Snatches of news came—from husbands on staffs, from the war office, from roundabout sources. When the items suggested a turn for their victory, the women shrieked and clapped their hands in joy. When the news was bad, the rooms grew silent, as the women stared at one another with blanched faces. Then some knelt to pray.

If the Confederates did not hold, their brief dream of independence was over. All their careers and fortunes would have been thrown away for nothing. Even here, in these rooms for transients, they might not be safe. No one could know what a conquering horde would do in this city they seemed to hate so much. Finally it was all personal—even to the men trying to block the enemy's drive. They were husbands and kinsmen and friends. . . .

Mrs. Chesnut had fallen sick and lay on her bed, not joining the waiting groups. Shadows of dusk filled the room, and through the open window drifted the mingled sounds of the anxious city. Mrs. Chesnut did not hear the visitor who entered softly, until she leaned over her bed. Mrs. Chesnut looked up into a face of desperate calm.

Varina Davis was holding a paper in her hand.

She said, "A great battle has been fought. . . . Your husband is all right. . . . Wade Hampton is wounded. Colonel Johnston of the Legion is killed; so are Colonel Bee and Bartow. . . ."

Mrs. Chesnut had no breath to answer. She lay stunned as Mrs. Davis went on in the same concentrated voice to recount the details of the death of their friend Bartow. (But, *your husband is all right*.) Then, "The President telegraphs me only that it is a great victory. Adjutant General Cooper has the other telegrams."

Still Mrs. Chesnut could not move. Mrs. Davis read from the paper in her hand. "Dead and dying cover the field. . . . Three hundred of the Legion wounded."

That was South Carolina. That was home. That got her up. She went with Varina Davis into Mrs. Preston's room. They put her on the bed in there, but the quiet was gone. Men and women and children streamed in and out of the room in mass hysteria. "We beat them," they all said, a little incredulously. They knew no details. It didn't matter. "We had been such anxious wretches," Mrs. Chesnut said, "the revulsion of feeling was almost too much to bear."

Slowly, as the meaning of the event sank to its personal levels, they thought of Mrs. Bartow, a few doors down the hall. Who will tell her? Each woman averted her face. It had to be Mrs. Davis. She did not want it, but they chose her. She had to do it.

She walked down the hall alone, the wife of the President of a real country now. When she knocked, an excited voice called, "Come in." When she entered, Mrs. Bartow sat up on the bed and started to rise. Then she got a full look at the set, pale face of her friend.

The spring left her body. She sank back and covered her face. "Is it bad news for me?" When Mrs. Davis did not answer, the woman knew. "Is he killed?"

From outside, the medley of uncertain sounds was changing to a triumphant chant. But it was low-pitched, more of relief than of joy. They were saved.

Judah Benjamin hurried from the hotel with Mrs. Davis's news and made the dramatic announcement in the war office. Now all the men who had sweat there all afternoon broke fast for their homes and bars. Each wanted to be the first to tell. . . .

3

There was no head of the government around to make an official announcement. The President, with his secretary, young Burton

Harrison, had rushed to the field by train, by commandeered engine, by horse—into a routed, broken mob of his people stumbling to the rear.

The erect man remembered Buena Vista, when his charge with the Mississippi Volunteers had saved the batteries that saved the day. The years fell away, and he became the invincible leader again.

"Go back," he shouted. "Do your duty and you can save the day!"

The shattered, powder-blackened men stared at the trim figure and brushed on past him. He moved through the thickening debris of battle. Here was a soldier crying as he buried his friend. They had promised each other before the battle to perform this duty if . . . There a bishop was giving comfort to a row of wounded men. One lad, covered to his chin with a blanket, was particularly pale and still, his fixed gaze staring upward, waiting for death.

"Is there nothing I can do for you, my son?" the bishop asked.

The boy shook his head. "My leg . . . it's gone. . . ."

The bishop, thinking it might not be too late to stop the flow of blood, pulled back the blanket. He saw two good legs, in striped gray trousers ending in stout boots. He felt of the legs gingerly. They were unmarked. The boy sat up.

He had seen a cannon ball strike the earth at his feet. One leg went numb. He tried to establish contact with the earth with that leg. It had no sensation of touch, as if suspended in air. As it happened, the leg was suspended in air. The cannon ball had plowed a furrow under the foot, at the same time it momentarily numbed the leg.

The boy jumped up and ran off, even more quickly than he had lain down and prepared to die. . . .

The President, moving frantically through the unheeding mob, reached a field hospital. A dour, brown-bearded officer in a battered cadet cap pulled low over his eyes, was having his hand bandaged. He was saying, "Give me five thousand men and I'll be in Washington tonight."

The man was obviously battle-crazy. The President did not know this man had just won the name of Stonewall by turning the tide from disaster to a victory of incredible size.

But there were other murmurs of success. The backwash Davis had first encountered did not truly represent the picture. . . .

He pushed on to meet the heroes, Beauregard and Joe Johnston. They had shared the victory. It was Beauregard's battle plan, only the battle had not been fought according to it. Joe Johnston, as ranking officer, had assumed command when he arrived on the field, only the point of danger had been established and held before either he or Beauregard was aware of where it was.

When they knew, Beauregard asked Johnston to leave the field to him and take charge of the reinforcements. Johnston instead rushed to the point of danger. Beauregard went with him, dramatically declaiming his willingness to die for victory. The soldiers died and the soldiers won it. It was their battle, on both sides.

Now luckless McDowell, who had planned and executed well, was carried along to Washington by the panic of his soldiers and the civilian spectators, and Beauregard and Joe Johnston sat down in a field tent to arrange responsibility for the victory. The President joined them there.

The three men lounged together, relaxed and exuberant, and talked vaguely of pursuit. An officer sent in word that he had found an opening to the Yankees' exposed rear, and relatively fresh Confederates were at hand. . . .

There was a stir of mild excitement. They talked it over. Someone pointed out that the officer had been known in the old army to be unreliable. Word came from another source of a column of Yankees moving across the front. That settled it; they never questioned this latter source. The reported Yankees turned out to be Confederates, but never mind—the day was won.

The President leaned back at ease, smoking a bland cigar, the picture of the victor in his gray suit and light felt hat. They talked some more about pursuit, but nobody took charge. "What do you think, General?" "After you, Mr. President." The hours passed. It was full night.

Jefferson Davis felt good. His people had accomplished what was necessary: they had driven the invader from Virginia—or rather, stopped him, and allowed him to run safely from Virginia. But that was the same now, as the idea of pursuit languished.

We are not aggressors. We have shown the world we can protect ourselves. England and France will see—and, anyway, tomorrow the men can harvest the field.

There were dozens of cannons and thousands of guns and—prisoners. Somehow nobody had thought of prisoners. They had nothing to do with them. As Richmond seemed an elastic city, with endless capacity to expand, the Union soldiers were sent on there. Somebody would look after them.

The next day in a drizzle, as Confederate cavalry looked impudently down on Washington from the Virginia hills, the President followed the Union prisoners to Richmond. There was a speech of thanksgiving to be made from his Spotswood window.

4

In Richmond the first prisoners received far less attention than they would have except for the Confederate wounded. No provision had been made for them either. Enthusiasm for the field of glory did not include the aftermath of battle. With all the bands and parades and parties that accompanied the rushing of men to the point of defense, somehow the people had forgotten the detail of those men returning as casualties.

The reality came as no pictures or words could simulate. Streets near the depot became cluttered with the suffering men and unprepared people trying to help. The gaily dressed groups in carriages were replaced by filthy, bloody strangers in agony. The parties for gossip changed to gatherings of ladies who volunteered to nurse. Nobody trained them. They tried—some timidly at the physical approach to a strange man, some becoming casualties themselves at the shock of blood and torn flesh. But capable ones emerged, and they all were so anxious to do something.

One young girl sweetly asked a bearded sufferer if he would like his face washed. "Well, ma'am," he said patiently, "it's been washed twenty times already, but go ahead if you want to."

As the three civilian hospitals were less than negligible, citizens worked with the few medical officers and detailed soldiers to set up crude makeshift quarters in hotels and warehouses, churches and stores, and in homes all over the city. Richmond became an extemporaneous hospital and its citizens the staff. Probably no wounded of any army ever received more personal attention, especially in the homes, where the ladies of the house and their friends provided all the tender care they would have to their own kin. After all, it was *their* war.

But nothing could have been less efficient militarily. Even Congress was stirred into action. Arrangements were made for general hospitals and the abolishment of the private system. For the present, the building best adapted for hospital use, the City Alms House, was used for wounded of the enemy. That would be straightened out later too.

For the unwounded, the chastened On-to-Richmonders who had unhappily accomplished their purpose, private homes would not do.

Their destiny was turned over to Major Winder, a stout, gray-haired apoplectic Marylander who had come to Richmond to volunteer his services. A West Pointer now too old for the field, he was appointed provost marshal, a role in which he combined the more belligerent traits of the M.P. with the sterner qualities of the martinet to make himself the most unloved official on either side.

First he selected an available building, Liggon's Tobacco Factory and Warehouse, a substantial three-story brick building at Twenty-fifth and Main, where the street curves close to the river. The commissioned officers were grouped downstairs and the non-coms and privates on the two top floors. There were no blankets and no furniture, but there were toilet facilities and gaslights. A kitchen was hastily set up, and the prisoners formed in messes. Those with money bought extra food from the outside, and Negroes wandered freely in and out, getting orders and making deliveries.

While some haphazard routine was established in the prison, guards were quickly chosen from raw recruits and a suggestion of organization brought to the prison staff. Being thoroughly untrained, and with no discipline in which to fit, the freshly uniformed civilians acted according to their natures and the feelings of the moment. After that first clash which turned back invaders, the feelings were antagonistic in what was still a personal fight rather than a war. In all truth it cannot be said that the majority of prisoners exhibited an attitude that would ease the situation.

Not yet soldiers themselves, they were unaccustomed to any sustained rigors, and imprisonment came as a shock to the volunteers who had marched so triumphantly from Washington to scatter the Rebels. Prison life under the best circumstances was an ordeal, and at Liggon's there was definite discomfort and inefficiency. The physical hardships were exacerbated by the prisoners' psychology, which, contemptuous of the movement they fought, resented every circumstance as a personal affront of the despised insurgents.

Winder apologized to them for the extemporaneous prison, and a chaplain, explaining that no provision had been made for anything like a thousand prisoners, said, "There was not a Confederate official in the land who had any experience in taking care of prisoners of war."

These bitterly complaining casuals were in no mood to make allowances and expressed their resentments by patronizing their guards and mocking their cause. Their diaries reveal a superiority from which they laughed at the Confederate—"an object of commiseration and curiosity"—for no understanding of the real issues of the war. A mere tool of his political leaders, he stupidly thought the North was trying to subjugate him.

The prisoners never seemed to think of the natural reactions of any man, especially an ignorant one, whose land they had invaded, whose kinspeople and friends they were trying to kill—and they forgot the handcuffs found among themselves which were on exhibition at the Spotswood Hotel.

Never calling Southerners anything except "Rebels," making a joke of the Confederate President, the prisoners were constantly outraged to read in Richmond papers of the hatred toward them. Their own self-righteousness in restoring the Union seemed to invalidate any responses the opponent might feel and, at least, did not tend to create in the Southerner a belief that any love of him or his region motivated the fight for the republic.

With this attitude, and the fact that the guards were neither of the highest type nor disciplined, it was inevitable that bad blood would come between them and the prisoners.

By averages, it followed that some guards would express their resentments and their natures in harshness or at times brutality. One of the two worst offenders was a stupid German named Wirz, who was to win his greater notoriety later at a Southern prison. The other menace was Lieutenant Todd, brother-in-law of President Lincoln.

Later, when Regular Army officers came in—Captain Gibbs and Lieutenant Hairston—conditions improved, and the prisoners all spoke well of these two gentlemen. By then the prison was being emptied, as some men were sent to Castle Pinckney in Charleston, where they were guarded by boy cadets, and others were paroled.

But from the first the prisoners were bothered by visitors who regarded them as "objects of curiosity," and some of the primitive spontaneous hate of those first days of regional clash was expressed in taunts and jeers. One old lady expressed wonder that Yankees had no hair on their teeth. And everybody wanted a look at New York's Congressman Ely, a bland and courteous long-suffering leader of the prison group.

Some few people showed the prisoners kindness, and Miss Elizabeth Van Lew, bringing delicacies and books and good cheer, became a favorite.

This mysterious woman was the daughter of a hardware merchant who had come from the North and prospered in Richmond. When he died he left his daughter a huge, spectacularly beautiful house on the most magnificent site in the city. Its garden, ending at a bluff, over-looked the hill below which was the prison warehouse.

It was known when Miss Van Lew took delicacies to the prisoners that she was a Union sympathizer with strong abolitionist tendencies. She had sold and emancipated most of her slaves and bought others to unite families. At this time she was a small erect woman in her early forties, with quick blue eyes, dark hair in ringlets about her face, and a nervous, tense manner. Though no one said so, she was also a great self-dramatizer. The guards just called her "Crazy Betsy" and let her alone.

Any news she could have gotten out would have been picayune compared to what the papers furnished daily, and when the New York *Herald* came out with lists of the Confederate forces, the fear of spies went to such high officers as Adjutant General Cooper.

This 63-year-old New Yorker, born on the Hudson River, boasted a father who had fought at Lexington and Bunker Hill, a great-uncle who had been president of Harvard, and himself with forty-six years in the U. S. Army had been adjutant general at the breakout of hostilities. He was married to the sister of Virginia's senator, James Mason, also of a great Revolutionary line. Having only his army pay as income, Cooper had come with the South purely in sympathy with their aims. Though he has not been regarded highly, he accepted with tact and generosity an office reduced to a clerkship by the President and brought to it a calmness and a cultivated mind. But he was a Yankee and, in those dog days of Richmond's smothering summer, talk was growing loose—because there was no more action.

Lincoln's effort "to suppress the combination" had failed, and the Confederate government waited for the United States to admit that the Southern states could not be forced back. Davis had never wanted the separation to come to fighting. He had been goaded into striking the first blow, and now that they had fought, he experienced the re-action of literally overwhelming relief. All through the government the shock at the size of their victory caused a suspension of action.

A fighter, who hoped to hold the champion to a draw, had knocked him down with one punch.

CHAPTER EIGHT

Siesta

THE way the Southern people interpreted the government mood was to mean that the war was over. Patriots who had arranged their affairs against volunteering unpacked and oiled their shotguns for a different kind of shooting as fall grew near. Congress, still following old American customs, began making eyes at its constituents and found an easy way to popularity.

The first issuance of treasury notes had met with such success with the public, while causing no depreciation of the currency, that Congress was emboldened to enlarge its field. From the first $20,000,000 in three-year notes issued before Manassas, it went in August to $100,-000,000 in treasury notes now payable "six months after the ratification of peace between the Confederate States of America and the United States."

When this issue took, it went up to $150,000,000 along with an issue of 6 per cent bonds which were used largely, in effect, as currency. Never before had there been so much folding money south of the Potomac, nor was there to be again until the WPA. Clearly the members of Congress had not adjusted their thinking to their more modest estate since they moved south from Washington.

Poor Secretary Memminger watched helplessly this cheerful financing, for Congress regarded him as no more than a bookkeeper. He had revealed an ineffectiveness to them when he got into trouble with the powerful planter class.

With their one-crop economy, the planters needed cash. As government bonds gave no help to their immediate needs, the less patriotic ones sold for cash to the North, and the others appealed to Memminger for aid. First he thought they should have it. Not knowing what to suggest, he tried futilely to get Congress to come up with something. Then he decided the planters shouldn't have any help.

Here he showed Congress that, outside routine, he didn't know his own mind. The untypical Charlestonian would never get anything through them now.

Cities and towns, counties and stores, joined in the currency-making carnival, and in Richmond the Southern Exchange issued fifteen-cent notes redeemable in wheat, baled hay, oats, or wood. The city issued over $300,000 in notes of less than a dollar, and the grand jury took action then, indicting Richmond. But that law was changed; Richmond was riding too high those days.

At all hours horse-drawn hotel omnibuses clattered to the depots to meet the trainloads of passengers—refugees and speculators, gamblers and "harlots and courtesans" from New York, Philadelphia, and Baltimore. With their coming, the city could feel established.

Among the speculators came spies, mostly cash-hungry petty adventurers selling to both sides. The hackmen, their prices soaring, asked no questions, and ancient hostelries opened their dusty doors to anyone with cash. The more respectable elements found shelter with families who, their men in the Army, turned their homes into boardinghouses.

The general populace, native and foreign, recovered from their fears and the shock of war and returned with enthusiasm to their pleasures. Sometimes pleasures got out of hand, as when a woman was committed to prison in default of $200 "for keeping a disorderly house where diverse persons assemble and get drunk and make great noise by fighting and swearing, all of which disturbed the neighborhood."

Another woman, arrested on a charge of keeping a house of ill fame, caused a jury disagreement over the question of whether a house of ill fame constituted a nuisance. A Mississippi soldier was tried for beating a woman on whom he attempted rape. Because of a girl, a South Carolina lieutenant committed suicide by jumping out of his sixth-floor bedroom in the Ballard House.

The old livery-stable section grew quiet on Saturday mornings as horse auctions disappeared, but workmen were needed in manufacturing firms turning to camp equipment, and in the Ordnance Department, where a newly invented machine was turning out Minié balls at 120 a minute. A boy turned the crank.

The Misses Clopton planned to open a school, "as a consequence of being reduced from comparable affluence to poverty by the seizure and ravage of their property now in the enemy's hands."

Richmond women felt the rise of peaches and grapes at the markets (brought in from the counties), which they bought to take to the hospitals. With the care of the wounded becoming organized, the ladies turned to knitting socks from coarse yarn. One soldier protested that he had received twelve pairs, and could he not get a shirt? He could not.

Editorials suggested using prisoners of war to operate the coal mines twelve miles out of Richmond, and proclaimed that when the Confederacy was permanently established, "Richmond will have the brightest future before her of any inland city on the continent." That their city would become the permanent capital of the new country was generally accepted, and the people laughed at renegade Winfield Scott, who had boasted he would lead his Yankee army into Richmond. They seemed indifferent even to the fall of Fort Hatteras.

This poorly prepared fort in name only, on the North Carolina coast, was the first inlet lost in the Sound country. Along the coast of North Carolina long sandy islets separate the ocean from the waters of the sounds into which the rivers empty. It had first been the job of North Carolina to protect these sounds, and the state had them patrolled with four captured steamers mounting one gun each. When the Confederacy took over the defense, no more than token "forts" were erected. The United States, immediately perceiving the importance of these sounds, sent in August several heavily armed ships that smothered the few defenders, and Hatteras Inlet was gone.

But as such things seemed not to disturb the authorities, the citizens lived happily in their sense of security. In truth the Administration was bothered more with internal troubles than with the enemy. The Cabinet was learning what states' rights could mean, and the chief sufferer was War Secretary Walker.

He was losing volunteers through inability to arm them. Though two hundred thousand men had already been rejected for lack of equipment, the governors of Alabama, Louisiana, and Mississippi refused to come to his aid on the grounds that their home guards needed the weapons. South Carolina's governor stated that, not only could he send no more arms, but he wanted some back. Furthermore he wanted powder. He had bought powder from Hazard's Mills in Connecticut until January, but that was all distributed, including loans to North Carolina and Florida. Florida wanted more powder, fuses, and larger-caliber guns. "Florida wants arms. She has never received a musket from the Confederate States."

That great comic, Brown of Georgia, who most vehemently called for arms for his own state's defense, declared it a punishable act for officers to carry arms out of the state for their soldiers, and then seized a Confederate cargo at Savannah shipped from Europe. Furthermore, Brown wanted the Georgia men themselves back to repel an imaginary invasion from the coast.

Virginia was no less vigilant of her rights than her sister states, but, with the fighting on her soil, home-guard questions were beyond the realm of pure theory. Her governor, however, did find other little ways to heckle the central authorities.

While misfit Walker fussed over these discouraging matters, and Benjamin smilingly eyed his job over a glass of sherry, Jefferson Davis returned to the military details which absorbed him.

His faith in the intervention of Europe was strong after their victory, and to that end he need only continue the threat of a cotton famine. In the North he saw signs of disunity, such as the movement against the war by the Copperheads, and the agitation by Senator Bright of Indiana. While at home, troops occupied practically all of their own country, and the situation seemed ideal for engaging himself in writing his generals to regroup their troops. He wanted the men of one state to be commanded by officers from the same state.

In camps the soldiers grew bored and restless. In Richmond thoughtful people began to ask why nothing was being done. Virginia's Senator Hunter, also eying a cabinet job he expected to be vacant, when asked by Mrs. Chesnut why the Confederates didn't go on to Washington, smiled and said, "Don't ask awkward questions."

But when the Texan Wigfall, who had left the President's staff with reported bad feeling, told her there was no reason the Confederates had not gone into Washington, Mrs. Chesnut recorded these thoughts: ". . . We will dilly-dally, and Congress orate, and generals parade, until they in the North get up an army three times as large as McDowell's. . . ." A friend told her that "this victory will be our ruin. It lulls us into a fool's paradise at our superior valor, and the shameful farce of their flight will wake every inch of their manhood. It was the very fillip they needed."

Mrs. Chesnut's friend called it close, as did war clerk Jones, who grew frantic at the inaction. While they argued in the South as to why the victory was not followed up, the defeat was followed up in the North. From "suppressing the combination" of insurgents, the United States began to gear for full-scale war which was to smell no sweeter by another name. There was no more talk over what constituted "coercion" of a state. Manassas wrote the tacit definition to mean "conquer."

Never was so much accomplished by headlong flight. Had the Unions only failed to carry the field and stubbornly retreated to a new line which still presented a solid front full of menace, the Confederates would still have been fighting. But the North inadvertently brought in a Trojan horse.

On their side of the Potomac, stung into new and greater efforts, they were free to rebuild at their leisure under that superb organizer, McClellan, while the South went back to its favorite game of politics —which even the generals entered.

2

There was even time for finding fault with the new postal service. If any job was lower than Benjamin's—Attorney-General in a country without courts—it was Postmaster in a country without stamps. Texas' John Reagan had not wanted the position, as did nobody—he was the only one they could talk into it. But once committed, he brought to it all the single-minded devotion to a task that characterized a life more typical of the American success story than anything associated with the Old South's plantocracy.

In the back country of Tennessee he had grubbed for what education he got in traditional frontier fashion—farm work, boat trips to the academy, finally to Natchez for a teacher's job. That failed to pan out, and to sustain himself he had for the next few months his first association with slavery. He worked as an overseer until, when the owners refused to give the Negroes more meat, he left for Texas. He arrived there, at eighteen, with a few dollars and his clothes in a kerchief. He fought in the Cherokee campaign, made friends, became a surveyor and militia officer, and at twenty-six started the study of law. Then steadily he became judge, state legislator, congressman on the postal committee, and commissioner of Indian affairs.

In politics he stood alone. Against both Secessionists and abolitionists, against all political parties, he was re-elected as a Unionist. His turn away from Washington came when states' rights were attacked by the new party under the banner of abolitionist fanatics. He said, "When we appealed to the Republicans to grant our rights under the Constitution, they answered . . . 'We have the majority, and you must submit.' It came to the point where I felt I could not sit with them and retain my self-respect and be faithful to the rights and honor of the people I represented."

He went to Montgomery to offer his services to the forming nation. When he conferred with Davis, rugged Reagan told him that he would not have voted for him for President, "not that I distrusted his fitness for the high office, but because I wanted him at the head of the Army." If this was a blunt statement of a forthright man, no guile could have been more effective. Though the job assigned him was thankless, it was an honor—and it was also his honor to perform all tasks as well as they could be performed.

Judge Reagan had to start right at the beginning—getting blanks, sealing wax, wrapping paper, twine, stationery for post offices, and dies, printing press, and perforating machines for stamps. As there could be no stamps immediately, he got by until June through the continuance of the United States postal service. When the shooting ended this and still no stamps were ready, clerks accepted cash and marked the mail paid—though some ingenious postmasters had their own stamps made.

These "provisionals" showed all the variety of the Southern soul. They went from crude hand-stamped impressions (one carved on the end of a piece of poplar wood) to beautiful lithographs and woodcuts. The majority were typeset, and most carried prominently the post-master's name. They used every conceivable kind of paper, some old U.S. government.

The stamped envelopes were even more elaborate. Those from Norfolk's post office carried a hideous Virginia seal (*Sic Semper Tyrannis*), and Lynchburg's bore a poem:

> On, on to the rescue, the Vandals are coming—
> Go meet them with bayonet, sword and spear;
> Drive them back to the desolate land they are leaving—
> Go, trusting in God, you'll have nothing to fear.

Reagan's real job was mapping mail routes, contracting with railroad and steamship companies, and with individuals for star routes. Though this was helped immeasurably by several key men coming over from the U. S. Post Office, everything was slowed by Reagan's plan of making his postal service self-sufficient. The U.S. postal service had nearly a two-million-dollar deficit in the Southern states, and Reagan thought the Confederacy could not afford such wastefulness.

He got the railroads to agree to half pay for the duration of war. He lessened trips on some routes and discontinued others. He gave no franking privileges—which lessened the weight of mails—and he raised rates on letters, papers, and packages, making five cents the lowest stamp.

He ran the department without a deficit, but by the time he came to Richmond newspapers were taking pot shots at Reagan for inefficiency, and people complained that it took a letter longer to go to Petersburg (twenty-two miles) than through the blockade to New York.

As an indication of their distrust, a newspaper notice announced that "all persons desirous of sending parcels, letters or packages to their friends belonging to the Richmond Light Infantry Blues can do so by leaving them at the Blacksmith Shop of T. C. Epps, corner of Broad and First, by this (Sat.) evening at 6."

But Reagan operated his department in terms of the present practical needs. Assuming that the struggling country could not afford a deficit, and that it could be sustained even without a mail service comparable to that of an established concern, he gave the Southern states as good a service as possible under all the circumstances.

The point was that the Administration endowed the whole setup of the new confederation with such an atmosphere of permanence, of tradition and custom, that the people did not *think* as revolutionaries. Reagan did.

He disapproved of Vice-President Stephens on the obvious ground that seems to have occurred to no one else—that he led a revolution he was known to be opposed to. This Texan by adoption, growing up in the wilds of a new republic, was not bound by legalities. At this time, when both sides were handling Kentucky with kid gloves, while she toyed with neutrality, Reagan was for sending troops right in. "If we were at peace, deliberating as a convention . . . that is one thing." But this is rebellion!

Sh-h, sh-h. Everything must be legal and honorable. Every act must go into the pages of history in such a manner that posterity may always read of our irreproachable conduct in a just cause. Reagan knew that the winner writes history, or else he didn't care who wrote it. No explanation helps when you lose; when you win, the act of victory explains everything.

They needed him in that makeshift crew, and Davis appreciated him. They became friends. Plain, solid Reagan, a self-reliant doer in his forty-third year, had an almost childlike admiration for the highly keyed gentleman of pure intellect. There was something protective in his affection for this wondrous and complex mechanism so different from anything he could be. There was also probably something awed in him to see Davis's moral courage and unyielding integrity—simple virtues like his own—in this planter-statesman with so much else.

Davis was responsive to affection, for by nature he was sweet. And by nature, and all that he had made of himself, he admired the stalwart values wherever he saw them.

Reagan and his second wife (his first, like Davis's, died of illness) were scarcely the sort to decorate the Davises' drawing room or make small talk smaller. In fact they cared little for the fluffy side of official life, probably not even knowing that their plainness was laughed at by the more elegant cabinet wives. They lived simply, outside Richmond society, which was little aware of them.

Reagan's real place was in Davis's heart. Though the President evinced no interest whatsoever in the Postmaster's department, Judge Reagan continued at his thankless task and spoke his mind freely in cabinet meetings.

In the early fall his lithographers—Hoyer & Ludwig—eased the public's pain by producing the first batch of Confederate stamps. Five-cent greens, they were the first stamps to bear the likeness of a living American—Jefferson Davis. He looked handsome on the engraving.

3

In his suite Jefferson Davis looked less well than in his likeness. During the lull in larger action he increased his detail work and fell sick. The old neuralgic pains twisted his nerves beyond his endurance, and he had to take to bed.

His wife administered to him well. Visitors were cleared through her, and she took messages or conferred with the less important ones. In a few days he was up and around again, but vague aches continued to plague him intermittently, and his stomach went off when he was overtired. When the long city summer dragged on, he was frequently overtired, as he had learned nothing about delegating authority, and problems increased with the Union efforts on distant fronts and internal dissension close at hand.

Robert Toombs, his Secretary of State, was the first enemy with whom he had to contend. Even before Manassas, this undisciplined malcontent had applied for a brigadier's commission in exchange for his portfolio of Secretary of State. That his military experience was limited to captaining militia in some Indian trouble did not bother Toombs in the least. In fact one of his arguments with the Administration was its preference for West Pointers, for whom Toombs held only colorfully phrased contempt. Yet because of his attacks on the West Point clique, Davis was forced politically to give the dissatisfied cabinet member his chance for the real glory.

Toombs was too chummy with Vice-President Stephens and, now the natural rebel leader (rebelling against whatever was authority), was too ready to buck over the traces. If his tumultuous energy could be diverted into military leadership, the Army would gain and Davis would lose an enemy in his official family. After all, there was the precedent of other political generals. Davis signed the commission.

Editorial opinion disapproved, but burly Toombs, ignoring that, resigned from the State Department and blustered off to the field. The only revolutionary in the Cabinet was gone. . . .

His place was filled instantly by the first Virginian, R. M. T. Hunter. Though he was at that time Davis's choice, Hunter's selection in its way was inevitable. There had to be a Virginian in the Cabinet. Robert Mercer Taliaferro Hunter was significant as a prototype of the Old Dominion politician among the Johnnies-come-lately.

An aristocrat in comparison with his colleagues, the label gives a false impression of the man against a broader canvas. As the states produced distinctive colorings in Americans, so sections produced distinctive colorings in Virginians. Hunter came from that pleasant Rappahannock River country, rolling from the east central part of the state down to Chesapeake Bay, influenced both by Tidewater and Piedmont to form a distinctive character of its own.

While its people were as conscious as any Virginian of breeding and manners, they bore more on the stalwart virtues than the fripperies usually associated with the ante-bellum Bourbons. A representative citizen would have come close to being a composite Virginian—and Hunter was that representative.

In the whole state the legend of their "Cavalier" origin had passed with time from an assumption into history. The codes and values and customs evolved to fit the legend had continued so long as to become characteristics, and their validity was no less real because they originated in a myth. Because this long-perpetuated culture (for America) had settled into uniformity and conservatism, it has been thought to have been fixed in rigid lines from pre-Jamestown days. Not at all. While variety was discouraged and extremes regarded as bad taste, the society was by no means without fluidity for those who could conform.

Without the spectacular successes of the rags-to-riches saga (which would have been an extreme in any event), families and individuals could definitely improve their position. The stakes were not so large as in the Deep South (or of course the industrial-financial North), but they were consistent with the solid societal structure, and the drift away from large one-crop plantations offered continued diversity for men of resourcefulness. Hunter was such a one.

Of a merchant family of Scotch descent, his father had run a farm and sawmill and untypically preferred the lamp to the field. Robert Hunter, serious-minded and ambitious, followed his father's studious bent. At the University of Virginia he eschewed the frivolities with which a more familiar Virginia type expressed his sense of his own glamour, and worked on intellectual self-improvement. Leaving college before graduation, he started the practice of law and the development of a plantation.

Within the moderations which his own people admired, he became an early success at both. At the time of the war, he owned seventy-seven slaves over twelve years old, had advanced through the state legislature to the U. S. Senate, acted as chairman of the finance committee, and refused the Secretary of State portfolio—because it might interfere with his own presidential ambitions.

Politically he definitely was a composite Virginian—states' rights and proslavery, but unradical and a believer in compromise. While the fire-eaters called him "milk-and-water," his lack of extremes provided an asset in Davis's government of conservatives. In addition, as Virginia's favorite son in 1860, he carried the prestige of the state, and he had his own reassuring presence.

With his short, plump body, firm features and fine brown eyes, his air of Victorian respectability, he looked what he was—a successful planter-statesman from the stronghold of the time-honored virtues of the gentry. "Sound," he would be called rather than anything so flashy as "brilliant."

He did not make the mistake of looking sleek or citified. His hair was somewhat unbrushed, his waistcoat rumpled, his mien grave and reserved. He was a family man, very happily married, and enjoyed the pleasures of seclusion. He relished the gay world no more now than he had collegiate high jinks in his youth, but he was agreeable, a good conversationalist on serious subjects, and critical Mrs. Chesnut found him most rewarding and always looked forward to his company.

The President also found him agreeable, but there was nothing intimate in their relationship. Without being antithetical, they were miles apart. In derivation and direction they shared no common ground except ambition.

Hunter was one of those contained, methodical workers who, of firm convictions and obvious integrity, are desperately ambitious. His aspiration for the presidency had changed only from Washington to Richmond. Davis probably knew this, but he knew Hunter for a sound and honest man too. Finally the new Secretary possessed the necessary qualities for getting along with the President—dignity and tact and, above all, the proper procedure in his approach to the constituted authority.

Davis could turn over to him the dead-end office of State in the assurance that Hunter, though not of a sanguine nature, would bring a cheerful competence to the department that was getting nowhere in foreign diplomacy.

In the Montgomery days the Confederate commissioners to Europe could not have been chosen better for the purpose of defeating Southern aims if Lincoln's agents had done the choosing. As there is no hint of treachery and Davis certainly was not acting out of whimsy, some reasons must be ascribed to the selections.

Rost must have been chosen because he could speak French (so badly he excited ridicule in the Parisians, and DuBellet, Confederate sympathizer there, thought him a complete fool). Mann must have been picked out of sheer ignorance, on his record of having held small diplomatic posts. His talents were just about adequate to his past jobs, though he did possess charm and made friends in high places. He was so pleased with his social success ("I have succeeded in opening up realms of communication with the most important personages of the realm") that he was impervious to official snubs.

Yancey—the most rabid of the Secessionists, the most outspoken defender of slavery, the prototype of the fire-eater, whose regional rhetoric had inflamed the South for years—could have been picked only for the purpose of getting him out of the states.

More revolutionary even than Toombs, Yancey was unfitted for diplomatic pussyfooting, could not accept official snubs and was disgusted with Mann for so doing. Yancey had received two informal interviews with Lord John Russell, British Foreign Minister, and after the victory at Manassas he requested another. Instead, the Confederates were asked to state their proposition in writing. Yancey (of all people) stressed that this was no war over slavery and pointed out that the fighting demonstrated the Confederacy's ability to maintain independence.

Russell replied briefly that England would maintain neutrality until the position of the belligerents was more clearly established. Yancey knew then that defending, as at Manassas, was not enough.

Although the Confederate commissioners were encouraged by France's DeMorny, who said he thought recognition was only "a question of time," Yancey correctly read DeMorny to mean it was a question of England's time. He believed that England would wait until the South "obtained some decided advantage" or cotton necessity "becomes pressing."

His health was bad, he was sick of England's shilly-shallying and his own anomalous position, homesick for the languorous days of Indian summer in his own land, and he resigned.

It devolved on Robert Hunter to select new commissioners and new methods. Doing nothing hastily (irritating his critics who found him indolent), bringing order to his office, he went methodically at his problems while the newspapers received his appointment with enthusiasm as mild as was everything about the new Secretary himself.

Hunter's department and what people thought about it was of small interest to Davis, absorbed in the growing complications of his favorite department, the war office. During the lull in action, generals as well as politicians grew restive and personality conflicts began to arise with no common enemy to fight.

The President felt the need of an ally, a confidant, someone he could depend on to think as he thought, to act as his deputy as he himself would act. There was only one who filled the bill—Judah P. Benjamin.

The other departments were moving all right, as far as Davis knew, and the Virginians had their man in the Cabinet. The only place for Benjamin was in the war office. Walker had to go.

4

The poor "gentleman" in the war office was a setup for the modern technique of having things made sufficiently unpleasant until he resigned. The public, long against Walker, turned on him for the inaction following Manassas, though he was in no way responsible for the policy of defensive waiting. Davis did not defend him.

The President did not reciprocate Walker's admiration (Walker wrote to him that "you were the only man whose greatness grew upon me the nearer I approached him"). Nor did Davis seem impressed with the accomplishments of the sick lawyer who, despite his clumsily run and feuding office, had organized, armed, and equipped an army that, starting from nothing, had in four months broken even on its minor engagements, held shut all avenues into the country, and won its big test.

When Walker left, papers of the forming opposition defended him out of proportion to his merits, but his patriotism was unquenchable and he had received unjust treatment. He was made, in compliance with his request, brigadier of Alabama troops at the defense of Mobile —only the regiments were not armed. Then half of the men were taken away. Finally he resigned and became military judge of northern

Alabama, useless to the cause to which he remained devoted to the end.

Davis's treatment of this stanch supporter is not pretty, but the President acted with the unaware cruelty of a kid in the first flush of infatuation. Walker's goosed-out departure opened the door for the Harry Hopkins of his day, the Du Barry of the court in Richmond. Judah P. Benjamin assumed his place as the official mistress.

His plump person could absorb the torments racking the oversensitive idealist like a black mammy with a child's fear of the bogies. All fears were like bogies to Benjamin. To him another day, another dollar —or another fortune. He never indulged in retrospect or worried about tomorrow.

Where Davis's self-concepts caused him to suffer from criticism and misunderstanding, Benjamin cared little whether he was understood or not, and criticism was like water off a duck's back. Using no emotion and wasting no energy, he was never tired, never nervous, never depressed.

Russell mentioned his bright "large black eyes," his "brisk, lively, agreeable manner" and "vivacity of speech," and found him "the most open, frank, and cordial of the Confederates whom I have yet met." His "full, olive-colored face" showed always the smile—that concealed everything else.

The danger in Davis's dependence on him lay in Benjamin's desire to please the President. Even more than Hunter, Benjamin knew the ways to Davis's approbation. If an adviser said to Davis, "I think so-and-so," he would receive in reply an almost automatic, "I don't." To get a reasonable hearing, one must say, "Mr. President, do *you* think there is anything to so-and-so?" According to war clerk Jones, Benjamin was not only adept at pleasing Davis, but more importantly he knew how not to displease him.

Where it did not matter, Benjamin was indifferent. He had his smile, his courtesy, and he went his own way ("purring," DeLeon called it) about the offices. In the War Department he instantly brought order to the office, just recently built in din and confusion by partitioning off the assembly hall.

He knew all the tricks, as poor Walker had not, for delegating work. Details were done by detail men. Letters were short, interviews brief. Portly Colonel Bledsoe resigned and came back, still chief of the bureau. Though the harassed colonel's ankles were too weak for his body, he could "shuffle along briskly enough when in pursuit of some refractory clerk."

Petitions for commissions no longer flooded the office. Up at

Manassas, the forty thousand of Beauregard and Joe Johnston grew restive in the hot idleness while McClellan received a hundred thousand reinforcements of the five hundred thousand called for by Lincoln. Benjamin's problem was to lengthen the twelve-month enlistments by cash bounties and furloughs to keep men in the Army against the next Yankee invasion.

This new menace was growing more slowly and purposefully than the first zealous "On to Richmond." To meet it, Benjamin inherited all of Walker's woes in obtaining arms, munitions, and transportation. The state governors still competed with the war office for home-defense troops and arms, and Georgia's clownish Brown exceeded himself in demands for his private war against his invisible enemy.

In Europe the Confederacy's Connecticut Yankee agent, Caleb Huse, labored mightily at his purchases. With the approval of Ordnance Chief Gorgas, who despised Memminger's dull parsimony, Huse worked independently of the Treasury Department and ran his initial paltry credit to half a million. But traffic was slow and uncertain, with even letters taking a month or longer.

In the home activity of the Ordnance Department, Benjamin had in Pennsylvanian Josiah Gorgas one of the real geniuses of the war. Though he had not been at it long enough to deliver many cannons, small arms, or munitions to the field, in converting Richmond factories into armament plants he obviously knew what he was about and was getting things started all over the South.

A West Point graduate who had studied arsenals and ordnance of European armies, he had been in charge of the depot at Vera Cruz and had spent the past twelve years at various arsenals. Now forty-three, Gorgas was married to an Alabama girl and, hating abolitionists, his conservative sympathies had thrown him with the South.

His little boy Willie, age seven, playing around the streets near his father's office, was to grow up to be surgeon-general of the U. S. Army, and achieve greater fame than his father through his sanitation work in the building of the Panama Canal and on yellow fever—in association with another little boy then playing in another Virginia town, Walter Reed.

In the Commissary Department, Benjamin drew a Davis pet who was in every way as unfitted for his work as Gorgas was fitted. Lucius Northrop, fifty, a classmate of Davis's and Colonel Bledsoe's at West Point, had been furloughed from the Army after a wound received in the Seminole War and turned to the practice of medicine. The connection of this background with the post of commissary general is one that only Davis perceived. But, like other Presidents, once having made his choice, nothing could induce him to change.

The howl at Northrop was deafening, but Benjamin ignored it. As Jones pointed out, Benjamin knew what Davis disliked—and one thing was advice, especially pertaining to his favorites. Benjamin proffered none, though it was clear his War Department would never be efficient as long as commissary was handled by that peevish, obstinate, secretive incompetent. Preferring to prove himself right over being right, Northrop regarded all suggestions as interference and displayed gigantic energy in finding fault with others. Nevertheless Benjamin let him alone, and he also let alone Northrop's rival in the people's hatred— (now General) Winder, the provost marshal.

Winder had brought in a crew of detectives—called "plug-uglies" by the natives—from Baltimore, Philadelphia, and New York. They had been trained for running down military lawbreakers and enemy aliens by chasing petty thieves in "barrooms, ten-pin alleys, and such places." They were getting the aliens out, though letting in some far more purposeful and dangerous.

In the cavalcades moving freely in and out of Richmond were blockade-running mail carriers and speculators of all sorts, among whom were spies. War clerk Jones, who had charge of issuing passports, frequently suspected individuals (at least once rightly) and refused them passports. They would go over his head to Benjamin, and the one later proven spy, rejected by Jones, boasted that his passage came personally from the Secretary of War.

This gullibility is uncharacteristic of the shrewd Benjamin. It could possibly be explained by his policy of playing along with Davis's appointee, Winder—in his own person, a good man to stay on the right side of. This is indicated by Benjamin's refusal to pass out some innocent Southern sympathizers against Winder's wishes. The test over one of those cases clearly pointed which way the wind was blowing in presidential favor.

Secretary of State Hunter had asked for safe passage for a kinsman of his from Maryland. Benjamin supported Winder in refusing, and the matter ended there. Hunter must have known then where he stood, but Benjamin presumed nothing.

Still Acting Secretary of War, he proceeded cautiously. Letting Winder run Richmond and Northrop the commissary, he did the best he could everywhere else on details. As for policy—his policy naturally was the President's.

In any case he was an administrator and not a military man, and apparently he held in low esteem those who were. He never attempted to deal with officers through the procedure to which they were accustomed and evinced no respect for their spheres of jurisdiction. If their vanity was hurt, let them grow up. If they made trouble, he had the President's support. If they became the President's enemies too (which some did), they probably would have anyway.

Knowing only that they were people required to execute orders, he thought little about them. When his vast routine for the day was dispatched with comparative ease, if anything annoying had happened he walked from his Ninth Street office over to Johnny Worsham's gambling parlor for the sporting element. Benjamin loved to buck the faro bank. In an establishment like Worsham's they also served fine wine to the players.

Life in Richmond was proving to be very interesting, and it was clear that Davis could not get along without him.

CHAPTER NINE

A Star Falls

THE Davises now enjoyed the dignity of living in a presidential mansion, the White House of the Confederacy. When they took over their official residence there was one point unmentioned by either critics or friends—Varina was pregnant. Mrs. Davis was carrying a child when she came to Richmond, and when in the still summer heat she moved into her new home there was a new heaviness in her naturally full body.

No one outside her family knew her deep pride and fulfillment in childbearing, after an early fear of barrenness. With all else she had, maternity became her final integration. In the clearly defined position of woman of her day, childbearing was matter-of-factly accepted as an integral part of marriage. With her great love for Jefferson Davis, wanting his children, it was also a vitally necessary part of their marriage and of her life. When he was away in the Mexican War, and she had not yet conceived, Varina Davis was terrified that her husband might be killed and leave her childless. It was more than missing a product of their union; it was a mortification to her womanhood.

She was married eight years before she bore her first child, and he died. Then, two years later, she had a girl, Margaret Howell, called Maggie, who was six when the family moved to their official residence. Following Maggie, Mrs. Davis had a child every second year—Jeff, Jr., now four, Joe, two, and the new baby expected.

Family life was important and very pleasant to both Mr. and Mrs. Davis. Aside from his political life, Jefferson Davis's satisfactions centered in his home. He liked a sense of well-being, as did Mrs. Davis, and she was able at providing it. She was an immaculate housekeeper, of order and system, and one of her first approving remarks on Richmond women was that "they felt the dignity attached to personally conducting their households in the best and most economical manner." The same could have been said of Varina.

While she enjoyed the prestige of occupying the Executive Mansion —"Queen Varina," some of her critics started calling her then—probably the deeper gratification came from having her own home for her family.

The White House has been variously described, from a mansion to a pleasant modest house, but to the average American citizen of that day (or of this) it would be a fine city home—of good lines, spacious high-ceilinged rooms, and handsomely set beside a garden on a hill.

The house had been a private residence, bought by Richmond to be presented to their President. Davis refused to accept the gift, and the Confederacy paid the city for it. Though the city was not permitted to make a present of the house, at least their selection was ideal.

With Capitol Square the center of downtown Richmond, the broad parallel east-and-west streets, Main, Franklin, Grace, and Broad, ran into the square or skirted its northern and southern borders. Other parallel streets to the south, like Cary and Canal and Byrd, ran along the slope going down to the canal Basin and the river. To the north of the square, the parallel streets ran along a plateau, variously designated but most commonly called the Court End of town from the days of John Marshall and Wickham, at whose house Aaron Burr had visited during his trial. The new White House was in this neighborhood.

It was of a style of big city homes, built in the early part of the century, that greatly influenced the houses of the following decades. Their chief feature was the two-story-high columned portico facing on the garden.

At the very end of Clay Street, where one of the city's hills sloped down to Shockoe Valley, stood the new White House. Originally built by Dr. Brockenbrough, it was brick, plastered over, with a gray slate roof, and consisted of two main floors, a full basement, and a lower top floor.

Directly in the center on Clay Street, white marble steps rose to the small entrance porch. There were poplar and sycamore trees in the sidewalk and a new wooden sentry box. One side was on Twelfth Street. The other faced the edge of the plateau, and there were built the handsome brick outbuildings which characterized the later period of Richmond houses—kitchen, stables and carriage house, servants' quarters and a greenhouse.

At the back of the house, facing south, lay its true life. Here the huge, colonnaded balcony opened on the garden, with the horse-chestnut trees so loved by Varina Davis, and beyond the house the garden sloped in terraces toward the valley below. This enclosed little world of flowers, which Mrs. Davis tended, became the favorite spot of the President and his wife.

To a couple coming from the Deep South, their new home lacked the sweep and splendor of plantation houses, nor was it set apart like the Executive Mansion in Washington. But for an all-purpose city house, for all seasons, their new home offered comfort and dignity and grace. Mrs. Davis was proud of it and said she felt the sense of the builder in the house—a cultivated, liberal gentleman, who "dwelt in peaceful interchange" with his neighbors.

Before the Davises moved in, a committee of Richmond ladies had arranged the furniture, but Mrs. Davis started right in making changes. First she moved things around upstairs to provide a playroom for the children. Downstairs she moved the dining room entirely, putting it in the outside room to the east. There, over a balcony and beyond the outbuildings, the family could look toward the distance of the valley.

Mrs. Davis put her tropical flowers in that room, for mealtime was a fine time to her family. They rarely dined without a guest, and talk was good then, except when Jefferson Davis suffered the strain of overwork and could not eat. Bad news and unpleasant encounters would also throw his stomach off. His wife probably hoped that cheerful surroundings would aid his digestion.

The center room downstairs, nearly square and of boldly high ceilings, served as the main drawing room. There were double white-paneled doors on either side of a Carrara marble fireplace, much liked by Varina and enjoyed by the boys. There were figures of Hebe and Diana in the fireplace pilasters, and the boys would climb up to kiss the "pretty ladies." Mrs. Davis made her own changes in there and was pleased that her husband "liked the arrangement of the drawing room."

Another drawing room adjoined this, an outside room to the west. As both these rooms opened on the balcony overlooking the garden, on summer evenings, with the connecting doors open, the family enjoyed a cross ventilation from the west and the south. In front of the western drawing room was a small, cozy private reception room for the President. This room, with a white marble fireplace and cream-colored rug, opened both on the drawing room and directly into the hallway.

From the fairly large hallway rose extremely steep circular stairs. There were niches in the walls of the hallway, the stairway, and the upper hall. Upstairs Mrs. Davis selected the southwest corner room for the master bedroom, off of which opened a dressing room for herself. The center room was used for official meetings, and it contained a lattice window on the hall, through which letters could be dropped.

The east room, above the dining room, big and bright, was the children's nursery. Their bedrooms were on the top floor.

They were barely settled before the old-line Richmonders came to "pay their respects," and incidentally to see what the new tenants had done with the house of their old friend. They seemed to like things well enough, but, with no display of tact, the old-timers harked back to the days when Mary Brockenbrough lived there. They probably were casting no reflection on the Davises. It was a resistance to the change represented by the Davises; a nostalgia for the simple days of tranquillity, when their city belonged to them.

Mr. and Mrs. Davis took their sighings in good spirit, though they did feel the house to be haunted by the "maiden in meditation." Mrs. Davis reported that she could tell to the minute when an old gentleman would say wistfully, "This house was perfect when Mary used to walk there, singing among the flowers."

Varina's sharp sense of humor helped her through these comparisons, and she and her husband made a house joke of their ghost. When they moved some of the furniture one would ask the other, "Do you think Mary would approve?"

They could find simple pleasure in making their home in the cool house during the long summer days in the hiatus following Manassas. Jefferson Davis, with his small gift for relaxing, found respite from the strain of office in playing and singing with his children, and most of all in the company of his wife.

With the passing of summer his respites grew fewer. In the prolonged inactivity, the President's troubles with Beauregard and Joe Johnston reached a head. The co-heroes, who disliked sharing top billing, disliked even more their relations with the war office.

2

In late September, Jefferson Davis journeyed to confer with his generals at Fairfax Court House, within twenty miles of the enemy capital. They thought it was time for some action, and Davis used the conference as an opportunity to visit the idling army. The panoply of military life drew him as a fire engine draws a kid.

At army headquarters, the President and the two heroes were joined by a third general, new to the Army. Gustavus Smith was unique in being able to speak out for his ideas without offending Davis. He was one of those powerful men, vibrant with energy and self-confidence, whose air of command lend weight to their words.

A forty-year-old Kentuckian, a West Pointer, G. W. Smith had been an engineer in the Army and then in civil life, and at the outbreak he was street commissioner in New York City. He was greatly acclaimed when he came South, and though he had never commanded troops Davis had no hesitancy in commissioning him. He had the kind of masterfulness that imposed itself even on the President.

When the four men gathered in the headquarters house, and Beauregard outlined a plan of action, Smith strongly supported Old Bory. Joe Johnston, the gray bantam, high-bred and charming, cautiously agreed to the plan. He was playing it close since the fortuitously won battle which rocketed him into fame equal to Beauregard's. He was keeping his neck well in, avoiding all limbs, remaining watchful of the enemy and very watchful of his shiny new reputation. He went along, letting Beauregard spin the grand strategy.

The Hero of Sumter and Manassas wanted invasion before the enemy reorganized. The Confederates had forty thousand men sickening from inactivity. They were equipped, trained, and half of them veterans of battle. With twenty thousand more armed and trained troops, they could cross the Potomac west of Washington. The additional troops would be drawn from the various defensive positions where they were dispersed throughout the South.

But dispersal was of the essence of Davis's concept. Undoubtedly he was influenced by his effectual period as U. S. Secretary of War when, in peacetime, the disposition and organization of scattered troops constituted the bulk of the work. Buttressing his predisposition toward this familiar activity was his belief in the holding of territory as a living proof of the Confederacy's existence as in independent country.

Though reports indicated that decisive victory would influence recognition, Davis could not think beyond his own armed patriots standing firm on every foot of Southern soil. From this conviction nothing could shake him—not even tactical victory for the purpose of preventing the enemy from growing in strength.

In football the only way a team can hope to defeat an opponent stronger in man power is by keeping possession of the ball. They must outscore. Davis, committed to his negative policy of justice prevailing, could not perceive that he must outscore the enemy. He played to contain the enemy, not to beat him.

With this inarticulated policy, he advanced to his generals the argument that it was unsafe to remove troops from "threatened" areas. However, if the troops here needed action, Davis suggested that the men could cross the Potomac to the lower shore of Maryland and attack the Yankee corps lurking there.

These Yankees (acting on the plans of Lincoln, who vied with Davis in keeping troops inactively dispersed on the defensive) feared an invasion of the Maryland shore for an odd reason. The *George Paige,* one of the little river steamers captured in the early going by Virginia's "Navy" and now armed, had been scooting out of creeks, under protection of shore batteries, and chasing Potomac River steamers. Occasionally she had also thrown shells on the Maryland shore. That was the entirety of the threat of invasion, but it had caused ten thousand Unionists to be alerted there.

As the generals saw Jefferson Davis's counterplan, they would be crossing a wide part of the Potomac with very little transportation; going where they were expected, with nothing to accomplish beyond this action for action's sake, where it would be most hazardous. (A month later Grant, also hungry for action, tried the same sort of thing, crossing the Mississippi at Belmont and, though he outfought the Confederates and should have won the small battle, he was extremely lucky to get away with his life.)

So in Virginia, with two months left of the open season, the troops spent October's bright blue weather in waiting for spring—and the North's new armies.

3

Back in Richmond, the President's complacent mood was reflected by the people reciting "The Run from Manassas Junction," which appeared in a local newspaper:

> Yankee Doodle went to war
> On his little pony.
> What did he go fighting for?
> Everlasting money.
>
> England offering neutral sauce,
> To Goose as well as gander,
> Was what made Yankee Doodle cross
> and Did inflame his dander.

Their mood also expressed itself in less innocent ways. A local paper stated that the city was "full of the vilest licentiousness. Among all loathsome vices imported, gambling became so prominent and brazen as to defy public decency as well as law." It was said even that the law winked at the license and corruption of the times, and there were enough gamblers in the city to form a regiment.

Editorials complained of the disorder caused by soldiers stationed near the city and said that "people had begun to entertain a well-gained apprehension that pandemonium had broke loose." Others thought the soldiers had been placed too near the city where they were "exposed to all kinds of temptations—whiskey included." Assaults occurred at the more disreputable places, and a soldier was found murdered on the street. There were constant arrests for prostitution and drinking, and robberies made unsafe some of the dark hilly streets.

The worst area loosely comprised several sections of such names as Butchertown and Bird-in-Hand, named for a run-down tavern which had once been a famous establishment. Going east from Capitol Square, the land sloped steeply to Seventeenth Street in Shockoe Valley, and from Broad Street steeply south to the river.

Through here were the buildings from where Negroes were bought and sold, and the section abounded in every type of tavern from the lowest dives to hotel bars, such as the Ballard and Exchange and St. Charles. The last stood on the site of the old Bell Tavern, where Washington and Lafayette had dined, and where Poe had his toddy when he worked on the editorial staff of the *Southern Literary Messenger* across the street. Along Main and Cary, the more evil spots ran east for a mile to the wharves at Rockett's. Grocery stores joined in the illicit trade, opening darkened doors at night, speakeasy fashion, to soldiers seeking their liquor in rowdy surroundings.

Farther toward the center of town near Main Street, a Confederate Reading Room was opened for the quieter soldiers. Richmond and Southern papers were on file, and writing material was provided.

Theaters were filled nightly. At Metropolitan Hall, which presented "singing, dancing and Negro delineations generally," Wells & Warwick's Southern Harmonions held "undiminished and successful sway." There also appeared two local girls, one of whom was to become the Confederacy's sweetheart with her singing of "My Southern Soldier Boy."

4

Aloof from all this, President Davis had returned to his work of writing the generals on troop organization. To assertive Smith he wrote, "How have you progressed in the problem I left—the organization of troops with reference to the states? . . . The authority to organize regiments in brigades and the latter into divisions is by law conferred only on the president; and I must be able to assume responsibility for the action taken by whomever acts for me in that regard."

Then are listed the damning facts that, while Kentucky had a brigadier but no brigade and Louisiana had a brigade but no brigadier, Georgia had two brigades and two brigadiers, but one of these was with other troops, and "Mississippi troops were scattered as if the state were unknown."

He seemed oblivious to the reasons why general officers in the field resisted interference with effective organizations as they were. Davis was only outraged when Mississippian Whiting said he did not want a Mississippi brigade, for, as he wrote Smith, the policy was foolish and suicidal when the men "are used to me, and I to them, and accustomed to act together."

This need of order in the President caused an immersion in detail, not only to the neglect of the larger plans but to an unawareness of personalities. Thinking only in concepts, while acting in detail, he so missed Beauregard's itch for glory, with his spinning of grandiose schemes, that he wrote the general, "in the tedium of waiting for spring, men from the same region will best console and relieve each other."

He was completely unprepared when Beauregard relieved the tedium of waiting for spring by writing a Homeric epic in the form of his report on Manassas. Published in the newspapers, his apologia went on to claim credit for a pre-battle design that would have resulted in the invasion of Maryland.

This was not the first outburst from Beauregard. Earlier he had written a couple of congressmen friends that at Manassas "the want of food and transportation has made us lose all the fruits of our victory. We ought at this moment to be in or about Washington, but we are perfectly anchored here, and God only knows when we will be able to advance; without these means we can neither advance nor retreat."

At that time Davis apparently dismissed the sad-eyed Creole's repinings as misguided heroics and wrote to quiet him. He mildly defended the commissary and transportation services and said, "Enough was done for glory." Beauregard then seemed tractable enough. He even reassured Davis that he had no presidential aspirations—though his backers, according to a Richmond observer, "were adding to the confusion of the day."

November 4th elections were to be held for the permanent government, in accordance with their gestures of form designed to give the new nation authenticity. Beauregard, in disclaiming any intention to run, said he felt fit only for private life after this victory was accomplished, when "I shall return to my home, if my means permit, never again to leave it, unless called upon to repel again the same or another foe." Never considering Beauregard as a rival anyway, this ended the matter as far as Davis was concerned.

But this new public outburst of purple prose was something else. It invaded the field of Davis's constituted authority, it assaulted his honor as a gentleman. "It seemed," he wrote to Beauregard, "to be an attempt to exalt yourself at my expense." That was the crux, and he let Beauregard know it in a rebuke of icy formality.

But Beauregard was off in clouds of his own. Ever since Fort Sumter he had been living in the reality of a boyhood daydream of playing Napoleon. (Had he not been so hailed in the Confederate press?) The dream and the actuality, however, had blended imperfectly, and now he was under the spell of his own vaulting imagination, acting out a personal grand opera.

He wrote an open letter to the Richmond *Whig,* dated "within hearing of the enemy's guns." In this he rhetorically disclaimed all political ambitions for himself and pitied those who held them, and asserted again that his ambition was limited to fighting for independence in their sacred cause. As the letter appeared the day after the November 4 elections, Beauregard's denial of political aspirations seemed a *non sequitur* at best, and at worst theatrics so irrelevant as to make his soundness suspect.

Formerly friendly newspapers viewed him with amazement. His friends and supporters were embarrassed, and his enemies grew bolder. Benjamin was one of his enemies.

Benjamin had been inimical to the general, according to Jones, even before he became Secretary of War. Possibly Benjamin, no hero worshiper, regarded his reputation as overrated and his vainglorious rhetoric as foolish. Certainly he answered the Hero in very harsh terms, quite unlike the respect to which he was accustomed.

Beauregard, along with writing heroic legends of his battle plans, also chafed at having Joe Johnston his superior. He wanted the army divided equally, to share the glory equally. Benjamin stated with more point than tact that Beauregard was second-in-command of one army, and not in full command of half of it.

When another item bothered Beauregard, he wrote directly to the President, complaining of Benjamin's attitude. Davis refused him balm, explaining that Benjamin's legal turn of mind possibly made the attitude appear discourteous and suggested Beauregard "dismiss the small matter" from mind. But Old Bory, fixed in his historic role, could no longer dismiss grandeur from his mind.

5

The way hurt feelings were snapping during the silence of the guns, Davis unfortunately could not follow his own advice. This lack of humanism in a mind of rigid concepts made the Cause subordinate to his need of being right. With the campaign to regain territory in western Virginia ending disastrously and Lee, who had led it, falling in general disfavor; with the second Union blow struck on the Atlantic coast in the fall of Port Royal, South Carolina, a deep-water harbor which provided a base for a blockading fleet; with the farther Western news becoming darker, the President occupied himself in proving that Beauregard was wrong long after everybody else already knew it.

He wrote Joe Johnston to ask if for "public consideration" he would say whether Davis "obstructed the pursuit of the enemy after the victory at Manassas, or have ever objected to an advance or other active operation which it was feasible for the army to undertake."

Johnston wrote:

To the first question I reply, No. . . . To the second question, I reply it has never been feasible for the army to advance farther than it has done. . . . After a conference at Fairfax Court House of three general officers, you announced it to be impractical to give the army the strength which those officers considered necessary to enable it to assume the offensive.

This answer did not please Davis at all. After thinking it over later, he wrote that Johnston "added a statement about a conference at Fairfax Court House, which . . . could have no relation to the question of pursuit of the enemy after the victory, or other active operations therewith connected." But as the President did ask if he "*ever* objected to an advance or other active operation," it would appear Davis found acceptable only that part of the answer which proved him right. What was not answered according to his liking became an irrelevance of Johnston's.

There had been bad blood between them before that. When the ranking of full generals was published, Joe Johnston was outraged to find himself fourth—below Adjutant General Cooper, Albert Sidney

Johnston (no relation, and on his way from the West), and R. E. Lee. In one of the most ill-considered communications imaginable, Johnston wrote Davis nine pages of almost hysterical wrath at this mortification.

The whole ranking, he thought, "seeks to tarnish my fair name as a soldier and a man, earned by more than thirty years of laborious and perilous service. I had but this, the scars of many wounds, all honorably taken in my front and in the front of battle, and my father's Revolutionary sword . . ." and now he, who had served in this war from the beginning, was to be degraded for "the benefit of persons neither of whom has struck a blow for this Confederacy."

This was worse than Beauregard. Davis was not only questioned in violent language, but that "father's Revolutionary sword" was dragged in too. Who did this Virginian think he was? He would be shown what Davis thought he was.

First, Davis's violated feelings were relieved in a long letter to his wife. Then he was ready to dismiss this other family-proud Hero with a quick cut.

"Sir," he wrote, "I have just received and read your letter of the 12th instant. Its language is, as you say, unusual; its arguments and statements utterly one sided, and its insinuations unfounded as they are unbecoming. I am, etc. . . ."

He probably felt a full measure of cold satisfaction when he signed that letter. There's nothing in this of any discredit to his character.

The world is full of honorable citizens who had rather put someone in his place than save friendship or serve a common cause. We rightly apotheosize those few of our heroes who rose above the pettiness of strutting little egos.

The trouble here was that Davis was a leader. It should have been more important to him to deny a personal gratification than to make an enemy of the commander of his first army. But it was not. He was right, and his detractor must be shown he was wrong.

Benjamin took the cue. In his drive for longer enlistments, with furloughs as a lure, the Secretary furloughed Johnston's men with little regard to the general's feelings. Why should he have, when the Number One had none? When Johnston protested, reasoning partly with emotion, Benjamin brought to bear all the fancy logic that had won him fame at the bar. Johnston's soldier's mind could only write in protest to the President that Benjamin "has not only impaired discipline, but deprived me of the influence of the army, without which there can be little hope of success."

Johnston was not entirely in the right. He had been lax in his reports and must have seemed unco-operative with a Secretary whom he held in as little esteem as a lawyer as the Secretary held him as a soldier. But the President sided with Benjamin, as he had against Beauregard, until it began to look as if the President and Secretary of War were more interested in defeating their generals by legal arguments than in building up morale or freeing them from behind-the-lines friction.

The only friction they did work on was that between Beauregard and Joe Johnston. Obviously both could not serve in the same army. For all the Creole's jealous and futile manipulations, Johnston was the superior, and Beauregard's feet of clay were being pointed at by everyone.

Mrs. Chesnut said, "to think that any mortal general . . . could be so puffed up with vanity . . . as to intimate that any man, or men, would sacrifice their country, injure themselves, ruin their families, to spite the aforesaid general!" And Secretary of the Navy Mallory, pleasing at dinners, said, "How we could laugh, but you all know it is no laughing matter to have our fate in the hands of such self-sufficient, vain, army idiots."

So Beauregard, the first hero of the new country, had to go like Toombs and Walker. They took him at his word, on his willingness to serve, and appointed him second-in-command to the one who was unquestionably first in the whole Confederacy, Albert Sidney Johnston.

Here, as dramatic Beauregard's brief star fell, the new star of the new country arose—in the West.

CHAPTER TEN

Providence Intervenes, at Last

ALBERT SIDNEY JOHNSTON took his place as the new hero much more quietly than Beauregard had accepted his Napoleonship. Nor did Richmond accord him the adulation they gave their first hero.

Now their attention was diverted to such mundane problems as coffee and calico rising in price, salt and shoes growing scarce, and rent in the overpacked city skyrocketing to where even some government workers could no longer afford to keep their families in Richmond.

Ice for sale had returned to the streets, at two cents a pound. Huckleberry leaf was suggested for tea. The first faint hint of currency depreciation was indicated when Richmond, Charleston, and New Orleans market quotations showed that a gold dollar was now worth 1.2 Confederate dollars. In the currency-making carnival, complications increased with the appearance of counterfeit treasury notes. A sad commentary was the newspaper warning that the lithography on the counterfeit bills was better than on the genuine. Other counterfeit bills represented bogus banks.

With the newspapers more concerned over such items, General Johnston arrived and departed with comparatively little fanfare. They commented on his fine physical presence. At fifty-eight he was strong and fit and definitely commanded respect.

Albert Sidney Johnston might not have deserved the President's opinion that he was "the greatest soldier, the ablest man, civil or military, Confederate or Federal, then living," but his reputation was firmly built (no overnight meteor), and he possessed one of those symmetrical, selfless characters which, like Lee's, suggest grandeur and nobility.

He was a Kentuckian by birth and Texan by adoption, having commanded the Army and served as Secretary of War during the Republic. In the Regular Army he had been colonel of the famed Second Cavalry, brevet brigadier, and when his state seceded he was commanding the Pacific forces at Fort Alcatraz. Refusing a major general's commission offered by Lincoln, he made the long and hazardous trip across the Southwest deserts. Avoiding Indians and Union scouting parties, it was not until September that he reached the Confederate capital. There he offered only to serve in any capacity. But his work was all waiting for him.

Citizens of Tennessee and southern Kentuckians had petitioned Davis for his services. They considered Albert Sidney Johnston the only man able to handle their troubled affairs. By then conditions in the two states created a real danger point to the Confederacy.

The Confederate government had violated Kentucky's neutrality in such a way as to gain little while being made to bear the onus of aggression.

Kentucky's neutrality, like all such, had been more favorable to one side than the other. While the Confederates were held strictly to the letter of the state laws, the Unions not only freely evaded the technicalities but had a force under Grant all ready to move in and occupy Columbus, Kentucky, on the Mississippi. At this point the Confederate administration, after months of honorable observance of the neutrality, was goaded into rashness. They beat Grant to the punch by one day and took over Columbus themselves.

Grant switched to Paducah, inland from Columbus, near the juncture of the Tennessee and Cumberland rivers. If the Confederates were ever to invade Kentucky, this Paducah area was what they should have taken. There, with one fort they could block these two rivers which sliced down into Tennessee.

As it was, in their neutral period, they had built forts on the rivers where they entered Tennessee and where their forts stood twelve miles apart. Now, with Grant controlling the juncture of the rivers, the Confederates found themselves occupying only a hostile state.

For Kentucky immediately abandoned her fiction of neutrality, left the Yankees alone and ordered the Southerners out. Confederate Kentuckians advised the withdrawal of these troops, but the government, having committed its impulsive act, stuck to it. Kentucky still had a rebel governor and legislature, congressmen in Richmond and some good soldiers in the Army; but what the Confederates had was a line across the southern section of the state, which they had to hold to protect Tennessee.

To central and west Tennessee, Kentucky had been a buffer, but east Tennessee yearned for the Yankees. Strong Unionist elements, led by Andrew Johnson and "Parson" Brownlow, needed only armed support to strike at the Confederacy. This mountainous region, having nothing in common with the planter class, was inspired by the secession of Virginia's western counties. Hundreds of the hardy men had slipped through the mountain passes to enlist with the North, and insurgents formed armed bands and burned bridges.

From Richmond, Benjamin showed both his iron and his realism. He had the bridge-burning leaders hanged, Brownlow escorted out of the state, and his strong hand got the South the only kind of respect it could hope for there. This expedient would not serve if the Yankees drove the Confederates out of eastern Kentucky.

The rest of Tennessee was even more important to retain as a granary. To hold this irregular line of 300-odd miles in Kentucky, and then on across the Mississippi to Kansas, there were scattered groups of half-armed, ill-trained volunteers, under bishops and patriot politicians, called by courtesy an army.

This was the sizzling area presented to Sidney Johnston, along with a title as long as your arm and no over-all plan beyond the customary defense.

To make his defense even more difficult was the tacit policy of the Confederates to fight two wars with two armies—one eastern, one western. Accepting the geographical division of the Appalachian Range, the government defended with one set of plans on one side and another set on the other. Virtually no connection, strategical or physical, existed between the two.

When Sidney Johnston arrived at his new post he instantly wired the war office for thirty thousand urgently needed rifles. He was answered that only thirty-five hundred had come in by the last shipment, of which one thousand went to Georgia's Brown "to repel an attack now hourly threatened at Brunswick," and fifteen hundred to regiments who had been waiting for arms for months in Richmond. He could have the thousand remaining. When Johnston requested engineers for fortification building he was advised that "the whole engineer corps comprises only six captains together with three majors, one of whom is on bureau duty."

Johnston soon began to find out what being in the West meant, and he turned to Westerners. Governor Isham, of Tennessee, with energy and resourcefulness gave very real help in the way of arms and supplies. For men Johnston received such leaders as Simon Bolivar Buckner, who, earlier resigning command of Kentucky militia, joined the Confederates when hostilities broke, and that arresting man John Breckinridge, who reached the general as a fugitive.

Vice-President in the last administration, Southern Democratic candidate in 1860, Breckinridge resigned his seat in the U.S. Senate when Unions invaded his state. He got out of Washington one jump ahead of the Federals who planned to arrest him for his pro-Southern sentiments. Just forty, of powerful physique and commanding personality, he inspired confidence from his first speech at Bowling Green. "To defend your birthright and mine, I exchange with proud satisfaction a term of six years in the Senate of the United States for the musket of a soldier."

With such more or less spontaneous support as this, Sidney Johnston applied himself to the task of molding his mobs into three military units in the presence of the enemy. Never admitting a word of his difficulties, he presented a bold front to the Unions and even harassed them with cavalry dashing about in furious demonstrations. His front was so effective that his own people complained of his want of action and contributed less than they would have if alarmed.

Their sense of invincibility was also given a boost by Grant's repulse at Belmont, Missouri, an outpost across the river from their occupied city of Columbus, Kentucky. Though Grant demonstrated his hard fighting, the whole thing seems a pointless action, and the South's hailing it as a great victory made the small battle a minor version of Manassas in its effect of deepening the false sense of security.

2

In the leaders, indifference rather than optimism would explain their attitude to the situation west of the Mississippi. That river subdivided the war in the Confederate West as the mountains divided the Eastern and Western theaters.

In Missouri, Sterling Price had organized the state militia—*not* in the Confederacy—down in the southwest corner where the government had taken refuge from the Unions. Further south, in Arkansas, Ben McCullough commanded some troops in the Confederate Army. After many difficulties, Price finally got Ben McCullough to join him in a battle, by giving McCullough nominal command in the field. Together they won the action, called Wilson's Creek. But as no harmony existed between the two generals, McCullough took his Confederate forces back to Arkansas.

Sterling Price, with his state troops, went north to Lexington, Missouri, where he captured a garrison and valuable supplies. When a powerful force began forming against him, Price could only retire again to the hilly southwestern country. There he tried to build up a stronger organization, while he sent a representative to Richmond, "Colonel" Snead—the quotation marks are his. Knowing nothing whatsoever about anything military, he had merely filled any post vacant and was acting adjutant general on his trip to the capital because that seemed a suitable title.

By then Missouri was officially in the Confederacy, with senators and congressmen, but without any real working basis. The problems of the harassed Governor Jackson were too distant to interest Davis. The President practiced his cold repartee in letters designed apparently to put the unhappy patriot in his place, and achieved the unprofitable result of gaining another enemy.

In all truth the handful of Missouri Rebel government fugitives and their collection of followers were not reassuring. The troops were partly unarmed, and some had shotguns and flintlocks. One group of seven hundred frontiersmen—they couldn't be called a regiment or any known unit—were commanded by their natural civil leaders, who knew nothing of military organization and cared less, and had as the head man a patriarch who was called "Jedge" by the squirrel shooters.

For nearly all the men in the West, except some of education, the fighting was pretty well local. Yet, in their provincial home-front private war, they were curiously indicative of the whole struggle. Those with the South had joined up with the people they liked and understood, and the enemy represented people whose customs and methods they were agin. As the Administration in Richmond saw them as peripheral and unrelated (no part of a central plan or, even, command), so the men fought their own fringe warfare in indolent ignorance of the central Confederate government.

Typical of the isolated action out there, before the Northern forces themselves were powerfully organized and purposeful, was the passage of a U.S. fleet from the Gulf through the passes into the Mississippi.

To meet this fleet the Confederates sent down some fire ships, led by a strange-looking object resembling a floating cigar. The *Manassas* (one of the Navy's early originalities) had been privately built from an old tug, with the upper works cut away and lined with a convex oak frame covered with iron. Mounting only one gun, it was primarily a ram, and as such it bore down to strike one shuddering but unlethal blow to a Yankee ship. Then, as so often happened with Confederate boats, the engine went off and the monster limped away under a hail of fire.

Meanwhile the fire ships darted about harmlessly, but adding to the confusion, and the Union fleet received the order to retire. One Yankee captain, interpreting the order to mean abandon ship, left his ship to blow up and reported dramatically to the fleet commander with a flag wrapped around him. In unrecorded language he was ordered back to his own ship (which he had failed to blow up) without the flag around him. By then the fire ships had run aground. Everybody went home and the excitement was over.

This violent action was of little if any importance. But far more than the formal battles, which climaxed months of preparation, they give the color of those early days. For then the land battles were fought the same way and were won by the side making the fewest blunders, and they are undeserving of the dignity with which they are treated— except for the valor of the men on both sides and a study in national unpreparedness. . . .

To all these doings on the river and west of it, Sidney Johnston could add little. He was working conscientiously and steadily, building defenses and not planning attacks, the manner approved by the Chief Executive. Though many found fault with the inactivity, and with the generals involved in it, the star of Albert Sidney Johnston was bright in the West in the fall of '61.

3

In Richmond, at the moment, the people had matters of more local interest. Though not a particularly bloodthirsty people, in the days before neo-Romanesque sport spectacles they found hangings a great spectator sport. One of the most colorful parades in Richmond's history had been that of the pirates who, on their way to the gallows, rode sitting atop their coffins. Now there was the promise of the greatest hanging ever in the city, the most consequential affair since the trial of Aaron Burr.

It all started when the crew of the privateer *Savannah* was imprisoned in chains in New York, where they had been kept since June awaiting trial for piracy. While the United States government made no answer to Confederate protests and threats of reprisal, the Northern newspapers—which at first supported the Administration—changed their tunes after the big haul of Yankee prisoners at Manassas.

The Confederate government wished an exchange of prisoners, man for man. Lincoln evaded exchange on the grounds that it implied recognition of the Confederacy as belligerents. However, on the grounds of "humanity," Confederate and Union officers practiced informal exchange, especially with the sick and infirm, and the Union prisoners in Richmond and Charleston began to petition their congressmen and/or friends to get them out of there by opening up a formal exchange of prisoners.

By November not only had nothing been achieved, but another privateer's crew came up for piracy trial.

This was the *Jeff Davis*. With several other raiders she had been more businesslike than the skylarking *Savannah* in sinking and capturing Northern cargoes, and the *Jeff Davis* had cruised the whole Atlantic coast as far north as Canada. And the court in Philadelphia, where the *Jeff Davis* crew was confined, was grimmer than New York's. They found Captain Walter Smith guilty of piracy and sentenced him to be hanged. His thirteen crew members awaited trial for a similar fate.

From the beginning this treatment of the South as rebels, with no legal rights, had burned into the soul of Jefferson Davis. He had consistently leaned over backwards in conducting his country's exchanges with the high-minded observance of the customs and international laws that prevailed between honorable nations. This final indignity was too much. If the United States was willing to carry its fiction of no war to the extent of barbarity, then its barbarity would be met in kind.

The proper order was given Provost Marshal Winder.

It was his duty to inform the prisoners in Liggon's tobacco warehouse that thirteen of them were to be selected to be hanged, on a man-for-man basis with the crew of the *Jeff Davis*. Poor Congressman Ely was to draw lots. One look at Winder and the men must have known the threat would stick. To an observer, he looked near sixty, his hair white and tufty, his face harsh, dry, and cruel, with clear cold eyes and a "mouth on which a smile seemed mockery." Twelve officers were led to the gloomy, walled building of Henrico County Jail.

Colonel Michael Corcoran, the top ranking officer to serve as reprisal for Captain Smith, had been moved to Charleston. This Corcoran, an Irish politician who had commanded the New York 69th Regiment, was considerably of a character in his own right and a known troublemaker with a large following. When he exploded, they heard that one in the White House.

The United States tried some desperate shilly-shallying on the whole question of exchange without implying recognition, offered Captain Smith for Colonel Corcoran, and came up with other devices for evading the main issue. But Davis held firm, and in the North home-front political pressure grew too strong. You couldn't sell the wife of a man about to be hanged on the principle that he was dying to prove that no war existed—not when there were a thousand others with him who had been captured on the same battlefield. The whole deal was called off.

It was a hanging Richmond was glad to miss. They did have ideas of old-fashioned chivalry in war, and they had tried to play their end of it that way.

The result of the unpleasantness was to bring the question of pris-oner exchange in for a good deal more attention. Though nothing came of it then beyond more dodges of the United States—which persisted in pretending there wasn't any war—there was *one* personal exchange.

The wretched Congressman Ely was at last "exchanged." He went to the war office for his passport, and now he could even smile to see the cheap brown paper on which it was written. He went to the R. F. & P. Depot on Broad Street at Eighth, across from the big colonnaded Marshall Theater, and in a way he was a real loss to the city's life.

His departure released Charles Faulkner, of Virginia, the prewar U.S. minister to France. On returning to Washington to resign, the diplomat had been thrown into prison, where he was held until some-thing had to be done about Ely. Faulkner received a fine welcome when he reached Richmond, in those early days when the fate of one individual native was still held of some consequence.

Entertainment was offered him in the homes of all his friends, for, with the coming of autumn, local parties got into full swing. There were private balls and receptions, street bazaars and big military balls in public halls. In the fine, mellow weather tournaments were held at the camps, where the victor's lady was named queen, in a game close to their hearts. Everywhere ladies gathered and sewed in little groups, making a valid contribution to the needs of their country.

4

In the White House less entertaining was provided than the new capital desired, and complaints began to be heard. Of one of the few Davis receptions, Mrs. Robert Toombs said, "Was that not a humbug? Such a failure. Mrs. Reagan could have done better than that."

Of course Varina Davis's friends dismissed that as springing from the anti-Davis sentiment shown by Mrs. Toombs since her husband left the Cabinet. But others were dissatisfied by the lack of receptions.

This official quiet was only partially explained by Mrs. Davis's advanced pregnancy. Varina would have enjoyed more partying, for, while she believed quietude was helpful to the spirit, she regarded socializing as a tonic. She loved the fanfare of fashionable society, liked to dress up and said, "Everyone should always look their best, especially if they have a distinguished husband."

Actually it was her husband who disliked parties. He was always tired when he came home, and contact with his fellows did not relax him. In explaining his aversion, he said with rather heavy sarcasm that he presumed he had been elected to run the government and not perform as a social leader.

Here Davis used logic, in defending a natural choice, to pervert the real issue. When he reduced contacts to mean formal society, he could reduce the criticisms of him to absurdity. The point was, however, that his avoidance of small groups in his home indicated an indifference to the group life of the people.

His wife, that pitilessly observing and adoring woman, said, "Perhaps I attach too much importance to the humanism of great men, but I have observed that the quality is oftenest found wanting in men of great intellect."

Davis was great intellect to her, and, as she found humanism wanting in him, her love would not attach importance to it.

As she saw the President at home, he was always warm and considerate. He liked good living, though he always put his wife and children first and made very few demands. With his intimates and young people, he was invariably pleasant and interested, and, while he avoided the large crushes, he enjoyed friends dropping in during the evening. With them he could talk without guarding himself, have a cup of tea, and then, trusting his wife to carry on, retire to the absorbing work which more properly belonged in the war office.

This absorption, indicating the bureaucrat, revealed the deepening division between the abstractions of the movement and the immediate details which could be met. Here Davis seemed to cling to an activity in which he had proven his competence, as a refuge from the mounting problems of correlating the forces of the new country.

From the moment when Lincoln maneuvered him into the position over Fort Sumter, of backing down (with the possible consequence of dissolution of the movement) or committing an aggression (which he feared), the enormity of the events had oppressed rather than stimulated him. He had plenty of courage (which can be acquired), but little audacity, and no flexibility with which to meet unpredictables.

At the crux of the movement the irrefutable logic of states' rights was used by the governors to thwart and bedevil him, and well-laid plans in support of the Confederacy's appeals abroad refused to follow the blueprint. In withholding cotton from England and France, to arouse the textile interests to force their governments to intervene, the South's unofficial embargo had certainly been effective. Only 10,000 bales were shipped in the last four months of 1861 from five leading Southern ports, where 1,500,000 bales had been shipped in the same period in 1860. But this happened to be a year when England held a large surplus of raw cotton.

The mills had used less cotton because earlier overproduction had driven down the manufactured price. England held half a million surplus bales in June, and, even by the end of the year, with virtually none from the South, the warehouses held 700,000 bales against 500,000 the year before. Of course this situation could not last indefinitely. But neither could the Confederacy without money.

The price of cotton was up, some mills were on half time, and France felt the pinch now, but nobody over there was hollering "Uncle." On the other hand, at home defenders were hollering for heavy guns from Evansport on the Potomac to Texas. Fifteen hundred, they wanted, and all large.

Everybody wanted powder. Until Sumter the South bought from the North, but now farmers were converting a couple of small crude mills, mainly for blasting powder, into "wartime production," and starting new mills. Niter came in through the blockade in some quantities, but chiefly the newly formed Niter and Mining Bureau had men digging in caves, and officers formed working parties of disaffected mountaineers in what was described as "a wild, rude sort of service."

Other groups scoured the land to get copper where copper never grew before. Miners worked day and night to get lead, and contracts were let to stimulate iron production. Benjamin was able at making contracts, but that was small help in manufacturing items without experienced workmen, tools, or materials.

Knapsacks had to be abandoned for haversacks, which women could make. Even the genius of Gorgas could not produce more than fifteen hundred rifles a month in Richmond and had not as yet gotten new arsenals into production. Without the Tredegar Iron Works, artillery would exist virtually in form only, and the enemy seemed obsessed with the determination to take Richmond.

Moving the armies around, as Davis had in the old war-office days in Washington, was not simple either. These deficiencies in equipment, arms, and ammunition always rose between the decision and the act. The generals were stubborn in their own ways of doing things and always misunderstood him.

These misunderstandings, and his need to explain, to demonstrate his rightness, took a heavy toll of the overburdened man. Though his pride never permitted him to reveal it, Jefferson Davis longed to be understood. Only his wife knew. "Even a child's disapproval hurt him," she said. "It was because of his supersensitive temperament and the acute suffering it caused him to be misunderstood, I had deprecated his assuming the civil administration."

His indifference to a larger popularity extended naturally from the unimportance to him of being liked as a man. He wanted to be respected, admired, in terms of his concept. To the world he could show no weakness. To his wife he showed them all.

Edward Pollard, the brilliant and biased associate editor of the Richmond *Examiner,* one of the loudest voices of the growing opposition, claimed that Davis was "wax in the hands of his wife." Davis was never wax in anybody's hands, but the statement was a distortion of the fact that he depended too heavily on his wife without realizing the extent.

Varina loved him, not for his weaknesses, but certainly *with* them. They gave her the means with which she could make him more completely her own. She was strong in all the places he was weak. With her fierce possessiveness, it fulfilled her womanly pride to be so necessary to her lover, the man who she believed was the greatest on earth. At all times she believed his weaknesses and needs of her were inevitable facets of the qualities that made him great.

5

In the midst of the far-flung makeshifts of the struggling country to defend itself, fate struck the first favorable blow. Mason and Slidell, Confederate commissioners to England and France, were forcibly removed from a British ship on the high seas by a rash U.S. naval captain.

The prayers of the religious people were answered: Great Britain stood on the verge of a break with the United States, and this could bring at last the desperately needed help from Europe.

CHAPTER ELEVEN

"My Bonnie Lies over the Ocean"

MASON and Slidell entered history with their names intertwined like a vaudeville team, but no two men could have been more dissimilar in gifts and character, background and experience. They symbolized the Confederate merger of fact and legend. Mason was the façade of the Old South; Slidell the reality of the new.

John Slidell (probably not pure Aryan) was born in New York City, the son of a tanner who prospered. He graduated from Columbia at seventeen, took a master's degree, then plunged into the extravagant life of the metropolis as a young man of affairs. After a duel over an actress and money entanglements, he migrated to New Orleans, the frontier for adventurers with brains rather than guns.

There he founded a political machine on the model of Tammany and became enormously wealthy in various speculations, some of a dubious nature. Despite criticism and opposition, he became Louisiana's senator to Washington and also kept in the Senate his younger friend, Judah Benjamin.

Russell said:

> I rarely met a man whose features have a greater *finesse* and firmness of purpose . . . his keen gray eye is full of life, his thin firmly set lips indicate resolution and passion . . . not a speaker of note, nor a ready stump orator, nor an able writer; but he is an excellent judge of mankind, adroit, persevering, and subtle, full of device, and fond of intrigue; one of those men, who, unknown almost to the outer world, organizes and sustains a faction, and exalts it into the position of a party—what is called here a "wire-puller." . . .

Though he worked behind the scenes and was now over sixty, he liked to enjoy the fruits of his manipulations in the gay world. He possessed distinguished social gifts, and his wife, a Creole beauty, was a most graceful companion. In Washington she had been a famous hostess, and she had deeply impressed Varina Davis. The Slidells had two enchanting daughters, of whom the old boy was very vain, and the four of them made a charming family group—as devoted to one another as they all were to the pleasures of fashionable society.

The Confederacy could not have found a better representative to France. For John Slidell, as American as Jay Gould in his ambition drive, loving the great world as did Benjamin, unlike Benjamin gave himself heart and soul to his adopted land. He fought for its success as savagely as any hard-bitten country boy who fought only for the soil beneath his feet.

The country boy was Slidell's companion, though there was nothing hard-bitten about James Mason, and even the country part was a proudly asserted provincialism. Mrs. Chesnut said that even in England he would say "chaw" for chew and call himself "Jeemes," as natives for no known reason always call the James River the "Jeemes."

Virginians to this day look suspiciously on sophistication. They affect a superiority to it, and in their long line of senators none will be found with smoothed-down hair and a taste for dry martinis. To his people, then, James Mason was what they liked to think of as "the best type of Virginian."

He *was* the legendary aristocrat, one of the few samples of the type generally thought to compose the Confederacy. Of a fabled plantation, "Gunston Hall," he was the grandson of George Mason, one of the chief framers of the Constitution—who refused to sign it because it permitted slavery and did not stress state sovereignty.

James Mason was accustomed to his name meaning something where he lived, and he had lived nowhere else—except in the Washington Southern colony—since he attended the University of Pennsylvania. With graduates from Columbia and Pennsylvania, along with Yale, Harvard, and Princeton, and the many graduates of West Point and the Naval Academy, these Rebel powers sound more like representatives of the Ivy League than any Solid South. But Mason, though he had married Miss Chew of Philadelphia, was warp and woof of his native state, and in Richmond when they said "everybody was there" they definitely meant Jeemes.

Slightly over sixty, he was a gregarious soul in bounding good health. Typically Southern in his love of social gatherings where talk flowed easily and plentifully in a frame of local reference, he enjoyed nothing more than visiting and entertaining—his social equals. Physically impressive, though a little pompous, full of virtue, though a little obtuse, his fine, hearty charm seems to have spread thin when it reached his inferiors. Caleb Huse, the very able Yankee acting as purchasing agent in London, found no magnetism in him to attract younger men. Huse said that Jeemes "seemed never unmindful of the presence and importance of the Honorable James Mason of Virginia."

Perhaps he was at his best only with his own kind—those others aware of their importance, who spoke a common language. But within the limitations caused by personal responsiveness to the caste system in which he was born, he was what is generally called a good man. He was conscientious and industrious and lived in simple acceptance of the prevailing standards of moral behavior and codes of honor.

Some of his obtuseness was another face of a certain naïveté. This was a credulity which accepts a man's words at their value and does not search deeper for what the words might be hiding. He was probably always a little astonished, even disappointed, to discover subterfuge and guile.

Mrs. Davis approved of him in spite of his affectations (though, like her husband, she was predisposed to things aristocratic). But Mrs. Chesnut thought his choice as commissioner to England a catastrophe. She said, "My wildest imagination will not picture Mr. Mason as a diplomat." However, Britisher Russell thought the English would like him, as he was so manly, straightforward, and truthful. "A fine old English gentleman, but for tobacco. I like Mr. Mason and Mr. Hunter better than anybody else."

This was his personal response to Virginians, products of the planter caste patterned on the British landed gentry. However, it did not blind Russell to Mason's lacks in comparison with Slidell. He thought Slidell had more tact, more subtlety and depth, more understanding and mastery of political maneuver. Slidell "loves the excitement of combinations and . . . in his dungeon, or whatever else it may be, would conspire with the mice against the cat rather than not conspire at all." Mason, on the other hand, loved the excitement of being Jeemes Mason; in Virginia it had been quite enough.

Russell suspected that Davis appointed both of them, as perhaps with Yancey earlier, to get rid of them. They both had considerable standing in the arch-Secessionist group, and Mason was identified with everything archaically aristocratic—slavery, one-crop pride (tobacco, as a Virginian), superiority to trade and manufacture, and ardently states'-rightist. He was born in the mold to which Jefferson Davis fitted himself, and he was ambitious.

With all that, it is not likely Russell's theory would hold water—or certainly not much. With Slidell, Davis's indifference to political expediency for the Confederacy would blind him to Slidell's usefulness at home. Mason, who had shifted to the Confederate Senate from the

U. S. Senate, where he had been chairman of the Committee on Foreign Affairs, must have seemed qualified to Davis.

His vast dignity would appeal to the President. With Davis so aware of his own gentleman's status and being under the influence of the environment of the original Southern aristocrat, he might well think the British would be as impressed by the Virginia baron as was he.

Personally the two men, whose destinies were to be so strangely joined, had little in common, and Slidell seems to have had no liking for Mason's company and no high regard for his talents. They met in Richmond late in September, to begin their joint voyage to destiny.

2

John Slidell, coming up from the South, arrived at the depot where the hordes of boisterously arguing hackmen created a "scandalous conduct" that was much complained of. It is doubtful if that wiry, hawk-eyed old boy complained much of anything that suggested thriving business. He probably looked with satisfaction at the canal boats filling the Basin and at the vast rectangle of buildings around it, where flour and meal were being made and tobacco stored. He would like the sweet tangy odor of tobacco, of which a foreign visitor said the city was redolent, and he would like the sight of the ocean-going ships down at Rockett's Wharf, where the flat space in back of the open-sided shed was jammed with cargo and carts and wagons and omnibuses.

With all the smoke up the river, where Tredegar and the ordnance plants were getting volume on the matériel of war, and the obviously overcrowded streets, the city looked solid, like a going concern. There was a reassuring, undisturbed quality in the way the red-brick slant-roofed buildings looked down on the river, and behind the Confederate Treasury Building (where Slidell was to meet the Secretary of State), the Capitol Square looked like the proud park of a permanent people.

Old trees shaded the brick walks that climbed the grassy hills toward the Capitol, and on the Ninth Street side, across from the war offices, stood the brick tower which served as the barracks for the home guard. Its bell had called out those guards in the War of 1812, had called the General Assembly, rung in welcome for Lafayette, and tolled for the funeral of John Marshall. John Slidell had absorbed the physical dignity of the capital he was to represent before he climbed the stairs to the State Department, first door on the east side of the passage at the top of the steps.

There the ex-New York, New Orleans manipulator met the two Virginians, James Mason, his companion, and portly Robert Hunter, the new Secretary of State. Each of the three men had been successful in his own way before he staked his fortune in this new country. Hunter had enjoyed a wide material success similar to that of Slidell's, though personally they were as antithetical as Slidell and Mason. Hunter and Mason were the plump sound men of provincial dignity, in the traditional statesmen's stance and the dark coats and black ties of the portrait for posterity. Slidell was all passion and determination, the hard fighter on his own, now in this strange company.

He and Mason listened attentively to Hunter's eminently sound instructions. There was nothing new, nothing bold, but all angles were covered with intelligence and, of course, their inherent justice. The men all knew, as of now, it was the best they had to offer Europe in their bid to be recognized among the nations of the earth.

The men shook hands. Mason and Slidell went to their hotels to get their things, and Slidell rode down the long hill back to Byrd Street station, for his last trip south. Perhaps, as his train crossed the bridge over the James, Slidell glanced back at the city on its hills, with the colonnaded Capitol bold in the center. He was never to see it again.

At Charleston, Slidell was joined by his wife and daughters. Mason, following what amounts in certain quarters to a Virginia custom of not making his wife a companion, came alone. He missed a beloved daughter, who acted as his amanuensis, but he insisted she stay with her mother, because they must leave their home and keep moving to stay outside the enemy's lines. However, to Mrs. Mason, Jeemes commented on the presence of Mrs. Slidell and daughters.

Then, on October 11, he wrote her they were ready to sail "as soon as the moon goes down at midnight." In the dark of the night their ship ran the then scattered blockade to Havana. They waited for a British ship, and Mr. Mason enjoyed being entertained "royally" by the wealthy, though the heat was oppressive and he longed for news of home.

Then, in early November, they put to sea on the British ship *Trent*. Relieved to have escaped the Yankees, the party relaxed to enjoy the voyage, and the Slidells were having a fine time. Suddenly the U.S.S. *Jacinto* appeared and started after them, signaling the ship to halt. Two shots burst across the bow, and the British Captain Moir was forced to bring his ship to in mid-ocean.

A U.S. naval officer boarded the British ship and demanded the commissioners and their secretaries. Captain Moir made an angry and formal protest against the act of piracy on a neutral ship. This was ignored. In a moment it looked as if the enraged passengers would make trouble. Then an armed guard came on board, and Mr. Mason and Mr. Slidell were ordered to get going.

One of Slidell's daughters became hysterical and clung to him until he had to be pried away. He was marched to the deck to the sound of her screams and weeping. He said to his wife, "I'll see you in Paris, my dear."

Mason said to a courteous and embarrassed United States lieutenant that he would leave the ship only by force. The young lieutenant reluctantly ordered four sailors to take hold of him. When they grabbed his arms, not hard, and led him toward the ship's ladder, he told them that was sufficient.

The secretaries followed with all the official papers, which the U.S. captain confiscated.

The U.S.S. *Jacinto*, with no means of communicating the news of her haul, set sail for Hampton Roads. When she put in there for coal, Mason was allowed to write a letter which the ship's officers put ashore. Under date line "U.S.S. *Jacinto*, off the Virginia Capes," he wrote, "My very dear wife, The date of this will show you that we have been captured . . ." and "I . . . presume the papers will tell you what disposition is made of us." He said that he was being treated well and asked her to write him "full details of domestic, but nothing of public affairs."

It was easy indeed for Mrs. Mason to learn from the papers what disposition had been made of her elderly husband. It was the prison at Fort Warren, Boston, and the papers of three nations were full of the news.

Captain Wilkes of the U.S.S. *Jacinto*, hailed as a hero in the North and denounced as a villain in the South, was in the British press regarded as a violator of neutrality (which he was). The British fleet readied itself, soldiers were shipped to Canada, and the official note was sent to Washington asking for the release of the two Confederate commissioners.

The highest hopes with which Robert Hunter had sent Mason and Slidell abroad were on the verge of realization—the break between England and the United States. Captain Wilkes had delivered the greatest blow for the Confederacy since First Manassas.

To the anxious men of honor in the government offices in Richmond, to the impatient men of action in bars and hotel lobbies, to the uninformed citizens of patriotism in homes and war workshops, it began

JUDAH P. BENJAMIN

As a member of the Confederate Cabinet. Courtesy of Confederate Museum,
Richmond, Virginia.

A TYPICAL REAR BALCONY OF A FRANKLIN STREET-HOUSE

In this house, Franklin is on the side, showing a walled garden. The slope of the street, from Fifth, continues to Capitol Square at Ninth. Photograph, courtesy of Valentine Museum, Richmond, Virginia.

to look as if the hopeful planlessness of Confederate diplomacy was to blunder into success.

They all knew that Lincoln had only the two choices: to lose face by backing down or to make war. They all did not know that England had offered Lincoln an out.

In a cordially toned note (a revision by Prince Albert of the first harsh demand) the British Foreign Office stated that they believed Captain Wilkes's action did not represent the official policy of the United States.

Against the bellows of the firebrands who would back down to no one, Lincoln took the out. He said the British were right; the commissioners would be released. . . .

While Richmond quieted down, the men whose names had rung around the world were rowed out on a bleak winter night to a ship in Boston Harbor, bound for England.

No break had resulted from the strained situation, but England, unlike Kentucky, had demonstrated a strict neutrality. The rights and dignity of the new empire were honored there, at least as belligerents. It devolved on the commissioners, with this opening wedge, to make it more.

3

When James Mason late in January registered at the Fenlon Hotel, in St. James Street, the Confederacy's diplomatic relations with England were at a stalemate. Before Mason came, and while the *Trent* affair was still hot, the commissioners then in London used that moment to reopen the blockade issue with Lord John Russell. Stressing that its ineffectiveness made it illegal, they hoped, in the event of a U.S. apology, at least for an immediate raising of the blockade.

Far from getting that, they were answered curtly with a refusal even to conduct official correspondence under the present circumstances. They could not know that Russell had been intimidated by the United States, who threatened action if England recognized the commissioners. But when Mason arrived he should have known that Russell's attitude plainly showed England's disinterest in any legalities save her own. While she would go to war with the United States over her own toes being stepped on, she would risk nothing in the interests of the Confederacy—whatever the rights of the new country.

Obviously the only way to bring England in was to entangle her in the strands of self-interest. The only policy toward this end, the use of King Cotton as a threat, also obviously was not doing so well.

In fact the unofficial embargo which withheld cotton had boomeranged in a curious way. It gave credence to the effectiveness of the blockade at the time when the blockade was little more than a nuisance —and England knew it.

British Consul Bunch wrote home from Charleston of the ineffectiveness of the blockade, as did Fullerton at Savannah, who reported seeing the *Bermuda,* loaded with arms, sail unmolested through the main channel. As by the turn of the year the United States had only 160 ships afloat for all purposes, it was manifestly impossible for them to blockade the thirty-five hundred miles from the Potomac to the Rio Grande, and the Confederate commissioners in London proved the passage of between five hundred and seven hundred ships by the end of the year.

But, as none of this brought England any cotton, the proof of the ineffectiveness of the blockade fell upon deaf ears. Mason and the originators of the policy in Richmond apparently failed to perceive this duality in their diplomacy. While they tried power politics with the cotton threat, they simultaneously tried idealistic appeals on the legalities of the blockade.

Once in England, James Mason bore more heavily on the rights of the Confederacy, honestly believing that recognition could not be withheld from a people whose dignity he so impressively represented in person. To confirm his conviction, from the beginning he was handsomely received in high places and found constant evidences of the sympathy with which the Confederacy was regarded.

Before he arrived the Confederate purchasing agents, with their smooth manners, had become social pets in the fancier sets. There were sufficient signs of their influence on opinion for the United States to start countermeasures. Mason found English friends already writing letters to papers, publishing pamphlets and books, and getting a lot of discussion in Parliament. He also perceived, in the prevailing attitude of the press, a drift in favor of his country.

At first England had been hostile to the seceding states. Disliking the United States in general, the British found the worst offenders among Southerners, from Washington to Jackson, and Mason himself. But as the states established themselves as a nation in the face of attack, and it became clear that no union would be re-established without a sizable war, this was a different matter. Such a situation would be ruinous to trade.

Correspondent Russell had privately written the British ambassador, "I do not see how the U.S. can be cobbled together again by any compromise . . . [nor by] any mode of reconciling such parties as these. The best thing now would be that the right to secede should be acknowledged." This opinion was shared by many, and, their dislike of the U.S. continuing, their sympathies turned toward the Confederates.

However, this expression was among the people, not the government. Then, any more than now, the British government could not be accused of letting its heart rule its head. And then, even less than now, did that coolheaded government give the slightest indication of what went on within. Actually much of the government favored recognition, but they pursued a cautious policy which naturally they did not confide to Mason.

For Mason in person the British Foreign Office had the same official snubs as for Yancey and Mann before. Lord John Russell granted one interview in which Mason presented Hunter's clearly reasoned arguments supporting the South's contention that their nation was no rebellion. In the icy formality of the minister's reply, there was no indication that he personally wanted to give them recognition but feared committing an act hostile to the United States.

He gave no hint that, with the pressure of the U.S. on him, the Confederacy's present physical status was too uncertain for England to risk involvement. Instead, because of this devious policy, he used an extreme hauteur as a national and personal face saver.

Mason, his dignity hurt by the surface rebuff, guessed none of this. Not trying to analyze His Lordship's motives behind the methods, Mason sought balm among his many socially distinguished and influential friends. How much he contributed to their solidification cannot be said, but a powerful Confederate lobby was growing in Parliament, and prominent figures were throwing their weight behind the movement. For all the duality in Confederate policy, there were portents enough to encourage Mason.

4

In France the prospects looked even brighter, and John Slidell enjoyed easier sailing in all ways. Free of the British stuffy international etiquette, the members of the French government received the Confederate commissioner most cordially. Napoleon III himself, more devious than the whole British Cabinet put together, talked frankly with a fellow intriguer.

He made it plain that he wanted to recognize the Confederacy and feared to act without England. He had made unofficial approaches to the Parliament, but they had rebuffed him with the same chilly formality they handed the Confederates. Now he only waited to discover another approach to the British, as, his dignity also involved, he could not risk another snub.

Napoleon backed these words with gestures of friendliness. The Slidells were invited to receptions of the Emperor, where, in his candid talk, Napoleon showed himself well informed and openly sympathetic "to our cause." The Empress Eugénie "received Mrs. Slidell and the girls most graciously." This led to all manner of invitations from the nobility. It was very gratifying to the old politician to see his daughters enjoying themselves hunting stags and wild boars with the hound packs of royalty and returning to the receptions of Empress Eugénie.

Slidell was getting around with the boys too. His chief pals were two real powers, DeMorny and Persigny. Both had been active in the *coup d'état* which made Napoleon III emperor, and, grateful or not, he had to be loyal. Persigny was an able man who had worked devotedly for the Second Empire from the early days when he attached himself to Napoleon's destiny. Now Minister of Interior, he did what he could for the Confederates.

DeMorny, illegitimate half brother of Napoleon III, illegitimate descendant of Talleyrand and Louis XV, had none of Persigny's convictions, but plenty of connections—and debts. These last were to be important. He was the old-fashioned royal rake—extravagant, dissolute, conscienceless. He found Slidell a good companion and used his influence with the Emperor for him.

The only cold touch was Thouvenal, the Foreign Secretary. Having no part in the *coup d'état*, he worked for the liberalism of France, on which platform Napoleon III first rode in. The difference was that Thouvenal believed in it. Unlike Lord John Russell, Thouvenal really was unsympathetic to the Confederacy. Hence, being honest, he did not have to be rude. He was the one who went right to the weak spot in the Confederacy's tricky diplomacy of withholding cotton while pooh-poohing the blockade.

Thouvenal asked Slidell, "If so many vessels have broken the blockade, how is it that so little cotton has reached neutral ports?"

Slidell could not well say, "We're deliberately withholding cotton as a threat to make you lift the blockade which we claim doesn't exist." He had to use his own guile to get out of the question, and he wrote back to Richmond that a cargo of cotton would be worth more than all the arguments the State Department could think of.

As for the rest, he knew it was a matter of waiting on England. When she moved, France would move—and not before.

CHAPTER TWELVE

The Favorite Goes—Up

IN RICHMOND, the people celebrated their first New Year's as citizens of the Confederate States of America. Traditionally they made the rounds of open houses, where groups gathered about the punch bowls of eggnog, and paid their respects to the governor, where it was observed that champagne had become a casualty of the blockade. But the main event was the public reception at the presidential mansion.

The ladies were disappointed not to see Mrs. Davis, who had recently borne a child (William Howell), but in all other things everyone could gratify his curiosity to his heart's content. The one dependable element in Richmond's weather is its changeableness. New Year's Day ranges from arctic to tropical, but in 1862, Nature outdid herself. The day was clear and balmy, like spring and without "unseasonable warmth," and the armory band played outside the front door during the bright noon hours.

The people came in carriages and by foot, arriving in a steady stream from eleven into midafternoon. The President's staff greeted them in the entrance hall and ushered them into the presence of Mr. Davis, standing just inside the parlor doorway. He looked well that day and was at his social best—at ease, with graceful dignity, a word for the least of old acquaintances, a smiling bow for strangers.

Disliking social functions as he did, when convinced of their fitness he brought a real charm and some of the gentleness which routine and duties of his larger concept usually hid. Playing host at a customary reception was also part of his concept and one that employed more appealing (and probably natural) facets of his character. As indicative of this he brought his own children from the nursery to play with those of an obscure Methodist minister.

Guests moved on back into the parlor to meet the hostesses, kinswomen of the President and Mrs. Davis. These ladies kept the reception flowing without groups forming, and there was free if brief intermingling between the government and state and petty officials, Richmonders of privilege and plainness, the shopkeeper and the planter, speculators and military leaders, and all the ladies of the new national capital. For that balmy New Year's Day the people of the Confederacy met together with their President.

But next day the local citizenry were caught up in more personal interests. Early in the morning, before daylight, downtown Richmond was awakened by "a lurid glow over the sky," and soon crowds were hurrying to the terrible fire of the Marshall Theater at Seventh and Broad. A handsome building, erected in 1818, it was the home of much of the city's theatrical history. The year before the war Joe Jefferson's stock company had played there, and the year before that young John Wilkes Booth, who, as a spectator, accompanied the Richmond Grays to the hanging of John Brown.

Before the fire companies could get into action, the old landmark was a mass of flames, throwing out "intense heat and livid sparks" as far south as the Basin. The falling rear wall crushed buildings on the adjoining alley, and the Marshall Hotel, well known "to all citizens of bibulous tendencies," caught next. Private homes on the parallel street, East Grace, were fired by flying sparks, and a tailor, whose outside kitchen caught fire, lost $250 "in goods carried off by people who undertook to help him saving his stock."

Most of the other buildings that were fired were saved from destruction, especially two whisky shops across the street, but everything in the theater, even musical instruments and sheet music, was totally lost.

This was the second great theater fire in Richmond. The hero of that earlier fire, 1811, a giant Negro named Gilbert Hunt, died soon after the Marshall Theater burned. A blacksmith, he had been given his freedom for his heroism and had gone to Liberia. Not liking it there, he returned to Richmond, where he lived in honor and respect.

In his day there was in Richmond an absence of the acute awareness of race consciousness that existed in the Deep South and later in America. Negroes had been in Richmond since recorded history, usually as house servants or skilled workers, and many were free. It was a custom for a slaveowner to hire out Negroes for $100 a year, the hirer providing food, clothing, and medical care, and from extra money earned in this way some bought their freedom.

Being originally of a more intelligent class of Negroes than the majority of field hands, and having for generations lived more closely with whites than the groups of their fellows in quarters on an absentee-owned plantation, they fitted more fluidly in the general community pattern than might be supposed from apologists or abolitionists.

Of course they occupied the same inferior position in white society that Negroes do in any American city, then and now, and there was much nauseous white sentimentalizing on the Uncle Tom theme. But, assuming the tragic difficulties of the whole problem of the Negro, and assuming the evil of any oppressed group for whatever reason, their condition was one of the less foul aspects of slavery.

Many of the Negroes lived in security and dignity and mutually exchanged affection and—free or slave—they enjoyed a genuine identity with the community and a pride in it. Naturally there were cases of devotion and loyalty to their owners, and cases of hate. Some yearned for freedom and some refused it. Among the free they ranged in prosperity and poverty, goodness and viciousness, like any people. But the point is that these Richmond Negroes of Gilbert Hunt's day were neither the field slaves of legend nor the faithful darkies of Stephen Foster, but an accepted, integrated social microcosm as varied and complex as the macrocosm of the city.

Of Gilbert Hunt personally, more would have been made of his funeral except for the prevalence of death that winter. Scarlet fever took a heavy toll, including three children of General Longstreet, and President Tyler's death in mid-January called for a state funeral. Then, a month later, came the epic funeral of the year, as fashionable as a wedding—that of O. Jennings Wise.

It was not only what he had been in his life that made his funeral an event, but the manner of his death. In dying he was strangely linked with the Confederate whom James Blaine called "the Mephistopheles of the Rebellion, the brilliant, sinister" Judah Benjamin.

2

Captain Wise was the son of Henry Wise, one-time governor of Virginia and U.S. congressman, now political general and always a tempestuous "character." Young Wise, as editor of the Richmond *Enquirer,* was widely known and liked beyond the world of formal society, where he was a favorite, and he entered the war dramatically as captain of the famed Richmond Light Infantry Blues. At their head, acting with wanton and gaudy rashness, he had been killed at Roanoke Island. The fall of Roanoke Island, and all lost there, was squarely charged to Secretary of War Benjamin.

With all possible extenuations Benjamin stands guilty as charged by the people—though his guilt was shared by General Huger, the elderly grandee commanding the Norfolk district which included Roanoke Island.

Earlier, the fall of ill-prepared Fort Hatteras had given the Union forces a foothold in the Sound country—the inland waterway—off the North Carolina coast. From that foothold Roanoke Island, the key situation, was their obvious objective. North Carolina's governor repeatedly called for stronger measures of defense there, and General D. H. Hill, observing the slow progress of fortification as early as October, had written Benjamin that "I would most earnestly call the attention of the most Honorable Secretary of War to the importance of this island."

Benjamin was neither a traitor nor a fool, and yet he did nothing beyond calling matters to the attention of Huger, who revealed himself to be completely supine. But Benjamin was primarily the Secretary of War of Mr. Davis and not of the Confederacy. As Davis, the commander, was his own Secretary of War *and* chief of staff, the cabinet member would be actually an assistant. As such, like poor Walker, he could be a harassed chief clerk; or, like subtle Benjamin, an adviser, expediter, liaison between the executive and the field. With his own ambitions for self-advancement, Benjamin was more interested in expediting for the President than in *what was expedited*.

During the lull of autumn and early winter, while the North was preparing with definite if limited objectives, Davis clearly called on Benjamin to expedite details of organization against the wishes of field commanders and to bring to bear his legal arguments to put these generals in their places. This naturally increased Benjamin's disrespect for military men and his own self-confidence in a job for which he was unfitted.

Always a fast and facile worker, to whom all things came easily, he would seem to have underestimated the requirements of the war office because he mastered its details. If bringing order to these details was enough for the President, it was enough for him—and his supple, realistic intelligence was not used on the larger and decisive policies of a war office.

Nothing else could explain his indifference to all warnings, his leaving the whole matter in the limp hands of General Huger. Pressure came to a head in January, when General Henry Wise was given command of Roanoke Island itself and immediately squabbled with the naval commander there and with Huger. It happened that this overbearing gentleman, Wise, was right—Roanoke Island could not be defended as it was, but it did offer excellent possibilities of defense. To his calls, Huger remained inert in Norfolk, holding thousands of troops inactive, and Wise arrogantly went over his head. He came to Richmond for a personal interview with Benjamin.

No two types could be better calculated to grate upon each other.

Wise, the aristocrat, proud of being outspoken and tumultuous, rants and bellows on the desperate need for more men and material, stronger and different fortifications. His passion breaks over Benjamin's smiling indifference like spray on a rock.

Benjamin, with his poor opinion of the military mind in general, finds a political militarist scarcely worthy of courtesy. Huger is not disturbed, and he at least is a trained militarist—and the superior. Has Benjamin not already had enough trouble with Joe Johnston over dealing with inferiors directly? And this inferior is not even a trained general. Benjamin smiles and hides his boredom at this bombast.

The general doubtless agrees with his son, who finds Benjamin "oleaginous . . . his overdeferential manner suggestive of a prosperous shopkeeper." Benjamin finds Wise a nuisance and sends him away.

In brief, each misses the other—and Roanoke Island falls, like a fat plum to one quick clutch.

3

Later Benjamin said privately that he lacked sufficient powder to reinforce the island and bore the blame rather than expose the weakness. This might be true, but there were many things that could have been done without more powder. Or, if the position was indefensible, the men and supplies should have been removed.

More likely unmilitary-minded Benjamin, accepting Davis's dispersal of troops, missed the importance of Roanoke Island. In a matter of days after its fall, the little "mosquito fleet" and the whole Carolina coast almost to Wilmington was gobbled up.

Clearly it was negligence, given personal drama in Richmond by the coffin bearing the body of O. Jennings Wise.

His father, the dramatic general, had cried when he saw it, "Ah, my boy, you have given your life for me." The newspapers in Richmond gave full space to requiems. "How sleep the brave." Crowds gathered in Capitol Square to follow the procession to St. James's Episcopal Church. "Thy will be done" was the rector's theme, and the choir sang "Come, Ye Disconsolate."

The procession re-formed and walked the winding streets south to Hollywood Cemetery, spectacularly rolling above the canal and James

River. The *Enquirer* employees followed the family; then came Blues and Masons; civil and military authorities, and "a large concourse of citizens." The body was buried near that of President Monroe. The State Guard fired three volleys. The *Examiner* said, "A sacrifice has been demanded and one sacrifice has been made and this victim had been selected to be offered."

Who selected the victim? Judah P. Benjamin, the people said. He had to go.

Nothing had gone right since he was Secretary of War. He had made trouble with the generals. He had shifted West two of Joe Johnston's trained field officers, Beauregard and Van Dorn, and almost lost Stonewall Jackson to the Army. He had sent Jackson direct a peremptory order to recall from a position an officer who had protested over Jackson's head, through politics, that he did not wish to remain where Jackson had placed him. Stonewall immediately sent in his resignation, through the proper channels, stating that "with such interference in my command I cannot expect to be of much service in the field. . . ."

To persuade Jackson to withdraw his resignation, it took Joe Johnston, Governor Letcher, and finally Old Jack's congressman and friend, who sold him on keeping his command by saying he had no right to withhold his needed services from Virginia. But that was not the end.

Joe Johnston then wrote Benjamin that, "having broken up the dispositions of the military commander, you give whatever other orders may be necessary." And to Davis direct, Johnston asked to be relieved of Jackson's Valley command, as a collision of authority between Benjamin and himself might occur at a critical moment and "disaster would be inevitable." Finally, driven frantic by furloughs being granted from Richmond, Johnston wrote asking that letters addressed to his command pass through his office, as "It would . . . create the belief in the army that I am its commander."

Davis supported his favorite against Joe Johnston and against the people, even after Roanoke Island. But a real storm was brewing when more disasters followed. These were in the West.

Albert Sidney Johnston, the new Hero, had lost the buffer state of Kentucky and much of the vital Confederate state of Tennessee in a quick succession of blunders that had his army and the whole South reeling.

With his huge assignment and scarcity of troops, Sidney Johnston tried to have men everywhere and had them in force nowhere—and wherever action occurred, he was somewhere else.

First eastern Kentucky went in a battle variously called Fishing Creek, Mill Spring, Logan's Cross Roads, and others, but definitely listed as a Confederate defeat. Zollicoffer, a promising Rebel, was killed there. His command was shared by Crittenden, a Kentuckian whose brother was in the Union Army. In the Kentucky battle the Northern forces were commanded by George Thomas, the doughty Virginian who had recently made his own hard decision. In any event the Confederates were cleared out of eastern Kentucky, back into hostile eastern Tennessee, and the way was open for rich western Tennessee.

The Unions had a clear plan: to cut down the Cumberland and Tennessee rivers with army and gunboats; then swing back to the Mississippi and on to Vicksburg, severing the Confederacy. The South, without a plan, had Albert Sidney Johnston.

He had three forces whose combined strengths about equaled any one of the three Union forces. With these forces he must check any thrust south from Kentucky—either toward the Mississippi or to Nashville, the Tennessee capital and storehouse of Confederate supplies.

His only chance lay in boldness, risking somewhere in order to combine his forces to defeat the enemy in detail.

He risked nothing and lost everything.

The separate forts, Henry and Donelson, guarding the entrance into Tennessee by the Cumberland and Tennessee rivers, fell to Grant's single-minded dogged determination when a three-cornered command of Confederates played "Button, button, who's got the button?" while Johnston waited elsewhere with an inactive force. Grant thought Johnston committed an error in not assuming personal command, especially with the incompetence of two of the generals.

As it was, Johnston's other two forces were nullified and hopelessly outnumbered with the surrender of the bulk of the men and guns at the two river forts. The Confederates could only retreat from Columbus, Kentucky, on the river, and uncover Nashville. Without a fight, the Tennessee capital was abandoned in a panic and riot that lost the Confederacy most of the supplies stored there.

Johnston combined what was left of his army and retreated deep into Tennessee for a defense of the Mississippi. With all possible extenuations, Albert Sidney Johnston had failed on a grand scale—losing a third of his force in a wretched affair, most of west Tennessee along with the Mississippi from Kentucky almost to Memphis, without one decisive action.

The public gave voice to a great clamor against this clay-footed idol, and their anger included Benjamin. As the war office was operated, Benjamin could not rightly be blamed for these heavy setbacks; but as he wanted the glory of the office, he must accept responsibility to the people for actions supposedly deriving from that office.

The actions derived from Jefferson Davis's defensive planlessness and the country's resultant lack of cohesive central forces. Only Benjamin would not say that, and Davis probably was unaware of it. The President knew only that, somehow, his favorite was not to blame and he must support him.

Newspapers and opponents in Congress, led by the vituperative Henry Foote, banded the pair of them together in attacks grown more forthright and vicious. Benjamin was called the tool of a despot, and it was clear that enemies were trying both to bring down Benjamin and get at Davis through him.

Though Davis was as loyal as he was stiff-necked, if he left unheeded the charges leveled specifically at Benjamin he would indeed appear the despot. The Confederate Congress, typically American, appointed a committee to investigate why Roanoke Island *had* fallen (and this was later to lump Benjamin and elegant Huger together as the culprits).

But the nerve-strained President needed the soothing personality of his friend. He could not bear the absence of the imperturbable sybarite padding around his office and home—especially now, with things going badly on other fronts of which the public was as yet not aware.

4

Robert Hunter had grown restless. Ambition itched beneath his plump Victorian façade, and, like Bob Toombs before him, he found the State Department a blind alley. He did not storm about, complaining, as had his predecessor. Such behavior was antithetical to a character founded upon self-control. This control only caused his efforts to escape to be more methodical and calculated.

Hunter wanted no break with the President. Their relations remained cordial enough, though not intimate. Nor did he lust after the true glory in the field, or sudden fame, unbecoming to a Virginia gentleman. He wanted merely what he had wanted his whole life long: the political position from which to maneuver steadily toward the White House, now of the Confederacy.

In his orderly office on the second floor of the Treasury Building the days droned quietly away. He could see visitors climbing the stairs at the other end of the hall, going to the President's office; he could hear passers in the hall talking of going over to the war office across the Square. Nobody had any reason to come to see him. Nothing ever happened in the State Department.

Abroad, France still waited on England and England still waited on decisive Confederate victories, and these manifestly were out of the hands of the Secretary of State. Nearer home, their official relations with neighbor Mexico had failed dismally through the ineptitude of the Confederate commissioner. But all that happened before Hunter took office.

In June of 1861 the ill-advised choice had gone to Mexico—Colonel John Pickett, Kentuckian, West Pointer, and professional revolutionary. His mission was to obtain use of Mexican ports for European supplies and to maintain quiet along the border where bandits kept everything unsettled. Physically aggressive and blustering, fancying his own harsh sense of humor and the recounting of his highly colored exploits, Pickett at best was personally handicapped in dealing with the gentle-mannered, patient Mexicans.

Also, he regarded all of Mexico solely as something for the Confederates to exploit, despised the ruling Juarez government, and favored the clergy-landowner combine under some European power (probably Napoleon). To climax all this, he was arrogant enough to state his attitude clearly in dispatches which the Juarez government intercepted and carefully read before sending on, months later, to Richmond.

Pickett was now on his way home to an unhospitable welcome at Richmond, leaving the Juarez government to U.S. representative Corwin, whose hold was as simple as it was binding—gold. Corwin offered (without ever doing it) to pay the interest on the Mexican debts to Europe. What could a Secretary of State do there?

As it happened, there was a very bright side to the practical aspects of the Mexican situation, but this offered Hunter no chance for noticeable activity. In fact even today little has come to light of the unobtrusive accomplishments of Juan Quintero, who was getting everything for the Confederacy that Pickett was sent to get.

This young Cuban, who had lived in Mexico and Texas (where he handled the land office at Austin), was superlatively qualified to manipulate for the South's ends the border situation.

At the southern tip of Texas, where it meets the Gulf and adjoins Mexico, Brownsville is across the Rio Grande from Matamoros. The port of Matamoros was in one of the northern Mexican states ruled by Governor Vidaurri, powerful and strongly anti-Juarez, to whom he gave only nominal support. It was Quintero's job to swing Vidaurri's allegiance to the Confederacy. This he did so well that all manner of supplies crossed the border regularly in exchange for Texas cotton.

That Quintero achieved this smooth flow of supplies across a border kept quiet in spite of bandits operating from both sides, conflicts of purchasing agents and quick-money agents, machinations of U.S. agents and the volatile temperament of Vidaurri, added nothing to the credit of Robert Hunter in a dead-end office overlooking Main Street in Richmond.

Who thought of Matamoros when the permanent Congress and the permanent Cabinet were about to be seated in the capital? Certainly not Hunter, who, covering all angles, had managed his own election to the Senate against considerable opposition. But the final returns had been decisive—not so halfhearted as those of Toombs, who had refused his seat with such little confidence shown him by fellow Georgians.

That revolutionary without a cause, now sowing undirected dissension in the Army, simply indicated the perils of impulsiveness.

In contrast, the Virginian proceeded cautiously. It is not known if he and Davis reached an amiable decision regarding Hunter's change of office, but there is little to indicate anything else. Blindly anti-Davis Pollard claimed a rupture, caused by the President's domineering manner, but Mrs. Davis, much closer to the inside, felt that Hunter feared to injure his own cause by identification with the Administration.

Davis probably told that to his wife on one of the winter nights when his neuralgia racked him and she soothed him with hot tea before the fire of the high-ceilinged drawing room. Davis would not mind the ambitions of the courteous gentleman as long as he intended to support the Administration with which he did not wish to identify himself. Davis could use a respected voice in the Senate and an experienced hand assisting with the troubled finances.

In any event Hunter resigned his cabinet post before the permanent government was established, took his seat in the Senate, where he could make himself known, and the President faced his inaugural without a Secretary of State.

He also faced his inauguration with his country in a very grave condition and the wolves howling. The Charleston *Mercury*, as antiadministration as the *Examiner*, said, "The President has proposed to hand his name down to history as one who combined in his own person all the best qualities of Napoleon and Wellington." To this end, the "despot" refused high command to Toombs and Beauregard.

The sensitive man might well have been hurt by the senseless charges of which the *Mercury's* was a sample. But their blind hatred stiffened him against all charges, and he made no effort to reach the people who in the main were still for him. In his torment, Davis turned to God.

> "I'll strengthen thee, help thee, cause thee to stand,
> Upheld by my righteous omnipotent hand. . . ."

In the night Mrs. Davis heard her husband repeating this hymn in a call from the loneliness of his proud soul. Outside, the city was black, except down by the river where sparks flashed from the works where Gorgas used his genius to turn land-loving agrarians into munition makers. The hill on which the mansion stood was removed from the occasional revelry that split the silence and the fierce sudden brawls that flared in the shadowy streets where vice was pandered. In the old city residence the man from the magnolia South sought succor in the struggle that was too big for him and in which he knew not the ways of sharing the struggle with his earthy fellows.

5

On the Saturday morning of his inaugural he went early to his office (though he was due at the Capitol before eleven-thirty) to check any news or details that might have come in. Mrs. Davis, at home, made a final survey of the house for that night's reception. Things were not so simple here in a strange wartime city, where she had brought only a few of her servants from Mississippi, and those she hired came and went. "Birds of passage," she called them, and one was suspected of being planted as a spy.

That day anyway she missed her usual anticipation for entertaining. Perhaps it was the gloomy day. Showers fell steadily, and at intervals a heavy rain. It was not good weather for Banny to be out in. Or perhaps she was depressed by the inaugural, where he assumed permanent control of these vast affairs. Varina had never liked politics— only the socializing attached—and now they were saddled with such vicious politics as she had never imagined. She went upstairs to see if his things were in readiness.

Her husband had already returned from the office and there he was in their room, on his knees, praying. She heard him say, "for the

[151]

divine support I need so sorely." Poor man, he was not happy at his lot either.

She watched him leave the house with no lightness in his steps, though his carriage was erect and his chin held high. Her depression deepened. When she followed, she huddled in the carriage against the rain. She had not far to go, but the carriage moved at a snail's pace. As the Capitol came into view, she moved impatiently and saw on either side of her carriage four sedate Negroes, in white gloves, creeping along. She cried to the coachman, asking what was going on here.

"This, ma'am," he said, "is the way we always does in Richmond for funerals and sichlike."

"Well, you order those pallbearers away."

Then she sank back again, feeling a sense of bad omen which she could not throw off.

Once at the Capitol, her wretched mood became almost unendurable. The two houses of Congress gathered in the Virginia Hall of Delegates—the Virginia lawmakers having moved to another floor.

The room now used by the Confederate Congress was not large, but it was magnificently proportioned, with huge windows and an extremely high ceiling. Every point was jammed around the little brown desks where the members sat. At either end of the room little balconies were overflowing with the ladies.

From the impressive circular hall outside, with black-and-white marble floors, the President, "pale and emaciated," entered with the Vice-President. Stephens, his boy's body huddled inside sepulchral clothes, stared with his haunted scholar's eyes in a white little face like a frustrated pixie.

The ceremonies passed in good order and due solemnity, and at eleven-thirty the long procession moved out by the eastern door of the Capitol into the rain. There were senators and congressmen, clergymen and judges, members of the Cabinet and governors and their staffs, army and navy officers, Virginia congressmen and the mayor of Richmond, Masons and benevolent societies and newspapermen, and a band.

They proceeded to the equestrian statue of George Washington (it was his birthday), and a small crowd from the procession clustered around the President on a platform. Below them was a "waving grove of umbrellas." Near the statue the crowd jostled and pushed in the deep mud.

The President spoke, but few heard. Mrs. Davis heard, and she saw him lift up his eyes and hands to heaven. "O God, I trustingly commit myself and prayerfully invoke Thy blessing on my country and its cause."

Some people wept, and Mrs. Davis turned away.

"Thus Mr. Davis entered his martyrdom," she said. "He seemed to me a willing victim going to his funeral pyre, and the idea so affected me that, making some excuse, I regained my carriage and went home."

6

A week later the permanent President decreed a fast day—with shops closed, business suspended, and services in the churches. War clerk Jones, the acidulous observer, said of Davis that "All his messages and proclamations indicate that he is looking to a mightier power than England for assistance."

But neither powers on heaven or earth poured oil on the waters roiled by his opponents, who sneered at his "telling of beads." Even plain, faithful Reagan wanted to resign his Postmaster's job under the hail of criticism.

Leaving his Main Street offices, the Texan crossed Capitol Square to Ninth and Broad, where in a long low-pitched room his lithographers were bringing out a new issue of five-cent stamps, the color changed from green to blue. At a window in the northeast corner, Charles Ludwig worked at his drawings and engraved his stamps. Behind him the polished big stone lay on the worktable ready for the transferring of the panes of stamps. Along the back wall the lithographic printing presses were ranged.

Hoyer & Ludwig had done, and were doing, good work considering all their handicaps of material and workmen, and Reagan knew he had chosen his stamp suppliers well. Now they had nothing to worry about except the artistry and perfection of their own work and getting paid with the Confederate money. God knows there was plenty of that around, with every town and county in the country printing its own bills, and he had even seen a Shockoe Hill bank note redeemable in meat or currency.

That was all that stiff-necked Memminger could do in his Treasury Department except fool with other people's departments, like the Postmaster's. The fact that their dollar was still quoted at 1.2 only showed the people's faith in their country, despite politicians. Reagan had never been a party man in his life, and if he was being nagged and nipped now by feists because he was an administration man, then let some of them come in and do better. . . .

Jefferson Davis calmed him down. He was warm and winning when he talked with a friend, and he could point out that losing the administrator's supporters was what the enemies wanted. The Administration needed his support. It needed him.

Well, he would stay—but that problem to Davis was just one of the multitude that came as regularly as his dyspeptic pains. The man he really needed, the indispensable one, was the one whose head the people as well as the politicians demanded. He just could not keep Benjamin in the war office, and he could not do without him.

There was only one way out: relieve Benjamin of his War portfolio and appoint him to the vacant seat of Secretary of State.

In mid-March, Jefferson Davis made his decision public and official.

It was the public, and not the politicians, who were astounded. He seemed to be flaunting his will in the face of their wishes. It made no difference that Benjamin was eminently qualified for the position, probably more than any other man in the South, and only at last had his proper place been found. That was not the point. The people wanted to be shut of him. They wanted him gone, and the President retained him.

In Virginia particularly, where Benjamin was regarded as the murderer of O. Jennings Wise, the move was universally unpopular. A Richmond lady, friendly to the President, said, "This act . . . in defiance of public opinion was considered as unwise and arbitrary, and a reckless risking of his reputation and popularity. . . ."

It is scarcely possible that Davis failed to consider this reaction. But he considered more his sense of right. Benjamin had been unjustly chosen for the sacrifice. If his record in the war office made it impossible politically to keep him there, it was equally impossible to administer the country without his uncluttered brain and cheerful spirit. The President's need could not be measured against the senseless emotions of the mob. Besides, *he was right.*

Benjamin personally shrugged off the clamor against him. He had found a place to get anchovy paste which, he said, spread on bread from Richmond flour, made a delicious hors d'oeuvre for sherry. It was of no consequence to Benjamin, in any event, what the people thought of him.

But it was to the President.

The chart of his popularity turned sharply downward. New people agreed there could be something in that accusation, "despot." In new places his hold slipped. In their heavy spirits, weighted by the accumulation of disasters on all sides, the people ceased to be united behind the newly inaugurated leader.

If Davis knew, he gave no indication. The disasters demanded longer hours devoted to the details of organization, more letters to write, more worry. He was immersed in his job of Secretary of War, for the nominal office of which he threw another sop to the Virginians by appointing a grandson of Thomas Jefferson.

CHAPTER THIRTEEN

Lost Enchantment

FOR Varina Davis the bloom was off the peach. The first excitement had passed before the inauguration, and since then she had adjusted to the responsibilities of her position in a life of enmities and jealousies and intrigues, where naturalness was out of order and calculation of the essence. She could not be above the sniping of her husband's critics.

When sharp-penned Pollard, of the *Examiner,* accused them of hoarding their salary and feeling superior to the common herd when the White House was not open for entertainment, she felt called upon to entertain more to disprove his lies. Yet, as the winter of '62 flowered into a subtle and early spring, she missed her old enjoyment at parties. Since the inauguration, when she had been caught up in the feeling that her husband bore the whole weight of the experiment, Varina had resented the demands of people.

Her temper grew shorter, even with servants, with whom she usually was most considerate. Colonel Blackford, Stuart's engineer, observed her on Franklin Street when a young groom was fretting one of Mr. Davis's horses to make him prance and show off. The courteous colonel said, "She burst out in a fury of invective, the like of which I never before heard from lady's lips."

In those days that tried the nerves she turned more to her own family. She was pleased that her little boys, Joe and Jeff, made friends with the neighborhood kids and joined in the rock battles between the Hill Cats and the Butcher Cats, the tough urchins from the underprivileged families of Shockoe Valley.

Mr. Davis was troubled by the antagonism between the boys of the two sections and one day climbed down the long terraces from his garden to a gang of the Butcher Cats below. He talked to them with real understanding of children, and they listened gravely to his appeals for peace.

Then the leader answered, "We like you fine, Mr. President, and know you mean right, but we ain't *never* go' be friends with them Hill Cats."

Mrs. Davis probably had no objections to the rough play of the kids and enjoyed their mock battles in which the inferiors were forced to assume the role of "Yankees." Jeff and Joe made friends with Jim Limber, a Negro boy, and he was an intimate of the secluded garden on those fragrant Sunday afternoons in April, when Margaret's friends played dolls with her under a cherry tree, and Varina held her new baby, while Banny drank tea and talked of the bad turn things had taken for the Confederacy. . . .

The heavy blow had fallen on the North's route to the Mississippi near where the Tennessee River passes into the state of Mississippi. At Shiloh, the door to Memphis and Vicksburg, the Confederates lost the battle and lost their Hero, Albert Sidney Johnston.

He seemed an ill-starred soldier, this truly great character who gave up everything for his belief in the rights of a state, and so soon died for that belief. On his actual record for the months he fought for the Confederacy there is little to justify his huge reputation—except for his character. When the people clamored to Davis for his removal, Sidney Johnston, unlike the Heroes who justified themselves at any expense, wrote the President that "The test of merit in my profession, with the people, is success. It is a hard rule, but I think it right."

George Washington, with more luck against bullets than Johnston, carried a revolution successfully on his shoulders with character as his largest asset. To accomplish that on character, apparently one needed the lackadaisical foe who faced Washington or some equality of man power and equipment.

Johnston, facing enormous odds of a determined enemy with a single driving plan, inheriting badly planned forts and poor concentration of supplies, needed some audacity or imagination beyond his very sound training. With all his qualities, he lacked the one his situation demanded. A lesser man, a scoundrel or buffoon, a traitorous, greedy megalomaniac like Benedict Arnold, could possibly have accomplished much more in the same circumstances.

At the same time Grant, his enemy, brought to his situation the exact qualities most valuable at that time and place. Had Grant used his exact same methods against Stonewall Jackson he would probably have been destroyed. Had Johnston used his against McClellan they would be waltzing yet, feinting for position.

But Grant bored toward the center through the periphery of Johnston's poorly co-ordinated subordinates until, at Shiloh, with relative equality of forces, the two head men locked horns in the climactic battle. With all the counts in, it is undeniable that Johnston surprised and outfought Grant. He had the borer-in rocked back on his heels, in retreat, desperately turning toward reinforcements. Grant got them; and Johnston got a bullet. It wasn't much of a wound, so he kept fighting and bled to death.

The command devolved on Beauregard, who felt the troops needed reorganization in the confusion of victory. The next day, when Grant was also reorganized, *and* with fresh troops under Buell, the field that Albert Sidney Johnston might have won was lost to the Confederates. Because of that "might" at the one brief noon of his fighting career, Johnston passed into legend.

His star had faded rather than fallen before that one flare-up in the Gettysburg of the West. With his death the people in the White House, and over all his harried country, felt a sense of loss that his deeds had not justified. But he was a great character, selfless and large-seeing. He was the greatest of the first Heroes, and he was gone. . . .

2

Along with the loss of Davis's favorite soldier and the battle for the Mississippi, other defeats hit the Confederacy from end to end. New Bern, inland from the coast, went in North Carolina, threatening a railroad to Richmond, and Fort Pulaski, at the mouth of the Savannah River in Georgia. Off the coast the Union blockade began to clamp down, and one of the few new Confederate cruisers, the *Nashville,* was lost at sea. In far-off New Mexico the Confederates began their retreat from near Santa Fe and at home, in the battle for Richmond, Joe Johnston started his retreat from Manassas. The long-held line on the northern plains of Virginia was abandoned before the menace of McClellan's newly and superbly organized fresh army. And the Mississippi River, seemingly nature's gift to the South, became a sword through its vitals.

The fortified Island Number Ten went down with losses and, on the west bank, Missouri was shoved out of the war. The last fighting was done by the combined Confederate forces of Ben McCullough and Sterling Price, just south of Missouri in western Arkansas. As personal friction between the leaders had prevented concerted action, command was given to Earl Van Dorn.

A Mississippian and West Pointer, a cavalry officer from the old army who had risen rapidly under Joe Johnston in Virginia (and was one of the officers Johnston had hated to lose), Van Dorn had one of those anti-bellum faces of tumult and recklessness, which truly expressed his spirit. He attacked the Union forces with boldness of plan and vigor in action, but the co-ordination was faulty and the Confederates lost at one of those variously y-clept battles, Elkhorn, Pea Ridge, and what not.

Finished in Missouri, Van Dorn hustled his forces eastward to the Mississippi to help in the fighting there. Needless to say, he arrived *after* Shiloh was over and the concentration of Northern troops was preparing to move on the rail junction of Corinth in northern Mississippi.

Poor Sterling Price came to Richmond, with generous recommendations from Van Dorn and other Western officers, with a plan to take his Missourians back home, so the state would not be helpless and Union troops would be occupied. After receiving warm receptions in his home state, the lawyer-patriot was not prepared for Davis's cold rejection of his plan, and he grew angry.

Price's aide said that "no one who ever encountered Jefferson Davis *in authority,* especially when he was President, could ever forget the measured articulation with which he gave force to words addressed to one who presumed to oppose his wishes. . . ."

The President gained another enemy. Missouri became in effect a Union state and Arkansas a breeding ground for guerrillas.

With everything lost by dispersal, and the end not yet, Jefferson Davis, talking of the failures with his wife in the warming April garden, where tulips and bright forsythia bloomed, did not look within himself for the cause.

Stemming from the all-controlling executive, the division of authority which operated over the territory of the South also operated at specific points. What happened at Donelson between three generals happened again at New Orleans on a larger scale.

There was a command of the city proper and of the exterior defenses; there was the Army and the Navy; there was the state and the Confederacy. To complicate this further, Benjamin (when Secretary of War) put in his oar, literally. With his low opinion of professional soldiers and confidence in his own methods (based upon achievements in other fields), he went for a gold brick and spent a million and a half on something called "The River Defense Fleet."

Fourteen river steamboats were outfitted as a flotilla under riverboat captains, and placed under *army* authority. The army commander, however, said the captains lacked either brains, system, or discipline, and no hope existed of them acting in concert.

He was unhappily more than right. Eight went upriver to be wiped out at Memphis, and the other six, when the sea battle opened for the New Orleans forts, flitted about, bringing confusion to their own side, until they attempted to escape—and failed even at that.

They serve as a fair example of the defense methods of the most important city in the West—though not of the courage and determination of the fighting men, whose efforts and lives were wasted. The evacuation was equally confused, and such order as prevailed was maintained by the city's European Brigade of forty-five hundred, representing virtually every Continental country.

After the U. S. Navy had cleared the way to the city by reducing the forts, General Butler, hurrying to win his name of Beast by his treatment of civilians, swaggered his legions through the narrow dramatic streets, took over the colored secret houses of iron grille and shadowed courts, and grew outraged that the inhabitants resented being dispossessed. Benjamin's sisters were among those ejected from their home, and Butler personally confiscated some of Benjamin's property.

With his brutal measures against civilians, climaxed by his harsh proclamation regarding women, the fiction of preserving order within a single country came to an end. He was a conqueror of foreign people. The Southerners, far from being urged back into the fold, were undeserving even of the laws of common decency.

Jefferson Davis and his wife were horrified. Not only did the President suffer for his people, but he was genuinely shocked at this violation of his sense of justice and his belief in the abstract rights of the struggle.

While the people of Richmond recoiled in a new kind of fear—deeper with the awareness of the hatred outside their own gates—Davis's suffering was beyond personal fear. Something terrifying had been turned loose on the land outside all his carefully evolved theories of secession and destiny of caste. He was a swordsman who had delivered a challenge on a point of honor and then been set upon by thugs who kicked his womenfolk while they spat on his rules of combat.

Nothing in his character prepared him to comprehend the real nature of the fight into which his proud words in Washington had led him. Like the people of Richmond, he was backed against the wall fighting for his life.

3

In the official family in Richmond, Stephen Mallory went his good-natured way, presiding over his wife's superb dinner parties and apparently unperturbed that more of his original accomplishments had been nullified at New Orleans, as elsewhere, by lack of co-ordination.

His Navy Department lost in that blunder two powerful ironclads which, given more time for completion, would at least have been formidable factors for the South. The *Louisiana,* nearly seven months along, found her engines non-working but as a floating battery made valiant use of her guns until blown up at the surrender of the forts. The *Mississippi,* larger and more heavily armed, was also more ingenious. Compensating for his lack of ship designers and builders, Mallory had this ironclad built like a house—with straight lines and pointed ends. She was not ready for action and, instead of being towed upriver, was burned in the general confusion.

Two powder mills the Navy had established also went, along with a large laboratory for fuses and primers and the like. Another gunboat had been similarly destroyed on the Tennessee River when the army retreated before the Federals. In Virginia, when Joe Johnston started his retreat from Manassas and McClellan started his water-borne invasion of Richmond from the east, the Navy again lost good guns and river fortifications by army abandonment.

But nothing daunted Mallory's spirits or inventiveness, and his resourceful department offered the one bright spot to the harried nation —actually involving McClellan's vast scale of new attack.

Straight from Richmond the flat Virginia Peninsula runs, between the James River and part way the York, to Chesapeake Bay. At the tip stood Fort Monroe, impregnably held by the Federals and with its approaching waterways guarded by powerful ships of the U. S. Navy. This was the base to which McClellan planned to bring his army and from which to launch his attack on Richmond from the east, up the broad highway of the Peninsula.

Across Hampton Roads from Fort Monroe lay the great Norfolk navy yards, early occupied by the Confederates. From these yards on a bright March day there emerged a strange and terrifying object. Built low in the water with the fore and after portions awash, the dark, ugly, visible part, squat and spiked with guns and topped with a single sputtering smokestack, looked more like some imaginary sea monster than a ship. But as the *thing* seemed bent on trouble, two fine

U.S. frigates, mounting fifty and thirty guns, sailed out to meet her.

Neither returned. One went down in deep water with guns blazing and colors flying, and the other, hopelessly grounded and afire, finally struck colors. Three others were grounded in trying to escape, one of which presented a fat target for the next day.

Stephen Mallory, the unwilling rebel from Florida, had revolutionized naval warfare. The scuttled U.S.S. *Merrimac,* reborn as the C.S.S. *Virginia,* was the first realization of Mallory's cherished dream of an all-destructive ironclad.

The credit went to fellow Floridian, John Brooke. Thirty-six years old, Brooke had served in the U. S. Navy since fifteen, when he entered as a midshipman under Farragut. Later he entered the naval academy when it opened and, after graduation, worked in hydrography on coastal survey and with Maury in the Washington Naval Observatory, where he invented a deep-sea sounding apparatus. He was a natural scientist researcher, highly trained and experienced, and he brought to his work in the Confederate Bureau of Ordnance and Hydrography a driving determination and high idealism. His rifled Brooke gun was the Confederacy's most powerful.

For the *Merrimac-Virginia,* he first had the ship cut down to her old berth deck. Then both ends for seventy feet were covered over and, when the ship was in fighting trim, were just awash. On the 170-foot midship section, at a 45-degree angle, a roof was built of pitch-pine and oak, twenty-four inches thick, from the water line to seven feet over the gun deck. Both ends of this shield were rounded, so the pivot guns could be used as bow and stern chasers, or quartering. The wood backing was covered with iron plates, two inches thick and eight inches wide, rolled at the Tredegar. A cast-iron prow projected four feet and was badly secured. The rudder and propeller were unprotected, and the engines, typically Confederate, were terrible. They could not be depended on for more than six hours.

Indifferent to defects, she lumbered bravely out into the Roads on a trial run that was to end in her taking on the Union fleet. According to one of her officers, the fabulous John Taylor Wood:

She was crowded with workmen up to an hour of sailing. Not a gun had been fired, hardly a revolution of the engines had been made . . . from the start we saw that she was slow, not over five knots; she steered so badly that, with her great length, it took from thirty to forty minutes to turn. She drew twenty-three feet, which confined us to a comparatively narrow channel in the Roads. . . . She was as unmanageable as a water-logged vessel. . . .

An hour before noon, accompanied by gunboats *Raleigh* and *Beaufort,* she puffed ponderously out into the Elizabeth River, past cheering crowds at Norfolk, past cheering soldiers and marines on the C.S.A. batteries, on toward Newport News—and destiny. . . .

Wooden ships were rendered useless. Lincoln's blockade would come to an end. Every detail of McClellan's plan of invasion was halted by this 1862 version of the atomic bomb. In Richmond they hailed their deliverer. In Washington they expected the White House to be shelled after their fleet had been decimated.

But—also in Washington—months before, a foreign inventor had persuaded the tradition-bound Navy to allow experiments on one ironclad. Though the gold braiders' interest in this invention was less than negligible, now a second strange-looking object was towed frantically through the night to Hampton Roads.

The next day Ericsson's *Monitor* and John Brooke's *Virginia* fought to a draw. Though the *Monitor's* shots fell on the *Virginia* with the relative harmlessness of those of the wooden ships, so did the *Virginia's* shots fall harmlessly on the *Monitor*. In trying to ram the *Monitor,* the *Virginia's* engines gave her insufficient power, and when in desperation the crew tried boarding, the *Monitor's* agility evaded that. It was clear the rival monster had come to stay.

They fought again, and many times again the *Virginia* tried to lure the *Monitor* in another stand-up fight. But the *Monitor's* job was not to try consequences with the *Virginia,* but nullify her. This the *Monitor* did, and once again the Chesapeake Bay was safe for McClellan's transports.

The great Union organizer proceeded with his plans for invasion— while the frustrated *Virginia* morosely eyed the *Monitor* and Secretary of the Navy Mallory went on amiably with new experiments and talked personalities with his lovely wife.

CHAPTER FOURTEEN

The Wolves Gather

SPRING brought no renascence to the heart of Jefferson Davis. When he walked through Capitol Square, with the world young and warm and green again, he was headed for his fortress (his office) from which he fought the private wars being waged on him by the political leaders of the country. Now beyond personalities, politics, and theories, these internecine fights involved the existence of the Confederacy. This was man power: Conscription.

If the President failed to understand his mistakes, he fearlessly faced the consequences. His righteous and planless non-aggression did produce periods of false security, causing streams to the recruiting offices to dry up—though earlier volunteers were turned away also from shortage of arms and others were diverted to the political uses of moronic governors. His foreign policy, a weak mixture of idealism and King Cotton, had hopefully depended on England. *But* . . .

Now that physical defeats threatened to finish off his infant empire, the President perceived that only man power in the armies could save the experiment even in defensiveness. Then, against the most violent opposition, he carried through the passage of a bill conscripting men from eighteen to thirty-five and, more importantly, holding in the Army for three years the men whose twelve-month enlistments were nearly up.

With the low pulse of Confederate spirits, Davis unquestionably maintained the armies in the field. Not only were the existing units saved from at least partial dissolution, but thousands of men enlisted in preference to (what was in their time and place) the stigma of draft. And, despite exemption dodges which should forever disprove any lack of Southern ingenuity, some thousands of more men were conscripted. It was probably Davis's greatest moment, and for it he was treated as a combination of Benedict Arnold, Caesar, and Judas.

The ground swell from the average citizen's grumbling rose from sound objections. The types of exemptions which let off a planter with twenty slaves, and the legalized practice of buying substitutes, caused complaints of "a rich man's war and a poor man's fight."

But the highly vocal attacks of the political opposition were based upon theories of constitutionality which recognized no practical need.

The leader of this opposition was Davis's Vice-President. Stephens had gone home to Georgia, where, undisturbed by governmental duties, he could think up speeches attacking his own administration. "Despotism" was his favorite charge, and his proof was the suspension of habeas corpus and introduction of martial law—both designed to facilitate conscription and maintain much needed order.

As the United States had already started conscription and suspended habeas corpus, he found the North "a despotism complete and fearful," where there would never again "be anything like constitutional liberty," and it "today presents the spectacle of a free people having gone to war to make freemen of slaves, while all they have as yet attained is to make slaves of themselves."

For his own people under the heel of Davis, Stephens despaired of the readiness with which they "surrender most important and essential constitutional rights to what for the moment they consider the necessity of the case. . . . I do not question the patriotism" of acts of enforcement of these laws, but "it is the principle involved."

Stephens, as the main drafter of the Confederate Constitution, had copied from that of the United States the plain statement that habeas corpus would not be suspended *"unless when in case of rebellion or invasion the public safety may require it."*

In this deification of abstract principle to the denial of danger to the public safety, Stephens here divorced himself from reality. Under the shock of rebellion he became the first Confederate to retreat into the world of fantasy.

His ally in Wonderland by no means retreated in similar delusion. Governor Brown, of Stephens's own Georgia, was the prototype of a Southern politician who has become unfortunately all too familiar. A fool with cunning, a demagogue without principles, Brown was obsessed with states' rights as they applied to Georgia's immediate interests and resultant votes for himself. If his fanatically provincial mind was capable of conceiving anything beyond his own state's borders, his rabble-rousing commitments would prevent his revealing it.

Born dirt-dog poor, he contributed as much as anyone to disunion on the grounds of states' rights. From the founding of the Confederacy he did as much as anyone (Grant and Sherman included) to cause the downfall of the confederation which made possible the existence of Georgia in a states'-rights nation.

He attacked conscription in speeches, pamphlets to Georgia troops, and letters to anybody who would read them, especially the harried President. Not only did he, with Stephens, find conscription unnecessary and humiliating, but it was a constitutional violation (so was everything, all over the South, they did not like). It made chattels of freeborn citizens; it was subversive of state sovereignty and would disorganize Georgia's militia. The last objection was the basis of Brown's real fear: the more men he kept at home in militia, the more votes he had in Georgia.

When Davis went ahead over his protests, Brown suspended conscription in Georgia until the state legislature voted on it. When they passed it, he appealed to the Supreme Court. When they upheld it, he damned them as tools of Richmond and went about using his own privilege of exemption to appoint two thousand justices of the peace, countless petty officials, until Howell Cobb claimed that Brown exempted more men than went into the Confederate armies.

To make this a tripartite alliance against success of their own country, Governor Vance of North Carolina attacked conscription so successfully that he could proudly point to his state troops as leading all others in desertion. (North Carolina, a big state, furnished so many troops to the Confederate armies that, even with the high desertions, the battle records of Tarheel units were magnificent.)

Vance, unlike Brown, was a capable man of convictions. One of the many pro-union states'-rightists, elected to U. S. Congress three years before secession at the age of twenty-eight, he went with his state on Lincoln's call for volunteers. When he was elected governor in 1862, he showed the same hostility to everything outside his state as did Brown—though for different reasons. Vance was blinded by a monomania. He conceived of North Carolina as independent from the other states as if the rest were temporary and untrustworthy allies.

These three men in their practical idiocy possessed the strength of knowing precisely what they were fighting for. Their enemy inside (Davis) was fighting for abstractions, and their enemy outside (the United States) was fighting, as always, against something. But these opposition leaders were fighting for their states as simply and directly as a dog fights for a bone. Their way of fighting amounted to "divide and be conquered." Though this might make no sense, it was the way of states' rights, and, by God, they would fight for that if it killed them, against Lincoln or Davis or whoever it happened to be.

The President's behavior was strange with these intransigent men. With his generals he was so vigilant of his authority and demanding of the proper procedure that nothing seemed more important than "putting them in their place." But with these vicious politicians he was conciliatory.

With apparent magnanimity he placed the movement above the coarsest stupidity with which they forced him to contend. Far from being the despot of his enemies' charges, the meaner and more subversive their behavior, the gentler and more long-suffering he became.

The obvious explanation might be the true one. Being supreme military commander formed the center of his vanity; exercising its prerogatives was his strongest compulsion. Anything that infringed on that sovereignty caused a reflex rebuff. When Congress passed a bill for a commander in chief of the armies to curtail his control, Davis instantly vetoed it and instead appointed Lee as military adviser to the supreme authority.

Years later, when Lee's greatness was an American heritage, Davis wrote that "General Lee was charged with the conduct of the military operations of the Army . . . *under my direction.*"

But governors and politicians at large made no transgression on his realm. He was indifferent, in effect, to what procedure they used because nothing they did invaded his area of ego. As their imbecilities, however, did interfere with the armies he led, he used all the persuasiveness of his logic to hold them in line. Even to Brown he wrote a 2,500-word essay on "my own views on the power of the Confederate government" in relation to states, a definition of "troops" and "militia," and of course an interpretation of the Constitution.

There are revealed the man's innate idealism and bloodlessness. He appealed to these buffoons on the grounds that he respected—logic and justice—when a strong arm or skillful politics was all that could possibly help.

Dealing with generals had been too simple. He controlled their destinies through his control of the war office. His long and fine relation with Lee proves nothing about Davis except his freedom from jealousy. The harmony indicates the extent of Lee's tactfulness. Always careful to approach Davis through the proper procedure, Lee never rubbed his fur the wrong way.

Davis's political enemies were outside his control, and he lacked the means to manipulate them. He feared too constantly being misunderstood himself to be able to understand other men's motives.

Bearing the burden of their opposition, along with the South's severe losses, he worked as best he could through the hours, through the days, through the nights, guided solely by what he, before his God, believed to be right.

Born without an outgoing warmth and too proud to reveal his weaknesses (if, indeed, they were revealed to him), he was labeled as cold and tyrannical when he was all too human.

His wife knew.

2

The repercussions of the South's defeats went to the President's favorite, the new Secretary of State. Judah Benjamin, now in his third Cabinet within a year, was finally in the slot best suited to him and where he would be most useful to Davis. The President would not have to study over papers of Benjamin, who could "compose a most important state paper of twenty pages at a single sitting in a clear, neat chirography, and with hardly a single word interlined or erased."

At the time (March 18) the plump little man moved into the office down the hall from Davis, the effect of Confederate disasters was being carefully studied abroad. Though not ready to recognize the Confederacy, neither the British nor the French government wanted the new nation to quit. France, particularly anxious to know how the leaders reacted to adversity, sent the U.S. minister, Count Henri Mercier, from Washington to interview Benjamin.

The Richmond newspapers hoped for nothing from the visit, and the *Examiner* commented, "Whatever may be the object of Mercier's visit it is likely to make at least two persons happy in giving occasion for half an hour's work to Messrs. Benjamin and Brown of the State Department, who, no doubt, will consider themselves relieved to this extent from the arduous occupation of assisting each other do nothing."

Pickups from Washington papers attached no importance to the visit and repeated a rumor that Mercier had come to close his connections with the Confederacy, while later Richmond editorials assured Mercier that "if he continued in Richmond two to three months, he would there meet the armies of the North and have the advantage of returning to Washington by a direct and uninterrupted transit."

This attitude not only reflected the people's pessimism but revealed the newspapers' ignorance of the accomplishments of their European agents. It is true the work abroad had not been directed from Richmond, and much of their agents' achievements had been made in spite of the government, but that happened prior to Benjamin.

From the beginning he worked closely with Slidell, his old political partner. By April, Benjamin was aware, through Slidell, of the extent of government agitation in France toward recognition. It was clear that the Confederate lobby, with powerful British shipbuilder Lindsay

Davis House, at Richmond.

WHITE HOUSE OF THE CONFEDERACY

As seen from the foot of Twelfth Street. The house fronts on Clay Street. To the right of the house can be seen a sentry box, to the left the stables on Clay Street. The garden, at the rear, sloped to the left, toward Shockoe Valley. The house was not so isolated as it here appears; to the right, outside the picture, Clay Street was built on both sides with homes of similar style. Wood engraving from a drawing by A. R. Waud. Courtesy of Valentine Museum, Richmond, Virginia.

VIRGINIA STATE CAPITOL

Used as the Capitol of the Confederacy, looking south. From a photograph. Courtesy of Valentine Museum, Richmond, Virginia.

and other influential Englishmen, was closer to Napoleon than either the British or American embassy. Their working understanding was such that, as Napoleon could not risk another British rebuff, Lindsay in effect represented him in petitioning Lord John Russell to move in denial of the blockade's legality.

Though England refused, the British ambassador to France confessed that he thought the two sections would not act together again and hinted that only U.S. successes made the time inopportune for intervention.

Napoleon, denouncing the British government as schemers, was obviously trying to bolster his nerve to act alone in defiance of the U.S. blockade. To him, naturally, the state of Confederate courage was a matter of vital information. Mercier came, then, to the Confederate capital to feel of its backbone. No one could have given him a better impression than his old friend, French-talking, wine-serving Benjamin.

Mercier tactfully mentioned the "possibility" of defeat by asking what would the South do if ports and big cities continued to go, and alluded to a possible reunion. Benjamin assured him that possibilities of union did not exist between "two distinct peoples" and stressed that, no matter what fell, they would fight on until the end.

But the bland gentleman with the bright olive-colored face could reveal a determination in effective contrast to his well-dined smile— and he obviously did not anticipate any end at all. Benjamin also brought out other charming gentlemen in Richmond, with Washington experience to give their words weight, whose manners and fiery ardor would please the Frenchman.

Senators Wigfall of Texas and Clay of Alabama (whose homes had been famous social centers in Washington), Senators Orr of South Carolina and Conrad of Louisiana and Catholic Bishop Maguire, between them pulled out all stops, and Mercier left with the conviction that the Confederacy would definitely continue.

Naturally Benjamin did not take into his confidence the newspapermen, who consistently used him as a whipping boy for the President. He had other fish to fry—the big fish, England.

Despite the waltzing and the studied rudeness of English officials, despite the steady defeats of the South, movement for recognition was more active in the British government than at any time since the war began.

Beast Butler's outrages in New Orleans acted as a diplomatic boomerang, especially his proclamation announcing that all women who were rude to his soldiers were to be treated as prostitutes plying their trade. Palmerston denounced this as infamous in Parliament, saying that "any Englishman must blush to think that such an act has been committed by one belonging to the Anglo-Saxon race. . . ." And the London *Times,* coming out for intervention (with the *Economist*), used Butler's behavior as a sample of what the South dreaded of the "tyranny of victor over vanquished. . . ."

Along the same line, the British had pointed out to U. S. Secretary of State Seward that the fifty stone-filled ships sunk in Charleston's harbor to block the channel scarcely seemed an act upon fellow countrymen. "Such a cruel plan would seem to imply despair of restoration of the Union, the professed object of the war . . . [and] could only be adopted as a measure of revenge and irremediable injury against an enemy. . . ."

There was in London at the time a young man (unknown to the people of the Confederacy) finding means to bring all this to the attention of the British people. Not needing to mention that the sunken ships physically did no permanent harm, as the tidal currents broke up the hulks and washed the fragments away, he could stress the unlikeliness of such a blockade by a government against her own cities. In his anonymity, as far as the South was concerned, Henry Hotze was introducing what is now known as psychological warfare.

A twenty-eight-year-old Swiss, with newspaper experience in Mobile, Alabama, he had been sent to England in November 1861, with very limited objectives. Hunter, then Secretary, had wanted his own sound arguments to reach the English people, and he instructed Hotze "to impress upon the public mind abroad the ability of the Confederate states to maintain their independence," to attack the despotism of the Lincoln government and contrast the U.S.'s high tariff with the virtual free trade in the South.

Hunter apparently regarded the assignment as a minor effort, and Davis evidenced no interest at all. They threw the job to whatever nonentity would accept it and showed their evaluation of the chore by allowing Hotze $750 a year for expenses. Then plainly they forgot him.

In fact, shortly afterwards, they sent to Paris a Davis pet, with $25,000 a year expenses and authority that took no cognizance of Hotze's existence.

But young Hotze had already been taken into the inner circle of the powerful Confederate purchasing agents—that group whose energy and resourcefulness and coolheaded purpose combined them into something of an independent government abroad. At once those men appreciated that the quiet journalist was, of them all, probably the most coldly clearheaded with a broad and realistic understanding of European politics and motives.

Henry Hotze perceived at once that England was concerned only with material interest. Far from being outraged, he went to work on their point of interest with the skill of a first-class diplomat, the detachment of a first-class analyst, and a sure understanding of the nature of his phase of warfare. He wanted the news colored favorably to the Confederacy while maintaining accuracy *and* telling people what they wanted to know about the American war. Inside information would capture attention; he must slant the information also to arouse sympathy.

First he went to work directly on British journalists. Observing that the strident aggressiveness of the U.S. agents made a poor impression, he set out to do the opposite. He met the journalists through the elegantly mannered Mason and then entertained them with good whisky and cigars, good conversation and some facts they could use. Mellowed by conviviality and grateful for the stories, the journalists not unnaturally wrote them through Hotze's coloration.

From there it followed that editors went to the source of these stories, and Hotze was asked to write a leader. His first appeared in Lord Palmerston's London *Post* and created a fine effect. Immediately other columns were opened to him. He went slow—one here, one there—never injected a controversial note but always gave interesting facts that any reading public would want to know of a foreign war that affected and might entangle them. Gradually through the *Standard* and Lord Derby's *Herald* a picture of the war took form, sympathetic to the South and indicating where England's interests lay.

Shortly after Benjamin became Secretary, Hotze branched out with a magazine, the *Index*. Its standards were high: to be cosmopolitan and yet have a country; miscellaneous and yet have an objective; tolerant but not indifferent; moderate, yet not dull, and entertaining without being frivolous. His purpose was to reach the Cabinet direct through his well-informed columns; to supply the British press with a source of Southern information and to draw journalists to the Confederate cause.

Because of the astuteness shown in all this work, young Hotze was brought into the councils of the Confederate agents.

This group occupied a curious position. As Davis had no more centralized plan or co-ordinated operations for this vital work abroad than he did on the home front, it devolved on these agents to develop a common purpose and co-ordination. Everything was against them.

With little money or credit, they must obtain arms and supplies for their army and navy and people, *and* get them delivered through a blockade to a country without ships or seamen or plan. Also they were to obtain cruisers to operate indirectly against the blockade, and ironclads to act directly. They must accomplish this behind the scenes in competition with an established country of vast money and credit and intangible power, who used every maneuver and threat against them—from a co-ordinated home office with a very definite plan.

For manufacturing and financing, they must create sympathy for their cause or arouse greed by selling their cause as a gamble, or raise money to pay cash where they must. Parallel with this, they must influence two of the mightiest governments on earth to aid them and, as an ultimate end, bring these governments in as interventionists.

A small group conceived these vast and complex needs as facets of a single plan. These men, in the main, were Caleb Huse for the Army, Captain North for the Navy, Captain Bulloch for cruisers, with commissioners Mason in England and Slidell in France, and propagandist Henry Hotze. They banked through Fraser, Trenholm, the British agents of South Carolina's Trenholm, powerful shipper and international financier.

Unlike the Richmond setup, their separate tasks did not move in separate channels unrelated to one another. Agents became diplomatic advisers, commissioners became bankers, and Huse and Bulloch, for example, worked together in hiring ships and charting routes to deliver arms in a simplicity which the home government failed even to comprehend.

Finally it was their government—easily as much as money shortage and physical difficulties, much more than the enmity of the United States—which handicapped the agents abroad. Pets of Davis were sent over on all manner of duplicating jobs, causing Confederate agents to compete against one another to drive up prices. Some were scandalously cheated.

Plausible men with their own ideas and ambitious men using vanity for acumen caused conflicts of authority. They gave Caleb Huse more trouble than all his other problems together. More agencies were set up than in the New Deal's heyday, all to create a tangle of cross-purposes, acrimony, and exacerbated nerves.

There are no monuments in the South to this handful of able men who gave Davis, in spite of himself, an army to be Secretary of. But when Judah Benjamin moved offices across the Capitol Square, at least there was an awareness of their impossible conditions. Benjamin knew the Confederacy depended on this Swiss, this Yankee, this uncle of Theodore Roosevelt, this ex-New York New Orleans politician, with the legendary Virginia aristocrat to front for them.

The backwater office of the State Department—that had driven Toombs sputtering into the Army and Hunter easing into the Senate —was not too quiet for Benjamin. He liked a place where he could keep his fingers in many pies, and what the boys were doing in Europe occupied his brain in a manner to his taste. Besides, he could never be bored with the opportunities for advancing himself as the President's unofficial adviser.

Finally, at the moment he must have been pleased that the continuing consequences of his maladroit acts in his old war-office job no longer had the political wolves howling on *his* trail.

3

From the beginning of the war a system of "underground" passage had operated between the two sections. Women crossed the Potomac carrying medical contraband, largely morphine, in their vast petticoats. Letter carriers (at $1.50 a letter) and smugglers enjoyed relative immunity and frequently used this to act as minor spies. Straight-out spies took their chances at night against enemy scouting parties (who might also have crossed in reconnaissance), but their way was made easier by the naïveté of both armies and governments. They seemed only too eager to believe that persons engaged in spying invariably favored their side. Because of this, these men sometimes actually received passes through the lines.

When Benjamin was War Secretary, with his astuteness evidently focused in other directions, he was extremely openhanded with these passes. One man in particular whom he favored, over the objections of war clerk Jones, was a personable fine-looking man named Timothy Webster. About forty, above the middle height and powerfully built, he was frank and resolute, amiable and self-contained, according to his boss, Allan Pinkerton.

Webster had worked as a Pinkerton detective before the war and became one of his most valued men when Pinkerton took over the U. S. Secret Service. Webster had Southern friends in Baltimore, and from them he got letters to their kinspeople and friends in Richmond. With that start, he worked on his own, not even trusting Yankees on his trips through the lines. Apparently he also avoided the number of "spies" supposedly honeycombing the Confederate capital.

These subjects of much melodrama and inaccurate glorification were in the main a sorry crew of self-dramatizing busybodies and Unionists who sincerely wanted to help without knowing how. They were mostly Northern residents in Richmond, a freed Negro, and the famous Elizabeth Van Lew. Still ostentatiously carrying dainties to Northern prisoners, she did everything possible to attract attention to herself as a mysterious figure and succeeded only in being called "Crazy Betsy."

Timothy Webster realized that the spy business, like any other, needs talent and training, and he conspicuously appeared only with Southerners and Confederate soldiers. Probably from their generally unguarded talk, the fake Englishman garnered the tidbits which his experience could piece together in a pattern of information. Pinkerton, who exaggerated everything and had the mind of a dime novelist, placed great value on Webster's information. But there is no reason to suppose that he did not send in facts regarding the South's coastal defenses. The North's attacks from Roanoke Island on indicated a knowledge of what they were up against and precisely where to proceed.

None of his activities caused the least suspicion, and the sheerest ill fortune brought about his trouble. First he was taken ill and, trusting no one, sent no word out. Pinkerton grew worried at the silence and sent to Richmond two other agents, John Scully and Price Lewis, to investigate. Contrary to all of Webster's wishes, they came to his hotel room, where sympathetic Southerners visited him. One of these Southerners recognized the two agents from Washington, where they had searched his home.

Price and Lewis were hustled off to jail and promptly convicted. But the Richmond authorities still could not bring themselves to believe the worst of their manly, pleasant friend with his strong connections in the war office. Lewis and Scully also believed in Webster's influence—until the day of their hanging. Then they turned state's evidence to escape, themselves proved Timothy Webster to be the spy head, and were let off with twenty-one months. The usual woman "accomplice" or companion of Webster, Hattie Lawton, was given a year.

When Webster was convicted and sentenced to be hanged, he believed that he too would receive a reprieve. But his old chum Benjamin, now in the State Department, remained as quiet as a mouse in that office to which no one ever came. Still Webster remained confident, even on the day when he was driven from his prison to new Camp Lee in the Fair Grounds. He could observe that the spring-green streets were too quiet for a hanging.

He could not know that on the day set for Lewis and Scully's hanging there had been great excitement, and the biggest traffic jam in Richmond was occasioned by every whore in town hiring a carriage from which to view the spectacle. They were so disappointed that this second hanging came as an anticlimax. Few attended except a couple of hundred little boys and Negroes who perched in the budding trees.

Arriving at a house near the grounds, where he was to await his hour of execution, Webster rudely dismissed the preacher who came to offer consolation and, with seeming unconcern, lay down and slept for half an hour. He was awakened by the bustle of self-important officials strutting about with horse pistols and swords, and he began chatting with his guards on general subjects like any man with nothing to dread.

Then the military escort, militia, formed a cordon around the grounds and the immediate guard took their stations about the scaffold. Quite suddenly Webster broke. It was as if he had expected a reprieve and at that moment realized he would be dead within an hour.

He moaned and wept and called for a chaplain. The Reverend Dr. Hoge tried to comfort the man, but Webster was obsessed with the horror of hanging. He begged the minister to intercede to commute his sentence to being shot. Hoge convinced him it was useless to try to change the manner of his dying.

His jailer came, and Webster had to be helped to his feet by Dr. Hoge, whom he beseeched not to leave him.

Then, as he left the building and was placed in the carriage again, his manner underwent another change. He regained complete composure. Pale and obviously not well, he held his gaze steady, and not a muscle moved in his face. He was dressed in black, still wore a silk hat, and his eyes, to an observer, seemed a cold disagreeable stone-gray color.

The newly built scaffold was a simple but substantial wooden structure on the edge of the parade grounds. Guards assisted Webster to the top. He stood alone and silent while his hands and feet were bound, and Dr. Hoge offered a prayer. Then he bade farewell to those nearest him and the black cap was pulled over his head.

When the trap was sprung, the hangman's noose slipped and the big man thudded to the earth below.

He was again helped to the top, and he said, "I suffer a double death."

The rope was again adjusted, and someone below said, "That rope is too short."

"Oh," said Webster, "you are going to choke me this time." But they did not. According to the newspapers, he died on the instant. His body was allowed to swing half an hour before it was let down. Detectives cut up the rope and put pieces in their pockets as souvenirs.

He accomplished more for his country than Nathan Hale, and the Richmond *Examiner* commented that no execution had ever taken place there that produced so little excitement.

4

In early May the Charleston *Mercury* opined that "Jefferson Davis now treats all men as if they were idiotic insects." In Richmond the people claimed that General Winder treated them worse than that. For this cold-eyed, bristly-haired martinet personified the new martial law in the capital.

It was not that military law was unnecessary in a city where a story head read:

A MAN SHOT—
SMALL MATTER
NOW-A-DAYS.

But the people, like the wolves howling "despot," resented this infringement on their personal liberty. And they loathed Winder. War clerk Jones, to whom the provost marshal was more hateful than a horde of Yankees, began his complaints of Winder with his office. The grim plain frame building on Broad Street, near Capitol Square, was a filthy one, according to Jones. "It was inhabited—for they slept there—by his rowdy clerks. And when I stepped to the hydrant for a glass of water, the tumbler repulsed me by the smell of whisky. There was no towel to wipe my hands with. . . ."

Jones went on from the foul office of Winder's "plug-uglies" to some of their methods. He claimed they forged prescriptions in order to "catch" the apothecaries at selling brandy. "They drink the brandy and imprison the apothecaries." Winder threatened to shut down the Richmond *Whig* and arrest the editor for mentioning the existence of arms and ammunition, and Pollard said that Winder would accept any gift for anything from exempting conscripts to winking at illicit liquor trade. Later he conscripted the donor anyway and impounded all liquor. He liked playing with victims, and he had for recalcitrants a barred factory on Cary Street—a "political" prison named by its inmates Castle Thunder.

Worst of all, to the suffering citizens at large as well as his personal detractors, was Winder's turning himself into a one-man OPA. He called his ceiling prices "tariffs" and fixed the limit at which hucksters could sell their butter and eggs, meat and chickens, and the like.

As it happened, the fall of New Orleans sent the price of sugar soaring, all imported goods grew higher as the blockade became tighter, and restaurants and hotels in Richmond began to charge exorbitantly. The hucksters naturally resented selling on a low market and buying on a high, and—like Americans of any time, place, or cause—protested at being kept out of a good thing.

Farmers driving their carts in from the counties turned around and went back rather than sell at low prices. Hucksters in the market, with nothing but vegetables to offer, told the people to "starve" if they weren't satisfied. On Saturdays they offered turnip greens and hominy, sweet and Irish potatoes, but these were forgotten when one patriotic citizen brought two barrels of eggs to the Old Market and was promptly mobbed by women. As no sale was possible and the cart was in danger of capsizing, the purveyor of a military hospital took all the eggs.

When the people grew hungry for meat they turned to fish, and those prices rose with the demand. DeLeon said, "We lived on canvasbacks and green-backs." Even with the rising prices, fish markets grew so jammed that it was necessary to shop early in the morning, and sometimes then crowds were too dense for women to make purchases.

Speculators flourished in this atmosphere. Strangers took over the once tranquil streets and, despite Winder's bully boys, disorder was everywhere and nowhere was safe at night. Fierce brawls emptied public halls, and any door below Capitol Square might open into a bawdyhouse or gambling den or illicit saloon.

All this frayed the nerves and lowered the morale when, with nothing but news of battles lost and cities gone and their country shrinking, the people knew the war was shifting toward them again. Fighting had been brought to a standstill in the West by the ponderosity of the Union commander, Halleck, and once more the main drive was "On to Richmond."

The new army under McClellan, the North's Young Napoleon, was poised to strike eighty-five miles east on the Peninsula.

The citizens had been momentarily cheered when their own Virginia troops passed through town, hurrying toward Yorktown, where Joe Johnston's forces were concentrating to meet the thrust. It was a beautiful spring day when the leathery, hairy veterans marched through the green tunnels of the thick-foliaged trees where they had paraded a year before as knights. Ladies waved handkerchiefs more urgently now from windows and balconies, and civilians ran out to shake hands more fervently with friends and kinsmen in the ranks. Officers visited briefly with their wives before riding on to overtake their commands.

Longstreet, grim and stolid since the death of his children, looked particularly impressive with his staff trotting along Main Street. Everyone crowded to see young Jeb Stuart's cavalry swinging past the lindens on Franklin Street and around Capitol Square to Broad Street hill.

Then they were gone. An uneasy silence lingered where all the spurs had jingled and the bands had played "Dixie." Apprehension deepened after the interlude. Rumor ran ahead of disaster, weakening resistance when the blows fell.

First went Yorktown, the protecting line against the Union thrust. This was abandoned in the face of overwhelming odds, and the army began its retreat toward Richmond. Next Williamsburg, the ancient capital fifty miles away, was given up in a rear-guard action, and the army kept retreating.

Then came the shocker. Norfolk, on the south side of the James River, was evacuated. With it went the great naval yard and, affecting the people more personally, the *Merrimac-Virginia*. Their prize, their proudest possession, their only victor in the long roll of defeats, was destroyed by her crew. Then the people's voices joined the politicians' in complaints of their leader.

At the end of that May day, with the sweet wistaria blooming as it had a year ago when he first came to Richmond, Jefferson Davis walked erectly home through the streets of stricken people. Once in his house, the erectness fell from him. Dropping his hat on the tall rack in the hall, he turned into the little reception room and collapsed on the sofa.

His wife ran in with ready words of comfort, but Davis confided that he felt a terrible sense of responsibility. Nothing Varina said lifted his dejection. It was a moment when he seemed to feel personally inadequate for his task. His mind must have been a kaleidoscope of dead events that he might have handled differently. . . .

Back in March, when Joe Johnston at Manassas started worrying about McClellan's coming campaign that might turn his flank, Davis's confusion had started. He hated another retreat, another deep enemy penetration—especially this one, down the roadway of the only untouched Southern section. In Richmond people said it was time for attack. Defensive warfare had proven a failure. . . .

But Joe Johnston said if McClellan turned his flank, the Federals would be between his army and Richmond. . . . So Davis had agreed on retreat.

But he evaded the inevitable. Giving up more ground was a terrible loss of face abroad. It certainly did not prove their ability to defend— yet. Arms and ammunition were desperately low. Tredegar, in the midst of expansion, was suffering the shortage of raw material. The new ordnance shops had hardly time to set up their tools, and supplies from abroad came pitifully slow with the hazard of the tightening blockade. Lee talked of making pikes for Jackson's men. No, attack was not possible. Let Johnston retreat. . . .

He did, and McClellan shifted his whole army by transports down to Fort Monroe. Johnston could only follow, piecemeal, a brigade, a division, while "Prince John" Magruder imposed on McClellan by making threatening gestures with his handful down on the Peninsula.

Then Johnston joined Magruder in person, and immediately found fault with his defenses. In fact the whole Peninsula was indefensible, he said.

The army should concentrate at Richmond, Johnston maintained. Gustavus Smith, one of his commanders, pointed out that, with such a concentration, they could move on Washington.

Randolph, the new Secretary of War, opposed abandoning the Peninsula. He was an old navy man and he stuck at evacuating Norfolk and the navy yard.

Lee, the military adviser, also opposed surrendering the Peninsula without a fight. He was looking at larger angles, problems of supply from North Carolina—a total picture.

Each one seemed right when he spoke on that warm April afternoon in the President's office, when the six men talked until long after dark.

Smith, his chin beard thrust out below his willful mouth, spoke with energetic self-assertion. He held no doubts.

The commander of the other wing of Johnston's army, burly Longstreet, had mentioned that he thought McClellan would not attack before May. He had been cut off. What else had he meant to say? After that, he said no more. Slightly deaf, he strained to hear what was going on, his tough, stolid face showing nothing.

Then there were the three Virginians—Randolph, Lee, and Johnston; Randolph, the grandson of Thomas Jefferson, a courtly man who handled the details of the war office without asserting his views but gave his opinion when asked in the meeting; Lee, flower of a great Colonial line, son of a Revolutionary hero, husband of a descendant of Mrs. George Washington, tactful as military adviser, quietly taking the side of Randolph, though for different reasons; Joe Johnston, small and peppery and high-bred, holding with tart stubbornness to his views.

All were right. Compromise offered the only solution. So Davis sent Johnston back, with aggressive Smith and silent Longstreet, to hold the Peninsula line as long as possible *and* concentrate.

Nobody had been pleased. Johnston held until McClellan threatened, and then he retreated. Now they would have to concentrate here at Richmond, piecemeal again, with Norfolk gone and McClellan pushing on, flanked on the rivers by his gunboats. . . .

What should he have done instead? He had held Cabinet meetings almost daily. He had sought advice from everyone. But he made the decisions, and the responsibility was his alone.

What could he do now?

Mrs. Davis saw that she could not help him with reason or consolation. She could only try to divert him.

All their married life they had read together. He preferred history and biography and anything pertaining to governmental problems, but this surely was not the time for political treatises. He eschewed novels as "only a means of driving out more serious thoughts," but escape was necessary now. However, "the stream of light literature, which was just then gathering into a flood, had swept past him with few exceptions, from 1845 to 1861," and his wife had little selection. She recalled that he had enjoyed the adventures of Jorax in *The Handley Cross Hounds*, which ran serially, and she thought *Guy Livingstone* might be the book now.

She read as animatedly as she could the descriptions of Guy and the horses, though her husband showed only vague interest. But slowly, as she persevered, his imagination was caught. Gradually he forgot the Confederate army retreating toward Richmond and grew absorbed in the words his wife read.

The house grew silent, the city still, as he lay on the sofa all through the night while Varina's voice filled his world.

From his side she saw the dawn come, the slope-roofed houses smudged against the pink sky. . . .

CHAPTER FIFTEEN

Duel of the Heroes

IT HAS been pointed out that Richmond was an unwise choice for the capital because of its proximity to the enemy. This caused a concentration of troops far from any central point in the South, which, with obvious logistical advantages, would also require longer for Union armies to reach. This overlooks at least one simple point. In 1862 Richmond had to be defended: it was the arsenal of the Confederacy.

Also, if placing the capital there did cause a concentration of troops and material for a more determined defense, then it can be argued that Richmond was spared the quick fall of Nashville, Memphis, and New Orleans, all farther south in the Western sphere. Long after Tennessee had been occupied, northern Mississippi and Alabama desolated, the states south of Richmond in the Eastern sphere were still protected by this concentration and were producing for the Confederacy.

Finally Union armies, as well as Confederates, had to be concentrated there, for the proximity of the two capitals worked both ways. Threatening Washington formed part of Confederate strategy and immobilized Union troops, who would have been feeding happily in the Upper South if the Confederates followed a supine defensive policy which simply placed the capital as far away as possible.

If such a policy had been adopted, and Richmond had fallen and its adjacent country lost, the South would have lost—in addition to the arsenal—most of its salt and lead, much of its coal and iron; farm country from which the Army drew, and the only railroad lines running from northern Virginia to southern Georgia with direct connections—at Richmond, which also connected with the West.

These lines had to be protected *from the North* against cavalry raids or temporary loss, as the South lacked the means to repair or rebuild. Even at their best the railroads offered almost as many hazards to travelers as they did supplies to the armies. They had to be known to be believed.

Perhaps the simplest description of their fame, even today, came from an Alabama soldier in the recent World War. On a weekly radio show in London, broadcast to Americans, he was a guest when the program featured a quiz on American geography. When the question was asked, "What is the American physical phenomenon which, contrary to natural laws of running forward, runs backward," the Alabamian promptly answered, "Southern railroads."

In 1862 the same answer would have been more complicated. The lines were laid in every possible direction—all single-track, with insufficient sidings—and union depots were unknown. Wherever two railroads came to a town there were two depots (in Richmond five), and it was said that the only attention railroads gave the arrivals of their competitors was to make sure their own train left before the other got there. But such as they were, railroads fanned out from Richmond, which also manufactured practically everything for locomotives and trains.

As Richmond was being protected (as the capital and/or the arsenal), ordnance manufacture developed through the existing facilities and afforded ready access of material to the armies. The Ordnance Department, separate from the great plant of the Tredegar Iron Works, though helped by it, reactivated the large State Armory, converted several tobacco factories at the foot of Seventh Street, and used the facilities at various iron mills in Richmond—the center of iron manufacturing in the South. Under the genius of Gorgas, the arsenal and armory were turning out rifles, cartridges, caps and powder, infantry and cavalry accouterments, gun carriages and caissons and artillery harness, artillery ammunition, primers and fuses, and much else.

Gorgas was also having arsenals and powder mills developed at Fayetteville, Atlanta, Columbus, Macon, Selma, and other places, but in 1862 the production from these was negligible. Even those in Richmond were still woefully insufficient to supply the armies concentrated on their defense. Of all things, they needed time to develop equipment, skilled workmen and routine in order to profit from their groundwork.

The long shadow of the conscript catchers caused such a rush of "skilled" workmen to these plants that examinations had to be given, as in Civil Service. Under the direction of Gorgas, Major Brown— former artillery officer—abridged the U.S. *Field Ordnance Manual* in basing his examinations on mathematics, physics, and chemistry.

The examination scared away many, but those who passed were mostly able and qualified workers.

A small group of highly skillful men in the naval laboratories, under Matthew Fontaine Maury and Hunter Davidson, were developing the torpedoes which a U.S. naval historian said contributed more to Confederate water defenses than all else.

But the real vital core was the four acres of buildings along the Kanawha Canal—the Tredegar. Founded in 1836, it was owned by Joseph Anderson, a West Point graduate and brigadier in the Confederate Army, who was drafted back to run the Tredegar. The administration of this plant was as complex and difficult, on a smaller scale, as that of the government itself.

Rebuilding the plants for expansion in the midst of production, Anderson was likewise forced to change methods of obtaining supplies while virtually financing the business by turning into gold the Confederate money and cotton certificates with which he was partly paid.

He stimulated Virginia founders to set in blast furnaces which had been idle for a decade, only to have them break the contracts when the government fixed the price of pig iron at $50 a ton. In April, as McClellan's "On to Richmond" poised to strike, Anderson leased and purchased and equipped the furnaces on money advanced by the government.

He also bought subsidiary ironworks in Virginia's southwest mountains, where they were safe and their material could be hauled to the main plant on the canal. As the canal boats were inadequate, Anderson obtained a fleet of his own, with crews and their food and mules and their forage.

He fed at cost all his white workers (which necessitated his becoming a cattleman and keeping a standing herd of cattle), and the Negroes were largely convicts who the state fed.

Fortunately his coal came from the nearby Midlothian and Clover Hill mines, though he expanded production by reopening old mines—for which he built the machinery and hired the hands. From mining ore, felling trees to be converted into charcoal, smelting pig iron in primitive blast furnaces and hauling to the Tredegar, to producing widely varied finished products while converting, Anderson blended all details into a smoothness which few Confederate activities ever exhibited.

When the Union army slugged through the mud toward Richmond, the Tredegar was supplying virtually all the Confederate cannon (heavy and field) and much ammunition, caissons, and carriages; had rolled the iron for the *Virginia-Merrimac* and other ships, and was supplying the government shops with material from its shops, mill, and foundry.

This was the prize in the city for which McClellan had prepared since the Union defeat at Manassas—this and the prestige accruing to a nation's capital. A symbol and a stronghold, Richmond in that May was the heart of the new country's life.

The Western country and the Mississippi had collapsed at both ends, and only the grandiose immobility of the Union's Halleck saved the Confederate forces retreating under sick and apprehensive Beauregard. The East Coast had been battered by amphibious attacks, and the blockade was getting a real grip. The Richmond line was all that stood.

Against it moved the North's finest army, superbly equipped and heavily gunned, commanded by the Union's top general and assisted by the might of the U. S. Navy, using both the York and the James rivers.

2

Opposing McClellan was the South's last Hero, Joe Johnston. His halo had grown a little dim through successive retreats. Outgunned and outmanned, his forces possessed barely sufficient arms and ammunition, and the men themselves, some of whom stumbled into Richmond after the Williamsburg action, were anything but reassuring.

These convalescents, scarcely able to walk, had been sent ahead to save the ambulances "for those worse than they." According to DeLeon, these "mud-encrusted" men, wan, hollow-eyed and "utterly emaciated—many of them fell by the wayside; while others thankfully accepted the rough transportation of any chance wagon or cart. . . ." Stragglers came too, escaping from Winder's clutches into the warrens of dives around the wharf. Others, too exhausted to care, slept in cellar doorways and even on sidewalks. The Richmond observer, speaking for the people, said, "Were *these* the only dependence of their hopes and their cause?"

For fear of defeat went deeper into the vitals than it had last year at Manassas. Then the two sections, after arguing so long, went from words to blows—but somehow the fight was still a family row. Since then New Orleans had suffered Beast Butler, whom the President proclaimed an outlaw (he probably would have hanged if captured), and the angry cousin had changed into a foreign conqueror.

In victory the enemy showed none of the spirit of what the "rebellion" was supposedly about—to return the errant sisters to Abraham's bosom—and Butler's vengeful actions denied all of Lincoln's inaugural assurances. *We denounce the lawless invasion by armed force of the soil of any State or Territory, no matter under what pretext, as the greatest of crimes.*

On his way to Washington, Lincoln defined "invasion" as the marching of an army into a Southern state "without the consent of her people and with hostile intent toward them." But, he went on, "if the United States should merely hold and retake her forts and other property, and collect the duty on foreign importations . . . would any one or all these things be invasion or coercion?" Now those year-old words belonged with the dead abstractions of secession that had gotten the people into this.

The realities were the wanton plundering of personal property, citizens removed from their homes under cheap pretexts and put at hard labor, and women exposed to insult.

Even on the Peninsula, where McClellan's personal policy was humane and chivalrous, one of his privates reported:

We pitched our tents amid the charred and blackened ruins of what had been the beautiful and aristocratic village of Hampton. . . . The only building left standing of all the village was the massive old Episcopal church. Here Washington had worshipped, and its broad aisles had echoed to the foot-steps of armed men during the Revolution. In the church-yard the tombs had been broken open. Many tombstones were broken and overthrown, and at the center of the church [was] a big hole . . . [where someone] had been digging for the cornerstone and its buried mementoes.

Ahead of this army, like wildlife before a forest fire, the refugees came pouring into Richmond. In homelessness and fright the women came in carriages and wagons and carts, some with Negroes, all with belongings hastily packed, all with stories . . .

Remembering Butler, the men began sending the women and children out of Richmond.

Government records were packed and millions worth of tobacco made ready to burn.

The Yankees are coming meant alien, enemy, conqueror, despoiler —all the dread unknown that had nothing to do with union one way or the other.

Only Jefferson Davis bothered about the rights and theories any more, and he preserved his outward calm by absorption in tables of organization. With enemy gunboats moving up the James River (under orders from U. S. Secretary of Navy Welles "to shell the city to surrender"), with Joe Johnston holding his shaken army together on its retreat through the mud, Davis reproached the general for not complying with the law regarding the organization of brigades and divisions. He wrote:

I have been much harassed by the delay to place the regiments of some of the states in brigades together . . . while some have expressed surprise at my patience when orders to you were not observed. . . . I hope you will, as you can, proceed to organize your troops as heretofore instructed, and that the returns will relieve us of the uncertainty now felt as to the number and relations of the troops.

There was justice in this untimely appeal for more accurate information from Johnston. The general was secretive with the government. He claimed it dated from the time when he attended a cabinet meeting on military plans and, before he left town, a Richmonder related to him the decisions arrived at. This would tend to uncommunicativeness, and Johnston was naturally lax in his reports. Seizing on this dereliction and frantic at the imminent fall of the movement, Davis clung to bureaucratic order in his desperate need for certainties.

To the public he presented a brave front. He was helped in this by his wife and by the increasing importance of religion in his life. During the retreat of Johnston's army, the President was baptized at his home by Dr. Minnegerode of St. Paul's and privately received into the Episcopal Church. His wife, attending to temporal matters, gave a big levee at the White House with the armory band going full blast.

It was in the midst of the party that Jefferson Davis was called into his study to receive a messenger. When he returned, there was no change in his manner, but he drew his wife aside.

"The enemy's gunboats are nearing Richmond," he said. "You and the children must leave town tomorrow."

Varina needed a moment. She knew as well as anybody the sketchiness of the river batteries hastily improvised at Drewry's Bluff, and in the Union fleet was the dread *Monitor*. Only a few days before, after the destruction of the *Virginia,* one of its officers had brought her a flag captured during its brief glory. It was still damp with blood, and she had to go to her room, "sick over the dead and dying on both sides." The officer who had brought her the flag, John

Taylor Wood, an in-law of her husband's by his former marriage, was now collecting sharpshooters to fight against the *Monitor*.

Varina knew all right what her husband's words meant, but she needed only the moment. The party went on, and the guests, diverted from their fears, stayed late.

The next day, against her will (for she wanted to stay with Banny), Mrs. Davis took the children to Raleigh, North Carolina.

3

Seven miles below Richmond, where the river is only a mile wide, the last shore battery before the city was erected on a 200-foot cliff on the south bank, known as Drewry's Bluff. The action at Drewry's Bluff gets short shrift in history. No fabled names led on either side, and only a few were engaged in a simple straight-on fight between gunboats and land guns. Yet it decided the fate of Richmond and directed Union plans for the rest of the war. The city could not be taken by water.

On the May day when the Union fleet steamed toward Richmond, the people did not know that. These boats, driving the few armed steamers of the James River patrol before them, had passed all the river forts on the way, and there was no reason to believe that the guns behind the makeshift entrenchments could accomplish what the New Orleans forts had failed at—especially against the ironclad *Monitor*.

The few guns, including several of Brooke's rifled guns removed from the steamers, were mounted on naval carriages, with all the tackle used on a man-of-war, and manned by the ship's officers with the crews filled out by survivors of the Mississippi fleet and farmers from Chesterfield County.

Below them the river was obstructed with logs and stones and iron rubbish in piles driven in the bottom, and several schooners and sloops in the main channel—leaving only a narrow, intricate passage directly under the guns.

The connection between the city side and the fort side of the river was a brand-new pontoon bridge, even more extemporaneous than the defenses. Entirely the idea of a recently commissioned captain, also recently transferred from cavalry to engineers, the bridge showed what could be accomplished with singleness of purpose. Captain Blackford (later Jeb Stuart's engineer) ignored red tape as completely as those hard-minded agents in London.

Given authority, as no one else seemed interested, young Blackford took one look at the ring-around-a-rosy setup of government agencies (a minor though more charming version of the Pentagon) and went straight to two civilians—a carpenter-contractor and a shipbuilder. They were willing to help, but all the skilled workmen were in the Army. Captain Blackford then went to Winder and gave that grim old army man a task to his liking.

Winder's plug-uglies impressed five hundred able-bodied men from the streets. Black and white, they were dragged out of the dives around the wharf, in Rockett's, and up toward the tough bright-light section south of the Square. Even house servants were snatched, and the owners knew nothing of it until there was silence in the kitchen at dinnertime.

A fleet of canal boats and schooners was raised at the same time. Blocks from local stonecutters' served as anchors, and lumber from local yards provided the planking. They worked toward the center of the river from the two shores—the carpenter at one end, the shipbuilder at the other, and Captain Blackford in the middle.

Five days from his arrival in Richmond with the idea, a four-mule wagon was driven across the bridge.

But the people's faith in these measures was indicated by a paid ad in the *Dispatch:*

I will be one of 100 to join any party, officered by determined and resolute officers, to board the whole fleet of boats and take them at all hazards, to save this beautiful city from destruction. I am not a resident of this state [but] my name can be had by applying at this office.

Early in the morning when the first fire was heard, muffled by moisture from a heavy rain the night before, Governor Letcher and old Mayor Mayo gathered a crowd in Capitol Square, to arm themselves and defend the city to the end.

Down on the north bank of the river John Taylor Wood collected a group of sharpshooters to fire from rifle pits. This Wood, from Louisiana, a grandson of President Taylor, had resigned his instructor's post at the Naval Academy at secession. Joining the Virginia Navy, he first served in the early batteries on the Potomac, and more recently as lieutenant on the *Virginia-Merrimac*. With his improvised warfare on the gunboats, he began an irregular career as archaic in its personal adventuring as the culture for which he fought.

Across the river the fort's guns opened confidently and strong. The wooden ships, unable to maneuver or run the gauntlet, kept out of range. Another ship dropped out from an accident, and the fearful *Monitor* could not get the elevation for her guns. The shore gunners bounced shots off her iron hide for the hell of it, though no harm was done. The real fight settled down between the batteries and the iron-clad *Galena,* who moved as close as six hundred yards.

She showed that she could not seriously damage the fortifications and, often hit herself, suffered over thirty casualties in what shortly proved to be a hopeless assignment. The firing opened at seven forty-five in the morning. At eleven that chapter in the fight for Richmond was closed.

As the boats returned downriver out of range, the *Monitor* passed close to the sharpshooters in the north bank and got a yell from John Taylor Wood.

"Tell Captain Jeffers that's not the way to Richmond," he said.

4

Jefferson Davis knew that the people of Richmond realized their salvation from naval bombardment only narrowed their danger to occupation by ground troops—and no Union army had been defeated since Manassas. Their fears showed in frantic flights from the city. Hastily packed carriages and wagons rattled through the streets from morning until night, and, in a housing shortage greater than today, families left their homes standing vacant. (Refugees, who had already run to town from the countryside, moved in.)

The President could admit that government actions did nothing to reassure the people. Packages of archives moved steadily through the streets toward the depot. Canal boats loaded with other packages were towed beyond the city. Steam was kept up in an engine to haul the Treasury's gold. Congress, some of whose members had wanted to be near the fighting so they could exchange the robes of state for the sword of the field, hastily convened and exchanged almost anything for a railroad seat south.

Postmaster Reagan, with all his troubles, had to arrange for a new contract. Hoyer & Ludwig, at the enemy approach, sold most of their presses and many stones and their Confederate stamp equipment to a jeweler who decided to switch to lithography as more profitable during a war. He took a dozen or so of Hoyer & Ludwig's apprentices and headed south—to failure.

At this time the Virginia legislature and Richmond City Council convened and passed a resolution to defend the city to the end, even if it were reduced to ashes. They formed a committee and came to visit Mr. Davis, alone in his big gray house. This heartened the President in his ordeal of bearing alone the fate of the experiment.

No matter what came of defending the capital, he could always say it was the people's choice. From that one choice, anyway, he would be free of charges of despotic and wrong decisions.

He wrote his wife:

The great temporal object is to secure our independence, and they who engage in strife for personal or party aggrandizement deserve contemptuous forgetfulness. I have no political wish beyond the success of our cause, no personal desire but to be relieved from further connection with office; opposition in any form can only disturb me insomuch as it may endanger the public welfare. . . . I wish I could learn to let people alone who snap at me, in forbearance and charity to turn as well from the cats as the snakes. . . .

From this credo, he tried to use all forbearance and charity in dealing with General Johnston, who had now retreated so close to Richmond that, from rooftops, the enemy's tented villages could be seen.

The crucial, all-or-nothing battle must be joined. Joe Johnston had to fight.

5

Joseph Eggleston Johnston had achieved, through no acts of his own, the position of his heart's desire. He held top rank in the Confederate armies in effect—in the minds of the people if not on Mr. Davis's list. One of the men whom the President had placed above him, Albert Sidney Johnston, was dead. The other two, Lee and Cooper, no longer in the field, were lost in the anonymity of office work.

Adjutant General Cooper, settling "his head on his cravat with the aid of a forefinger," tugging nervously "with the something that is always wrong inside of his collar," performed nothing more exciting than inspection tours, and at that sometimes to Charleston, where the people complained of his being a New Yorker.

Charleston also had pecked away at Lee's crumbling reputation. Already called "Granny" for his retreats in western Virginia (where he suffered the impossible task of co-ordinating political generals Wise and Floyd), Lee aroused the ire of the blue-blooded South Carolinians by putting them to work at fortifications. Now, as military adviser, he performed the milk-and-water chores of liaison between the chief clerk then in the war office (called Secretary) and the decisions of the supreme authority.

Even Beauregard, Johnston's old rival from The Victory (Manassas), lurked in the shadows of the all-conquering Union armies of the West. But those Yankees, gorging off the fatness of the occupied country, were far away, a side issue. They were minor characters who, acting out the subplot, had now retired to the wings.

The stage was cleared for the two great protagonists, McClellan and Johnston, in the death struggle for the pearl of the Confederacy. The winner could hold the center of the stage alone for all time to come.

In this last war of the individual the battle for a nation's capital became a personal battle for immortality in which the antagonists, strangely, were not enemies. Their enemies were their own civil leaders. For Lincoln had plagued McClellan as Davis had plagued Johnston. He had interfered with McClellan's plans and strategy and bothered the general with his own ideas. For his part, McClellan, growing imperious as his moment with history neared, became highhanded with the civilian and refused to share the confidences of his grandiose plans.

McClellan, also conceiving of the rebellion in terms of what his President said it was about, fought as a duelist in a contest—to win, not to destroy. General Richard Taylor said that "he and a gallant band of officers supporting him impressed a generous, chivalric spirit on the war." In that spirit he approached his rival for posterity. In that spirit Joe Johnston retreated warily before him.

6

Johnston had not engaged in fighting since last summer, when, at Manassas, he became co-holder of the Southern Hero title with Beauregard. Since then, becoming sole holder by default, Johnston had cherished his reputation like a champion reluctant to risk his title. In pursuing his cautious policy, he was true to his essentially defensive military nature. Finally, he was one of the Confederates who never thought in terms of a rebellion—its specific and special needs.

Remembering the limitless U.S. supplies from his quartermaster days, he was wasteful with resources. When he abandoned the Manassas line he burned clothes sent from states, burned and scattered a million pounds of bacon, and left heavy guns at the time Gorgas and the Tredegar were so pressed that citizens of Richmond put on a drive for "scrap iron about the house, broken ploughshares about the farm," the iron railings from their homes and yards, anything. Tobacco factories gave some of their machinery, and money was raised from a bazaar to which the people contributed the goods. Even church bells from Marietta, Georgia, were accepted. Then, when he retreated from Yorktown, he again abandoned heavy guns, fifty-six.

In contrast Forrest, who did understand the specific needs of a rebellion, armed two whole commands by capturing weapons and ammunition from the enemy in action.

When Johnston went down to hold the Peninsula "as long as possible," in accordance with Davis's compromise plan, he had no intention of fulfilling the order. He said himself that "events on the Peninsula would soon compel the Confederate government to adopt my way." Here is the clear indication that Johnston thought in terms of his own personal position, of being justified to history regardless of rebellion.

Yet, at the age of fifty-four, with only his pay for the support of his family, he gave up the fruits of a lifetime of service with the U. S. Army and came with Virginia with the noblest of sentiments. He said:

The revolution begun was justified by the maxims so often repeated by Americans, that free government is founded on the consent of the governed, and that every community strong enough to establish and maintain its independence has a right to assert it. Having been educated in such opinions, I naturally determined to return to the State of which I was a native, join the people among whom I was born, and live with my kindred, and, if necessary, fight in their defense. . . .

Their defense did not take precedence over that of his honor and reputation. He was as touchy as Davis over his personal honor, as small and mean in defending it; and vigilance of his reputation made him jealous and petty. To the end he underrated Stonewall Jackson. To Lee, who had been fond of him since they were classmates at West Point, Johnston gave no credit for the present Peninsula concentration which he now led, though it had been entirely the work of the military adviser.

However Lee disliked his anomalous position (as he wrote his wife), by tactful suggestion and patient persistence he forced the President and Joe Johnston to meet the same type of military problem which had defeated Albert Sidney Johnston at Nashville.

In Virginia and in Kentucky there were three enemy forces and one main city. Sidney Johnston, using three separate forces of his own, lost one in action; the other two were nullified and retreated, uncovering the city to fall without a defense.

Lee kept only a single brigade to observe one Union force, of forty thousand, in northern Virginia. He put a striking force of thirteen thousand under Stonewall Jackson in the Valley to hit the scattered Unions there in detail and immobilize the other forty thousand. Then he concentrated the bulk of all available troops against what he had perceived to be the main thrust.

To gain time for the concentration, the thirteen thousand men under Magruder, who held the Yorktown line against McClellan, demonstrated so convincingly that McClellan waited until every detail of his vast army was perfected and siege guns brought up. Magruder, as General Taylor said, "was a man of a singular versatility, of a boiling headlong courage . . . too excitable for high command. Widely known for social attractions, he had an histrionic vein, and indeed was fond of private theatricals. Few managers could have surpassed him in imposing on an audience a score of supernumeraries for a grand army."

If McClellan brought a chivalric spirit, "Prince John" Magruder brought a color and splash and fine theatricality to those early days of armies fighting armies.

But for all the success of "the great demonstrator," Johnston gave Magruder short shrift. After Magruder suffered the comedown from commander of eastern Virginia to that of one of Johnston's lieutenants, Johnston found fault with his fortifications and said "no one but McClellan would have hesitated to attack." Then Johnston planned the retreat against the known wishes of the recent military council in Richmond.

It is true, from other evidences, that the fortifications were inadequate, and McClellan, watchful of his destiny, showed "a slowness and hesitancy" to commit. But Magruder *had* achieved the necessary objective in Lee's larger plan and made possible Johnston's command of the large army against McClellan.

With all this smallness Johnston, when there was no rival or impinger on his honor, was a man of honest and warm affection that endeared him to his family and friends, fellow officers, and soldiers. Many mention his charm, his humor and flashes of real wit. Though he could be spiteful and vindictive when aroused, ordinarily his dignity was a natural and fine quality. As a rule he got on well with his subordinates and not well with equals. His real feud was with his (unacknowledged) superior, the President.

Johnston and Davis had known each other at the Point, where their dislike was mutual and probably chemical. When they met they were like two well-bred men who loathe each other but, in common interest, behave with constrained courtesy and all the form of their day. But when not in personal contact their letters read like the ill-natured exchanges of a couple of cranks who have nothing better to do than to excel each other in insults.

Because the fate of the Confederacy was virtually at stake, and because Davis believed that Johnston, despite everything, was the best man to defend the city, the President tried not to interfere as the decisive battle approached. Even when Johnston lifted the screen on his movements to advise that he intended to defend the Chickahominy, twenty-five miles from Richmond, and the whole Cabinet turned against Johnston's army having the river at its back, Davis would not interfere. Naturally Davis was relieved the next day, when Johnston advised them that he had crossed the Chickahominy and would defend the *crossing* of the river.

In friendliness of spirit Davis got his friend, Postmaster Reagan, to ride with him for a visit to the army at the Chickahominy. They passed through Rockett's, the section east of the wharf, and came upon high ground which gave a view ahead. Davis halted in surprise at seeing a tented encampment half a mile away.

"Whose tents are those?" he asked.

Reagan told him they were Hood's Texas Brigade.

"No! Hood's Brigade is down on the Chickahominy."

Then Reagan realized that the President had not been informed of a new shift of Johnston's to the outskirts of Richmond. Reagan explained that he had visited his Texas friends there the night before. "And," he added, "General Johnston is in that brick house off to the right."

Again the President said, "No. He's down on the Chickahominy."

Reagan perceived that the President was unable to absorb the shock and explained again that he thought Davis had known that the army had changed plans. When Davis at last understood, "the look of surprise that swept over his face showed a trace of pain."

Immediately with Colonel Ives, one of his staff, he rode to Johnston's headquarters. The general informed him that the ground along the Chickahominy was low and marshy, poor for defense, and the water bad. Here the ground was high, the water good, and they were closer to supplies.

The President absorbed this and then asked if Johnston intended to fight here. Johnston's answer was unsatisfactory. Davis then grew alarmed and hurried back to Richmond to call another cabinet meeting.

There was nowhere else for Johnston to retreat. If he went backward any farther, Richmond would be abandoned. Davis could not accept the idea of surrendering Richmond without a fight. The cabinet members were equally anxious. It was then that Lee, on being asked his advice, showed the emotion so seldom seen by anyone. With tears in his eyes he said, "But Richmond must not be given up—it shall not be given up."

On this line, then, Johnston had to commit his ambition and bring McClellan to commit his.

7

In neither of those men was there the instinct to kill or the trained habit of hitting to hurt. They were crafty, military-wise counterpunchers, trying to feint the enemy out of position, lead him off balance. Either could be counted on to take advantage of the other's mistakes.

Johnston's reports reveal the clearest and most comprehensive grasp of any military situation. He eliminated every move his enemy was unlikely to make and weighed accurately each of the possible moves. Then his purpose was to frustrate the enemy's intention by evasion or, if the enemy blundered, to strike a counterblow.

But now the two Heroes had sparred for months without either striking a blow, and now for weeks they had reconnoitered and maneuvered, watched and guessed, one advancing, one retreating, and neither had made a mistake. They had covered eighty miles with consummate skill in doing nothing, except . . . McClellan was at Richmond and Johnston could go no farther.

Once Johnston's men dug in, McClellan stopped. To cover his reluctance to tangle, he turned back to his very real talent for arranging details in order. He built entrenchments to protect his base at the headwaters of the York, thirty-eight miles from Richmond, where one of Virginia's few good railroads had recently been built. Near by the White House, formerly owned by Martha Custis when Washington came courting her there, was now owned and occupied by Mrs. Lee, who reluctantly left under a full escort supplied by McClellan with all possible courtesies.

Aside from arranging angles for supply, McClellan, who was due east of Richmond, hopefully placed a corps north of Richmond to meet the forty thousand Unions under McDowell, only fifty-odd miles away at Fredericksburg.

When McClellan had started up the Peninsula a month before, his was the main advance in an over-all pincer movement. Supported himself by river gunboats, he was to receive the co-operation of McDowell's forty thousand striking straight down from the north while McClellan moved heavily from the east. With the James River to the south of Richmond, the Confederates would have been forced to retreat west and abandon the city—*if* McDowell came.

But Lee, the military adviser, handled his own President while McClellan did not handle his. With a counter over-all plan, Lee used the genius of Stonewall Jackson to wreck the Union plan.

In the Valley of Virginia, with thirteen thousand men, Jackson struck in detail two Union forces (under Fremont the fake and Banks the buffoon), defeated them, and not only immobilized McDowell's forty thousand but caused one of those divisions, under Shields, to come after him.

After Jackson defeated Shields too, Lincoln forgot all about the pincer plan on Richmond and thought of McDowell only as the savior of Washington. The combined forces of the Unions in northern Virginia and in the Valley aggregated around seventy thousand, but Jackson's name suddenly took on a dread magic and the Northern forces became paralyzed in waiting for his next thrust.

While Washington waited for him, and McClellan waited for McDowell (who was never coming), Joe Johnston hit McClellan.

McClellan's pause for order, which possibly prevented Johnston from retreating right through Franklin Street, gave the Confederates time to complete their concentration, rest their bodies, and regain their morale, and gave Johnston the decision to try consequences.

So, at long last, the two posterity seekers, the fancy boxers, were forced to slug it out.

It was not their game.

Alexander, great Confederate artillerist and literate observer, said Johnston's attack (at Seven Pines) was "phenomenally mismanaged."

Units of McClellan's were pushed back by the fury of some of the clumsy blows, but they were not routed.

For all the long-laid plans of both generals, the confusion was terrible over the whole field, and about the most decisive action occurred in late afternoon when Johnston, recklessly exposing himself in order to gain information, was struck by a bullet and a shell fragment.

He was being carried to the rear on a stretcher, and looked about gone, when Davis saw him. The President, unable to resist the battle-field, had ridden about with his staff all afternoon, getting in every-body's way but oblivious to the lack of welcome. Now, at seeing the commander laid low, he forgot everything in the "great concern" which even Johnston said he manifested.

Characteristic of Davis's sweetness when natural, and naïveté in relations with men, he impulsively offered his home to his old acquaint-ance. Past squabbles held no meaning before the suffering of the man who, finally, was his comrade in arms. But Johnston's staff had already arranged for a house in the quiet old section on Church Hill, and the President's offer was declined.

Davis watched the staff carry their general on toward an ambulance. Then Davis had to find Gustavus Smith, second-in-command, and advise him to take over. The day was not yet done. In the smoky twi-light much could still be accomplished before the long May light darkened.

Unexpectedly then on the understudy fell history's moment. Only forty-one years old, powerful and vigorous, Gustavus Smith was one of the few whose assured assertions Davis would accept. Since he came down with the army last summer from his position as New York's street commissioner, the Kentuckian had talked for boldness—at the Fairfax conference last fall, and in April in Richmond he advocated the concentration in front of Richmond from where they might attack Washington.

Now the chance came to the proud-mouthed man whose action under fire was as bold as his words. He had been noticeably cool all day, seemingly unmoved under the heaviest fire. He needed only to go from following orders to delivering them, from execution to de-cision.

He spoke . . . he faltered . . . the assurance slipped, fell away. . . .

The units bungled through the deepening dusk. The battle was over, and so was Smith. Between sunset and nightfall his hour came and passed.

As hungry for glory as any man on either side, when he walked into the bright light alone on the empty stage his nerve failed him. Was it possible he would not live up to his own self-evaluation, and what he had led others to expect? The man who had not been afraid of any enemy guns grew afraid of himself.

By next day a physical paralysis had set in. His adjutant warned the President against giving him any responsibility. . . .

But by next day the President had already appointed a new commander, Lee, and given his opponents a new reason to attack him. Lee, called the "King of Spades" for forcing the hotbloods to dig trenches, at that moment would have been voted the least likely to succeed.

The day he took over Johnston's army Lee did nothing to change the opinion. A second indecisive battle was fought. Lines were straightened. And McClellan, his rendezvous with fame postponed, settled down to a siege against another opponent.

Davis went back to his empty house alone. At least Richmond was safe for the moment. Maybe they could attack McClellan again. . . .

He climbed the long, narrow curving steps to his room upstairs. Now he could unpack the books and sword, the pistols used when he was a hero at Buena Vista, which the day before he had packed in readiness to send to his family.

He had written his wife, "These articles will have a value to the boys in after time, and to you now. . . ."

He raised the windows for the cool night air, and as he undressed before the marble-topped bureau he heard the wagons of wounded rumbling over the cobblestoned streets.

CHAPTER SIXTEEN

The God Emerges

THE month of June after the battle (called Seven Pines) meant to Jefferson Davis, in varying degrees, what it meant to Richmond—more wounded, a new hero, and new hope.

For the people, the wounded started coming in a grim parade all through the night after the first day's battle, and once more life was disrupted to find room for them and to arrange care. Though hospital facilities had been greatly expanded since the summer before, the casualties were much heavier (6,134 total), and churches and dry-goods stores and tobacco warehouses again provided shelter.

For Davis, though he could not endure suffering in others, the detail of medical service occupied his mind little. He had forbidden Mrs. Davis to nurse in the hospitals on the grounds that her presence might cause constraint. This, of course, was used against him by enemies whose own wives did no nursing and were not obligated, as was she, to perform official social chores. It was primarily the plans and organization leading to combat that absorbed him, and here he shared more wholly the South's enthusiasm for their new hero—Stonewall Jackson.

From "Fool Tom" to "Old Jack" he had come in a year from eccentric to legend, and his fabulous deeds were recited from end to end of America, in France and England. In lonely farms all over his own South, in the crowded homes and on the disorderly streets of Richmond, the tales of his lightning strokes kept hope alive.

He was one of them too, a simple countryman from Virginia's western counties, molded by a hard life to pray and to kill. Even his eccentricities became lovable manifestations of his genius. His fire-and-brimstone Presbyterianism gave grim right to the fabled marches of his legions.

There was romance in his invincibles too. Jackson's "Foot Cavalry" they proudly called themselves. Among them was Company F, Richmond's cream, who had dropped their leather-compartmented knapsacks for the loose haversacks swinging by a cord, and more likely to hold a few grains of corn and a stolen apple than a change of linen and crested stationery.

Then there was his fierce cavalry, led by black-bearded Turner Ashby on his milk-white horse. But all of "Jackson's men" had the color and mobility of cavalry. Something new and bright and terrible had flashed in the war, and it was a new song in the hearts of the battered people: "Stonewall Jackson's Way."

Davis saw him less romantically, less as a meteor than as a weapon to be used in larger plans. Old Jack's silences and brusqueness, his lack of side and society-column newsworthiness, made the people's hero less interesting to Davis as a man. He was too impressed with the status of gentleman to evaluate at his highest this iron-visaged rustic. The President did not envision new independent exploits for Jackson. He was to collaborate in a strategy devised by General Lee.

General Lee did not cease suggesting the larger strategy when he changed from military adviser to army commander. Only now the suggestions, though still tactfully given, were less devious. They could be more direct, because they applied to his personal execution. And Davis accepted them wholly, for he trusted this soldier who had not yet won the people's hearts.

Because of Lee's new plan, Davis's hopes were more specific than those of his countrymen. Richmond had a reprieve and a new hero; but Davis hoped, with Lee, for a Cannae.

2

The Chickahominy is a mean little old river, hardly more than a creek as it passes in front of Richmond on the east at an angle from north to south. In a wet spring, as in 1862, the water overflows its marshy banks and becomes a wide and sinister swamp which forms a not inconsiderable military hazard.

When McClellan settled down with deliberation before Richmond, the bulk of his forces were in front of the swollen Chickahominy, on the Richmond side of the river. To the north of Richmond, where he wistfully waited for McDowell, one corps was across or behind the river. Thus one segment of his army was separated from the major force by the Chickahominy.

Lee's plan was to contain this major force of McClellan's with a small but fiercely demonstrating unit of his own. There he planned to use Magruder, "the great demonstrator." The bulk of his own forces would strike McClellan's separated force straight on, from west to east, while from the north Jackson would slip down and strike it in flank. Not only would this sizable Union force be destroyed, but so would McClellan's flank, and he would be forced to retreat with the river at his back.

To execute this plan Lee had to divide his numerically inferior force in the presence of an enemy *and* leave the three Union armies in northern Virginia with no more threat against them than the name of Jackson. Old Jack was to steal away to Richmond. Though this was audacious, it was not reckless. Lee counted on McClellan.

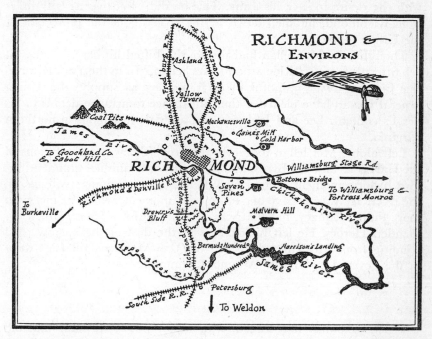

Pinkerton's "shrewd and daring operatives" had already played on the hero's apprehension by bringing reports of two hundred thousand men in Lee's army, and he was concerned with his own safety. So Lee, unlike Joe Johnston, who figured what McClellan would do when attacking, figured what he would do when attacked.

As it happened, everything went wrong except the audacity and Lee's estimate of its effect upon McClellan. The bold strategy failed in sloppy tactics, but offense caused reputation-conscious McClellan to worry what Lee would do next. Worrying, he evaded the blows by retreat—but it was retreat away from Richmond.

The Confederate strategy was too grand for inexperienced and unproven subordinates and the poor staff work from Lee on down. Jackson suffered an unexplained relapse. In addition to arriving late the first day, so that the original trap was exposed, he fought only one engagement (Gaines' Mill) in a manner to live up to his reputation. When, despite incredibly poor co-ordination in the parts, Lee caught McClellan in another trap (Frayser's Farm), Jackson showed so little vigor or initiative that the enemy again slipped away.

In fact, in six pitched battles and constant skirmishing, McClellan lost only one engagement. But he lost the initiative and became obsessed with the desire to save his army. This he did—but over twenty miles from Richmond, huddled down by the river under the protection of the Union gunboats.

Thoughtfully McClellan had previously shifted his base, because of Jeb Stuart's famous "Ride around McClellan," from the York River to the James. Always mindful of such matters as supply, the Union general was to have plenty of time and peace to arrange details to his heart's content. Lee and Jackson went after those Unions in northern Virginia.

Left alone, McClellan rode over the great Tidewater plantations of the Harrisons and the Byrds, and there, in that vanished grandeur, his own historic moment faded slowly like the long summer twilights on the river. He was to have one more brief moment, which he met with more than adequacy, but that was not enough for a nation which demanded Heroes. He left his chances in the dust of the narrow road winding from Mechanicsville (first day) to Malvern Hill (last day) in the Seven Days' Battle Around Richmond.

3

When that dust had settled, with new reputations made and old ones broken, the man who emerged was Lee. In appointing Lee, Davis had shown judgment and courage, though the President could not have imagined that the quiet tactful gentleman was to emerge as the God, and ultimately the Symbol, of the Confederacy.

His victory had the size and authority that turned the tide of the people's spirits. All over the South faith revived, and in the collection of forces he had handled during the Seven Days an *esprit* was born. In the damp, dusty, hazy heat of the Virginia Peninsula, Lee reorganized those forces into an army which fused into the unit the qualities of the individual Confederate soldier.

Out of the frontier's individualism, the hot land's romanticism and violence and pride, came the swaggering fury that needed only to be blended, given direction and unity. Discipline would never accomplish it. Ready to hand was their kinship born of the fierce eagerness to fight for their native land. That, properly led, would use their undisciplined aggressiveness toward the enemy.

Lee gave them the leadership, the sense of their own unconquerableness that made them more terrible than the sum of their parts. Out of the cross section of the South—the rail-lean mountaineer and the thin-boned city dandy, the scrawny dirt farmer and the droopy swamp rat, the lordly plantation master and the humble family-style planter; out of the red clay and piedmont, the piny woods and deep timber, the bayou and the brush, from sun-baked villages and Charleston's Battery, from New Orleans's Vieux Carré to Richmond's West Franklin—out of the blood of the regional self-image came that dirty, ragged, stinking fighting entity striding toward immortality as the Army of Northern Virginia.

With that one army and one campaign behind him, Lee rose beyond fame or popularity. He was never spoken of with the other heroes. Only militarily was he spoken of as the commander of the Army of Northern Virginia, which is the only army he ever had or evinced any interest in. Historians even today write of "Lee's armies." They were Davis's armies. But from the end of the Seven Days, the one army that Lee actually commanded could no longer be Davis's toy. This was to have a profound effect upon the Confederacy.

For now Jefferson Davis knew an exultance that must have more than compensated for every burden and ill, large and small, he had suffered during the birth of his nation. As he walked to his office, in his Confederate gray suit and light felt hat, he could see and hear on every hand a new confidence in the people.

They felt more solid about their new country than they had a year before. They had stood the ordeals, fought off the invader, and molded a new empire not with abstractions but with deeds.

They faced the future with steady gaze, looking to their independence as the Yankees must eventually abandon hope of conquering them.

Essentially romantic rather than realistic, the people returned quickly to their natural buoyancy. In the days the sweet heavy heat, tanged with tobacco, and the slow-falling misty dusks, like a haze, were not conducive to practical thinking. The people again tended their gardens, large and small, from the walled secret worlds of the Court End of town to the modest lawns on old Church Hill; they cleaned the fanlights over their white doorways, looked at the shadowed designs of iron grille on blue nights, and they could not believe anything could destroy their enduring pattern.

Their leader, taking the summer alone in his city home like any native, and worrying about his sick son, wrote his wife of their high hopes—at home and abroad.

CHAPTER SEVENTEEN

The War Gets a Slogan

IN THE long hot summer when the people followed the continued successes of their god and new hero, Lee and Jackson, and could even look toward the West with sudden expectancy, Judah Benjamin was unobtrusively turning the favorable events to the use of his department.

Cool in the deserted quiet of his office, uncluttered by details or advisers or even assistants, he worked effortlessly at his green-covered black walnut table from nine to three. He had only five clerks and a Negro porter, and the total salaries of the Confederate State Department, including the Secretary's, amounted to little more than $12,000 a year. His former assistant, Browne, a British-born Washington newspaperman, had been drafted to the President's staff (along with John Taylor Wood), and Benjamin had not replaced him.

The only physical difficulty of his office was the awkwardness and time element in communicating with Mason and Slidell. Sometimes months passed before the dispatches reached Europe, and occasionally Benjamin read his own dispatches in Northern papers. Even this failed to disturb his equanimity. Working easily on the basis of doing the best he could, he never worried about failures beyond his control.

When the office door was shut, if there were no conferences with the President, he strolled home through the fragrant heat and, in his red-brick house on upper Main Street, settled down with unmarred pleasure to his dinner. Though not a heavy eater, he relished fine foods and managed to get almost everything he wanted except hors d'oeuvres. This loss really pained him, but still he had his sherry, which he imported by the cask.

Having some cotton of his own at Mobile, which he continually shipped abroad, he was undisturbed by the rising prices and certainly never experimented with coffee made of parched sweet potatoes. That summer calico went to $3.00 a yard, bleached cotton to $3.50, muslin to $6.00, and shoemakers cut boot tops out of old sails, colored them with gun blacking, and sold them for $50 a pair.

No more interested in the people now than before secession, Benjamin passed the evenings reading or playing cribbage with his brother-in-law. Jules de St. Martin was as equable as Benjamin. On coming to Richmond after the fall of New Orleans, when friends asked him of his losses, he shrugged and said, "I am ruined, *voilà tout.*" Of an affectionate nature, Jules seemed to enjoy sharing Benjamin's home more than did his sister, now in Paris.

Benjamin was freer of the President's demands than usual. Though Davis was coming to lean more heavily on him, the President was more occupied in the summer by the armies.

Oppressed by the heat and dust of that summer, Davis sought relief by riding out in the afternoons to the camps around Richmond. Then, when Lee's reorganized army had moved to northern Virginia after fresh enemies, Davis had the satisfying dispatches of victory to read.

Lee and Jackson gave a couple of bad beatings (Cedar Mountain and Second Manassas) to the new Union general, Pope, who concentrated all the forces still in northern Virginia, and drove him from the state. Defeating this John Pope, a personal selection of Lincoln's, gave Davis a deep gratification which everyone in the South shared.

Pope had come swaggering out of the West, puffed up by his victory at Island Number Ten. With brash phrases he dismissed precautionary measures regarding lines of communication, boasting that in the West they had only seen the backs of the enemy, and now in the East his "headquarters were in the saddle."

Along with his vainglory, Pope brought to Virginia a change in the war. He ended the days when Confederates could speak of "chivalrous enemies," and he started the war on civilians. Having no truck with the later-day American philosophy of feeding occupied countries, Pope seized the property and food of any civilians in his path to subsist his soldiers.

As some of the people resented being robbed, Pope followed with his personal notions of showing Virginians the error of their ways in not wanting the blessings of One Country. He seized civilians of any age or condition and held them as hostages to be murdered if any of his men were fired at by what he termed "bushwackers." With this, the brutality of Beast Butler changed from an isolated horror to the color of the war.

From Washington new orders went to Grant to live upon the resources of the civilians and "to handle rebels within our lines without gloves"—to imprison them and expel them from their homes. Grant did not follow the last part of the order, believing it "better a few guilty men should escape than a great many innocent ones should suffer." Because Pope relished and exceeded the order, a sense of outrage stirred the whole South, causing an enlistment wave out of sheer hatred.

Davis, as always deeply shocked by violation of rights, made strong protests simultaneously with an appeal for civilized usages of war. He hoped that the barbarities would cease before the South should be forced into retaliatory measures. Before things came to such a pass, Pope was driven by Lee to the safety of Washington's forts.

> Little Be-Pope, he came at a lope,
> "Jackson, the Rebel," to find him,
> He found him at last, then ran very fast,
> With his gallant invaders behind him!

Benjamin was less interested in the humanities Pope violated, and in the satisfaction of his subsequent defeat, than in using Pope's expulsion for diplomatic ends. With McClellan's forces already drawn away from the Richmond front to concentrate with Pope, the whole state was as free of the enemy as it had been a year ago. This time there would be no lull, no waiting for intervention while generals held vague councils of war on possible invasions. This time Lee would invade directly.

The two armies had to get out of Virginia to give the farmers a chance to harvest their crops, give the people a rest from occupation, and give the Confederates a chance to subsist off the enemy without the hazards of capturing Yankee supply trains and depots. They had sickened themselves feasting off Pope, and they had pounced so regularly on Banks's supplies that he had been called by Jackson's men "Commissary" Banks. Going into Maryland, the Confederates would raise more recruits from pro-Southerners suffering under "the despot's heel . . . on thy shore, *Maryland, My Maryland.*"

Davis now agreed, under the spell of Lee's victories and boldness, that defense seemed insufficient. A blow to the enemy would provide Benjamin with a weapon in his fight for European recognition.

And in the West, Braxton Bragg, who had superseded the ailing Beauregard, started similar plans regarding Kentucky. With enlarged and reorganized forces, Bragg ended the supine watching of Union plans to carve up the Western Confederacy and took the initiative suddenly. Aided by the raids of Forrest and Morgan, he struck out for Louisville, to live on the way off Kentucky's fat grassland and rally the pro-Southerners there.

Everywhere the ebbing tide changed and came in with a rush. At Vicksburg, their last river stronghold since the fall of Memphis, Farragut's fleet, combined with Porter's, had enjoyed no such success as at New Orleans. Not only was the combined fleet held off, but at last one of the sea monsters of Benjamin's friend, Mallory, got in its work in the West.

The homemade ram *Arkansas* had escaped from Memphis to be finished up on the Yazoo River, far away from shipyards, shipbuilders, or supplies. When covered with railroad rails and moving spasmodically with the usual Confederate engine, she plunged out into the Mississippi to take on the whole Union fleet. She was badly battered, most of her crew casualties and her wheezing engines about gone when she made the safety of the Vicksburg shore batteries, but Farragut's ships knew they had been in a fight.

The days of making free with the river around Vicksburg ended right there, and the water siege was lifted. The Union fleet retired to New Orleans. This time Mallory's inventiveness paid off, and it can be presumed that he and Benjamin lifted a few glasses of champagne, which Mallory managed to get as Benjamin got his sherry.

To complete the list, the Union progress on the Atlantic came to an abrupt end at Charleston. All the captured fortified points had supplied the Northern fleet bases from which to attack the hated city, the seed-bed of secession, and in the summer the fleet confidently came on. But there was nothing wrong with Charleston's defenses (by preparing which Lee had gained the citizens' opprobrium), and there was no divided command. Officially the U.S. fleet was "repulsed."

This high tide was Benjamin's moment. All that could be done indirectly in England and France had been done. Benjamin had even offered Napoleon the bribe of free trade and 100,000 bales of cotton for his hard-pressed textiles. Still the Emperor, trying to screw up his courage, waited on England. And England waited on "more decisive military victories. . . ."

Well, here they were.

Pussyfooting time was past. Now they must officially demand, boldly and flatly, recognition for the new country among the race of nations.

2

From the first Benjamin worked on total plans of supply, finance, and diplomacy with Mason and Slidell abroad and with friend Mallory at home. For his Navy, Mallory would try anything once. This combination handled practical finances toward definite ends almost as if Memminger's Treasury Department had no existence.

On the floor under Benjamin, with the old U. S. Customs vault stuffed with archives, the long-suffering German kept his books in customary order while up the hill, in the high-roomed Capitol, Congress playfully pulled his money policies to pieces.

During the preceding winter, after the permanent government was inaugurated, Memminger stated that $215,000,000 would be needed for the next nine months, of which even optimistically only $40,000,000 could be counted on. Again he suggested more taxes, more government bonds, and, though he was alarmed at the increase, more treasury notes for currency. On bonds he advocated acceptance of wider produce, for use abroad—following a practice of individuals in purchasing shipments against produce.

Again the popularity-minded Congress eschewed taxes, indifferently issued more bonds, and brought their real enthusiasm to the printing presses for more treasury notes. They were real pretty too—with trains and steamships, milkmaids and cotton-picking Negroes, of course one of the Confederacy striking down the Union and one two-dollar number with an unflattering bust of Benjamin himself.

To make a Rube Goldberg cartoon out of the whole thing, bondholders sold their bonds for treasury notes until the sale of bonds (depressing their value) approximated using them as currency. The states, allowing the government nothing they did not have except responsibility, issued bonds and notes of their own for cotton, and in Texas the state buyers competed openly with government buyers. "I wish I was in the land of cotton" made "Dixie" truly the national anthem.

While Memminger could remain oblivious of the effect of these didos so long as his conscience was clear regarding his own department (for no larger co-ordination was demanded of him), none of this helped the purchasers to obtain supplies.

The agents had long since spent the $15,000,000 of the original Confederate loan, and from then on they had scraped along from hand to mouth on practical uses of cotton in evasion of the unofficial cotton embargo. This continued through congressional debates, and actual laws were passed in the spring to curtail the growth of cotton and burn it before the advance of the U.S. armies. Individuals evaded this last measure by selling to black-market operators in the U.S., who also evaded their laws against buying Southern cotton. The cotton necessary for purchasing agents was shipped directly or hypothecated, and agents drew on Fraser, Trenholm.

However, the government was unwilling to relax the embargo officially on a large scale because, as Mason wrote, King Cotton soon would "turn the screws further." In England the cotton shortage was indeed acute. In July cotton stock was down to 200,000 bales compared to 1,000,000 more than that the year before. By September it reached the low mark of 100,000 and was going at 30,000 a week. The price was up to fifty cents. Mills were closing, and the industrial population averaged half-time employment.

The loss of American markets, the cheap price of manufactured goods against the high price of cotton, all contributed to this frightening depression. But Henry Hotze in his magazine, *Index,* kept before the British public only the specter of complete loss of cotton.

He pointed out that $10,000,000 worth was burned at the fall of New Orleans and 100,000 bales at the fall of Memphis. All over the South only one third of the amount of 1861 was being grown. The closing U.S. blockade would shut off the leaks of private sellers and speculators, while Confederate military victories assured at least a long war, with no cotton confiscated by the U.S. With this propaganda preparation the Confederates prepared to strike with their diplomatic weapon, the cotton embargo.

While using this weapon against England the South had to get credit within the restrictions of their own policy, to pay for the volume of supplies that had swelled geometrically since the innocent days when Caleb Huse went to England with a few thousand dollars.

Benjamin and Mason, and Mallory for his ships, tried several hard-bargained methods of floating limited loans on cotton bonds, to be paid on the lifting of the blockade. When those failed, the Confederates settled on straight loans on cotton to be collected at fixed places and prices by the bondholders. This plan was then taken downstairs by Benjamin, and Memminger gave it the O.K. of his department.

There was then a correlation of Confederate resources, events, and policy toward one purpose. As these new loans went for ships to be used against the blockade, the building of them involved the whole diplomatic structure of England, the United States, and the Confederate States.

3

Captain Bulloch, the able and resourceful purchaser for the C. S. Navy, waged a private war with the U.S. diplomatic and consular agents over his ships. As a private citizen, he contracted with shipyards for the building of two ships, called the *Oreto* and ✲*290*—destined to be Confederate commerce-destroying cruisers *Florida* and *Alabama*. He got it rumored about that they were intended for a mercantile firm, and he supervised the building with no haste and no mystery.

From the first, U.S. spies swarmed around the shipyards, and the U.S. embassy made strong presentations to the British government. Though the ships were unarmed, their requirements were unusual, and they were definitely designed for specific assignments other than mercantile.

Captain Bulloch recorded that these ships had to be as nearly self-sustaining as possible at sea. While the U.S. had four large dockyards on the Atlantic, consular representatives and established credit and prestige in every port of the world, the Confederates had no home port, and, except for England and France, their treatment depended on local sympathies and U.S. pressure. Usually they could obtain no resupplying, but only "a grudging allowance of the barest necessities." The ships, then, must be of ample supply space and, as they took long voyages without putting into coaling stations, he fitted them with sail and steam—sails for ordinary cruising, steam for action.

The *Alabama,* which the Lairds built, was a first-class ship for her day—brass screw with lifting apparatus and barque-rigged with "very long lower masts, to get large fore and aft sails." There was a double suit of sails, five boats, including launch, cutter, and whaleboat, and engineer's stores and spare engine gear of the sort used by the Royal Navy on distant voyages. She could do ten knots at her best with sails, over eleven with sail and steam. £47,500 in five equal payments was considered a fair price.

Toward the end of July she neared completion, and, the *Florida* already having slipped out, the U.S. agents grew determined the *Alabama* should not sail. Bulloch was warned that their pressure for the ship to be detained was growing too strong to ignore and he'd have to get her out within forty-eight hours—if ever. He gave no indication around the yards that anything had happened.

He had hired a British captain and crew, and with them he arranged for a trial run. It was all very gay. Ladies came aboard and drinks were served, and there was only the small crew necessary for a run down the river.

At dusk the ladies were sent back by tug, and at night the tug returned with more seamen. In the morning the ship was gone.

Off the Azores the *Alabama* met another ship with stores and armaments. She was armed with six 32-pounders in broadside, a 100-pounder Blakely rifle in the forecastle, and an eight-inch shell gun abaft the mainmast. The rest of her crew and officers came aboard, including the retired U.S. naval officer, Raphael Semmes, destined for a new and strange fame as her captain.

He had previously commanded the *Sumter,* the first successful cruiser, which in six months captured eighteen American ships, burning eight. Run down by the U. S. Navy at Gibraltar, and blockaded there, the *Sumter* had been sold, and Semmes went to England and then to his new ship.

The *Alabama* was commissioned at sea in late August. In early September—when Lee crossed the Potomac on his invasion of Maryland, when Kirby Smith defeated the Unions in Kentucky, and Braxton Bragg led the Yankees in the race to Louisville—the new sea raider ran down her first victim.

Bulloch had won that battle in his private war. Now the stakes went higher and the going grew tougher. New ships contracted for were the ironclads of Mallory's cherished dream. Not the homemade affairs whose engines broke down on rivers, these were under construction at British shipyards—two rams at the Lairds', who made the *Alabama,* a floating fortress on the Clyde, contracted for by Bulloch's rival agent, Captain North, and the *Pampero,* contracted for by still another agent.

These were not designed to prey on commerce in the scheme to draw off blockaders. These aimed for the destruction of the blockading fleet. By them, the old *Merrimac-Virginia* was a crude affair, and the U.S. agents knew it. These they had to stop, and it would be impossible for them to slip out.

It was the U.S. pressure on the British government against the Confederate, and for the first time in the war the Confederates held a basis from which to press.

4

From France, Benjamin had the assurance of support in a formal demand of recognition from England. Slidell wrote him in late July that "I am more hopeful than I have been at any moment since my arrival." Slidell had made the formal demand on Napoleon and learned, at a pleasant personal interview at Vichy, that France dare not act alone. The Emperor was full of sympathy, but Europe was too unsettled, and, alas, "The policy of nations is controlled by their interests and not by their sentiments."

Napoleon's "sentiments" drew him to the Confederacy because of his own dynastic ambitions. Pushed by Eugénie's Catholicism and the greed of speculators, the tinhorn emperor centered his ambition in Mexico. He had tricked England and Spain into sending ships with his own to Mexico for the ostensible purpose of collecting debts from the Juarez government. When England and Spain smelled a rat and pulled out, Napoleon showed his hand and moved inland.

His troops were surprisingly defeated midway to Mexico City during the period when Lee lifted the siege of Richmond and was blasting Pope out of Virginia. With the United States thus occupied, Napoleon was emboldened to send over hard-bitten Bazaine with reinforcements to destroy the Juarez government. In its place he planned to enthrone Maximilian, the vaporous Hapsburg archduke who lacked anybody to rule. For this defiance of the Monroe Doctrine a friendly Mexican neighbor was vital.

For his more important homeland the friendship of England was even more vital. Hence for Slidell he could do no more than promise unofficial communications with England to indicate his willingness to act. This he did.

In England the Confederate lobby made a concerted move for debate in Parliament, led by their powerful sympathizer, Lindsay. He gave figures on England's cotton famines and, coincident with Confederate victories, stressed that the nature of the war was for a people's independence and not the support of slavery.

At the same time Hotze, whose expense account had been upped to $10,000, encouraged his *Index* writers to write for other papers. He also stressed the nature of the war, the ineffectiveness of the blockade, and Confederate resources, and pointed out that the competition of U.S. industries made an independent South advantageous to England. As he gave fair accounts of the fighting, his veracity was trusted, and he could make appeals to the imagination on the exploits of Jackson and Lee.

At the end of July (as the *Alabama* stole out to sea) James Mason sent the fateful note to Russell, asking for a personal interview on the subject of recognition.

His note contained Benjamin's flawless legal arguments on the ineffectiveness of the blockade ("a predatory cruise") and the rights of secession.

Russell's return note, refusing a personal interview, stated that the time was not opportune for a discussion of recognition. England was not involved in the moral issues of the struggle but in the Confederacy's ability to maintain its independence. This was accompanied by a few gratuitous jabs denying Mason's claim that the South would never return to the Union.

The Confederates were shaken by the tone of the refusal. James Mason, a man of genuine dignity despite his pomposity, was hurt and angered. His pride long anguished by the preceding snubs, he had to be restrained by British friends from an impulsive response. They assured him that Russell's attitude was actually covering activity in the British Cabinet on the subject of intervention.

Even coolheaded Hotze mistook the Foreign Minister's manner for his convictions. Only Benjamin remained untroubled by the discourtesy. Not interested in the personal aspects, he feared only the "apprehension by Earl Russell of the displeasure of the United States."

Benjamin hit it close. Actually Russell was working in the Cabinet for Confederate recognition. And Gladstone was working in Parliament. In early October he made the famous speech including the words, "Jefferson Davis has created a nation."

Everything that lobbying and propaganda could do was now done. The issue was reduced to might.

At that moment Lee's army was defeated in Maryland at a little town named Sharpsburg, through which the Antietam Creek flows. He was not beaten on the field. The actual battle was a draw. But, insomuch as it checked his invasion and forced a retreat to Virginia, it climaxed his campaign in failure.

McClellan had been yanked from the shadows to save the Union when Lee's bloody-footed legions swung toward the Northern vitals. Knowing McClellan, Lee boldly dispersed his men. He grabbed the arsenal at Harper's Ferry a second time while his starved scarecrows gathered the fat forage of the Maryland countryside. At the peak of Lee's audacity one of his generals lost an order and one of McClellan's found it. Knowing for once his enemy's intentions, and with no Pinkertons to exaggerate the opposing forces, McClellan struck with decision and power.

It was not to his discredit that in the crucial sector his men opposed literally Stonewall Jackson; or that in a flanking movement that still could have turned the tide, his Burnside faltered and Lee's "A.P. Hill came up." However, when McClellan adjudged his own roughly handled army too spent for vigorous pursuit and was slow to take on Lee in his own lair, he was relegated to the shadows again.

Though McClellan missed his bid for immortality on his brief second chance, he took the weight out of the Confederate arguments abroad.

5

The indecisive check of the Confederate military forces was used for a most decisive defeat to their diplomatic forces. With Lee defeated, Lincoln played his ace. He issued the Emancipation Proclamation.

This Proclamation was not the way Lincoln had wanted to do it or believed in. He believed the emancipation of slaves was an injustice to Southerners, and, if it came to that, the government should pay the compensation. Of all things for the South, Lincoln desired that region in the Union, and he explained in the Proclamation that the war was for that purpose and not abolition.

Of all people, he understood the complications missed by the self-righteous do-gooders. He said to Negroes, "When you cease to be slaves, you are yet far removed from being on an equality with the white race." In urging Negroes to leave America and colonize, he said, "It is better for us both to be separated."

That the Proclamation was a war measure was indicated by the members of Cabinet who urged it as a penalty against the seceded states, wishing to incite the Negroes against all the whites, while leaving slavery untouched in the loyal border states. On this Russell said, "If it were a measure of Emancipation it should be extended to all the States of the Union . . . [it] is not granted to the claims of humanity but inflicted as a punishment."

Lincoln had written Greeley as late as August, "My paramount object . . . is to save the Union, and is not either to save or to destroy slavery. If I could save the Union without freeing any slaves, I would do it. . . . What I do about slavery and the colored race, I do because I believe it helps to save the Union. . . ."

A British schoolteacher in the South, who had been blockaded by the war and had just returned to England, also said:

Horrible scenes have undeniably occurred in the slave states, as in other countries; but let any upright reader judge, whether it would be a fair representation of English society, to collect from a year's, or even a week's newspapers, the terrible list of crimes and sufferings, and concentrating them in one volume, to send it forth to the world, saying, "Such is England." The second American Revolution is producing remarkable changes throughout the civilized world . . . but in all sincerity the author ventures to assert that the most calamitous and unmerciful infliction that could befall both master and servant would be the sudden emancipation of the slaves of the Southern states.

Whatever Lincoln said privately or a qualified observer said publicly, the simple dramatic appeal to humanity seized the imagination. The public did not question the odd fact that slaves were not to be freed in loyal states, such as in the dubious ground of Kentucky, where slaveowners might turn against the Union. No one asked what the 90 per cent of non-slaveholding Southerners were fighting for. No one investigated the harsh treatment of Negroes by Northern soldiers.

The war had a slogan. The Unions emerged as crusaders for freedom, and the whole South was stamped in the minds of the world (for generations to come) as fighting for slavery.

The character of the war changed to the British public, and workingmen's organizations held mass meetings in praise of liberty.

Awareness of the English people's reaction joined the government's fear of the United States. In October, Lord John Russell (considered by Southern people to be their enemy) proposed intervention on the side of the South in the British Cabinet—and was defeated.

To the British it was clear the Confederacy had failed to *win* its independence. Saddled with an odious and archaic cause, its only chance was to outlast the enemy. In achieving this, time was against it because of the incomparably greater U.S. technological potential. In that time England could wait for cotton.

At Sharpsburg, Maryland, the cotton embargo lost its puissance as a weapon. Always its power depended on military success. This the government missed because of its faith in their king, Cotton.

While the political theorists misjudged the situation, a naval scientist from the beginning exposed the basic fallacy. Matthew Fontaine Maury, in newspaper articles, attacked the government as "political dreamers" for expecting cotton to accomplish "what other nations require armies and navies" to do for them. In urging early appropriations for ships, he asked: *"Did ever unprotected wealth secure immunity to its owners? . . .* The breadth of our plantations and the value of our staples will be of small advantage if the others may have the mastery in our own waters."

With Maury this was not in the realm of theory. He remained steadily committed to the torpedoes which the U.S. naval historian praised for their effectiveness, and to light ships, readily constructed and of short range, that could mount one or more heavy, long-range guns against a large target. Secretary Mallory, committed to the government's policy, devoted his energies to the raiders, like the *Alabama,* and the huge ironclads.

When the Confederate policy failed, Maury was sent quietly to England to purchase materials for his torpedoes. In any large way his talents were lost to the nation for one of whose states, Virginia, he had sorrowfully left his Washington work. In a final way the diplomatic goal of the policy he opposed began to recede.

Politics without power was failing.

CHAPTER EIGHTEEN

The Favorite Far Away

MRS. DAVIS returned to Richmond in September to find her house in a mess. Fall cleaning, through the somnolent dust of four hot months, became a real problem with the now chronic servant shortage. Negroes had been drained off the domestic market to work on fortifications, in war plants, and in less savory activities, and the general agitation made others undependable.

For the first time in generations Negroes worked for families without a sense of identification, without looking to them for their final security, and on that condition came the little understood Emancipation Proclamation. A vague sense of the new forces at work caused restlessness, largely undirected except for those pulled toward the factitious dream of the North. Mrs. Davis lost a nurse in that flight; the woman simply disappeared and went with her husband.

Probably from that phase stems the Negro's "irresponsibility," by white standards, toward his jobs. The manner in which they simply fail to show up for work, disappear overnight from the ken of their labors, and leave the dependent housewife with her curtains down and ready for laundering goes back to the time when it was simpler just to vanish.

In those first days the Negro could not comprehend that freedom meant opportunity to select his own work and boss and assume responsibility for his family's welfare. To the majority it meant a perpetual holiday. Like democracy to many today, it carried no responsibility—only privileges and slogans.

This type of attitude was expressed in the story of the Negro who followed a Northern soldier, leaving his wife and children behind. The Northerner was shocked that the husband would leave his family at the mercy of the world. "Oh no," said the Negro gaily, "the white folks won't let them suffer for nuthin'."

For others the new freedom meant an undefined hostility to the whites, a justification to plunder and destroy. Another of Mrs. Davis's servants attempted to set fire to the house, and others stole. Yet, as the war meant the same to many Northern soldiers—who showed a predilection for silver and jewelry and a curious vandalism toward china and pianos—this proved little about the Negro.

Another segment of Negroes remained steadfastly addicted to the *status quo*. Some of these were of a settled type, really contented where they were, and among these were many cases of the later romanticized loyalties and genuine affection on both sides.

Because this type of intimacy was indicative of the relationship wherever Negroes worked closely with whites—as house servants, artisans, and workers on small plantations—there was an interweaving of the two races in the societal pattern that made any single cut through it leave the edges ragged. Lincoln knew the Negro and the white could not be separated by edict where for two centuries each had been formed by the same hot, slumberous land and each insensibly influenced the other.

The majority of Negroes were bound by primal ties to the familiar land, and many, with no particular loyalty to any family, stayed where they were out of associations with place. With some of these, fear of the unknown operated. Others were repelled by their liberators, especially when they demanded amorous rewards.

Northern soldiers expressed surprise at the numbers who silently rejected freedom and stood, clustered in groups, watching the blue armies pass. But the Negroes were not left untroubled. They were not the same as before. . . .

Confronted by the change, the Southerner acted like any controlling power in the world's history: he resisted trends unfavorable to his position. With the existing relationship too deep in his consciousness for him even to conceive of it differently, he was chiefly exacerbated by the untimely inconveniences and, what a Richmond judge called, "their insolence."

Mrs. Davis, having grown up with Negroes in her house, had always known them as individuals and shown real interest in their lives. While she was careful of their dress and taught them "all the niceties of service," her attentions extended into all the details of their living. Like women of another day and other places, she thought she had done her part. The implications of their changed ways and attitudes were not her pressing concern. She had a house to run for a nation's President, for her lover and their children, and the behavior of her servants became another and somewhat baffling problem.

More acute were the prices she had to pay to restock the pantry, woodshed, and linen closet. Bacon had gone to 75 cents a pound, sugar to 80, butter to $1.25, and coffee $2.50—with clerks in the war office using parched corn meal. For the Southerner's hot bread, rolls, and light-bread, flour went to $16 a barrel. With her servant shortage, to fill out with store-bought bread, she must pay twenty cents for a loaf the size of a fist. For cooking in the wood range, a cord of wood brought $16. Twenty-five dollars was asked for six-dollar blankets, and to replace sheets a four-dollar pair cost her $15. For home laundry, soap was at 75 cents a cake. With fall coming on, bringing sharp mornings and evenings, the grate fires were made from black gold, with coal at $9.00 a load and rising.

Even though the prices were high, the markets were full again since both armies had been out of the state. Skinny little chickens brought a dollar, potatoes climbed above six dollars a bushel, cucumbers and cymblings brought a dollar a dozen, and tomatoes $1.50. Fruit was so high that little canning could be done. For a thrifty housewife like Varina Davis, who, as the First Lady, had no special channels, such conditions worked a real hardship, especially as she must always serve attractive food to a husband who gave scant attention to his bodily needs.

But the most disturbing adjustment on her return to Richmond was to the lines of opposition that had hardened against her husband. She saw this reflected in countless ways to herself, and was probably not unmindful that Mrs. Joe Johnston had changed her original description of Varina from "a Western belle" to "a Western *woman*." Someone else added a "coarse" to the "Western woman."

Varina was no longer in a mood to exert tact where her nature opposed it. By now she expected deference for her position. The days were gone when the movement was new, routines extemporized, and all made do in the exultance of a common cause. The country was established, divisions emerged with the passing of the early enthusiasms, and Mrs. Davis had changed with the times—even in appearance.

Close up, blue veins could be seen in her brows and cheeks. Her assurance was now spoken of as "hauteur," and Pollard called her "a brawny, able-bodied woman . . . excessively coarse and physical in her person . . . full of social self-assertion . . . [and with] more of masculine mettle than feminine grace. . . ."

Pollard's hatred of Varina Davis, which must have been some glandular reaction, could well have been caused by his male resentment of intelligence in a woman when accompanied by strong will and independent spirit. Pollard might have revealed more about himself than about Mrs. Davis by his emphasizing her vitality in uncomplimentary terms.

Certainly she was never called pretty, though known for her looks. It was "comely," and her face was proud and her full mouth determined. She needed the softening of her eyes, which everyone mentioned as "soft, liquid, dark." She was also mentioned for her clothes, and dressed to advantage in white silk, usually wearing a flower in her dark hair. There were ample admirers and unbiased observers who found her graceful and imposing in the self-assurance which drove the newspaperman to splenetic outbursts.

Another newspaperman, a country editor, bothered her more than Pollard when, in paying her a compliment, he called her "a handsome, portly, middle-aged woman." In her middle thirties and vain of her figure, she laughed at the well-meant words—too loud.

This occasional strong laughter, in contrast to her deepening dignity, rang out at odd times. Annoyances might provoke it, but more often it came from some incongruity, and sometimes at another's mistakes. While the laughter could be full of humor and irresistible, it could also be of an unseemly loudness, and other ladies were known to have felt uneasy when she laughed out of all proportion to the provocation.

Also other women observed that what they had regarded as easy repartee had become more barbed, was more apt to be satire. Her tongue so quick in conversation became as quick with sarcasm. They remembered from the old Washington days that critics even then found her too individualistic, with too superior an air and manner. Now that she was First Lady, they inferred that her natural inclinations flowered until she became quite regal.

But her own friends continued warm, though she missed Mrs. Chesnut, down in South Carolina. Even their gatherings lacked the gaiety of the first days at the Spotswood. Sitting on the balcony in the fine fall weather, they knitted socks now and talked of the blockade and other women—spitefully and interestedly. Varina was not one of the women who disliked her own sex; she was always fascinated with their affairs.

With her friends, as with her husband, she kept her troubles to herself. The one subject on which she blew up was unjust criticism of her husband, and in the autumn of her return she found plenty of that. The coalition of his enemies amounted virtually to a second front, and he was worn from trying to get along with them.

The hot city summer had been hard on Davis anyway, and only the buoyance brought by victories had kept him up. Now the victories had ceased. Their high plans had failed, and new measures were desperately needed at the time these obstructionists put obstacles in the way of his every move.

Mrs. Davis used all her ability to create an atmosphere of comfort and ease to carry him through the nerve strains of the war within.

2

Vice-President Stephens had returned from Georgia in August apparently to direct in person his attacks on the Administration. The spearhead of his crusade was directed at the suspension of habeas corpus, including martial law. It was of no concern to him that these measures offered the only means of enforcing law in districts unsettled by war or actually occupied, and in vast areas where courts were disrupted and virtually no civil law existed. What mattered was that "I have pointed out six plain and palpable violations of the Constitution in these military orders!"

That the government pointed out thousands of violations of conscription was only a matter of satisfaction to the self-intoxicated pedant. It proved the people would not willingly surrender their constitutional liberties. Abuses of the substitute clause gave him no alarm, even when it was clear they formed the nucleus of forces that would undermine morale.

Substitutes were just as popular in the South as in the North, and newspapers regularly ran ads.

WANTED—A SUBSTITUTE TO GO IN A Cavalry company, to whom will be given Sixteen Hundred Dollars in cash, and a fine horse fully equipped.

A SUBSTITUTE WANTED—For a Virginian, none other need apply, over forty-five years of age, who can come well recommended, a liberal price will be paid.

These ads produced results increasingly, though the system had clearly proved a failure. Some substitutes were subject to military service anyway. Others were sorry physical specimens who took sick right off and burdened the meager commissary.

There were countless exemptions—cotton-factory workers and all forms of transportation workers; ministers, teachers with twenty pupils, printers, one apothecary to a shop, postmasters and mail employees. Reagan was vastly helped in his economical post office by the low contracts submitted for star routes when mail deliverers became exempt.

But Stephens agreed with his ally, Governor Brown, that a standing army was unnecessary in any case. Let the men work cotton, Brown advised, and rally only at time of battle. A squirrel shooter didn't need all that drilling to be able to shoot a Yankee.

What this country needed, Stephens maintained, was protection from its own national government. To this end he boasted of his anti-administration lobbying in the Capitol:

I have not been idle in attempting to arouse our members of Congress, both in the Senate and the House, to the importance of arresting these proceedings. . . . I got Mr. Semmes, the most sensible man in the Senate, to introduce resolutions there requiring the Judiciary Committee to report on these questions. That Committee is now at work, and matters are progressing favorably. I have got Semmes to agree with me that *no power* in this country can establish martial law; neither the President nor Congress, much less a general in the field. Congress may suspend the writ of *habeas corpus;* but that is the utmost extent to which they can go. . . .

He could boast that his "efforts have thus far met with more success than I anticipated when I saw the general apathy prevailing at first."

With Davis's long-time personal enemy, Henry Foote, vituperating in support of Semmes, the opposition carried the fight into October. However, though much historical attention has been devoted to Davis's enemies, the President did have his own strong supporters. They obtained an extension of the habeas corpus law, though technically the martial-law phase had to be eliminated.

Stephens's opposition lobby (elated over their partial victory) even denounced General Hindman for trying to bring order to guerrilla-infested Arkansas, on the principle that any ill was preferable to the President's possessing authority which the military could enforce. In his legalistic fight against the military, Stephens was strengthened by Robert Toombs, who came in on purely personal grounds.

This early Danton of the Cabinet had fared as badly in the Army as in Richmond. His undisciplined ego could not submit to military procedure. Toombs considered his opinion as good as the next, and an order to him was not something to execute but to debate about. Regarding no man as his superior, he attacked all his ranking officers as Davis's "Janissaries" and. as Mrs. Chesnut said, he was ready for another revolution. Cursing everything in the Confederacy, "he thinks there is a conspiracy against him in the Army."

Just as he had stormed out of the Cabinet, he stormed out of the Army—and ran for senator. When Ben Hill received the largest majority in Georgia, and Toombs won the second seat in close balloting, he refused that too. His pride was hurt that he was not a hero even to his own state, and Mrs. Chesnut said he went "out on a rampage."

Like others of the former U.S. politicians, Toombs's gifts were wasted in a movement which required constructive legislation for preservation. The dangerous element in Toombs, for Davis, was his unquenchable energy in a rebellious nature. The one person in the Confederacy who could use that destructive energy was Alexander Stephens.

Toombs, to an observer, was powerful and magnetic, "his fine head set well on his shoulders, was covered with long, glossy, black hair, which when speaking he managed to toss about so as to recall the memory of Danton." But Stephens's "head was unshapely and immature . . . and his beardless, wrinkled face gave him the look of one born out of season. . . . His voice was thin, and piercing like a woman's, but there the resemblance ended. His was a virile mind sustained by an inflexible will; and, in all matters of importance, Mr. Toombs came up, in the end, on Mr. Stephens' side."

Stephens offered Toombs a needed direction, and under the personal influence that would control him. Both had been states'-rightists along with Howell Cobb, but Cobb had become what they now called a *"Confederate Nationalist."* He was supplanted by Stephens's younger brother, Linton, a shrewd, political-minded under-cover worker. These three had a ready-made mouthpiece in Governor Brown.

In returning to Georgia in this alliance, Toombs seems to have been unstrung by the pattern of events that left him ineffectual. It was passion, not deliberation, which drove the chafed ego of the rebel.

With Stephens it was different. He was coldly deliberate in the treachery, conscious or unconscious, of a monomaniac determined to destroy everything that was not done the way of his abstractions. From Richmond he wrote his brother that he preferred to see the city fall and the whole country engulfed rather than "that our people should submissively yield" to the laws of the government to which he objected.

Out of this background—and with Hunter usually presiding for him in the high-backed, red-upholstered chair in the Senate—Stephens commented with some surprise that the President had sent for him only once since the government had moved to Richmond. It does not prove Davis a "despot" that he wanted no advice from Little Aleck. It is to his credit that he could treat him civilly when they were forced to meet in public.

In that fall, during the collapse of their long-term plan for recognition, Stephens could only say, "Were I the President, I should forthwith recall all my ministers or commissioners abroad." He believed that England and France "rejoiced to see strife now raging here which . . . will . . . end in the destruction of republicanism on both sides of the line." With that blast he went back to Georgia.

This theory, while not without some element of truth, both oversimplified the foreign situation and missed altogether the practical implications of the failure abroad. And this theory was important not only because the opposition leader held it, but because the Administration advanced no opposite working theory.

Davis's cotton-threat plan, unsupported by military victories, had failed, and he must devise a new and, of necessity, makeshift plan. What Davis missed, along with his enemies, was that the nature and philosophy of the war had changed—and a new *kind* of plan was needed.

They missed this because, wanting only what they had, they lacked from the beginning a total policy expressive of political dynamics. Fighting for the *status quo,* they gave the initiative to the revolutionary forces of economic determinism.

The Confederacy's most significant military defeats (Lee's invasion of Maryland and Bragg's of Tennessee) culminated the South's nearest approach to a total aggressive plan within the limits of their static defense. Bragg's campaign, along with European collapse, marked not only the end of that plan, but a turning point in the whole conflict.

However, instead of studying the strategical consequences of these setbacks, Davis's enemies only attacked the individual responsible— Bragg—and Davis could only defend him. Lee was enshrined, beyond criticism; but Bragg, especially as he was a Davis pet, offered fair game.

3

Davis's new favorite was, of course, a West Pointer. While the critics like Toombs foolishly attacked the "West Point clique," the President was overdisposed in their favor (as he was to gentlemen). They were more apt to do things the "regular" way. Records showed that trained soldiers were far more apt to produce, on both sides, than untrained; but there were some great natural untrained soldiers whom Davis underrated, and some inadequate trained soldiers whom he overrated. Braxton Bragg was one of the latter.

He was a strange character. Conscientious and hard-working, by no means without ability or courage, and apparently free of Hero aspirations, he was another of the nervous dyspeptics—irritable, contumacious, and unstable, harried by responsibility. In preparing his army Bragg was a fine organizer, but he buckled under the commitment of combat, worried himself sick, and seemed more relieved to have any action over than follow it to its conclusion.

His good record in the old army was topped in the Mexican War by a famous American battle crack made to him. He was commanding a battery at Buena Vista where the going got very tough. When a Mexican charge seemed about to swallow up his guns, Old Rough and Ready Taylor said, "A little more grape, Bragg." It was one of the lines that caught the imagination of the day.

Previous to that, appointed to West Point from North Carolina, he graduated fifth in his class. After the Mexican War he grew bored by garrison life and became a planter in his wife's state, Louisiana. Originally a non-secessionist, when the break came Bragg told Sherman (an old garrison mate then head of a military academy in Louisiana) he thought the sections should separate peaceably—or, in any event, part.

With those convictions he first entered the state service, shifted to the Confederate forces at Pensacola, then to the Department of West Florida and Alabama that included Mobile. Everywhere his work was marked by a strong sense of organization and stern discipline, and he showed a sound sense of total strategy. Bragg advised Benjamin, when he was War Secretary, to concentrate at a few points against the enemy instead of trying to protect all land. As his letter arrived just before A. S. Johnston's failure in Tennessee, through dispersal, Bragg made something of an impression. In the following concentration of troops at Shiloh he commanded a corps.

When Bragg joined the Confederates on their retreat from that bloody battle they were in a bad way. They had just lost their leader, Albert Sidney Johnston; and Beauregard, his successor, was not in a confident mood. The original Hero, who had chafed under sharing his glory with Joe Johnston, was suddenly full commander of a big army in a huge territory, and if ever he was to live his Napoleonic dreams the time was now. The Union armies that had driven from Kentucky to Mississippi were concentrated against him and still coming on.

Whatever Old Bory might have liked to do, he could only hole up in the little town of Corinth, south of the Tennessee border and strategically important as a railroad junction. There his army licked its wounds and sought reinforcements while the Federals, with unwitting mercy, gave him time and peace.

Halleck, the commander in the West, took personal charge of the gathered Union armies, and a clammy hand fell on their confident drive to end the war. On Halleck, whose battles had been won by field commanders like Grant, reputation sat heavily. Nothing was to be impetuous.

He crept ponderously toward Corinth, building fortifications before him as he went, with a system of crisscrossing corduroy roads behind. At Corinth his elaborate preparations for attack went on so long that the Confederates slipped away intact. Beauregard gave up the rail junction (which was inevitable anyway), but he saved his army and, deeper in Mississippi, had more time to ready it for a fight.

Halleck apparently felt that his mission was accomplished (HALLECK TAKES CORINTH). He settled down to give his engineers a chance to demonstrate their skill by building vast fortifications against attack by Beauregard, who asked nothing more than to be let alone in Tupelo, Mississippi. While Old Bory grew puny from his apprehensions (his Hero title was further tarnished from Shiloh), Braxton Bragg used his abilities at organization to rebuild a fine army.

Then, in July, Halleck was brought to Washington, as commander in chief, and the character of the war in the West changed. The Great Reputation turned to large-scale strategy and gave the South some overdue dispersal from their enemies. It was all the Confederates needed to bounce back. It was all the Unions needed to slump.

The rise and fall of those opposing armies was like that of individuals. The struggle was too personal for troops to function as mechanical units. For a year the Union soldiers had been exposed to hardships and dangers away from their homes, marching and fighting to end a rebellion and get back to their wives and jobs. They had done everything asked of them. They had driven the enemy deep in his own territory and occupied enough of the South for the Rebels to know it was all over.

But they didn't know it. Not only that, but back in Virginia a Confederate army was clearing the eastern South of Yankees. Disappointment set in as the delusion of a quick war faded. General Buell reported fourteen thousand officers and men in his army absent from their duty and stated that the men manifested a "weariness and impatience" at the routine of camp life, and "thousands of letters which poured from the camps into the soldiers' homes and the public presses were mediums for these manifestations. . . ."

In brief, the same sort of slump that hit the Confederates after Manassas, when they had thought the war over, hit the Unions when they discovered that it wasn't. In this lull the South, roused out of its own complacency, struck back.

Bragg was given the job. Beauregard, on realizing that his army was at last safe (and also his glory), went on sick leave. While he was gone Braxton Bragg was put in his place.

He was then forty-five years old, his unstable nature on an upbeat, and he possessed the initiative, the advantage of knowing what he wanted to do, and the enemy's halfhearted dispersal.

4

When Bragg assumed command, the Union forces had taken and occupied all of divided Kentucky, the granary of western Tennessee, control of the railroads in northern Mississippi and Alabama, control of the interior rivers and of the Mississippi down to the Delta, with only Vicksburg holding out. Southwest of Bragg, Vicksburg was under water siege by the combined Union fleets from the North and from New Orleans—and Farragut had already taken Baton Rouge and Natchez.

In breaking this concentration into a grandiose strategy, Halleck followed a political maneuver dear to Lincoln's heart. That was to take Chattanooga and the surrounding Unionist country of East Tennessee. While Lincoln wanted the loyal population freed from the Rebels, there were sound military reasons for occupying Chattanooga. In the heart of the mountainous country that divided the Eastern and Western Confederacy, it was the railroad junction from Richmond to the Mississippi (which made it a back door to Richmond) and the gateway to the Atlantic through Georgia.

But, for these reasons, it was an area that the Unions could reasonably expect the South to defend bitterly—except for their known habits of dispersal. Possibly Halleck, grown fatuous with successes others won for his reputation, unconsciously depended on continued Confederate ineptitude and did not realize he was beginning the same thing.

Bragg, however, did.

As Memphis lies virtually on the southern border of Tennessee to the west, so does Chattanooga to the east. The Tennessee border in a straight line passes Mississippi, Alabama, and, at Chattanooga, a slice of Georgia. Halleck's right rested on Memphis, his center was strung across Mississippi and northern Alabama, and his left became Buell's detached army advancing to Chattanooga.

Aside from this dispersal, a couple of minor events lessened the pressure on Bragg. The Vicksburg water siege was lifted by the redoubtable ram *Arkansas.* (Though she later had to be destroyed by her crew, when her engines gave out in another engagement, this one brain child of Mallory's had made a solid achievement.) Farther south, Butler, who had repelled one attack on Baton Rouge, grew apprehensive of another and retired to his more congenial warfare on New Orleans civilians.

Grant, commanding these armies in the Mississippi area, had vague intentions on Vicksburg, which under the circumstances could not materialize. All the forces, then, sprawled in unwieldy uselessness except Buell's army and a smaller force in the mountains north of Chattanooga.

In Chattanooga was an equally small Confederate force under Kirby Smith, who, wounded at First Manassas, had returned to this new command. According to previous Southern policy in the West, Kirby Smith would be gobbled up separately while Bragg remained fixed down in Mississippi.

At that point Bragg broke the fix and grasped the initiative at an extremely inopportune time for Buell.

Under orders from Halleck (who must have been a frustrated construction engineer at heart), Buell was forced to rebuild railroads through the enemy's country as he went. This opened him to harrying attacks by Confederate cavalry leaders, who constantly broke his line of communication, captured whole garrisons, and forced him to spread his forces thin.

John Morgan and Bedford Forrest emerged as cavalry leaders with a sounder sense of the essence of warfare than either President had, or Lincoln's commander in chief. As a case for non-West Pointers, Morgan had served only as a volunteer lieutenant in the Mexican War, and Forrest, a semiliterate slave trader, had no combat experience except of a strictly personal nature. But, operating separately, they set Buell's whole army up for Bragg.

In August, Bragg shifted his army to Chattanooga and, solid and swift, struck almost due north across eastern Tennessee towards Kentucky. At the same time Kirby Smith moved north on parallel lines farther east and drove at once into Kentucky.

Buell, from his laborious part in the awkward offensive, suddenly was forced to hurry his scattered army north, concentrating as it went, to protect Nashville. When Bragg by-passed Nashville and moved on into Kentucky, Buell could only follow, still concentrating.

Farther east, Kirby Smith defeated the Union forces in northern Kentucky and was headed straight for Cincinnati, or in position to turn on Louisville from the east. In Louisville and Cincinnati citizens were frightened and excited and meetings were held hourly. In Richmond newsboys sold extras, about one column in size, for a quarter— and their citizens laughed to see the boot on the other leg.

When Bragg gobbled up a Union garrison in southern Kentucky, he also had a clear way ahead to Louisville from the south. Between Buell and his base, Bragg could either fight him or race him to Louisville, with the advantage on his side in either move.

Up until this time, in September, Bragg had demonstrated the value of the initiative, which he used skillfully to keep Buell guessing. His soldiers were confident and excited, and Kirby Smith's victorious force to the east was as hot as a depot stove. Suddenly, at the climactic moment, Bragg's will palsied.

In the whole campaign he had been apprehensive and elated by turn. The farther he penetrated into the enemy country, the more oppressive the consequences became. When he started, he had been fired by the assurances of Kentuckians that Southern sympathizers only needed a chance to rise to his standards. Once there, he was quickly disillusioned. He said, "The people here have too many fat cattle and are too well off to fight."

With his political mission failing and the situation devolving more on straight military success, he grew timid of committing his army to battle. He said, "This campaign must be won by marching, not fighting."

So he marched—away from both Buell *and* Louisville.

Without a fight, Bragg surrendered to the anxious Union general the right of way to his base of supply, while the Rebels marched eastward to try to save the political stakes with a futile gesture.

Bragg inaugurated a Confederate governor who lasted exactly as long as Bragg's army supported him, which was one hour. By then the Unions, relieved after their close call, were concentrated and full of fight. Bragg, after marching all over hell-and-gone, and heavy with captured supplies, now started a backward trek. . . .

5

In his whole brilliantly conceived campaign Bragg had enjoyed assistance in the total plan against the Union's dispersal. Back in Mississippi, Price and Van Dorn had acted against Grant to keep his force under Rosecrans from reinforcing Buell.

When some Federals moved north in answer to Buell's desperate needs, Price attacked Rosecrans's weakened force at a town near Corinth. Price withdrew after an indecisive fight to collect his own forces for another go at Rosecrans.

At this point Van Dorn (the West Pointer) received presidential orders to supersede Price (whom Davis disliked). Actually the combined forces amounted to two commands. As such, they attacked Rosecrans directly at Corinth and got a very bad going over. They could only stagger away south and try to escape pursuit.

However, they had accomplished their primary purpose of holding the enemy dispersed. Unfortunately they could not resist fighting though not concentrated in force themselves. As a potential threat Price and Van Dorn immobilized part of Grant's army without exchanging a shot. Or, if they hungered for action, they could have followed Bragg northward, which would have brought Rosecrans after them and out of fortifications. But by early October, as Bragg seemed not to do any fighting, Price and Van Dorn were like the Irishman who said, as he moved sadly to battle, " 'Tis a poor fight, but 'tis better than no fight at all."

Now, after they erased themselves as a threat, after Buell concentrated against Bragg on equal terms, after the larger plan had collapsed, Bragg fought.

This action in Kentucky (Perryville, October 8) was a stand-up affair with no particular skill shown by either side. It was hard-fought, with honors about even. The Confederate soldiers, at last in battle, felt elated. They did not dream of defeat as they bivouacked on the field.

But Bragg, keyed up to bursting point, felt only his relief that he had gotten out of the fight with no disaster. He retreated well, leaving the field and the technical victory to Buell (who was rewarded by a congressional investigation into his failures, and he, an able patriot forced to execute Halleck's cumbersome assignment, was retired to the shadows with the glory hunters).

Bragg holed up in the strategic base of Murfreesboro, Tennessee, and seemed very well pleased with the whole thing. While the President's enemies attacked Bragg in the press, the general cheerfully entertained his staff with tales of the Mexican War. He particularly enjoyed telling them of Buell, Sherman, and Thomas, the last two of whom had been in his old battery.

In all truth his campaign had considerable accomplishment. He upset the enemy's plans and dispositions; subsisted off them for a change, bringing off vast supplies, and regained some territory which placed him in a strategic position for defense.

But there lay the basic failure—defense.

The political issues of the invasion, arousing Kentuckians, had failed as had Lee's in Maryland. Lee, instead of getting recruits, inspired an enemy poem, "Barbara Frietchie," about something that never happened. His soldiers retreated into Virginia singing bitterly, "Maryland, *Their* Maryland."

The major consideration of the joint campaign was ultimately military, in support of the cotton-threat plan on England. As such, Bragg or Lee (preferably both) had to remain at least in a threatening position. To fail of this and to retire in defense of their land, with whatever improved position, reduced the war to a time struggle—with resources against them. Bragg's campaign was the turning point strategically, as Sharpsburg had been diplomatically, in the Confederates' war for independence.

Though both campaigns had been extemporaneous, in reaction to the North rather than in pursuance of a basic policy, fortune had fitted them into a total plan. Now it was gone.

In Richmond, when Bragg came to see Davis in late October, no new plans, or even aggressions, were envisioned. As Davis had been without an over-all policy prior to the summer, he returned to planless resistance to what had definitely become in the North a determination to subjugate the South by arms. There was to be no end until that end, and no help was forthcoming from outside.

Lincoln had said, "The power confided in me will be used to hold, occupy and possess the property and places belonging to the government, and to collect the duties and imports; beyond what may be necessary for these objects, there will be no invasion, no using of force against or among the people anywhere." Now it became clear that "what may be necessary for these objects" was conquest of all the people everywhere.

While the "restoration of fraternal sympathies and affections" may have been Lincoln's personal ideal in his determination to maintain the geographic-political entity of the United States, he was supported by powers whose interests were antithetical to "affections."

The high-tariff boys needed that Southern agrarian area within their control, and subservient; the lice that attached themselves to the abolition movement. wanted a chance to exploit the freed Negroes, and investors friendly to the party wanted a chance to exploit land that would become useless to planters without slaves. Finally, in some (like Thad Stevens, who wanted to "reduce the South to a mudhole"), there was straight sectional hatred.

While this gang (as far as they were concerned) had Lincoln as a front, they had millions of citizens to follow him in honest belief in the Union and thousands in the armed forces committed to executing their program in duty to their country. Among military leaders, as the fighting itself became an end, their job to do, they saw the job in its basic terms of defeating a people by force of arms, with no incidental interest in "restoring fraternal sympathies."

The South could have been any foreign people.

When this became clear, as the South failed in its one concerted effort, their own money immediately reflected their sagging position. Their dollar, which had held at 1.5 until August, dropped in October to 2, in November to 2.9, and was clearly skidding.

Davis did not know the character of the war had changed. As he lived within the matrix of a legend—probably the loveliest legend of this country—the outer realities reached him a little muffled and blurred.

CHAPTER NINETEEN

Plumes and Corn Bread

WHEN November came cold and rainy, and a new "On to Richmond" drive was massing below Washington, the Davises, in their comfortable and now familiar house, enjoyed a more informal social life than in their first season. Though their fortnightly levees in the two big parlors grew more formal as Mrs. Davis grew more imperious, new young people gave an intimate tone to the casual evenings. Mr. Davis usually avoided the "at homes," except for sharing a cup of tea if the visitors were friends. However, when Mrs. Davis's younger sister Maggie came to live at the White House and the Cary girls came to Richmond, there was a lighter and freer atmosphere, and to them the President's home was virtually "open house."

Jefferson Davis had always enjoyed the company of women, and young people released the sweeter elements in his nature. He liked to banter with them and found interest in their affairs. And these three Cary cousins were the glamour girls of their day, the fabled belles in the last flowering of knighthood. They brought a freshness and a radiance to the whole social life of which the White House was the center.

Because of the disproportionate place this formal society occupied in the structure of the South, the effect of the group symbolized by the Carys was significant. Calling themselves the "Cary Invincibles," who went "where one was sure to meet the cream of society," these princesses were Constance Cary, from northern Virginia, and her cousins, Hetty and Jennie Cary, of Baltimore.

Connie's fame derived from her social inventiveness and a literary turn of mind. She published verse during the war and later wrote a chronicle of the court during the siege of Richmond.

Hetty was the great beauty of her day. In the New Orleans *Crescent* appeared this typical tribute: "Look well at her, for you have never seen, and will probably never see again, so beautiful a woman! . . .

[234]

It is worth a king's ransom, a lifetime of trouble, to look at one such woman."

The countless descriptions of her "Titian-haired loveliness" and "magnificent form" were always accompanied by references to her intelligence, sweetness, and humor. Either as one word or two, she was in every sense a gentlewoman. She had to leave Baltimore for doing what Barbara Frietchie got the credit for—waving her own flag at the enemy troops. Warned of impending arrest, she and her sister, Jennie, ran the blockade and eventually joined Connie in Richmond.

Connie and her mother first found lodging in the Clifton House, an old run-down narrow brick building "honeycombed by subterranean passages, and crowded to its limits with refugees. . . ." As the dismal rookery boasted no sitting room, Connie took possession of an abandoned doctor's office a short distance away, and there she entertained "many a dignitary of camp or state."

Because of the "pinch of war," occasionally the suppers were Dutch treat "when the guests brought brandied peaches, boxes of sardines, French prunes, and bags of biscuit, while the host contributed only a roast turkey or a ham, with knives and forks. Democratic feasts those were, where major generals and 'high privates' met on an equal footing."

Finally, when Hetty and Jennie joined them, the Carys escaped from the "gloom of the Clifton House to lodgings in Miss Clarke's pleasant home in Franklin Street, surrounded by a pretty garden and embowering trees." Like any people accustomed to their own home, they suffered the privation of having to share quarters, but Connie could always find exciting diversions in the panoply of war.

She enjoyed making flags and presenting them to famous military units, and she was not long at Miss Clarke's before she was rewarded by the Washington Artillery of New Orleans, who desired to "salute the donor of their flag."

Connie describes how the ladies gathered at the front gate for the event:

We stood . . . bareheaded under the canopy of green leaves above the sidewalk, I a little in advance, while the travel-stained battalion filed by us. My heart beat high with pride as the officers saluted with their swords, the band played "My Maryland," the tired soldiers . . . set up a rousing cheer; and there, in the midst of them, taking the April wind with daring, was my banner, dipping low until it passed me.

Helping with the wounded was another activity:

The residents of those pretty houses standing back in gardens full of roses set their cooks to work, or, better still, went themselves into the kitchen, to compound delicious messes for the wounded. . . . Flitting about the streets in the direction of the hospitals were smiling, white-jacketed negroes carrying silver trays with dishes of fine porcelain under napkins of thick white damask . . . surmounted by clusters of freshly gathered flowers.

Then there were weddings, followed by receptions, and constant gatherings in celebrated "salons." To these came the outstanding officers and the "high privates," distinguished visitors from the South and Europe, government officials and the literati.

This small segment of Richmond, with their courage before danger, their humor before sacrifices, their resourcefulness in gaiety, achieved a gallantry which was no less valid because it was self-conscious. They suffered material losses and personal anguish continuously, and their privations were no less real to them because, being privileged, they still lived at a higher level than the average individual. The point of their attitude was that in dramatizing their social-newsworthy group, they colored the Confederacy with their values and emphases.

To them the war was to maintain a privileged caste in a land they loved, and, as their class was conceived in chivalry, they behaved chivalrously. They brought a fine flavor of romance to the last stand of a civilization. But it was not the same romance that colored the anonymous masses in Richmond who (their goings on unchronicled) were indecently and miserably crowded, already suffering actual want and the deeper wants of the heart for not being able to provide their wounded with canopied silver trays.

Constance Cary describes vividly a moonlit burial of "a spotless knight" in the magnificently set Hollywood Cemetery, but she evidenced no awareness of the cemetery on the outskirts, Oakwood, where the thousands of unknown dead lie marked by rows and rows of simple white stones.

The emergence of Lee validated their position. With all the Stonewall Jacksons and Forrests of humble origin, the god was an aristocrat of aristocrats. That neither he nor his wife and daughters entered into their gay little world of a few city blocks could be regarded as a matter of personal taste. He symbolized the cause to these sincerely patriotic women whose "society was reinforced by a number of agreeable and high-bred women from all parts of the South, many of whom had previously graced a wider social sphere in Europe and America."

Though acutely aware of the drama of their makeshifts, the members of this small publicized segment did sustain an agreeable graciousness in the general neighborhod of the White House. In the lingering fall, the haze blurred outlines and gave the illusion of unchanged tranquillity to the tree-lined streets. Even when the foliage was gone the branches smudged against the mauve dusk sky; and at night, in the misty blue, lights were a powdered yellow. When inside the large-roomed houses the silver still shone and the linen gleamed and Negroes lent themselves to the air of dignified comfort, it was easy for one to believe in the security of their way and to enjoy old friends and new powers.

This society that developed was basically of the Confederate government, and its functions followed the pattern of the old Washington political set, in which many of these Southerners had been prominent. Starting from the Davises', an unofficial social detachment of the White House was the home of Colonel and Mrs. Joseph Ives. As Colonel Ives was on the President's staff and Mrs. Ives was a most gifted hostess, Davis turned over to this "elegant" couple much of the entertainment of distinguished visitors.

A brother of Mrs. Ives, Thomas Semmes, the Louisiana senator, and his wife lived across the street from the White House and provided a center for the more mature mental types who also liked good living. Benjamin, who selected his hosts with great care, was seen at their receptions. As Mr. Semmes was one of the senators whom Stephens found sensible, it was not unnatural that the Vice-President, at times, stayed there. But this did not stop the President and Mrs. Davis from enjoying the hospitality too. Another blandly selective couple, the Mallorys, whose own home was widely known for its charm, also visited there.

A rival court to Varina's was held by Mrs. Joe Johnston. An extremely clever woman, she rallied some of the Davises' new enemies like the Wigfalls and Mrs. Clement Clay.

Wife of a senator, Mrs. Clay had been known in Washington as one of the top-flight hostesses, and in the early days in Richmond had been one of Mrs. Davis's friends. Her house too was a pleasant center.

General and Mrs. Samuel Cooper entertained frequently, and another favorite spot was the Oulds'. Judge Ould, former D.C. district attorney, was commissioner of prison exchange. His daughter Mattie was one of the belles of the group led by the Cary girls.

Among other belles, both of Richmond and Confederate families, were Henrietta Semmes, Jennie Cooper, the Haxall and the Cabell girls, and the beautiful Mary Triplett.

The daughters of General Lee went about very little. Though the home, where all the Lee women were refugeeing, was cordial, Mrs. Lee felt that entertainment was inappropriate. Mrs. Lee was severely crippled by arthritis, and from her wheel chair she, helped by her daughters, was probably the record sock knitter of the Confederacy.

The older natives for the most part lived quietly, much as they had before the war, and did not as a group become a vital part of the social structure of the Confederacy. However, the younger Richmonders took very happily to the new gaiety.

The "men about town," like the belles, were from everywhere. Leaders among those were Will Wyatt and Willie Myers, Trav Daniel, a Washington dilettante; Harry Stanton, a Kentucky soldier and poet; George Bagby, who was to become Virginia's favorite humorist; Ham Chamberlayne, who wrote his mother and sister superb letters of war life; and Page McCarty, who was to kill a rival for Mary Triplett in a notorious duel that established the field of honor as illegal in Virginia. Two young Yale men on the President's staff were well liked —William Preston Johnston, son of Albert Sidney Johnston, and Burton Harrison, Mr. Davis's secretary, who lived at the White House and was to wed Connie Cary after the war.

Of the five young soldiers most loved in Richmond, none was to survive the war. In the fall of '62, two had already been killed in cavalry action—Turner Ashby, fighting with Stonewall Jackson in the Valley, and William Latané, the lone casualty of Stuart's "Ride around McClellan." Latané was destined for a curious immortality. In those early days of chivalry Latané's family was much grieved at some obtuse Yankee's callousness in preventing a proper burial. With the help of a couple of Negroes, the women buried the body near a farmhouse, and an engraving of this scene became familiar in every Southern parlor as "The Burial of Latané."

Two soldiers from Richmond were Willie and John Pegram, sons of Mrs. Virginia Pegram, who ran the fashionable girls' school in Linden Row. Bespectacled Willie was to become, at twenty-two, A. P. Hill's great cannoneer, and to be killed in the last week of the war. John Pegram was to win his greatest fame in the last winter of the war by marrying the gorgeous Hetty Cary. Three weeks after the fashionable event of their wedding he, like his brother, was killed at Petersburg.

John Pelham of Alabama, the beautiful dark boy called by Lee "the gallant Pelham" and famous as Jeb Stuart's brilliant cannoneer, was only a few months from his death. . . .

With young and old, native and Confederate, separate and blending, the society was distinctly defined, and its varying standards and gradations were understood by its few hundred members. At the undisputed top was Mrs. Robert Stanard, a native Richmonder, whose home admittedly most nearly approached a salon.

The wealthy widow of Edgar Poe's boyhood friend, Mrs. Stanard was a handsome and gracefully imperious lady. Purely socially, an invitation to her home was probably more an accolade than one to the Davises'. Her receptions were beyond any political lines. Her guests were truly distinguished in one way or another. It was the sort of house where foreign nobility or celebrities would be entertained.

Before the war Thackeray had found her hospitality very charming. During the war Benjamin, of course, was one of her bright lights, and even Stephens would emerge from his bookish villainies at her invitation. From New Orleans there was Pierre Soulé; from Georgia, Lucius Quintus Cincinnatus Lamar; from South Carolina, the great grandee, Wade Hampton; from Maryland, Robert Kyd Douglas, Jackson's engaging young aide-de-camp; from Tennessee, Judge Campbell.

(Judge Campbell was the Supreme Court justice who resigned when he felt the Southern commissioners to Lincoln had been betrayed through him. He now lived across from the Davises', and his wife was described as a "gentle and delightful" hostess of a much-sought wartime house.)

Mrs. Stanard, with her love of and flair for brilliant society, inadvertently performed a valuable contribution. Her vast entertaining, in contrast to most Richmonders' conservative habits, permitted the government newcomers to understand there was nothing necessarily hostile in the lack of social intercourse of the stay-at-homes. Those who went in for the gay life before the war still did; and those who hadn't still didn't. Of Mrs. Stanard, DeLeon said she "was one of the very first to break that thin layer of ice over the home society which formed at first hint of the white frost of social invasion. . . ."

2

As the fall passed into an unusually cold early December, all segments of Richmond were emotionally united in a common elation. The latest and biggest "On to Richmond" had been broken at

Fredericksburg, fifty-five miles away, where Lee ruined the third Yankee general's reputation in six months—Burnside's.

For a Union government hungry for a decisive victory in Virginia, to get momentum into its new war efforts, McClellan's cautious maneuvering became unbearable. This time his military career was officially ended, and the general who had failed him at Sharpsburg was given command of the greatest army yet in Virginia—150,000.

If the government wanted action and not maneuvering, Burnside aimed to please. With a river at his back, he sent his men straight up a hill precisely where Lee expectantly awaited him. The result was slaughter. Burnside lost well over twelve thousand men who, in a foot soldier's version of "theirs not to reason why," charged the impregnable lines with grim gallantry.

Strategically, besides keeping hopes high in the South, the battle proved nothing except that Virginia was a tough state to invade with Lee's army in the way, and pressure in the East must await for spring. Even the people's hopes lacked the early expectancy of the war's ending because of a Union defeat. They hoped it might hasten the end, contribute to their ultimate victory, influence Europe, but their preparations for a wartime existence became more businesslike.

When the wounded were returned on trains the city no longer turned to frantic impromptu efforts to provide shelter and food and care for the men. Carriages and hired hacks no more rushed through the crowded streets. After the Seven Days around Richmond, a group of military exempts, called "a committee," formed an ambulance corps at their own expense.

There were no more "smiling Negroes" carrying silver trays through the fashionable streets or careworn women carrying little baskets as they pushed with humble anxiety through the confusion for their own loved ones. Even the old extemporized hospitals were gone—tobacco factories and dry-goods stores, railroad depots with the workshop an operating room, the horror and stench of the St. Charles Hotel on Main Street.

By congressional act, all these hospitals were either discontinued or incorporated into the military medical organization. There was one exception. Miss Sally Tomkins had operated, at her own expense, a private hospital at Third and Main so efficiently that President Davis commissioned her captain and, assisted by other women, Captain Sally continued her private hospital throughout the war.

Among hospitals that existed before the war, Bellevue on Church Hill and the Medical College of Virginia Infirmary near the White

House provided care for civilians, as did the small infirmary of St. Francis de Sales, slightly north of Richmond on Brook Road.

Their prices had jumped along with everything else. Ward patients paid four dollars a day at the Medical College Infirmary as against six dollars a week before the war, and private rooms went from seven a week to five a day. Midwifery was ten dollars and for d.t.'s, euphemistically called *mania à potu,* eight dollars a day must be paid "invariably in advance."

Of the soldier hospitals, there were twenty-three in or near the city. As far as possible men from the same state were placed in the same hospital, and the same effort was made with doctors. The nursing situation was extremely confused. In the beginning the young women who rushed to help largely performed tasks which did not require skill or training. They made beds, washed faces and hands, served food, read to and wrote letters for patients, and tried to bring cheer in general. Some, who were put to assisting at operations, became casualties themselves at the gore.

As the military general hospitals became established, duties became more clearly defined. Actual nursing was done by men, at first drawn from the Army. As demand for nurses steadily increased, this proved too much of a drain on combat troops, and an effort was made to use military exempts and Negroes.

Women's work became that of hospital and ward matrons. These were regular full-time jobs with small pay, hard thankless work, and very little recognition (save in the affection of the wounded). When the job of "matron" was included in the military organization, the volunteers who liked to help on their own time were noticeable by their absence. The greatest number of applicants came from the ignorant and so-called lower class of women.

The administration of hospitals was under the supervision of Surgeon General Moore, attached to the War Department, and his office was in the same building as the Secretary of War. The whole medical department had fewer than three thousand medical officers (755 of whom were from Virginia), and this gave them a ratio to troops of less than one half that of a modern army. A large number of these doctors acted in the field, where much of the surgery was performed behind the lines. But as Richmond was in proximity to all the fighting in the east, more than 60 per cent of the Confederate wounded passed through its hospitals.

Nineteen per cent of war wounds were of the abdomen and chest, and those of the abdomen especially were regarded as fatal. Twelve per cent were gunshot wounds of the face, neck, and head. The vast majority, 65 per cent, involved the extremities. This is where the surgery came in, largely consisting of amputation.

The mortality rate from amputations in Richmond hospitals in the summer of 1862 ran from 13 per cent with forearms to as high as 59 per cent at the thigh. These deaths were caused mainly by infections following the surgery—such as gangrene, tetanus, erysipelas, and septicemia. Hospital gangrene, occurring most often in the lower extremities, was a horrible death in from fourteen to sixteen hours of great suffering accompanied by nauseous putridity.

Far more of a problem for the hospitals than wounds was illness. Before the war was a year old the troops in Virginia had averaged three illnesses per man; by the end of the war, statistically, each Confederate soldier was sick or wounded about six times. (Two hundred thousand died of wounds and disease—one in twenty-five of the Southern white population.)

Typhoid fever took one fourth of all the men who died of diseases in the Confederate Army, though malaria held first place among illnesses. Scarlet fever was rare; mumps was prevalent only the first year; smallpox came to Virginia with the army's retreat from Maryland.

Measles was a bugbear: "The diseases consequent to and traceable to measles cost the Confederate Army the lives of more men and a greater amount of invalidism than all other causes combined. . . ."

As close second, "diarrhea was the bane of the volunteer recruit. . . ." Nine tenths of new recruits suffered from it. This and dysentery were difficult to cure, and they disabled more soldiers than battle accidents. Of course there were venereal diseases, the "army itch," and a form of night blindness observed during Fredericksburg which the doctors came to understand later as a diet deficiency.

The importance of diet, as a preventive, was never realized during the war, and no conclusions apparently were drawn from the fact that active armies suffered much less from disease than armies in camp.

Jackson's army, during its strenuous days of the Valley campaign, was the healthiest of all Confederate units. In Jackson's instinctual aggressiveness, he may or may not have understood the effect on health of the morale resulting from action; but Davis certainly never learned from the facts of his hospitals the deleterious effects resulting from the boredom of troops in the idle occupation of land.

He had the facts available. All hospitals kept monthly and quarterly reports on the sick and wounded, a prescription and a diet book, and annual reports, all of which forms were almost literally identical to those of the old army.

In the treatment of both wounded and ill the hospitals were terribly handicapped by the lack of medicines, and the Union blockade of medical supplies definitely contributed to the spurts of primitive hatred of the enemy. None of the people in the hospitals could stifle all reactions to the cause, when they were unable to quiet agonized men with morphine or bring unconsciousness with anesthetics to the screaming men having their bones sawed off.

Laboratories in Richmond attempted to manufacture drugs, but the disadvantages were too great. Mainly the Medical Department, for hospitals and the field, relied on substitutes. Cottonseed tea and willow bark were used for quinine; American hemlock for opium; wild julep for ipecac; peanut oil and cottonseed oil for olive oil; hops and motherwort for laudanum; dandelion for calomel, and Jamestown weed for belladonna. Blackberry root was a specific for dysentery; dogwood bark for malaria; watermelon seed for a diuretic, and holly bark for a tonic.

For surgical supplies the Medical Corps had to be equally ingenious. The pliant bark of a tree served for tourniquets, the penknife as a scalpel, and a piece of soft pine wood for probing bullets. Splints were so scarce that a fence rail was used to set a broken arm.

The bandages were made largely by women of all classes. They scraped old sheets and clothes for lint; they carded raw cotton by hand and baked it in the oven. Cotton rags had to serve for sponges, and, as silk was very scarce, cotton with flax or horsehair was used for ligatures and sutures.

With all these makeshifts and inexperience, with all the improvisation and exhausting hours, this large new segment of Richmond's population came in for far less historical attention than those charming ladies whose inventiveness was turned to making hats and gowns out of damask curtains.

Those women and doctors who labored in candlelit buildings to return disabled men to combat did not lend themselves to romance. The ladies remembered are those who provided music for Jeb Stuart to dance to. From them comes the memory of how his spurs jingled and how his golden laugh rang out and how, on a clear winter night, the music of Sweeney's banjo drifted back as Stuart's staff rode away.

If you want to have a good time, jine the cavalry. . . .

But the color and music of Stuart's world was only the plume waving over the anonymous masses who fought, suffered, and groaned through the same clear winter nights without a song.

CHAPTER TWENTY

Arrangements for Disaster

FOR the first time, Jefferson Davis was in distant fields when a battle occurred. When Fredericksburg was fought (though he had known it was coming) the President was in Tennessee, setting the stage for a tragedy. It was to be a puppet show, and he would pull the strings.

In Virginia there were no more loose units under the control of the President. There was the Army of Northern Virginia under Lee, and clearly there was now no place for Davis. Though General Lee was "regular" in his procedure, and very tactful, it was *his* army—and he had virtually ordered Davis and his staff off the field when the President made a nuisance of himself during the Seven Days.

The frustrated militarist needed a new interest, and the loose units in the West provided it.

His enemies—brawling with his supporters in Congress, using knives and inkstands and turning Jefferson's old high-ceilinged Capitol into a battle-royal arena—were wrong in ascribing even the least admirable of his traits to despotism. (On many of the same issues Lincoln was equally despotic.) What neither friend nor enemy seemed to perceive was his need to *play soldier*.

Far from springing from a domineering source, this compulsion was rather pathetic. The damage it caused resulted from his sincere belief in himself as a qualified leader of the armed forces. He not only suffered delusions regarding his limitations, but, with his defensive concept, he thought bureaucratically in terms of departments that were artificial, unsound, and impractical for the existing conditions.

Because of the railroad connections and the mountains, which could have been a barrier for and not between the Confederate forces, the logical armies to co-operate were Lee's in Virginia and Bragg's in eastern Tennessee. Because of the proximity to open Vicksburg, the logical armies in the West to co-operate were those in Mississippi and across the river in Arkansas.

But Lee had the Army of Northern Virginia, and west of the river was too far away. As Davis accepted the division of the Alleghenies, and Bragg's army in East Tennessee and the Confederate force in Mississippi were both in the *West,* they were grandly incorporated into the Department of the West. The few forces west of the Mississippi River became even more grandly the Department of Trans-Mississippi.

In the last action in the Department of the West, Bragg and Kirby Smith had led in East Tennessee, and Price and Van Dorn in Mississippi. When Davis recognized this situation as having too many cooks, he consolidated all the forces in eastern Tennessee under Bragg, and all the forces in Mississippi were grouped under General Pemberton, sent out from the Charleston defenses. To co-ordinate these two armies in the department, Davis appointed Joe Johnston vaguely as commander in the West.

Joe Johnston had fully recovered from his wound received at Seven Pines, where his date with destiny had been postponed. He was no longer the Number One Hero, but his reputation was still big and he still had his chance for posterity.

From the beginning Johnston perceived that the two armies under his nominal command had two separate and distinct objectives, as well as being too distant for physical co-operation.

The Union armies, after the debacle of Halleck's grandiose strategy, likewise were concentrated into two separate forces with distinct objectives. Rosecrans led the Tennessee army aiming for Chattanooga, and Grant headed the drive on Vicksburg.

As Grant was bold and pertinacious, it was evident that Pemberton needed reinforcements for the protection of Vicksburg. But as Bragg could not afford to be weakened before Rosecrans, in addition to the impracticality of Bragg's and Pemberton's armies working together, Johnston wanted for Pemberton the idle troops under Holmes across the Mississippi in Arkansas.

To Johnston this seemed very simple, as indeed it was—except that it confused Davis's departments. In this it involved the newest member of the Cabinet, George Randolph, the third Secretary of War.

2

Randolph's greatest accomplishment was a biological accident: his mother was the daughter of Thomas Jefferson. This genealogical fact allied Randolph with the top bracket families in Virginia's ruling class, and, in affirmation of the legend, Virginia regarded socially connected kinfolk as the highest individual merit. It was a well-bred, well-mannered achievement; it required none of the ruder qualities of assertiveness and did nothing to disturb the *status quo*. With this solid achievement behind one, to be called a fool or a knave carried little sting. The most foolish knave could always claim superiority over anyone he could call "plain."

Where a caste system had flourished for over two hundred years, a class consciousness developed among those who controlled the Negro and held the land through which he was exploited. With passing time, the possession of neither slaves nor land was required for a newcomer to be "accepted" in the master class, but it was required that his whole family, possibly for two or more generations, possess the personal and social attributes and values that had become synonymous with the aristocracy.

In this way there were no violent fluctuations or upheavals, no sensational conquests of formal society. Naturally, individuals with uncontainable drives had started leaving the state as early as 1800, to fructify the South and Southwest, and much of the sturdy yeomanry migrated West in philosophic disagreement with the class structure. The existing population, then, was clearly separated on either side of a shadowy borderland.

With Randolph, his family's rise (beginning with Jefferson's father) was so far back in the frontier-colonial period that he, beyond any individual activity, was warp and woof of the legend itself. As there must be a Virginian in the Cabinet, what more natural choice than this cultivated gentleman of "an illustrious family"? He had come in with the permanent government when Hunter went out of the State Department and Benjamin went up.

In a government based on the aristocratic concept, his choice was at least as reasonable as appointments made in a United States government based on the concept of political expediency. Also, on his record, Randolph was as qualified as the average American cabinet member before and since, and a good deal more than many.

He had served as a midshipman in the U. S. Navy before entering the college founded by his grandfather; while practicing law he was active in the state militia; and early in the war he commanded a battery on the Peninsula under Magruder, whose unstinted praise won Randolph a brigadier's commission. He had never served as a brigadier, as ill-health forced him into retirement from which he emerged as Secretary.

For War Secretary, however, his record was less important than his character and personality in meeting the curious and special demands of that office. During Benjamin's tenure in the war office, compatibility between him and Davis produced a teamwork between the President and the Secretary. Benjamin assumed responsibility for the operation of the office, at which he was facile, and never intruded on Davis's cherished prerogative of the appointment of officers. On strategy, in which Benjamin was uninterested, he advised when asked and gave the President a sense of support. Having the President's confidence and a supple sense of appropriateness, he made many decisions and assumed responsibility on department policy. He became the collaborator who does not instigate.

For Randolph to step into the role created by Benjamin was outside the realm of possibility. Without experience in adjusting himself to the convenience of a social inferior, he had no desire to acquire it. Not knowing how to advise without authority behind his advice, he advocated nothing at all. When his suggestions were overruled, he ceased making them. Temperamentally unable to fit into the teamwork on Davis's terms, Randolph slowly reduced his job to that of chief clerk of the bureau.

He continued the custom of conferences with the President, but Davis grew dissatisfied with his lack of initiative. Randolph, for his part, unquestionably grew to hate the job.

He had earlier disliked the military life that kept him from his books and home, and now he disliked the routine that was so different from what he called the "gentlemanly ease of private life." The detail work bored him; the anomalous position was distasteful, and the freely made references to his being a clerk nibbled at his pride.

With his state at war, even a Randolph could not well resign without reason. Though he cared little enough what Confederates thought of him, Virginians of his own class, like Joe Johnston, who admired Randolph, might not accept his quitting without question. His course was simple.

He could suddenly assume authority and act independently of the President. This would either make his position one that he could understandably and pridefully fulfill or it would force the President to fire him.

The event which he selected as the test was the movement of Holmes's troops from idleness in Arkansas to active support of Pemberton in Mississippi. Johnston wanted the move, and it was wise; but Randolph's manner of going about it was the same as a slap in Davis's face.

Far from advising, without even asking Davis's approval, he sent the order. Davis immediately rescinded the order and sent Randolph a very stiff letter.

That sour observer, war clerk Jones, saw the end coming. After acting "merely in the humble capacity of a clerk, Mr. Randolph all at once essayed to act the PRESIDENT." For the third day he "did not go to the President's closet," and "such incidents as these preceded the resignation of Mr. Walker."

Davis, after his rebuke, waited on Randolph. The Secretary answered the rebuke with his resignation.

His going was of no consequence. He was replaced by a better man and a better Secretary (who also filled the requirements of being a Virginian of the top drawer). But the issue over which he went, the movement of Holmes's troops for Johnston, was of the vastest consequence.

There is no way of knowing if Davis rescinded the order because Randolph made it or because he disbelieved in its practicality. But it is possible that he would have agreed to it had either Benjamin or Randolph's successor, Seddon, tactfully pointed out the wisdom of the move.

In either case Johnston, from virtually the day of his appointment in Richmond, was refused permission to co-ordinate troops according to his own plans. Once in the West the conviction grew that being department head there meant the same as War Department head in Richmond. He was to advise and suggest; yet, at the same time, assume responsibility for the result. Even if Johnston had not been mindful of his reputation, he could scarcely feel enthusiasm for an assignment that promised such little glory and so much grief.

Albert Sidney Johnston or Lee would have done the best he could with it; as Lee, in his desk job of military adviser, proved the unsung crucial factor in the Peninsula campaign. But Joe Johnston lacked the selflessness, the sheer size, of those men of heroic mold.

It would ask too much of that posterity-conscious generation to produce more than a few giants who found immortality by not seeking it. Too many others found only death, odium, and obscurity by following the same course.

In the unprecedented clash of forces, Lee and Lincoln grew with the demands of the unique struggle. Johnston, with the majority of others, did not.

By his own ambition and ill fortune, he was historically placed where the amalgam of talents through largeness of character was demanded.

Lacking that, he lacked all. Nothing commonplace—of skill and training and courage—could meet the needs of his exacting and huge assignment.

3

Joe Johnston had been in Tennessee only a short time when Davis joined him for "an inspection tour." Having always proven Johnston wrong to his own satisfaction, Davis saw no reason they could not be pleasant traveling companions (Old College Chums). But Johnston, his mind on his unenthusiastically regarded job, pressed on the President directly the need of transferring Holmes's troops to Pemberton. When Davis refused, and instead ordered him to get ten thousand from Bragg, Johnston started writing friends in Richmond.

They put pressure on the new war secretary, Seddon, who agreed with Johnston. By the time Davis and Johnston reached Mississippi, Davis had gotten around to admitting that maybe Holmes should come over. But he only *suggested* this to Holmes, and by the time Holmes got around to following the suggestion there were no more troops in Arkansas to send.

Earlier in the year, when Van Dorn and Price had taken their troops east of the Mississippi, Arkansas was left undefended and at the mercy of roving bands of guerrillas. General Hindman, an excellent organizer and administrator, by his own efforts raised from nothing a force of twenty-five thousand—infantry, cavalry, and artillery (fifty-four pieces), and five thousand unarmed men in camps of instruction. He not only lifted the Union threat on Little Rock but in turn offered enough of a threat on Missouri to cause a concentration of Union troops there.

When Hindman had achieved this his force was incorporated into the Trans-Mississippi Department under the command of Holmes, whom Lee did not want. Holmes, the inadequate field commander, was made administrator, and Hindman, the excellent administrator, became field commander. When Holmes called on him for the troops which he had organized, Hindman decided to take one crack at the Yankees first.

Alas, it was his last. The army, which Hindman raised, he could not fight. By the time they staggered back over the winter roads, illness and desertion whittled away to barely ten thousand troops the force from which Johnston had asked twenty thousand.

Then Davis got rid of both Hindman and Holmes, giving the department to Kirby Smith, but this gave Johnston no troops for Pemberton. Grant did get some troops, after Hindman single-handedly removed the threat he had created. However, some inconsequential fighting continued in Arkansas and, of course, the department still existed.

The President, apparently well pleased with the military phase of his tour, continued through the South on one of his rare personal appearances and made speeches. He returned to Richmond, buoyed by the Fredericksburg victory. He took to heart the praise of those sections of the British press favorable to his country. The London *Times* said, "Whatever may be the fate of the new nationality, in its subsequent claims to the respect of mankind it will assuredly begin its career with a reputation for genius and valor which the most famous nations might envy."

Davis seemed to enter a mental phase in which, from failing to comprehend the nature of the war, he began to lose focus on the physical realities of the fighting.

From secession Davis's conviction in the rightness and beauty and inviolability of the planters' feudalism was so personal that he accepted the existence of the Confederacy as instinctually as an individual does his own life. With this identification he buttressed himself with the same unreasoning hope that comes to any mortal. He expected a "break" from the outside and gave credence to such possible aids as the political power of the anti-war Copperhead movement in the Middle West.

In man and Confederate, with this elemental hope, there was the constant tension from failing to adjust to the two widening levels of idea and action. When the tension became unbearable, his neuralgic aches reached the peak, in illness, which broke the strain of the effort to adapt. Refreshed, he returned to ways that were efficacious in his earlier life—arrangement of military departments.

As the cycle spun faster and his control of the government remained rigid, the new phase of the struggle from the South's angle became the psychological drama of Jefferson Davis.

4

Davis's retreat to the safety of familiar patterns even permitted him to accept in the departmental organization a commander who was outspokenly dissatisfied with his job and lacked confidence in the arrangements. Conceiving of the Confederacy as an established country, where a man kept on his jobs whether he liked them or not, it followed for Davis that a subordinate must execute the supreme authority's arrangements regardless of his personal opinion.

Never understanding the human element, it apparently did not occur to Davis either to remove the cause of Johnston's complaints or remove him.

For Johnston, whose stronger interest seemed to be in the Vicksburg front, there was nothing at the moment he could do for Pemberton. Sherman, from Memphis, had tried a back-door attack on Vicksburg from the Yazoo River and got a bad going over. Grant had started an overland attack from the northwest, which was permanently ruined when Van Dorn with cavalry destroyed his base at Holly Springs, Mississippi. (In this kind of bold action Van Dorn had found himself, but he was killed shortly afterwards by the husband of a woman whose lover he was.)

Morgan and Forrest were embarking on destructive raids of their own into enemy territory, and temporarily the dangerous situation in Mississippi was in hand.

Back in East Tennessee, with the dyspeptic Bragg, things were different. After Bragg's army had been weakened by one fourth, against Johnston's advice, Rosecrans attacked him. It was another of Bragg's hard, tough fights (Stone's River, December 31) to no conclusion. He really had Rosecrans rocked back on his heels and, with the ten thousand taken from him by Davis, Bragg could have destroyed him. As it was, with his neurotic relief at having an action over, Bragg hesitated until Rosecrans was reinforced, then abandoned the field (with captures), gave up his base at Murfreesboro, and retreated toward Chattanooga—back where he had started from less than six months before.

After that his ranking officers complained so bitterly that he asked for a vote of confidence. Bragg generously stated that if they voted against him he would resign. The officers took him at his word and gave a resounding vote of no confidence, but Bragg went on as if nothing had happened. When one disillusioned officer sent the vote on to Davis, the President immediately ordered Johnston to inspect the situation.

Up to this point Johnston had complained of only nominal command of two armies and actual command of none. Now, in spite of the candid letters of Bragg's officers, Johnston professed to find the army in good condition and thought Bragg should not be replaced by anyone in his army or anyone making the inspection.

But, as Johnston was the department commander, Davis thought he was the one to assume command of Bragg's army. Johnston replied that it would "wound his sensibilities" to replace Bragg, and anyway he didn't think Bragg should be removed at all. Davis answered, in effect, that he would not think of wounding Johnston's sensibilities.

Though Johnston now clung desperately to his hateful nominal command, Seddon, the new War Secretary, began to press him to assume command of Bragg's partly demoralized army. Reluctantly Johnston went to do this—only to find Mrs. Bragg so ill that he could not intrude the unpleasant subject. When Mrs. Bragg recovered, Johnston himself fell sick and went to bed.

According to his codes of honor he might well have found the situation with Bragg distasteful. However, in the same period, after Lee won at Fredericksburg, Johnston wrote his friend Wigfall, "What luck some people have. Nobody will ever come to attack me in such a place." It could well be Johnston did not want Bragg's army, which, characteristically, he already found in a poor situation for defense, and he feared attack.

With Union troops occupying the same position in the West they had in early summer, only concentrated now in determined drives, Davis allowed this situation to continue. The lack of confidence in Bragg had been admitted to the point of trying to supersede him. Joe Johnston, in effect, refused the job and plainly disliked the one he had. Pemberton, on the river, was a gentleman and officer whose regular approach was pleasing to Davis, but he was untried in major battle and largely disliked for his manners of a Northern martinet.

Having completed this arrangement for disaster, Davis made speeches in Congress denouncing England and the U.S., and happily returned to the clerical details of organization. In one day he sent over to the war office one hundred papers, nearly all applications for office, which he had diligently gone over in pencil.

He brought this work home from the office, climbing the steep hill of Capitol Square, and his light burned long into the night.

These papers were becoming the Confederacy.

CHAPTER TWENTY-ONE

Gentlemen, Place Your Bets

I N THE bitterly cold January of 1863 Mrs. Davis selected that inopportune moment to announce that she reserved the right not to return social calls. This was the Fort Sumter of society's "irrepressible conflict." It squarely divided her adherents and enemies, and the *Examiner's* Pollard used the occasion to attack her edict as undemocratic.

Of course he attacked the Davises for everything. When they did not give receptions he accused them of snobbishness and hoarding their government pay; when they entertained he accused them of extravagance and pretense. He even blamed the President for the vice in Richmond. However, by denouncing everything he was bound to be right occasionally—even if not on the grounds of his reasons.

It is true that the Davises, as rulers of an aristocracy, felt no need to con what some today call the little people (though to ante-bellum Southerners it would have been more dangerous to call them "little people" than to ignore them). It was natural that Mrs. Davis limited her functions to social equals and/or government officials, and not to return calls was a prerogative of the busy wife of an executive—even though it had been different in the young days of the nation. But, as a leader of a movement depending on loyalty and freely given support, the President (as well as his wife) lost touch with the heart of the people—even those within a few blocks of his home and office.

War clerk Jones, struggling to find shelter for his family with unfurnished houses renting at $1,800, observed:

A portion of the people look like vagabonds. We see men and women and children in the streets in dingy and dilapidated clothes; and some seem gaunt and pale with hunger—the speculators, and thieving quartermasters and commissaries only, looking sleek and comfortable. . . . The President . . . should cultivate the friendship and support of the people, and be strong in their affections, if he would rule with a strong hand. If he offends and exasperates them, they will break his power to pieces.

The "strong hand" was the execution of necessary wartime measures—such as impressment of food which began in the spring, conscription, suspension of habeas corpus, martial law, the abortive price fixing, the curtailment of cotton and tobacco trade, and all the abuses and inequalities inevitably associated with such legislation. To the individualistic Southerners, with extremely personal ideas of liberty, such goings on were even more oppressive than equivalent legislation in contemporary America. Working on their potential "destruction" of the President's power was the fact, which he forgot, that to them it was *not* an established country. Many of the people had not wanted to secede in the first place, and the majority (including, with Lee, practically all the Virginians in the Army) had come in only for their state.

These people needed the warming assurance that their sacrifices were not the whim of a despot whose favorites flourished and who permitted speculators to wax fat off their privations.

The *Dispatch* published tables showing that speculators had increased the costs of a family's basic needs by ten times since 1860. Women grew bewildered when they had to shop all over town to try to find a pound of candle tallow for less than $1.25 or enough calico to make a simple dress for less than $30, only to read of a gambling-house raid where "it is said that a cabinet minister, who was in one of those inner chambers reserved for distinguished guests and sacred to the mysteries of 'blue chips,' effected his escape by jumping from the window." This was generally believed (probably correctly) to be Benjamin.

On the opposite side of this gay life was the explosion in one of Gorgas's ordnance buildings on Brown's Island. In a detached one-story frame building, where over sixty women worked on condemned cartridges, separating the bullets and the powder, the haste of one girl caused the explosion that killed thirty-three. The rest were badly burned, and one missing was believed to have jumped into the river with burning clothes.

It could not have heartened the families and friends of these victims to learn that the recent Secretary of War Randolph (who resigned his brigadiership along with his civil job) was defending in court the speculators who had bought substitutes and now claimed exemption.

Nor could they be cheered by the spectacle of the clerk of the House of Representatives being fatally shot at noon near the Treasury Building by the former assistant clerk whom he had fired.

These isolated incidents could not be blamed on Davis; but what was he doing to change conditions? Lee wrote the Secretary of War, asking him to discontinue the rule permitting officers' families in Richmond and other cities to buy government meat for their families; but Northrop, after what Mrs. Davis called his "usual delay," wrote that the practice was necessary. The President defended the hated incompetent running the Commissary.

The Virginia state legislature tried to pass a bill to suppress extortion, citing such instances as shoe-sole leather jumping from twenty-five cents to $2.50 a pound and boots from $7.50 to $60 a pair, but this got nowhere.

In the Senate, Robert Hunter suggested a sound refunding act to reduce circulation of treasury notes and stabilize prices. Aside from the impossible living conditions of the people, planters wanted cash, and the government produce loans on cotton began to fall off.

But without a quorum in both houses, a few tobacco chewers whiled away the time listening to the idiocies of Foote, and Crockett of Kentucky. Crockett believed that some Union states would also secede if the South made proper advances. Indeed, he wanted still a third country, formed of the Upper South and the Middle West, and was probably one of the hosts to the Union disloyalists from Indiana and Illinois who came to Richmond at that time with some wild idea of their own.

When they did fill the two rooms on either side of the great central hall, the members busied themselves adopting "the Great Seal of the Confederate States." It was to be a piece of solid silver, about three inches in diameter and thick, and designed with the best silver workmanship available in England. In the center was to be a reproduction of the equestrian statue of George Washington that stood in Capitol Square. This was to be surrounded by a wreath displaying the agricultural products of the Confederacy—cotton and tobacco, corn and wheat. The motto was *Deo Vindice.*

Benjamin occupied some of his slack time writing Mason the instructions. Benjamin worked so fast he never had enough to do, but he used no leisure studying the people. He kept himself fresh and available for the President.

Davis always welcomed his friend for exchanges of opinion, but in the long winter his attention was concentrated on troop movements. From the coast of North Carolina ambitious Union generals threatened inland movements at the railroads. Inland from the coast of Virginia at Suffolk, Unions threatened an advance on Petersburg, south of Richmond. Some of Lee's divisions had to be moved there to guard while resting.

Burnside puffed up for one more advance on Richmond. This bogged down in the mud, but necessitated more troops moving back and forth, and Stuart's cavalry was actively raiding. At Charleston a couple of Mallory's gunboats attacked the blockading fleet, and a later attack of the fleet on Charleston was repulsed. All of these matters were handled adequately in their own departments. It was the people who needed the President's attention. They needed the same sense of kinship that welded the men into Lee's Army of Northern Virginia.

2

The many who suffered from rising prices and inflated money, on fixed or reduced incomes, were too aware of the few coming into quick new money. This was the flush money of black-market operators, speculators, army and government swindlers in supply services, certain merchants and manufacturers with government contracts. Privately owned cotton and tobacco were sold secretly abroad and to the North; frequently these speculators sold in barter for goods rare in the South, which they sold in Richmond at fantastic prices.

Another element was the blockade runners:

. . . known on Main Street by their New York costumes of baggy trowsers, round sack, and oval tile, their segar alight, and the complaisant air with which they survey the show windows and themselves, as they saunter back and forth from the auction stores, with nothing on their hands and minds but the question, how shall they dispose of their cargo to the best advantage and the highest price? . . .

The money of all these people represented no permanent wealth. Tomorrow its source might dry up, and certainly its value would be less. It went as quickly as it came, for pleasure, for vice, for transient luxuries and excitement. Desperate people sold their furniture, china, silver, anything to the auctions that lined Main Street like a carnival concession; refugees from the country hired their slaves to the government for the constant building of fortifications around the city. Some of these took the sudden ready cash for a brief squandering.

The more fashionable crowded the new Richmond Theater, rebuilt on the site of the Marshall Theater that had burned the year before. It opened in February with *As You Iike It,* but the chief attraction was the theater itself. The colonnaded façade was severe, but the interior caused exclamations of awe. The gold leaf decorating the circular-shaped balconies was "so liberal it may be doubted whether the whole Confederacy contains half as much." Shakespeare was followed by a French comedy, melodramas, and tragedies, and Bulwer Lytton's *Richelieu.*

The more raffish people thronged to Metropolitan Hall and the Varieties, in the new bright-light district below the Exchange Hotel. In the same section a sweet narrow little street lined with locust trees, and bearing the pleasant name of "Locust Alley," became famous out of all proportion to its one-block length because of the quality of its bawdyhouses.

Less famous but more numerous were the dingy houses scattered in the poorer sections and in such places as "Ram Cat Alley" between Main and Cary. Their inmates, described as "squalid wretches in dirty calico and checked bonnets," trooped in bannerless parades through the mayor's court. Beyond the reach of the mayor's court, the aristocrats among prostitutes lived in the upper floors of the gambling establishments.

The forty well-known gambling establishments formed the core of Richmond's night life. They combined svelte speakeasy and club and served the best food in town. Some spent ten thousand dollars a day for the food, superbly cooked, which they gave to habitués. They sold fine brandies, champagne, and whisky. In the top places, like Johnny Worsham's, the decorations were engaging and the furniture "luxurious."

Richmond papers said that "nearly every third door in the most frequented part" of Main Street "displays the gilt numbers and painted glass which garnish fashionable gates to hell. At hotels, street corners, everywhere in Richmond may be seen sinister-eyed gamblers, glistening in fine clothes and waiting like a cat for his prey."

Despite the newspapers' constant plaints, "These faro-banks collected the leading men, resident and alien, of the Capital. Senators, soldiers and the learned professions sat elbow to elbow . . . in the handsome rooms, with soft lights and obsequious servants. . . ." They offered the only relaxation to many soldiers on brief leaves in a strange city, and many of these were offered the hospitality of the establishments even though they lacked the cash to gamble.

Naturally around these houses gathered adventurers of all sorts, what the newspapers called "thieves and garroters and bloated vagabonds from Washington," and bogus military men whose only title was what had "been given them in brothels."

These professionals got plenty of amateur competition, local and foreign, from civilians and deserters. Stabbings and assaults went hand in hand with robbery. Coats, hats, canes, pipes, hens—everything—were stolen—even a bay horse of the President's. A dry-goods store on Broad Street was robbed of over $10,000 in clothes and silks, which soon appeared again at auctions at double the price.

Bootleggers flourished as the government bought up alcohol for medical purposes and the prices in licensed saloons became prohibitive. "Nips" went up to fifty and seventy-five cents, with apple brandy about the best to be had. At the depot for trains from the South, Winder's detectives, ever vigilant on the scent of whisky, grabbed seven women who were carrying twenty gallons in beef bladders hung around their waists under their skirts. Winder's boys had no hesitancy in raising ladies' dresses, and the whisky was "confiscated."

One barkeeper they arrested, an Englishman, they could charge for his misdeeds only with "being very suspicious."

3

With all the problems in a city crowded and disrupted beyond its means to exercise ordinary controls, the Confederate government burdened it further by introducing a new kind of population—which was to grow to more than one third of the peacetime population.

Some years before, a ship chandler from Maine had come to Richmond in search of new opportunity. He went in partnership with a Richmonder and they built up a nice business down by the public wharves at Rockett's. In time the senior partner from Maine decided that the site for expansion lay toward the center of the city, where work on the river was opening up passage for larger boats nearer town. As the native Richmonder (typically satisfied with things as they were) resisted this change, the partnership was amicably dissolved and the Maine man took as partner his then grown son.

Shortly before the war they built a fine new brick warehouse, three stories high where it fronted on Cary Street and four stories at the back where the side street sloped down to the canal. Their business of ship chandlers, grocers, and commission merchants had hardly started flourishing when Provost Marshal Winder requisitioned their building. He ordered them to clear out in forty-eight hours. The harassed father and son moved so fast they neglected to haul down their sign.

When the new Yankee prisoners, from the summer of '62, were marched in, they saw the big bright letters: Libby & Son. Thus the name of the honest Maine merchant, who had prospered in Virginia, became excoriated throughout his native land, as Libby Prison became a symbol of all that was horrible in the Rebels.

It was bigger than the first makeshift prison in Liggon's warehouse. There was running water, and routine was better established, since the administrators now had some prison experience. But there was the same lack of furniture, less food than the Northerners were accustomed to, and crowding.

Though there were other prison camps in the lower South, and later very large ones were to be built, Jefferson Davis (as he insisted on being supreme authority of everything military) was supremely responsible for the lack of planning that permitted Richmond to become a prison center.

With both armies feeding off the state, and the doubled population of Richmond already suffering food shortage, prisoners added a needless strain to the inadequate commissary and railroads which brought foods from the South. With their proximity to their own armies the prisoners required a large number of experienced guards, and they presented a constant menace in the center of the capital.

The prisoners, forced to share the people's privations (for which they were at least partly responsible), complained almost as much as the first batch, some still with a sense of outrage. Others sneered at the "Rebel's ignorance of the great issues of the war."

Among the veteran Union troops there was more general adjustment, and many of those accepted as reasonable the Southerner's idea that he fought for preservation. A Middle Westerner, who found the food scarce but no unnecessary hardship imposed, understood the Rebel when he told a guard they should be natural friends, as their sections shared more in common than either did with New England. The Southerner answered, "No, you've tried to subjugate us and we'll have nothing to do with you."

However ignorant was his oversimplification and his unawareness of the greater issues, his viewpoint does not seem to justify contempt; and the denying of any dignity to his position showed an intolerance that contributed no less to wider misunderstanding than did his limited and primitive interpretation of liberty to mean the right to defend his own soil.

With the coming of the Popes and Butlers a growing vindictiveness and ruthlessness was shown the Southern people, but a type of prisoner consistently accepted his own occupation and destruction of homes and farms and towns as beside the point, before the theoretical rightness of the crusade for the republic. While other Federals accepted the prisoner's lot as unenviable and brought resourcefulness to relieve it, the righteous continued to condemn the contemptible "Rebel" for not making him happy in prison.

The prison facilities were certainly limited, and there was real discomfort among the prisoners even then. While the prison officials on the whole tried to do the best they could under the trying conditions, everything, including some of the prisoners' attitudes, exacerbated their nerves rather than promoted kindness. If their best was not enough, they let it go at that. Among the guards, as before, there were decent men and hard men, but there was no systematized brutality.

A major element in the whole prison situation was the fact that the Confederates did not want the prisoners there any more than they wanted to be there. From the beginning the government had tried to effect a cartel of exchange.

Individual exchanges had been made between individual generals. In the spring of '62, in the Valley, Jackson's surgeon gave unconditional parole to eight captured Union surgeons, who promised to try to institute the same practice. In an agreement with Washington, Lee treated Union surgeons as non-combatants and, after the Seven Days, paroled the wounded abandoned by McClellan.

Following the abortive measures during the threatened reprisal on Colonel Corcoran and his twelve brother officers, Benjamin continued to try for a working agreement with the United States, whose attitude he found puerile and devious. Some progress was made when the Unions got the big haul of prisoners at Fort Donelson, and negotiations broke down. But they opened again when the Federals, from the battles around Richmond, began crowding Libby. In late July a cartel arrangement was finally made.

Flag-of-truce boats took the men down to a point on the James River and met a boat from Fortress Monroe. This was necessarily a slow process, and it was evident the Northern prisoners were to form a permanent segment of Richmond's population.

This was all right with the speculators who sold the well-to-do prisoners food which Richmonders could not afford to buy, nor could the government find any means of obtaining for its own soldiers.

These leaks in an oppressive system, these inequities between rich and poor—whether the rich were extortionists or enemies or cabinet members—created in the people a susceptibility to anti-government attacks.

Mrs. Davis said that if her husband's enemies could see him as he really was, they would be won over. The element of truth there was that he could make himself extremely appealing. But with his enemies he could not, and with the people he did not. Expecting them all to believe as he did, he expected them to execute the arrangements he so painstakingly made on the papers in the office on the second floor of the quiet house on the hill.

CHAPTER TWENTY-TWO

Innocents Abroad

THE Haxall, Crenshaw Company in Richmond manufactured superb flour, and as the sister of Crenshaw, Mrs. Grant, lived in friendly neighborliness next door to the Davises, she often sent them flour and other delicacies. When Mrs. Davis had bread made from this flour, and a paste made from English walnuts which grew on her grounds, she saw that some went to her favorite epicure, Benjamin. With this and a glass of the Davises' small store of McHenry sherry, Benjamin said, "A man's patriotism became rampant."

His optimism also became more pronounced.

In that winter of heavy snows Benjamin received a visitor from the great French banking house of Erlanger & Cie, who came with a financial proposition which Benjamin regarded sourly. The Erlangers were to float a European bond issue—a loan—on cotton payable in the future, which would net the hard-pressed Confederate purchasers millions in gold immediately. As a straight business deal the terms were insulting to a cold touch, like Benjamin, on money matters.

On the five-million-pound loan the Erlangers would get everything above 70 cents on the dollar and an 8 per cent commission, which would net the Confederacy around three and a third million. On those details Benjamin cut the loan down to three million, lowered the commission to 7 per cent, and lifted the Erlangers' take to begin at 77 cents.

Even then he was not satisfied, but, from France, Slidell urged the loan because of its political power. Benjamin, with his awareness of the need for co-ordination in Confederate activities, consented to the bad business element on Slidell's assurances that the loan would influence recognition, as well as assist Confederate credit. Benjamin was the most optimistic official in Richmond as to recognition, and, once he agreed to the loan for that purpose, he went through the formality of walking downstairs and getting the signature of the Secretary of the Treasury.

Seared little Memminger had retreated to his bookkeeping from where he observed the incomprehensible antics of his fellows. He who had suffered the rejection of all his tax measures now beheld Robert Toombs, a most consistent opponent of tariff when he had been in Congress, bombard the press with letters clamoring for government bonds and taxes as the only way to run the Treasury Department. To what must have been the amazement of Memminger, these measures were now hailed as wisdom from the quarters which had opposed him. As an earnest administration man, Memminger had become one of the targets of Davis's enemies.

In response to the newspapers, Congress erupted in a passage of bills taxing everything—salaries and money, goods and slaves. By then much of the land was occupied and the hard-pressed people within the Confederacy would have nothing to do with revenue collectors. This reduced the states'-rights-Confederate wars from politics to personalities. It also reduced Memminger to a bewildered impotency in affairs involving personal contact.

For purchases abroad he had obtained credit from cotton certificates on the government-owned cotton acquired through produce bonds. But he worked slowly through Washington-style red tape and concentrated on his department as a bureau rather than on the total objectives with which finances should have been integrated.

Like many of his fellows, Memminger was wholly adequate for a country of abundance, but was unable to make the shift to emergency legislation with inferior resources while working through Congress on established democratic procedure.

It is not without point that the men working toward correlated total objectives operated outside any set department. Benjamin was technically in the State Department, but that had no rigid bounds to him. He was more of a co-ordinator with presidential support. Unfortunately for a study in what might have been accomplished from his unofficial post, his potential was largely nullified by the time lapse in communications abroad.

Otherwise he might not have been misled by Slidell on the Erlanger loan.

2

All of Slidell's talent for and experience in intrigue had been confined to American political machines. Master of the cloakroom deal, when he went abroad he represented for the first time a cause larger than himself. He became, unaccustomedly, a special pleader. His larger loyalties developed a disparity between his old skills and his methods of approaching the new needs.

Hope blurred his realism, and, as so many Americans before and since, he did not apply his back-room technique in dealing with Europe. Attributing qualities to France which he hoped were there, he failed to study motives with his usual astuteness. Nothing else could account for his expectation of honorable dealings from that sawdust emperor, Napoleon III.

This second-rate adventurer was clearly interested in the Confederacy for the primary reason of establishing Maximilian in Mexico in safety from the United States, and the French forces were soon to take Mexico City and drive Juarez north. Bazaine would become military commander, holding the country safe for the bewhiskered archduke. Maximilian was hesitating until the Confederacy's position assured his throne of some permanence.

As anxious as Napoleon was for the Confederate recognition, Slidell could not miss the fact that the Emperor was extremely timid of any action. When England threatened to close down the Confederate shipbuilding there, after the escape of the *Alabama,* Slidell called on his good friend the Emperor. With all Napoleon's assurances to help, he obviously stalled.

It required the best of Slidell's intriguing to get work actually started by Arman, largest shipbuilder in France. When Slidell tried to hurry matters through the new Foreign Minister, De Lhuys told him he didn't want to know anything about it and suggested the Minister of Commerce. Rouher then gave promise of clearance, but with seeming reluctance. Meanwhile Bulloch had come over from England and placed another ship order, and the total called for four armed corvettes and two ironclad rams. It required more pressure to get final permission indirectly from Napoleon, and when Slidell thanked him he found the Emperor very cautious.

The shipbuilding to Slidell was a relatively minor phase in his drive on recognition. Though England had refused in the preceding fall, Slidell's friends in the British Foreign Office assured him that the issue on some form of intervention was still active. Also when Davis, in his midwinter speech, had denounced England for its blockade stand, Russell had written Mason an evasive letter which indicated that the British government had not closed the door. Hence it was still possible that activity in France could influence the British, and they could certainly be influenced by involvement in money.

The Erlanger loan—a speculation in future cotton—would achieve both.

In this Slidell was not only deluded by hope, but it seems that personal vanity also played a part. The Erlangers were as powerful politically and socially as they were financially, and it must have been a triumph to the old New Orleans machine politician when one of them married his daughter. And to tie in his family ambitions with hope for his country, the Erlangers were sufficiently potent to get their Confederate bond issue advertised in French newspapers. Slidell could well think this was tantamount to official French backing, and the boy who could swing it was his son-in-law.

The conviction of the old intriguer caused him to override Mason and his English adviser, James Spence. Merchant, banker, and shipper, Spence was one of the Confederates' greatest friends and, at great cost to himself, acted as their purchasing agent abroad. Spence and Mason preferred the Confederate cotton bonds to such loans as Erlanger's, and when Spence saw the actual contract he openly opposed the loan. At this point, to complete the confusion through conflicting authority, C. J. McRae was sent over from Alabama to supervise the Erlanger loan. As Spence was not a Confederate and was avowedly anti-slavery, Slidell pushed through the loan by ignoring Spence's existence.

Everything seemed to justify his faith when the loan opened in March, and even Mason wrote Benjamin that it shows "cotton is King at last." After opening at 90, the bond soon sagged to 86. Spence feared the buyers might be willing to forfeit the 15 per cent they had paid rather than meet the next installment, and he offered to take over the loan himself. He believed that the Erlangers' greed for profits was the basic cause for the slump.

The Erlangers then threatened to keep all of the first installment if Mason did not put a million pounds of the Confederacy's scant money in to bull the market. Mason could think of no alternative to agreeing. By his buying, the second installment was paid and the market driven up above par, but the price soon started to drop again.

Though now it should have been clear that the Erlangers were little better than swindlers, who had used Slidell's filial affection for their own ends, the proud father only attacked Spence for criticizing them.

It was equally clear that no pressure had been brought to bear on the problem of recognition, and, over a year too late, the Confederate government realized that cotton had failed in everything except as a medium of purchase.

At the end of November '62 the textile situation in England reached bottom, with employment averaging one-quarter time. From here on it improved until, in the summer of '63, mills were running at half time, with cotton coming from India, Egypt, Brazil, and China. The legend is that the English working classes were willing to starve because of anti-slavery sentiment; the fact is they were not required to do so.

It was not so much that they were willing to get by without cotton, but that the South was unable to get by without selling it to them. The Confederate policy gave way before necessity. The unofficial embargo silently faded away while cotton was shipped increasingly through the blockade as a basis of Confederate credit on war material.

3

John Wilkinson, aged forty-one, arrived in England from Richmond in the fall of 1862. He had enjoyed a pleasant trip through the blockade, stopping off at Havana and St. Thomas, where he carefully observed their manners and customs. In England he made contact with Mason, whom he liked. Through him Captain Wilkinson met Southern sympathizers who received him warmly and the heads of shipping firms who offered him material and plans and even models. But time was a consideration to him, and he bought a Clyde-built iron steamer. She was a long and narrow side-wheeler, light of draft, strongly built, and fast, and had plied between Glasgow and Belfast. Captain Wilkinson named her the *R. E. Lee.*

Before leaving Richmond, Captain Wilkinson had been in a Northern prison. He had been captured during the fall of New Orleans when, as the executive officer of the ill-fated *Louisiana*, he had assumed command when the captain was wounded. At the beginning of the war he had commanded the Aquia Creek Battery on the Potomac, and before that he had served in the U. S. Navy, as had his father, a commodore. At the time of Virginia's secession (he was from Norfolk), his duties particularly fitted him for his new service with the *R. E. Lee*—he had commanded a U.S. coastal-survey steamer.

Loaded with supplies for the War Department, the *R. E. Lee* put out to sea and made for Madeira. Captain Wilkinson was accommodated by a Yankee hotelkeeper who salved his conscience by overcharging the Rebels and running up a U.S. flag at night. From Madeira he sailed to Puerto Rico and then to Nassau, "the El Dorado."

Ideally located five hundred miles from Charleston and 550 from Wilmington, this port was the trading mart for Southerners, Northerners, Britishers, and anybody willing to take a risk for high profits.

A Northern correspondent said that "Charleston and Savannah in their palmiest days were never so overrun with cotton" as Nassau now.

Speculators bought Confederate cotton on commission and shipped it under neutral flags to Europe. For the most part under neutral flags supplies for the Confederacy came into Nassau. Dealing through these speculators and private blockade runners was an unsatisfactory and extremely costly method of obtaining supplies.

Such heavy goods as steel and iron and other metals, with their proportionately low selling price, gave a much smaller profit than salt and coffee, which could be resold to civilians. As the government exercised no control over these ships, it was forced to take what adventurers brought.

Even when the government chartered its own ships, it had to pay $200 a day for a forty-thousand-dollar vessel. Crews were paid $100 in gold for the trip, usually about seven days, with a fifty-dollar bounty; captains received $5,000 a month and other officers in proportion. Clyde-built ships ran practically every night, as 51 of 57 steamers and 55 of 91 sailing vessels reached Confederate ports from the summer of '62 to the summer of '63. At the same time 44 steamers and 45 sailing ships reached Nassau.

For the Northerner, John Brown was in his heaven and all was right with the world of trade—and the Deep South Cavalier, under this example, discovered the new and heady pleasure of money-making.

The judge advocate of the fleet blockading the South Atlantic said, "The munitions of war were furnished in very large quantities . . . by citizens of the United States. Good old Horace Greeley used to say . . . that the ideas and the vital aims of the South were 'more generally cherished' in New York than in South Carolina. . . ."

Confederate states, wanting to get in on the gold rush, operated their own fleets for profits in competition with the horde of speculators and the few government non-profit boats.

The government boats before the spring of '63 were operated largely, like the *R. E. Lee,* by Gorgas's Ordnance Department and the Confederate group in England. Huse had four that completed twenty-two round trips from January to August. The officers on these boats, like Captain Wilkinson, were paid in gold at their grades.

While the profit-motive captains could afford to be reckless, where two successful runs would pay enough so they could afford to lose the ships thereafter, the Confederate captains were so careful that it was not until 1864 that more than one of their blockade runners was lost.

Preparing to leave Nassau, Captain Wilkinson observed the wharves piled with cotton and warehouses with Confederate supplies; the streets crowded by businessmen during the day and "drunken revelers" at night. Every nationality on earth was there.

Then he started on his last lap to Wilmington, heading for an inlet north of Smith's Island. He got through the blockade fleet but struck "the Lump," a sandy knoll outside the bar. He unloaded some Scotch lithographers bound for Reagan's post-office work, finally got his ship off and made it in to a small village between the bars, from where he could see the blockade fleet.

He unloaded his cargo and found Wilmington a Southern version of Nassau—with speculators from everywhere thronging the blockade auctions and the unlucky ones turning desperado at night. Nothing was clearer than that the profit-motive nature of most blockade runners was not meeting the ideal of cotton going out and arms coming back, with luxuries to fill up the cargo. Though rifles and caps and ammunition poured steadily in, too frequently this matériel of war only filled up the main cargo of luxuries.

The same activity went on in other Southern ports. The British consul at Mobile reported sixteen ships out with cotton and eleven in within five weeks during the spring of '63. At Matamoros, in effect a Southern port near Brownsville, Texas, from seventy-seven to 125 ships, chiefly British, were counted in a single day.

From Matamoros, that unknown Confederate, Quintero, got the ammunition, powder, lead, copper, blankets, and coffee to supply the Trans-Mississippi Army. He kept the Mexican governor happy while hauling this material across the border by paying heavy duties on the cotton he shipped out. Quintero's worst enemies were neither bandits, venal politicians, nor U.S. agents, but rival purchasing agents for Texas. That his accomplishments continued was due primarily to his own clear purpose and an effective blending of tact, force, and money.

More purpose of this kind was sought on a larger scale by the gradual introduction of blockade runners like Captain Wilkinson. Before he was transferred to another field, he ran the *R. E. Lee* in and out twenty-one times, taking over six thousand bales of cotton and bringing in matériel mainly for the Army of Northern Virginia. Captain Wilkinson never feared danger from the blockading fleets; even as they increased, they increased the chance of firing into one another. He always felt the greatest danger in the open sea and was relieved that the United States did not put more ships inside the Gulf Stream between Wilmington and Charleston and Nassau.

Ships like the *R. E. Lee* also brought in medical supplies. An agency in London was maintained to send quinine, morphine, and chloroform in exchange for cotton. Blockade runners usually took the mail to Cuba, Nassau, or Bermuda, and it went from there to England or France on neutral ships.

Though this freedom in running the blockade was a tacit admission that the unofficial embargo had ended, Benjamin hoped to use the facts towards diplomatic ends. Even with the Erlanger loan limping and causing no official stir in England, Benjamin believed that another decisive military victory would have effect.

The North was practically no further along in occupying the South than it had been a year ago. Lee and Jackson were clearly the military geniuses of their day (young Henry Hotze had busts of them sold in England). When they defeated the next "On to Richmond," with the North's drive in the West stalemated, England must see that the war would last too long for its interests.

Also Benjamin's lawyer mind could so irrefutably prove the blockade illegal that England would be provided with a reason in international law to intervene on the grounds of humanity.

Finally Benjamin, the subtle realist, like Slidell, the wily intriguer, came to believe, with the President, that the justice of their beloved mellow land must prevail.

CHAPTER TWENTY-THREE

"Let Us Cross over the River . . ."

THE unusually cold winter in Richmond was slow in passing, and on March 23 snow was still on the ground. In late March, when the weather turned fine, and green came with a rush to the streets, Jefferson Davis declared another of his days for fasting and prayer. From the war office the clerk groaned, "Fasting in the midst of famine! May God save this people."

Since the spring the year before, when he was baptized, Jefferson Davis had turned increasingly to religion, as he suffered more constantly the dyspeptic pains and neuralgic aches of tension. The clerical work, which tired his mind, was naturally performed in a sedentary position which, using only the small muscles, tired his nerves. The fatigue from work gave him the illusion of accomplishment.

While Davis found relaxation in his home—with his wife and precocious, willful children—and by riding in the afternoons, he possessed no understanding of the value of mental change.

The shift from details to military decisions did not constitute a change but an extension of the same type of thinking, and he never had any freshness to bring.

The decision over an army involved so much more than a decision over an appointment that, using the same tired mental process, the comparable enormity of the consequences caused him to vacillate, worry, and doubt. It also prevented him from conceiving the totality. Events of the spring, which he regarded as peripheral, were not related by him to the whole.

As the Union cavalry developed in strength and skill, the Unions adopted the Confederate pattern—practiced in the East by Jeb Stuart, and much more in the West by Forrest and Morgan—of raiding deep into enemy territory. Stoneman raided in Virginia to Ashland, a supply point twenty miles north of Richmond, doing considerable damage and causing great alarm. In Mississippi, Grierson paralleled the river unhampered in an extremely destructive raid. In Alabama, Streight attempted the same toward Rome, Georgia, but was captured with his whole command by Forrest in one of the great exploits of that native fighting man.

These raids were not only to destroy resources for the Confederate armies, and incidentally anything else (in Tennessee a Union general ordered burned the home and barn of every family with a man in the Confederate armies), but to divert strength from the main forces.

With the South's limited man power, the only way to meet these threats was by greater concentrations which offered a chance to defeat the enemy armies in the field. If that could not be done, nothing could be done, as dispersal could never stop the raids.

But Davis was importuned from all over the country to protect specific areas. Even Hunter advised him to divert troops from Lee to protect farm areas in Virginia. Lee was too powerful for Davis to interfere there, and the Army of Northern Virginia was already weakened by the troops detailed in southeast Virginia gathering its own supplies.

A new "On to Richmond" was forming along the Rappahannock under "Fighting Joe" Hooker, a general considered by Charles Francis Adams to be "little better than a drunken West Point adventurer." In the Richmond war office Hooker was considered "deficient in talent and character," and Adams said that his headquarters was "a place no self-respecting man liked to go and no decent woman could go. It was a combination of barroom and brothel." Legend has it that the old-fashioned word "hooker" for prostitute derived from a train car full of "Hooker's" women who were captured by the Confederates.

With all this, Fighting Joe was not deficient in courage and ambition for one of the quick war reputations. He was planning with bold determination and skill to use his huge army.

But in the West, Davis had, along with his worries over Joe Johnston's evasions and Grant's bulldog drives on Vicksburg, his many departments. Dispersal reached its ultimate through departmentation in northern Alabama and Mississippi. Called "a lost land" between the armies, the people desperately needed protection, and the Confederacy needed to bolster their failing morale.

This failing in morale was manifested everywhere except in the armies—at the peak of their physical powers—and the new food-impressment measure heightened it. Here was revealed the division between military unity and civilian disunity.

The men of the armies shared a common loyalty to their leaders and developed a morale through their units. Even with food, no matter how little, they all fared the same and, spared the spectacle of fat living, occasionally enjoyed a feast off captured Union wagons—an event to which they could look forward with reasonable expectancy.

The civilians, with only their individual morale, were subjected to the constant inequalities of starvation and comparative luxury. As during the World Wars, the people with money, who were willing to patronize the black market, could always get what they wanted. The difference from today was in the smaller proportion who did and more who struggled on sub-subsistence levels.

When the government started to impress a portion of the farmers' produce at government prices, the farmers evaded the measure in every way possible. Some sold even higher what they did sell, and others raised less—some only enough for their own use. Others hid their produce, which was frequently ruined by exposure or stolen. The shortage of supply officers caused soldiers to act without proper certificates, and farmers sometimes resisted physically, since robbers, posing as government agents, also frequently "impressed."

Although this measure was a crude precursor of the OPA, it was so alien to American personal philosophy that Schwab, the recognized Yale economist, wrote in 1901 that, "By forcing out of activity the usual, automatic, and regulating factors of an open market, the government necessarily encouraged the kind of wastefulness which the modern individual system aims to correct."

Naturally, Professor Schwab's theories were held by the states'-rightists—Foote in Congress, Toombs, Brown, and the brothers Stephens in Georgia, the governors of Alabama, Louisiana, and Texas (the last of whom was actively engaged in cotton business on his own), and Vance, of North Carolina, who threatened the impressment agents with the state militia.

In Virginia, with the army in its unoccupied areas, impressment was easy to force. In Richmond, if the chronically poor railroads brought no food from the South, when the farmers used their various dodges to withhold food or else charged prices beyond the average person's reach, the city suffered acutely. The ladies of Connie Cary's set, who could always manage the necessities, gave "Starvation Parties" at which no food was served but paid musicians were provided. The mute suffering of the poor, who were outside the legend, expressed itself in a starvation party without music. It was called the "Bread Riot" and played down as far as possible.

The women, with a scattering of boys, started collecting in Capitol Square early in the morning on April 2. Outside the Treasury Building, where Davis and Benjamin worked above Memminger, the crowd complained of their hunger as their numbers swelled. When they reached over a thousand, they marched out of the Ninth Street end of the Square. Past the war office they surged down the steep hill to Main—with its gaudy auction blocks—and on down to the produce stores on Cary.

There, when frightened speculators tried to close their doors, the women swarmed in by sheer weight of numbers. With arms and aprons and baskets full of foods, they turned to more spoils. By now the rougher element took command and headed for the auction shops of Main Street.

When the owners, warned of the mob's approach, bolted their doors, the women broke through the plate-glass windows. Excited by their own vandalism, the mob took anything in sight—boots and brogues, silk and clothes pins, ladies' slippers and washtubs, hats, shirts, canes and jewelry.

When they threatened to reduce the central blocks of Main Street the city battalion arrived, led by the mayor. He threatened to fire if they failed to disperse.

At this moment the President, who had heard the noise in his office, hurried from the Treasury Building down to Main Street. Climbing up on a dray, he spoke to the angry women.

Davis was deeply moved, as always before any suffering, and under the circumstances he made a fine appeal. Reasonably he explained that such acts would only keep all food out of Richmond, and the bayonets poised against them should be better used against the common enemy, so that want would be removed from their land.

The women slowly dispersed, though about thirty were arrested as the ringleaders. The newspapers, in covering their trial, were careful to point out that those who were not dismissed could, with one exception, furnish bail. They depicted Mrs. Jackson, the arch instigator, as "an athletic woman of forty with a vixenish eye," and the Bread Riot was passed off as the act of rowdies.

2

Jefferson Davis, ignoring the women's riot as a symptom, went back to his paper work. He took to Congress the troubles of Postmaster Reagan in holding his contractors against conscription. Though these contractors were, in effect, buying exemption, they were necessary, and the President felt he should send the message to Congress.

He also sent nominations of postmasters to Congress, who referred them to committee, and he wrote at length his reasons for vetoing their bill to mail newspapers to soldiers free of postage. Chiefly the President's reason was that Reagan was interested in keeping his department in the black to the exclusion of all other considerations—and Reagan was a loyal supporter.

As it was, Reagan's mail service west of the Mississippi depended on the hazards of adventurers crossing the river at night in rowboats, and from occupied Missouri to Missouri troops east of the Mississippi the "department" consisted of the impromptu one-man service of an old friend of Sam Clemens.

When Absalom Grimes first refused to take the oath of allegiance in St. Louis from a German who, in broken English, told him Secessionists were trying to disrupt the Union, he had to flee to escape arrest. On his flight he took letters from all the women of his friends to his friends in camp. From this humble beginning Grimes survived two captures and one sentence (as a spy) to continue his mail service along the borderland.

The President naturally could delegate these small matters where they had no relation to the war office. Many other matters were made easier by discussion with Benjamin. As related to the people, Davis's well-fed friend would, if anything, remove him further.

The bland Secretary of State had discovered a means of endearing himself to Mrs. Davis, while serving his own department. With the increasing difficulties of sending communications abroad through the blockade, Benjamin gave Mrs. Davis letters to send under an assumed name to Slidell's daughter, through whom she received the answers.

He never cautioned her not to read the dispatches, and Varina related how, when they were alone, he talked freely on the basis of her having read them. Mrs. Davis was particularly grateful for his tact and confidence because, as she observed, "no more reticent man ever lived where it was possible to be silent."

Through all this, Benjamin remained "serenely cheerful, played games, jested and talked as wittily as usual." His conduct was so markedly different from the President's, who, his wife said, "suffered like one in torment," that they asked Benjamin from what source he drew his comfort.

He answered that there was a fate in the destiny of nations. As he regarded the fortunes of his country with the same philosophy which he applied to his life, he found it pointless to upset himself, when the only result could be the use of energy he might need to meet the inevitable.

Jefferson Davis was not the man to draw any comfort from that philosophy. In any case, looking for strength to carry him as he was, he turned to religion, in the fragrant days when peach and apple trees shaded his terrace sloping down to Shockoe Valley.

But nothing sustained him when the blow fell in May. IIe was shattered by the wounding of Stonewall Jackson.

3

Hooker's well-conceived opening battle in his "On to Richmond" ran into a counterconception of Lee's which, executed by Jackson, performed one of the pure military masterpieces of the modern world.

Outnumbering Lee, Hooker, with a strong holding force at the pivot of Fredericksburg, swung in a great flanking movement to the west. Containing the holding force with a handful, Lee divided the rest of his army and flanked Hooker's flanking movement.

At the area designated Chancellorsville, from a farmhouse, Jackson made the actual turn which rolled up Hooker's flank, bringing confusion to his army. At dusk, riding ahead for personal reconnaissance, Old Jack was shot by some vigilant North Carolina pickets.

His left arm was amputated, and pneumonia set in. Jefferson Davis, forgetful of the great victory that wrecked Hooker's advance, lived only on reports of Jackson's condition. As Jackson sank, Davis realized what unique genius was passing and how he had failed to use him to the best advantage.

While the President stayed up until one o'clock, with a Negro boy waiting to bring telegrams direct to him, he must have thought of the departmentalized futilities of the West, where all the men together would not make one Stonewall Jackson. He, and not Joe Johnston, should have been sent to the West. And the West should have been two armies—one Jackson's and one either Johnston's, Pemberton's, or Bragg's. Those three men, less than their sum, were letting that half of the Confederacy falter, while the incomparable Stonewall was wounded as a corps commander of Lee's. . . .

Then came the news. . . . *Pass the infantry to the front. Tell A. P. Hill to prepare for action. Let us cross over the river and rest under the shade of the trees.* . . . With these words, the great Presbyterian warrior passed to his own God.

When his body was brought to Richmond and lay in state in the Capitol, the stricken city suspended its life to do him honor. In its whole history Richmond never so mourned for one dead. Davis joined the throng who reviewed the simple, rustic face.

He had been slow to recognize the eccentric who had been no gentleman. He had brushed him off at First Manassas. He had sided with Benjamin against him. After his fabulous Valley campaign, his brilliance at Second Manassas, his indestructibility at Sharpsburg—after everything that made him one of the immortals—Davis had given armies and departments away and left this strange giant in command of four divisions in the Army of Northern Virginia.

Now that he was gone the President realized that, with Tom Jackson, something irreplaceable had gone from the Confederacy.

When Davis returned from the funeral he just sat staring blankly. A visitor came, and automatically Davis tried to bestir himself. But he had to say, "You must excuse me. I am still staggering from a dreadful blow. I cannot think."

CHAPTER TWENTY-FOUR

And Then There Was One

FOR the crucial West, where Jackson might have been, Jefferson Davis oddly had another man doing his thinking for him. Virginian James Seddon, the new Secretary of War, was as strange in his way as had been Old Jack in his. He belonged to that type of Virginia family whose chronicler in a book of memoirs would come out flatly with a chapter headed, "My Family Relationships," and then sprinkle names, like a savage handling his charms, in the simple belief that they exorcised all evil and made everything right with the universe.

But, unlike his gentlemanly predecessor, Randolph, James Seddon was a highly accomplished man in his own right. Not the least of his accomplishments was a dignity of presence and a charm of manner despite an appearance which Jones described as that of "a corpse exhumed after a month's interment . . . gaunt and emaciated, with long straggling hair, mingled gray and black. . . . His eyes are sunken. . . ." And the sepulchral note was completed by a black skullcap which he wore at all times.

Though not yet fifty, Seddon was in very frail health and suffered much from neuralgia. The details of the office taxed both his strength and patience, but Jones, the harsh observer of favorites and aristocrats, held Seddon in real respect and found him "manly."

Jones was accurate in using that adjective. Seddon's force of character, along with his other attributes, was the quality that gave him his influence over Davis. From the assumption of office Seddon had no slightest intention of becoming anybody's clerk, and he possessed both the tact and mental gifts to offer his advice in a manner acceptable to Davis.

Prior to the war he had been an extremely successful lawyer in Richmond and at one time owned the house in which the Davises now lived. He had served twice in U. S. Congress but, because of his health, had retired from politics to Sabot Hill, his country estate. About twenty miles west of Richmond in Goochland County, this plantation was situated on a broad hill which sloped down to the James River Valley and gave a magnificent view of the green, rolling farm country. His home there became a great social center, as his wife was a "delightful hostess."

Described by everyone as "gay and charming Sally," she was vivacious and intelligent, knowledgeable in literature and accomplished in music. Naturally gregarious, she once said, "I would rather talk to the most stupid man or woman alive than to no one at all."

Young men, as well as his contemporaries, were attracted to Seddon by his conversation—learned, reasoned, and flavored with "colloquial eloquence." Though he was widely read and of intellectual habits, he also shared his region's interest in outdoor life and had been a great quail shot in his youth. He was courtly, a little short on humor, and generous. Deaf to music—of which he said the only difference between it and other noises was that the steady rhythmic beat made music more disagreeable—he patiently bore his wife's vocal and instrumental performances and the singing of his guests.

Of all members of the Cabinet none was more of the essence of the South than Seddon. From his Calhoun days he had been a separatist, so passionately convinced of the rightness of secession that he could not conceive of the necessity of war. He had gone with the Virginia commission to Washington in its effort to effect a peaceful separation.

Once war came he served in the Confederate Congress and was among the uncompromising Confederates who thought clearly in terms of actualities toward the one end of winning their independence through military victories.

When he entered the Cabinet he brought a concept of his job and a plan for shifting the emphasis in the strategy of the war. Coming in after the failure of the Maryland-Kentucky invasions and Bragg's retreats, the new Secretary perceived that brilliant defensive victories in the East were only producing a stalemate, while the war was being lost in the West.

Because Seddon, being what he was, approached the President with definite plans when Davis's doubts of the West were growing into uncertainty and confusion, he was welcomed as an adviser. From the first he supported Joe Johnston over Bragg, the presidential favorite, and even won Davis over against his own pet. Davis, whose earlier interference with Johnston's plans had created in that general a dissatisfaction with his "anomalous" position, now allowed Seddon virtually carte blanche in dealing with the reluctant commander of the West.

Seddon went to work on Johnston with appeals and persuasions. Far from the harsh treatment Johnston had received from Benjamin and occasionally Davis, he received from Seddon warm, considerate letters, mentioning his "high repute" and "distinguished talents" and attributing Johnston's shilly-shallying to his "self-abnegation."

If Johnston felt his position was anomalous, Seddon assured him he was only too anxious to make any adjustments that Johnston suggested. If Johnston felt no adjustments would make co-ordination possible between the two armies of Bragg in Tennessee and Pemberton at Vicksburg, then he could take Bragg's army. If it wounded Johnston's sensibilities to remove Bragg, then retain him as second-in-command and use his organizational talent. If Johnston could not bring himself, out of what Seddon called his "generosity," to remove or retain Bragg, then send him on to Richmond for a conference with Seddon.

To this last understanding and friendly letter Johnston replied with a telegram that Mrs. Bragg was ill and he would not even send Bragg to Richmond. He later wrote direct to the President.

Though Johnston had complained bitterly at Benjamin's treatment, he showed no response to Seddon's kindness, nor even respect for the man. Doubtless he held a low opinion of the War Office. The only Secretary he approved of was Randolph, whose loss he regarded as irreparable, and Randolph had gone in protest at being a mere clerk. Possibly resenting Seddon as his friend's successor, Johnston could have felt that Seddon was also no more than a clerk.

Certainly Davis had released no final authority. To some extent he continued the personal contact which would serve to relegate the War Secretary to a subordinate position, if Johnston so wished to regard him. At the bottom, though, it would seem that Johnston had gotten off on the wrong foot in the West and determined to stay there.

A pall of disaster hung over the West. The artificial department was awkward, and the two commanders—Bragg and Pemberton—failed to inspire confidence. Guarding his reputation, Johnston simply did not wish the authority and preferred to record complaints which shifted it elsewhere.

2

When Davis wavered on Johnston, after Seddon's efforts failed, the Secretary did not give up.

Johnston interpreted some rumors to mean that Grant, approaching Vicksburg from the south, was sending some of his troops to reinforce Rosecrans in front of Bragg. As at Manassas, in the spring of '62, Johnston immediately saw the difficulties of subsistence and the problem of having his right turned if Rosecrans attacked. He wanted reinforcements for Bragg, whose army he vaguely lurked around.

With this information Seddon approached even the god, Lee, and suggested some brigades from his troops collecting supplies in southeast Virginia. These detached divisions were forced to serve as commissaries because Seddon, concentrating on Western strategy, accepted the existing inefficiency of Colonel Northrop's Commissary Department. Though Lee allowed his troops to be so employed, he by no means accepted a policy of their dispersal.

Lee answered Seddon that if Grant were sending troops to Rosecrans, the way to get them back was for Pemberton to attack Grant while he was weakened. Lee even then, a month before Chancellorsville, was planning to invade Maryland and bring Hooker after him. Lee thought possibly this might divert strength from the West and from Beauregard, who, now at Charleston, constantly predicted attacks against which he would fight to the last man, even with pikes.

When Johnston's fears of Rosecrans proved groundless, and Grant was obviously making his bid against Pemberton for Vicksburg, Seddon began to have his qualms about Johnston. By then Davis, grown frantic with worry at the threat to Vicksburg and Johnston's inactivity, ordered him from a sickbed to take command of the forces in Mississippi. There was none of Seddon's solicitude about the order, and Johnston left, covering himself in his answering telegram by saying, "I shall go immediately, although unfit for service."

Now that Johnston was actually going somewhere, Seddon rallied to provide troops to give him his chance. He scraped the Deep South of garrisons to form a unit for Johnston at Jackson, Mississippi. Due west of Vicksburg, these troops were in position to co-operate with Pemberton, between them and the city. Again Seddon bearded Lee, this time directly, on the matter of sending troops to Vicksburg. Chancellorsville had been fought then, stopping Hooker's "On to Richmond" —and Hooker, as Jones said, "was going the way of all general flesh." Could not Lee turn defensive in Virginia and send Pickett's division West?

But the Virginians of that long-haired, perfumed young gallant's command had a date on a hill outside the cemetery of Gettysburg, Pennsylvania. Lee wired, "The adoption of your proposition is hazardous, and becomes a question of Virginia and Mississippi. The distance and the uncertainty of the employments of troops are unfavorable. But, if necessary, order Pickett at once."

Davis sent the wire over to the war office endorsed, "The answer of General Lee was such as I should have anticipated, and in which I concur. JD."

That was the end of Seddon's plan, evolved around Johnston, for priority to the West. He was probably not influenced by Davis's rebuke. Lee, going to the crux in the decision between "Virginia and Mississippi," changed Seddon's thinking from desirable strategy to possible tactics.

In an even choice, Seddon preferred Mississippi to be held over offense from Virginia, for he believed Virginia would remain safe on defense. But Lee's words, "the distance and *the uncertainty of the employment of troops* are unfavorable," were a clear implication that divisions which could possibly gain advantage in Virginia would be wasted in the conditions of command in the West.

Already supporting this was the absence of Longstreet's "commissary divisions" from Chancellorsville. Their added number in that battle could probably have turned Hooker's defeat into military destruction. As Seddon's dilatory detail work was partially responsible for their absence, he was not willing to do deliberately what he had done inadvertently—not with his growing doubts of Joe Johnston.

From that moment Seddon came over to Davis's opinion of Johnston.

With his awareness of the West, he shifted his emphasis to the Eastern theater, where results were achieved. After all his efforts, Seddon turned from the West as a strategical center because he lost faith in Johnston and never held any in Bragg and Pemberton. He could only struggle on to save the situation there with the makeshifts in hand, and that he did most desperately.

3

The mounting worries of Davis, now that his adviser Seddon had failed him, brought on his physical illness that released the strain. He took to bed with an inflammation of the throat, and the strain in his one good eye grew so acute that some feared he would lose the sight of that. At home he clung to the reversion to activities of a period prior to his problems, and sent over to the hard-pressed war office fifty-five letters mostly concerning appointments.

He had to pay the City of Richmond $79.20 for three months' gas and had to figure out where to cut down expenses in order to buy forage for his horses. Board in Richmond was $300 a month for a horse, and $15 a day.

He and his wife were deeply saddened to learn that Grant's troops had ransacked their home in Mississippi and stolen all the thoroughbred horses left there. But the reason that enabled Grant's troops to pillage all that Davis owned struck even deeper than the private losses.

As Grant, subsisting off the country, advanced from south of Vicksburg, Joe Johnston had ordered Pemberton to concentrate his troops with Johnston's. As Johnston was farther west of Vicksburg at Jackson than Pemberton was, to join him Pemberton would further uncover the city. When Pemberton received Johnston's order he also had one from Davis urging him to hold Vicksburg at all costs.

Pemberton was Davis's friend. Like Lee, he was "regulation" in his approaches and procedure. Johnston previously had evinced small interest in him and never before assumed any active interest in the department. Pemberton was torn between duty to the President and to the reluctant commander of the "anomalous" department.

He wavered.

Decisions on Pemberton are usually unfavorable. But opinions on Civil War leaders were usually formed from an Olympian detachment that considered neither character nor the circumstances of rebellion. John Pemberton was a Pennsylvanian of the Regular Army who had come in with the South because he had married a Virginian and believed in the cause of her people.

Rather than welcoming a Northerner, the Confederates suspected him. On the statement of his grandson, Pemberton's formal West Point, Northern manner was not conducive to good fellowship in the South. Though he was a trained soldier, personally brave and deeply patriotic, he lacked the confidence of his army, and, in the field before Vicksburg, he certainly faltered. Under the duality of orders and sensing the lack of confidence, he would seem to have lost his poise.

Not concentrating with Johnston, Pemberton did not concentrate his own troops. Grant, to whose hard slugging the Western Confederates always offered their own divided commands, defeated him in detail. Pemberton barely managed to save his army and collected it inside the fortifications of Vicksburg.

Left alone at Jackson, Mississippi, Joe Johnston was overpowered and retreated. Sherman put the torch to the countryside for thirty miles around the state capital, apparently to prove his point that war is hell.

From a safe distance from everybody, Joe Johnston advised Pemberton to evacuate Vicksburg and lose the city, rather than stand a siege and lose also his army. Grant thought that Pemberton should have abandoned Vicksburg and striven to unite with Johnston. But Grant was unaware of Davis's orders to hold the city, though he did say that Davis more than once "came to the relief of the Union Army by means of his *superior military genius*." (His italics.)

At this point Davis's fears broke through his absorptions in military details. When bureaucracy no longer supported him, he lacked resolution in the moment of decision. Without the order of small details, he was driven only by anxiety.

Seddon, who could delegate authority, had as his assistant Judge Campbell, the former U. S. Supreme Court justice. Campbell found Davis, "procrastinating . . . filled with petty scruples and doubts, and wanting in a clear, strong, intrepid judgment, a vigorous resolution. . . ."

It was a crisis in the life of a nation that called for greatness.

A year before, when Lincoln wanted to put heart in the war, he had come out with the Emancipation Proclamation.

Davis, with intelligence and courage and integrity, lacked that imponderable by which qualities become greater than the sum of their parts.

He called a cabinet meeting.

4

The only man who counted in the group which met on that Saturday morning was the only outsider—Robert E. Lee. They were all there—Reagan, walking the half mile from his modest home on Second and Marshall; Memminger, coming from the quiet of the old Queen Anne section of Church Hill; Benjamin from his urbane house on Main near Foushee; Mallory from the neighborhood of the President, and Seddon from the Spotswood Hotel.

Mallory and Memminger, running on the tracks of their departments, said nothing. Benjamin, close to his own failure as a War Secretary, remained a smiling and alert observer to an unequal struggle. The fight was between the great Lee and, unexpectedly, Reagan, the humble Postmaster.

There was nothing humble in John Reagan's manner. Bearded and powerful, stubborn in his own convictions, he stood out against the god, against them all, for the immediate sending of troops to the relief of Vicksburg. Pemberton's force was inside, withstanding a siege. Johnston's small force skulked without purpose behind Grant, waiting for reinforcements to move to the rescue.

Give Johnston the men, Reagan argued. Nothing at the moment was as important as Vicksburg. That last city on the Mississippi *was* the West. To abandon Pemberton was to abandon the Western Confederacy.

Bewildered and shaken, Jefferson Davis clutched the short arms of his black-upholstered swivel chair and swung from side to side, looking for someone with evidence to sway him. What said Secretary of War Seddon, the champion of the West?

He said with Lee. The invincibility of the Army of Northern Virginia was a certainty, not to be tampered with. The troops were all concentrated now in the terrible force Lee had made them. Let them march north and complete the destruction that the absence of Longstreet had deprived them of at Chancellorsville.

Silently the Cabinet agreed. The memory of these veterans of Longstreet, passing through Richmond to join the main body, was still vivid. Their official gray long gone now, they wore homespun dyed yellow-brown from the native butternut. There were black dress coats and Yankee breeches, and bright checked shirts made from old aprons. Haversacks swung loosely from a cord around their shoulders. Ragged shoes scuffled the dirt as they walked. Hats were anything with brims they shaped in rakish slants, and the shaggy hair beneath had forgotten barbers. Bearded-faced and hairy-handed, they looked like some horde of terrorists, laughing and cursing and clutching their shiny muskets. Could any living man save Lee lead them in the yelling fury that had made the Army of Northern Virginia, man for man, the greatest body of combat troops ever on this continent?

Except tough-bitten Reagan, no man in the Cabinet would assume the responsibility of opposing that tangible.

Then there was Lee in his own personal grandeur. His hair had turned gray, and the once trim mustache had become a whitening beard that nigh covered his face. Success sat in simple austerity on the native aristocrat, born of the legend to which most of them had aspired.

Only Reagan, the plain man, stood in no awe. But what could he do against a people's god?

The god chose to invade the North. He suggested it might relieve the West, though that was not his point. He had made his point in his telegram concerning Pickett's transfer. It was Virginia's safety against Mississippi's.

For that he has been accused of failure to view the war as a whole. He was not asked to. He was asked less than one year before to command the Army of Northern Virginia, and he was only one of half a dozen army commanders. The greatness of his exploits with his one army, in contrast to the others, caused history to think of Confederate armies synonymously with Lee—and caused some historians to think that Lee, in his day, should have so regarded himself.

But Lee, neither personally ambitious nor anything of a rebel, saw himself only in relation to the recognized authority of an established country. And, in the cabinet meeting, his opinion was asked on the limited subject of whether or not his troops should reinforce in the West. He had clearly expressed the feeling that troops sent there would not be well employed. Vicksburg would fall anyway.

If he went personally, with some of his troops, he faced new conditions, strange terrain, troops and commanders unknown to him, with the time lapse of distance that would threaten two fronts.

Bragg and Longstreet, after the fact, advanced brilliant plans for a concentration that would invade to the Ohio. That was easy from their tents. On Bragg's previous invasion he had turned back without firing a shot. As for Bragg's army, Joe Johnston, on the spot, had refused to touch it with a ten-foot pole. Longstreet failed woefully on his two independent commands, and, as a subordinate in Lee's invasion, he was only weeks away from the unco-operativeness that was to contribute to the failure.

In any case, whom would Lee leave in Virginia, with Jackson gone? Again the critics claim that uncovering Richmond was of no consequence. A capital was only the pawn in the old-fashioned thinking of a chivalrous war. But what else of a symbol did a country possess when it lacked even boundaries?

Were Kentucky and Missouri Confederate states invaded or Union states with Southern sympathizers? Were the Confederate boundaries at the Ohio River or the Tennessee border? Where did they stop and start west of the Mississippi? *What* constituted the Confederacy? What, beside the capital, symbolized the life of the Confederacy as long as it lived?

As the North subscribed to the same symbolism, their armies were magnetized by the few square miles of red clay hills climbing above the James River. Radiating in all directions from its physical bounds, the power of that city provided a breakwater to the Eastern South—the only Confederate breakwater that lasted in the whole war.

At the most, as Lee saw it, he was asked to *exchange* the safety of Virginia for the possible safety of Vicksburg. He was not asked to become commander in chief and think of total strategy, but only to decide between two *immediate* courses. His decision was based on his confidence to defend Virginia, which was by no means freed of threat because Hooker was defeated. His plan to invade Pennsylvania, as a means of defense, only indirectly concerned the West, in that a successful invasion might cause dickerings for peace.

With all else, a tactical reason for invading the North was that both armies again would get out of Virginia. The farmers needed to get their crops in. As it was, because of poor transportation, he had seen his physical position endangered by want of subsistence back in early April.

Davis, wanting to be convinced by somebody, was convinced by Lee. Seddon seconded him. The die was cast.

Lee went north, then, for supplies, for possible political pressure, and because he felt Vicksburg was already lost.

The Cabinet accepted the decision and dispersed. It was Saturday night. Only Reagan remained unsatisfied. He walked the floor long into the night, talking to his wife, and Sunday he went back to Davis's house.

He apologized for intruding, but he was so troubled that he must ask the President to reconsider. The sun came through the broad window in the little study where Davis listened. He looked pale and thin, really frail. His hollowed cheeks showed his own torment.

But he said the decision was final.

Obviously he was not satisfied with it either, but the mistake was imbedded somewhere in the past—back in the early days when the West had been neglected, and more recently when he had played soldier by creating departments—when Joe Johnston had been left in command.

Now the thing that had been created by makeshift tactics, within the grandiose departmental pattern, must be saved by makeshifts.

Seddon, with his misplaced belief in Johnston, must help Johnston rescue Pemberton.

5

Seddon tried. He was tired with the city summer coming on, and the demands of the office, but his spirit kept him going. Though he had shifted emphasis to the East in his disappointment in Johnston, he by no means abandoned hope. But abandoning his own basal plan and possessing no final authority, he could do little more than exhort.

When Johnston wired him that his only plan was to relieve Vicksburg and asked could Seddon send more troops, Seddon answered, "You know best about Bragg's army."

When Johnston evaded the decision on Bragg, Seddon wired frankly, "Do you advise more reinforcements from General Bragg? You, as commandant of the Department, have power so to order if you, in view of the whole case, so determine."

Johnston refused to take the ball. He wired back that it was for the government to determine if troops should be moved from Bragg, as, since he had come to the Mississippi, he no longer considered himself in any authority in Tennessee. Again he wired, "It is for the government to decide."

Seddon, in Richmond, knew too little about the physical circumstances to assume the responsibility—and Johnston would not.

Earlier Johnston had wired Pemberton that he would move to his relief as soon as he got ten thousand men from Bragg. Shut up in Vicksburg, waiting for Johnston, Pemberton's army and the citizens withstood the siege from land and water on dwindling rations, and the men fought well and showed a fine morale.

The soldiers arranged a HOTEL DE VICKSBURG bill of fare:

Soup: Mule tail.
Boiled: Mule bacon, with poke greens; mule ham, canvassed.
Roast: Mule sirloin—saddle-of-mule *à l'armée.*
Entrees: Mule head, stuffed *à la Reb;* mule beef, jerked *à la Yankie;*
    mule side stewed—new style, hair on . . .
Pastry: Cottonwood-berry pie, *à la ironclad;* chinaberry tart.
Dessert: White-oak acorns . . .
Liquors: Mississippi water, vintage 1492, very superior . . .

Meals at few hours. Gentlemen to wait upon themselves. Any inattention in service should be promptly reported at the office. JEFF DAVIS & Co., *Proprietors.*

In the middle of June, Johnston wired Seddon, "I consider saving Vicksburg hopeless."

Seddon answered that the "telegram grieves and alarms us. Vicksburg must not be given up without a struggle. I rely on you still to avert the loss. If better resource does not offer, you must hazard attack."

Finally, in desperation, Seddon pled with him to do something. "It were better to fail nobly daring, than, through prudence even, to be inactive. . . ."

Johnston could deride this as office heroics. Being on the ground, he knew there was nothing he could do. So he did nothing.

When Pemberton, inside Vicksburg, realized that no help was ever coming, he gave up to avoid more useless bloodshed. He could have held out a little longer, but he selected July 4, because he thought the sentiment might obtain more lenient conditions from the enemy.

In the South he was regarded as a traitor for selecting the national holiday.

On the same day Pickett's Virginians staggered back from the hillside at Gettysburg, Pennsylvania. They had failed of the military decision that might affect the war politically. They had achieved the limited purposes of the commissary raid—and Virginia was still safe. But the army would never be the same. It had suffered over twenty thousand casualties, nearly 30 per cent. Crack units were decimated. General officers fell like the men.

The Northern army, taken over in the emergency by George Meade, suffered even more casualties—but Lincoln had called for three million men. The South had passed its physical peak.

In the Department of the West the problem of the two armies that Joe Johnston had been sent out to solve had been solved for him. There was only one.

He advanced every sound reason for remaining supine, every justification for refusing to assume the military situation, but the Mississippi River was lost to the Confederacy. The process of carving up the pieces smaller was about to begin.

CHAPTER TWENTY-FIVE

End of a Mission

IN RICHMOND the people had survived so many lost battles and fallen cities that they missed the significance of Vicksburg—that they could not even defend their country. Gettysburg was the shock to their pride, in that Lee could fail to win, and there was the deep disappointment that the war must go on, but . . . life would go on with it.

Prices continued to rise and money to drop. By the end of autumn their dollar was quoted at 1 to 20 for gold. Drugs became scarcer, and the surgeon general asked ladies to grow poppies. Gamblers shot it out on the streets, and soldiers fought among themselves. Refugees continued to crowd in from the country, but at least one came in an expectant frame of mind.

WIFE WANTED—I am anxious to marry; have a sufficiency to take care of a wife; have been in service for 18 months, but am now exempt for the war; have heretofore surrendered to no *arms,* but am willing to surrender to *woman's.*

> I want a handsome, gentle wife,
> To share the joys and sweets of life;
> I'm neither old, ugly nor cross
> I'll give up the pans and won't be boss.

> "Volunteer"
> ALBEMARLE

Those who took their romance secondhand bought *Beulah,* a new novel by a Mobile writer, Miss Augusta Evans. They read *Romola* and *Thaddeus of Warsaw,* Trollope and Lever, a Richmond reprint of Wilkie Collins and of war clerk Jones's *Wild Western Scenes. Don Juan* and *Pickwick Papers* were on the forbidden list (the latter as too coarse), and *Devereux* and *The Disowned* were hidden behind other books. Romantic ballads went the rounds like a popular song on a juke box today.

Les Misérables was brought out in five parts (at $2.00 a part) by the *Southern Literary Messenger,* which was doing a fine job in maintaining its standards. Along with its book-review section, it carried Fashion Notes with engravings copied from *Le Bon Ton* of the previous year. Also for fashions (with never a mention of war), *Godey's Lady's Book* was sold at West's Bookshop, on Main Street near the war office.

Every Thursday the *Record* appeared on the stands, carrying a news summary, general informative material, reprints from English magazines, and poetry. On Saturday appeared the favorite *Southern Illustrated News,* with its eight uncut newsprint pages ingeniously and neatly folded into magazine format. On the front page it ran "Profiles" of leading Confederates, and inside it carried varied material of a livelier approach than the *Record* or *Messenger.* There were jokes and light verse, oddities and a word puzzle called Enigmas, housewife columns and always a romantic serial. They also offered a one-thousand-dollar prize contest for the best Romance. Their cartoons ran to topical subjects. These showed Yankee prisoners at Belle Isle, happy and fat, as they lounged outdoors smoking their pipes, while a lonely Confederate, gaunt in convict stripes, pined in a solitary cell.

For the "Dixie Children" the *Geographical Reader* had been published in Raleigh. Describing Virginia, it taught:

The higher class of society is noted for hospitality and for high living. Some of these claim to be descendants of Pocahontas, which they consider a great honor. . . .

Richmond city is the capital of the State, and also of the Confederacy. This is a goodly sized city on James river. President Davis resides there, and Congress meets there to make laws. Many of the large buildings are used for hospitals, and there are thousands of sick and wounded soldiers constantly there. There is said to be much wickedness in the city.

There are many planters who own large numbers of slaves. These are generally well treated, and are as happy a people as any under the sun. If they are sick, *master* sends for the doctor; if the crop is short, they are sure of enough to save life; if they are growing old, they know they will be provided for; and in time of war, they generally remain quietly at home, while the *master* spills his blood for his country.

For theatergoers, Tom Taylor's *Ticket-of-Leave Man* was very popular at the new Richmond Theater, and all restaurants were packed with civilians and soldiers despite the high prices. At the Oriental, with ham and eggs at $3.50, bread and butter at $1.50, coffee at $3.00, and a potato costing $1.00, the least supper would cost ten dollars with tip. If drinks went along, there was sherry at $35 a bottle, ale at $12 a bottle, and a drink of French brandy for $3.00 or apple brandy for $2.00.

For the epicures, delicacies were still obtained despite all restrictions. Though the Davises did not subscribe personally to the self-indulgence of some of the government members, occasionally Varina would come up with a dish that would provide the basis for an intimate supper. When she served some very good brains *en papillote,* she of course invited Benjamin.

During the meal her friend grew depressed because his brother-in-law had not come. "Jules would like these dishes so much, and he is young and values such things." Mrs. Davis instantly offered to send some to his house, but Benjamin said no, "The papillotes would fall flat and the salad would fade; but if I might take him some cake and lollipops, I should feel very happy."

Mrs. Davis was only too glad to provide them, and Benjamin insisted on taking the parcel himself. He wrapped it in a napkin and left for home, "beaming with the hope of conferring pleasure upon his beloved Jules."

Such pleasures for the Secretary of State grew more meaningful as he faced the collapse of his main job abroad. For with Vicksburg fell Confederate diplomacy. Lacking even the dignity of formal surrender, it fizzled out in recriminations and farcical blundering.

2

In the summer of '63 the final move left the Confederate lobby was the formal introduction of a motion for recognition in Parliament. This was to be done by a radical member named Roebuck who, independent of party, had a strong pull with the people.

Just before Roebuck made his move, with Hotze getting newspaper support, anti-Confederate newspapers got the rumor circulated that Napoleon was now against recognition. To counteract this, Slidell impressed on Napoleon that the moment had come to advocate recognition. Through inside friends Slidell learned that the French Cabinet, though against action now, definitely intended to deny the rumors to England. In fact Baron Gros, the ambassador in London, had approached Russell and, in diplomatic deviousness, gave as his opinion the belief that Napoleon was ready to come in.

At the same time Roebuck and Lindsay, the hard-working Southern sympathizer, went directly to the Emperor. Napoleon authorized them to deny the rumors and said the reason he could make no formal application to England was that the last time he did they told the United States.

On June 30, with Vicksburg still holding out and Lee marching triumphantly north in Pennsylvania, Roebuck introduced his motion. When opposition members repeated the rumors denying Napoleon's support, Roebuck grew excited and repeated his conversation with the Emperor. Carried away, he assured Parliament that Baron Gros had carried communications from Napoleon.

Both the Foreign Office and the Home Office denied any "official communication" from Gros. As their records showed no written documents from Gros, this amounted to a very fine hairsplitting; for, in effect, it implied *no* communication from Gros.

Furthermore, members of Parliament turned directly against Roebuck as the bearer of a message which implied British betrayal. They regarded him either as a liar or a dupe of Napoleon. He was more a dupe of his own hopes, who lost his poise in the labyrinthine dealings and suffered complete defeat.

When he withdrew the hopeless motion, it amounted to a clumsy exit of the Confederacy as a potential world power in Europe.

Before Benjamin realized that it was all over he sent abroad his blockade figures to offer England and France facts in the event they wanted to intervene. From January to May, $9,000,000 in merchandise had been shipped from Charleston, making the annual trade $2,500,000 more "during a blockade pronounced effective by neutral governments [than] the total foreign commerce of South Carolina while a member of the late Federal Union in 1858." At Wilmington the trade was four times that of all of North Carolina in 1858, with "ocean steamers running almost with the regularity of packets."

Hotze believed that England's interest in these facts was quite different from Benjamin's intention. While England wanted a Confederate victory, which would make a weaker United States, her industries were again getting the necessary cotton without antagonizing the United States, and, more importantly, the government wanted an ineffective blockade established as legal. The rights to search ships on the sea established a principle against the practice of which the United States had fought in 1812.

Hotze's letter to Benjamin might have been an opinion of that shrewd young Swiss, but England's action clearly showed Benjamin that the door was finally shut. Following on the news of Vicksburg and Gettysburg, the British capitulated under increased American pressure and seized the two large ironclads being built for the Confederacy.

Both Russell and the British press pointed out strongly the right of a neutral to sell ships to belligerents if it was right to sell munitions, and this was in accordance with American practices. However, it was not their beliefs involved, but the necessity of amiable relations with a powerful nation.

In London, Bulloch, seeing that nothing more could be expected from the British government, transferred the ownership of rams being built by Laird to Bravay of Paris, agent for the Pasha of Egypt. When the British seized the ships anyway, Slidell and Bravay petitioned Napoleon to demand them from England. By then the ships were hot potatoes and the Emperor was having troubles of his own with America.

United States agents were showing him evidence that ships for the Confederacy were being built in France, and they complained about the Confederate raiders being refitted in French ports. The involved empire gambler shilly-shallied against the toughening American tactics because he still hoped for Confederate victory. Only an independent South assured him of the Mexican empire, the crown for which Maximilian had finally been induced to accept. For these reasons Slidell still received a certain courtesy in Paris and kept active in garnering gossip from his official friends.

In England matters were different. Ever since the vast relief over the *Trent* affair, the British government had treated the Confederate commissioners with studied discourtesy. While Benjamin could shrug this off as British face saving as long as he hoped to achieve a concrete end, he saw no point in subjecting Mason to indignities when nothing could be gained from it. As Mason could not now hope for the courtesies extended an accredited minister from the least nation, and Benjamin felt no less pride in his own country than the old-line aristocrats like Mason, he wrote Lord John Russell, terminating the mission.

Russell replied civilly enough.

To Benjamin a closed door was as forgotten as if it never existed. Filing Russell's reply, he turned his agile mind to untangling the problems of foreign purchases. James Mason, with no official mission, enjoyed himself as best he could among British friends and Southern refugees and helped with the physical affairs.

[293]

3

As with most Confederate objectives interrelating policy and action, a plan of action was usually withheld until the policy collapsed. Thus, even when the action became effectual, it had no effect on any policy and was late in achieving physical results.

In a one-man government where the leader's interests were limited primarily to the war office, correlation of action was impossible except where individuals emerged with that type of thinking. Benjamin was such a man.

When the cotton-embargo threat failed to achieve recognition, Jefferson Davis realized that the only course left, in what was to be the Confederacy's fight alone, was to ship out all the cotton possible, get the most credit abroad, and import necessities for the government. To achieve this he was forced to heed the complaints of the hit-or-miss purchasing operations and shipping. Having small interest in such details, he placed this co-ordination in Benjamin's hands.

First Benjamin had to let go James Spence. As Hotze said, Spence occupied the difficult position of representing the Confederacy as "a disinterested alien." Though his strong anti-slavery sentiments strengthened the South's position of fighting for independence, they antagonized many Southerners, who grew bitterly critical of Spence. Also, his ill-defined position of necessity hampered accomplishments where War, Navy, Treasury Department, and other agents were at one another's throats.

In interdepartment rivalries the old college tie had snarled the machinery. Crenshaw, the Richmond flour man, who got a government contract through Virginian Randolph, next got a British purchasing commission from Virginian Seddon. Crenshaw's fight to get contracts over Huse led him to try to undermine the able Yankee by accusing him of accepting bribes.

This public scandal was only the most obvious incident in the complications caused by individuals who, hoping for a quick fortune as government purchasers, sought to demonstrate their superiority over the regular agents. The abuses of these individuals with contracts could only have been borne by a country as rich as the United States.

One agent charged a thousand pounds for an introduction to a firm Huse had been working with for a year. He sold cotton at 30 cents when its price was 45 and paid twice what rifles were worth. Another contract for clothing at three times its value was nullified when it was paid at 20 cents in cotton selling at 50.

Now that the policy phase of cotton had failed, the action phase revealed frantic, unorganized efforts to use it anyhow they could. Inevitably the green agents, hawking contracts through markets for the highest bidders, hurt credit and prestige with English firms. Hotze, watching "the clashing interests, the rivalries, the hostilities," doubted if "the credit of any other government in the civilized world would have withstood so successfully and so long as ours has done, such reckless and damaging hauling."

James Spence, having occupied his anomalous position during this panic, became inevitably associated with it. To bring order out of this chaos a new man was necessary. C. J. McRae, who had gone over to handle the Erlanger loan, was selected by Benjamin. Able and energetic, he was virtually drafted from his factories at Mobile, which he had built into valuable ordnance works for the Confederacy.

McRae received all the credit from cotton shipped, now increasingly by the government, and was in charge of all disbursements. With this control he consolidated purchasers and had the regular agents working smoothly through him. Conflict and delay were eliminated, credit improved, and even the Erlanger bonds eventually rose as a medium of exchange.

After the news of Vicksburg the bonds floated by Erlanger went to a 36 per cent discount. When the issue was finally closed out, the Confederacy realized only three million dollars—no more than the Erlangers themselves, in whom Slidell somehow still retained his faith. However, the Confederacy did own about seven million dollars' worth of these bonds which they had bought to keep the issue going.

At varying discounts they used these bonds to pay off debts, especially over a million to Isaac, Campbell, & Co. It was from these worthies that Huse was accused of taking a bribe, when it was proved that their double set of books had robbed the Confederacy blind. So with worthless bonds gotten from a French swindler, the agents paid off a British swindler.

The Erlanger fiasco climaxed the "policy period," during which the government held cotton bonds, and sold cotton direct through speculators and private blockade runners. With the coming of McRae, the government undertook to purchase all cotton and tobacco at fixed prices and take all exports and imports in its own hands. As the government could not buy sufficient ships, they forced private runners to carry one third or one half of war matériel in their cargo.

Even before this whole system functioned smoothly, a very real improvement was immediately noticeable. By the end of '63 Henry Hotze wrote in the *Index:* "Had the cotton been exported for its own account, instead of, for the most part, private speculators', the Confederate government might have dispensed with foreign loans, might have bought its warlike stores at the lowest cash rates and supplied its citizens with commodities of prime necessity at a moderate advance on cost."

It is clear that had the C.S.A. exported the cotton which reached Europe through the blockade, not only could it have obtained supplies for armies and citizens, but it would have removed all the confusion and delay of didos like the Erlanger loan. Only now—with ports gone, the blockade becoming actually tight, and inland cotton lost through invading armies—did the government adopt a vigorous and realistic policy to supplant the belief in the embargo as expressive of Cotton's royalty.

By then this was only the desperation of a fugitive against the closing machinery of established law.

ALEXANDER H. STEPHENS

During the war years. Courtesy of Confederate Museum, Richmond, Virginia.

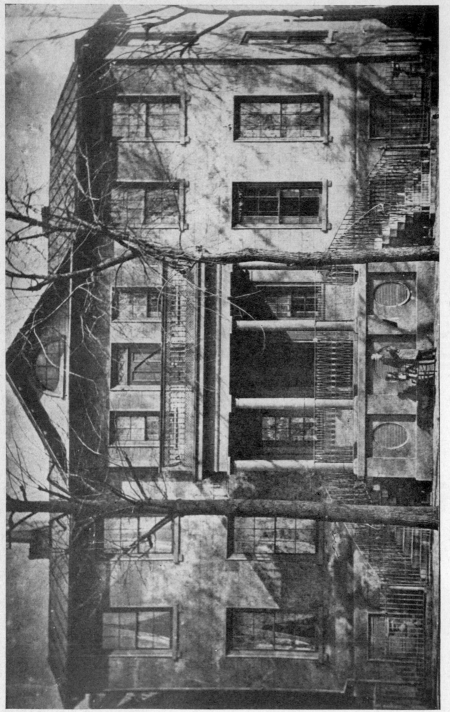

COURT END OF TOWN

Front view of a representative house in the general neighborhood of the White House, Richmond. Originally owned by Edmund Randolph, first U. S. Attorney-General. Photograph, courtesy the Valentine Museum, Richmond, Virginia.

CHAPTER TWENTY-SIX

We, the People

FROM the office down the hall from Benjamin, Jefferson Davis moved to the long stairs as erectly as ever. He descended the steps with the military carriage that gave him the appearance of being taller than he was and walked out the Bank Street entrance to the hill of Capitol Square. He might be alone or accompanied by one of his staff, usually Burton Harrison, the secretary who lived on the third floor of the White House. He would not talk much in any case, for the hill was steep and he felt drained of strength.

The lines bit deep in his face where his mouth was set in pride. This pride, like everything else, remained inflexible after the emergency to which he had proven unequal.

The Confederate movement had suffered irremediable defeat, but the President did not blame himself. As a man Davis suffered moments of fear of inadequacy to the burden, and he turned to his Lord in prayer. He prayed, not for simple humanity, but for the strength to lead, as commander in chief, where others must follow.

He perceived no specific failures of his own. For the larger failure, such as Vicksburg, he laid the blame on his old enemy, Joe Johnston.

In the White House the narrowly curving stairs were steep and very long. Out of sight of the world, he must have paused and rested his hand on the wide rail before he took the final turn upward. Then, into the office where cabinet meetings were held, his frayed energy was rallied by righteous rage at the general who had failed him.

Erect in his low, curved-back chair, he dictated a historic record in the form of a bitter letter to Joe Johnston. His precise voice grew cold as he listed that general's inadequacies. Point by point he took up Johnston's denials of holding command in the West, his refusal to accept it, and, with harsh logic, proved him utterly in the wrong. The letter bristled with, "My orders as your superior officer," "I differed with your opinion," "You were told to . . ." and clarified what or whom Johnston meant by Executive in a wire to Seddon.

With such letters Davis began his retreat further from the realities

[297]

of a region struggling through war for its independence as a nation. He had emerged briefly from his protective preoccupations in the crisis. Now he turned more to them.

There were enough serious details to occupy anyone. When Lee brought his battered army back to Virginia, the equally battered Union Army was unable to attack seriously on its own. Though the situation in Virginia remained unchanged, Lee felt a sense of failure and offered to resign that he might be replaced by a commander who could bring freshness to the task.

As almost always responding in kind, Davis wrote Lee a letter of real nobility. "My dear friend . . . Where am I to find that new commander who is to possess the greater ability which you believe to be required? I have but used the language of sober earnestness, when I have impressed upon you the propriety of avoiding all unnecessary exposure to danger, because I felt your country could not bear to lose you. . . ."

The opposite of Lee in humility was Stephens. He had come to Richmond in May, ostensibly to assist in the arrangement of prisoner exchange. The Vice-President wrote to Lincoln that he wanted to clarify the conduct of war where United States' abuses to civilians were becoming outrageous. Actually Stephens wanted to use the contact as a feeler for peace. He had gotten as far as Fortress Monroe, when Gettysburg toughened the Union administration. Stephens was halted by a wire which said, "The customary agents and channels are adequate for all needful . . . conferences between the U.S. forces and the insurgents."

Insurgent Stephens, his heart longing to return to the Union, lurked around Richmond until October and then returned to Georgia, where he could do more mischief. A guidebook, listing the offices and residences of members of the government, located Stephens simply as "the Vice-President resides in Georgia."

His friends in Congress had already defeated the renewal of the suspension of habeas corpus when it expired. With this, exempts and deserters could move much more freely in sections where the population, never too strong for the war, now wanted peace.

In the mountainous area of East Tennessee, southwest Virginia and northwest North Carolina, original Unionists were joined by increasing disloyalists against the Confederate government and formed the Order of the Heroes of America. They worked on undermining morale in the Army and in the civil population, appealing particularly to ignorant mountaineers. Never having any stake in the war and little feeling for any region beyond their neighborhood, these hill people, discouraged by hardships, were susceptible to Yankee promises of land in the coming division of the Confederates' property.

In northern Alabama and Mississippi and western Georgia, original Unionists formed a Peace Society, complete with signs, grips, and passwords, and proselyted the disaffected. In that "lost land" where Union soldiers, according to one of their generals, had killed, burned, and robbed indiscriminately, the Unionists were invariably spared and, indeed, frequently shared the fruits of plunder. Secessionists despairing of the war, or losing faith in the government, went over to the Peace Society both to spare themselves and to hasten a peace they believed inevitable.

Both of these societies gave protection to the swelling numbers of deserters and conscript evaders. No politics were involved one way or another with these. On strictly personal grounds they were just agin army life, and scattered authority was inadequate to control them. The more influential found grounds of exemption, and an observer in Alabama said, "There had never before been so much skilled labor in the South."

The majority hid out, and numbers of these formed in armed bands, defied and killed conscription officers, and terrorized the countryside. Probably the worst of the outlaw bands, sprinkled with Yankee deserters, operated through Texas, though the more famous "guerrillas" were Quantrill's in Missouri, who passed themselves off as Confederate sympathizers.

All through the South these bands and societies could defy authority because of the disharmony between government and state. Stephens and his crowd gave validity and encouragement to any action against the "Nationalists." Their states' rights, in the realm of pure theory, were promoting a second armed conflict—between the Confederate government and its people.

The boldness of the disloyal-Unionist combine in western North Carolina, spearheaded by a Raleigh editor, led to resolutions for the restoration of the Union and outright attacks on the government's war aims. Against this flagrancy Davis protested to Governor Vance, who replied that peace proposals would not be amiss as a means of showing the people the government was willing to "negotiate."

Regarding this as subversive, the President failed to read the sign of the times. With his own sense of the unconquerableness of abstract right, he apparently placed these manifestations of the fainthearted and disloyal in the same category with similar disaffection in the North.

There, Valladingham, the Copperhead leader, who made great claims for the possible power of the anti-war movement in the North, promised help to Southern moves in Union territory, and in New York the governor clearly revealed his lack of sympathy with the war.

Seymour had stripped New York City of troops during the anti-draft riots, when the mob routed the police and soldiers, burned buildings, and captured an arsenal. Negroes were hunted like animals, and at least eighteen were known to be hanged. A Union officer, striving for order, was tortured to death by civilians. Many persons were killed and wounded as battles between thousands ranged all over the city before regular troops arrived to take over. When Governor Seymour, antagonistic to the Republican administration, sent New York troops to Gettysburg, he did it for the same reason that Virginia first raised an army—for "the aid of a sister state."

While in the North these sentiments were isolated, contained, and their potential overrated, in the South they polluted the bloodstream of the movement. One of the worst causes of the disease was desertion from the armies, and in this Davis revealed his failing grasp on realities.

From the peak to which Seddon, by vigorous conscription, had brought the armies in the spring, casualties and hunger and the consequent failing morale began to reduce them. Desertions became steady. Lee, and Seddon who hated disloyalists as deeply as he did Yankees, advocated stern measures for suppression.

Davis's hatred of suffering acted on his growing unrealism, and he undermined the war office by granting constant pardons to deserters. When Seddon sent to Davis a recommendation of Lee's for more stringent methods of handling desertion in his own army, the President returned it to the Secretary with the curt comment, "That is not a proper subject for the criticism of a military commander."

As for Seddon, his misplaced confidence in Joe Johnston had permanently cooled Davis on him. They still conferred, though not so frequently, and Seddon still conducted the war office with his own conception of the Secretary's job. But the complete teamwork, where Seddon's influence was felt, was no more.

2

James Seddon, his frail health taxed by the strain, had too many troubles to be then aware of his loss of court favor. All during the absence of the army in Pennsylvania, threats had been made at Richmond from all sides. An attack on the salt works at the southwestern corner of the state had been barely beaten off by old men and boys aroused by a young girl who rode across the mountain at night with the alarm.

The South had imported much of its salt before secession, and early in the war Virginia had lost the saltworks in what became West Virginia. Later works were lost in Louisiana, and Union troops were particular to destroy salt whenever possible. Even small raids out of the path of the armies contained reports like, "We burned two dwellings, an outbuilding and ten barrels of salt." Though smaller works were scattered in the Lower South, by far the largest supply came from Saltville, Virginia.

Other states erected works there, and the operation was supposedly on a national basis, but there was the usual friction between states. North Carolina's Governor Vance, who held more uniforms in his state warehouses than there were in Lee's army, complained the loudest about Virginia getting the lion's share (which it probably did). But whoever got it, the salt had to be protected, and in September Seddon was rushing troops there against a more determined raid.

With his Western strategical plans gone awry, Seddon strove for more efficiency on detail work, especially of the commissary. Earlier war clerk Jones had addressed to the President a plan to appeal to the people for the direct contribution of food to the Army.

When this was referred to Commissary General Northrop, he rejected it on the grounds that he "had no acquaintance with that means of maintaining an army." Supporting this preference of red tape to food, Seddon had acknowledged his clerk's efforts with a brief note which explained that Jones's plan was "not deemed judicious, except in the last extremity. . . ."

By fall that extremity had been reached in Seddon's mind, and he now advocated the plan himself. By then the people showed less willingness to contribute. As the trickle of soldiers away from the armies began, the morale of people in isolated districts dropped accordingly. Resisting the impressment agents, many farmers raised only enough for their own needs, and less food came into Richmond.

The city, as the citadel, was to some extent unified by a group morale kindred to that of the Army. Even there, as want became more acute and more strangers overtaxed the city's capacity, segments began to split off from the dominant mood. The deserters in town made a strong impression among the oppressed element where they hid. Traces of Union sentiment became more apparent, in words scrawled on walls.

From all over the South, Union sentiment was expressed in poison-pen letters to the government. As fiercely loyal Seddon studied these signs, he read another kind of letter from a neighbor in Goochland County. That letter must have heaped fuel on the fires of his Southern passions, as well as causing some bitter reflections on human relation·ships.

This letter, intercepted by Confederate authorities, was from Mrs. Allan, wife of the son of Poe's foster father.

Mrs. Allan was from Cincinnati originally and, when not staying at her husband's plantation in Goochland, visited Mrs. and Reverend Dr. Hoge, on Fifth Street in Richmond. Dr. Hoge was the minister who attended Webster, the Union spy, in his last hours.

While staying in the country Mrs. Allan gave two letters to a friend to mail via the underground—one to a sister in Cincinnati and one to a Miss Haines in New York.

The letters reached the manager of a Main Street gambling house, named Burns, who also acted as a "depot" for the underground mail. Burns never adequately explained what prompted him to open the letters, but when he saw the enclosure in the letter to Miss Haines he promptly turned it over to Judge Ould, the socialite prison-exchange commissioner and lawyer.

The enclosure, addressed to the Reverend Morgan Dix, of New York's Trinity Church—and the son of the Union General John Dix —was the letter which appeared on the War Secretary's desk.

Seddon read that Dr. Hoge, the husband of his neighbor's Richmond hostess, was in Europe to propagandize for the Confederacy as well as to obtain Bibles for its army, and Mrs. Allan advised that he be arrested when he returned to New York on the date which she supplied. Then, coming closer to home, the Secretary read an accurate description of plantations neighboring his own, which Mrs. Allan marked for destruction on the next raid because of the residents' Secessionist views.

As a climax Seddon saw his own name listed in a complaint of the light destruction in Stoneman's spring raid, and Mrs. Allan was particularly critical of the Yankee failure to burn Seddon's home at Sabot Hill.

When Seddon jumped out of his chair on that, he did not need to go through the President for action. Mrs. Allan was arrested at the home of Mrs. Hoge, where she had come from the country. Out of consideration to her sex—on the part of General Winder!—she was allowed to stay at the Hospital and Asylum of St. Francis de Sales, out on Brook Road, until she appeared in court to answer charges of attempting to communicate with the enemy.

The Allan money obtained for her two distinguished lawyers— Judge Lyons and George Randolph, Seddon's gentlemanly predecessor in the War Office.

The prosecution, following the lead of her manner of address to the Reverend Dix as *"Caro Signore,"* established their acquaintance in Italy. Further evidence revealed that during Stoneman's raid she had entertained Federal officers, who carefully spared her husband's property.

With all this, the defense hammered on the identification of the letter, which had passed through three hands before reaching Judge Ould, and on the unsavory character of Burns, the gambler. On the technicality of the letter, Randolph won for the lady a hung jury.

She was released on $100,000 bail and was never again brought to trial. Shunning the streets of Richmond, Mrs. Allan "retired to her luxurious home on the James River," waiting, as the people believed, for the coming of the Yankees.

3

Gettysburg rather than Vicksburg affected Richmond with the influx of its two unwilling segments of population—prisoners and wounded. Since the early days of hopelessly confused inadequacy, the Confederate Medical Corps had developed not only sufficient hospitals, but one which, the largest in the world and greatly in advance of its time, operated with the self-sufficiency of a town. Its director, with the powers of a mayor, handled over seventy-five thousand patients with a mortality record unsurpassed until World War II.

Back in 1862, when most of nine thousand sick from Joe Johnston's inactive army were to be sent to Richmond, Surgeon General Moore, in the emergency, called on Dr. James McCaw. At that time the thirty-nine-year-old Virginian, educated at New York University, was serving in the cavalry. He was a well-built man with a contained, strongly designed face and resolute eyes, and his appointment was one of those happy choices that occasionally in wartime produce results far beyond the immediate requirements.

Dr. McCaw selected the eastern end of old Church Hill, where the Chimborazo plateau swept to a high bluff overlooking the river. It was sunny in the winter and the coolest spot in Richmond in the summer. Residential streets on Church Hill did not extend eastward beyond the wide ravine of Bloody Run Gully, where Nathaniel Bacon had fought Indians during his rebellion, and the hospital, built east of the ravine, enjoyed the physical atmosphere of the country. In the hillside toward the south were springs of fine water, cool on the most sweltering summer day.

From the first, Dr. McCaw worked to make his little village self-sustaining. Operated on a communal basis, the hospital never received money from the government and, with the originality of its staff, made the Commissary Department look, in comparison, as inept as it was.

From tobacco factories came boilers for soup making, and the factory workers made beds and other furniture of tobacco-box wood. In other boilers soap was made from kitchen grease with lye run through the blockade. Beer was brewed on a large-scale, and ten thousand loaves of bread were made daily in its bakery. On neighboring farms, the hospital pastured from a hundred to two hundred cattle and from three hundred to five hundred goats. The hospital had its own dairy and five icehouses. The men's clothing allowances for cotton, yarn, shoes, and such were used for bartering with farmers between Richmond and Lynchburg for eggs and fruit and vegetables. The hospital owned a canal boat which operated regularly for this purpose.

Slave labor constructed 150 ward buildings. They were painted white with lime, light and airy, with two rows of beds on either side of a center aisle. Wide streets were left between the rows of buildings and kept scrupulously clean. Waste was handled efficiently, draining into the gully. Thirty buildings formed a division, under a surgeon. The surgeons were from different states, and, as far as possible, patients from the same states were placed in their divisions. In a section-conscious people this sense of kinship with the doctor helped morale.

Roughly fifty assistant or acting surgeons were directly responsible for two or three wards each, and stewards assisted them. Diet and laundry were in charge of forty-five matrons.

Those long-suffering women of all work, whose invaluable contributions to the armies were made under most unladylike conditions, maintained to the end the legend of languishing Southern belles. The men with whom they worked—cooks and bakers, carpenters and shoemakers, baggagemasters and forage masters and wagon masters, quartermasters and commissaries, hospital attendants and the armed guard of thirty—interpreted the Southern ideal of women to mean people easily pushed around. Perhaps the greatest triumph of these matrons was in keeping the ideal undisturbed while pushing back—with diplomacy or persuasion or moral force.

Partly through these remarkable ladies, and chiefly through McCaw, Chimborazo Hospital developed the spirit of an old town in which the inhabitants feel a pride in the community well-being. Dr. McCaw was too little of a specialist to be labeled a natural psychiatrist, but in the entirety of his approach he possessed an understanding, unique in his time and by no means commonplace in ours, of the relation of mental and physical health.

Paying great attention to diet, he used sunlight and fresh air and space for mental therapy and created an atmosphere more of barracks than a retreat for the sick. No attendants slept in the wards, and convalescents were encouraged to perform useful tasks about the hospital. In addition to making minds and bodies well, he had the purpose of returning men to the rigors of a Confederate soldier's combat life.

Not only did Dr. McCaw keep the men flowing back to the Army, but in the primary job of saving lives his mortality rate of slightly over 9 per cent was not equaled until the new medicines were introduced in the recent war. And McCaw was frequently using substitutes for the medicines of his day.

Here again, as in places throughout the Confederacy, one man rose with and above the occasion, achieving an efficiency that was too often obscured by the failure of other key men, accustomed to abundance, to adapt to the emergency.

4

Though the Gettysburg campaign brought Union prisoners to Richmond, it was the big haul of Confederate prisoners at Vicksburg that indirectly affected the city and the war situation of the whole South.

In the exchange of prisoners, frequently men were paroled on either side without the physical exchange and the mathematics were figured out later. When the surrender of Vicksburg gave the Union many more prisoners than the Confederacy held, parole began to break down and eventually ceased.

The South complicated matters by refusing to treat captured Negro troops as soldiers, but in returning them to their states. White officers commanding them were technically liable, under state laws, to prosecution for inciting to insurrection. All this slowed down exchange to the point that the Union prison population of Richmond grew to fifteen thousand.

Libby Prison, for officers, had become an institution. In its neighborhood of Negro shanties, an old meetinghouse, a warehouse used as a Confederate hospital, stables and vacant lots, there was the now familiar sight of tents for the guards and the row of sentries in constant patrol around the barred building.

Inside, the prisoners, grown more philosophical since the early batches, more hardened and adaptable, had learned to subsist à la Confederate style on bread and river water, rancid bacon and wormy beans, occasional soup which they shut their eyes to swallow.

They arranged "permanent" bunks on the floor, sometimes without blankets, and used haversacks or whatever would make a bundle as a pillow. The more ingenious made, from barrels and crates, stools and chairs and tables, even clothes racks. Bureaus and closets were unnecessary where the men possessed only the clothes worn when captured and there were no replacements except what was sent through from the North.

Other men made backgammon boards and checkers, read books, and listened to sermons, paid a dollar for one week's subscription to the Richmond *Enquirer* and disapproved of it, found fresh beef an "agreeable change" from bacon, and rice from beans. As the weather grew cold they stuffed bags in the windows in which the broken glass could not be replaced. Three old cookstoves, on which the men did much of their own cooking, also served for warmth. But the nights were cold for sleeping.

The men observed with surprise the selfishness among their own officers, and every floor produced the shrewd traders who ended up as speculators and shopkeepers. The men observed with interest the field officers washing and mending their own clothes.

Nothing was demanded of the prisoners except to take turns at policing their own quarters. The cleaning was done "indifferently" by Negroes who swept once a day and twice a week sloshed the floors with water and brooms, chiefly bringing havoc to the men's few belongings.

For keeping themselves clean, and their clothes, the men used a common troughlike tub, usually without soap, for there was none in the South for anybody. While most of the early complaining had passed, some prisoners constantly listed their privations, such as soap, as though they were unaware that the other people in Richmond were faring the same or worse.

Some of the prisoners—like a very elegant Sardinian, who had been a staff officer in the Crimean War—complained of being searched and robbed of everything on entering the prison. But, by record, prisoners continued to buy food with their own money from the outside at fabulous prices (the same paid by the civilians and Confederate soldiers), and Abner Small, of Maine, mentioned selling his watch for $150. It could have been that the luck of retaining possessions depended on the guards the new prisoners drew.

The same obtained with the boxes sent by the prisoners' families and through the active Northern Sanitation Commission. The Confederate officers in charge had no system of robbing the prisoners of their gifts, but obviously individuals rifled individual boxes. That some of these boxes were untactfully addressed to "The Capital of Rebeldom," and the like, eased the conscience of the hungry Confederates. Or maybe they had a family whose home had been pillaged, or a refugee family in Richmond whose home had been destroyed. Neither the plunderer of a Virginia home nor the robber of a Northern box acted on the principles of the war: each was motivated by greed or hunger.

In the recent World War an American commission settled claims for damages done by exuberant soldiers. In that more personal war the Libby guards acted as a personal commission, and innocent Northerners suffered directly in repayment as innocent Americans today repay with money, through taxes, the vandalism of their fellow citizens.

There was still the type of prisoner who became a military lawyer in outraged demands for treatment according to the articles of war. Colonel Streight, who had been captured by Forrest on the cavalry raid deep into Alabama towards Georgia, had definitely designed to destroy civilian property on the way. In Libby the tough-bitten Indiana cavalryman ceased completely to regard the war as a rebellion, in which he was justified in practically anything against insurgents, and became a stickler for the provisions regarding prisoners of war between established nations. That the systematic destruction by other men like himself made it impossible for Rebeldom to feed him as he was accustomed in his own army never seemed to enter his head.

Later Colonel Streight escaped from Libby with over a hundred other men in a party led by Colonel Rose. With ingenuity and painstaking effort they dug a tunnel from under a lower room to a yard behind a building across the street. That self-dramatizing and dramatized Union sympathizer, Miss Van Lew, was credited with secret tunnels from the garden of her mansion, but these Northern soldiers made their way in ignorance of her romantic contrivances. Streight and others were secreted for a time in Richmond houses.

This escape, coincident with Union cavalry raids into civilian territory, caused a severe tightening of the discipline at Libby. As most of these guards were a lower type of man, many of whom were inefficient and venal, there was undoubtedly some meanness in their behavior and undoubtedly there were cases of individual brutality. Northern observers point out that Major Turner, the commandant, "might possibly have been a gentleman under favorable circumstances," and his policy was to run the prison as justly and as efficiently as possible. Observers also noted that a certain turnkey was "a scoundrel."

The prison for privates was in all details worse than that for officers. Belle Isle was a beautiful green island in the James River. Slopes rose from the water to a low hill, and around the banks of foliage the water rippled in eddies and falls. A favorite spot for Richmonders before the war, it was ideally situated as a prison. It was outside the overcrowded city proper, the rapids of the river made escape difficult (some prisoners were drowned trying), and the hill made it possible for a few guards with obsolete cannons to control the thousands below. But for living conditions, with the acute shortage of everything in the South, the island became a horror for the men.

There were never enough tents. The ground was usually damp and, in rain, boggy. Men sleeping out, some without blankets, suffered terribly from the cold that went through their bones, and some froze to death during a night. (Confederate troops fought under the same conditions.)

Northern prisoners observed that no unnecessary hardship was worked on the men, and the officials seemed to try to do all they could. That was simply insufficient—as were virtually all Confederate efforts to subsist and shelter people within its boundaries. With a large part of the country occupied, with a large portion of the blockade runners carrying arms, with the inefficiency that characterized the commissary from beginning to end, there were not enough food and equipment to go around. . . .

In the civilian population of Richmond, women unraveled and reknitted old stockings, cut down old civilian overcoats of their men for jackets. Worn-out silk dresses were cut up and stitched into handkerchiefs, window curtains served as petticoats, and mosquito nettings were fitted over cambric slips.

For paper to write to their soldiers they searched the houses for ledgers, albums, books, anything with blank pages, even tore off wall-paper. For ink they used the juice of pokeberry and green persimmon, with rusty nails to deepen the color. As there were no envelopes, the papers were folded and sealed with mucilage made from the gum of peach trees mixed with the starch from ripening corn.

Mattresses were stuffed with leaves and cattails. When families sold their China and glass lamps for cash, bottles and gourds and odd tumblers served as oil lamps, which burned cottonseed or peanut oil mixed with lard. The poor used torches from resinous pine.

The plentiful peanut was used as imitation chocolate and coffee, though practically everything grown in the South was tried for a coffee substitute—rye, corn, sweet potatoes, chestnuts, chicory, okra, beans, even watermelon seed. A rising generation knew only sorghum for sugar and associated salt with smokehouses and old storage barrels from which they scraped the brine for their families.

In the countryside around Richmond the papers reported that robberies "are so numerous they have ceased to excite comment. They are all, with rare exceptions, committed by straggling deserters and runaway negroes." Observing the sag in Confederate fortunes, Negroes were leaving their owners in greater quantities than a year before.

In Richmond a "semi-Yankee" was committed to Castle Thunder "to answer to the charge of running off negroes to the Yankees." In the mayor's court a Negro was charged with helping a slave run off and a free Negro charged with harboring the fugitive. But the mayor's court was crowded with plenty of other troublemakers.

A woman was sentenced to twelve months for taking a pistol, a glass tumbler, and a greatcoat when she left early in the morning the bed of a good burgher who had paid her to spend the night. Another woman, Belle Summers, who operated "a house of ill fame in Solitude" (Seventeenth and Cary, near where Byrd's first trading post once stood), entered a complaint about a drunken customer. He knocked a glass of ale out of her hand and urged other customers to join in his riot. When they refused "he laid upon the floor and kicked about." Finally evicted, he then stoned the house.

Drunkenness made the war-born Tenderloin section look like the later-day Bowery, but it offered no escape to the conscientious workers in the government departments. Reagan's poorly paid postal workers petitioned the War Department for the right to buy at government prices at the commissary stores.

Theories differed as to whether speculators caused inflation or inflation created speculators, but nobody argued with the newspaper that stated, "Every man in this community is swindling everybody else."

Virginia came up with a unique check on the printing of state notes when its legislature objected on the grounds of "the great expense it would be to the State, owing to the high prices of paper, printing and clerks." Even Virginia's Senator Hunter, expert adviser on finances, never offered the harried Memminger a more sensible reason for checking inflationary currency.

The same difficulty of paper and engravers provided also the only check on counterfeiters, though Northerners were untroubled by that. They circulated bogus Confederate money among the Union troops, and one group of soldiers tried their hand at it themselves. Most of the Federal troops, however, brought "greenbacks," and these formed another element in Confederate money. Even the Treasury held some, and a few lucky Rebel soldiers were paid in greenbacks at the 1-to-15 rate.

In North Carolina tenpenny nails passed for a nickel, and barter was freely resorted to. Hampden-Sydney College students paid their board in produce, and farmers exchanged food for manufactured goods. As faith was shaken in the currency, frightened people would pay anything for tangible property—land, cotton, tobacco—and this definitely favored speculators.

War clerk Jones, after despairing of even soup for his family with no shinbones under five dollars in the market, and then obtaining a good one for a dollar in the government commissary, evolved another of his ideas which he forwarded to the President. He suggested that any army surplus from the impressed goods of farmers be sold to the public at government prices. He believed this would be a blow to extortionists and by helping the half-fed and half-clad people "would give popular strength to the government."

The President had too many worries over one of his favorites now to bother about the people.

CHAPTER TWENTY-SEVEN

I'd Rather Be President than Right

WHEN Seddon was failed by Joe Johnston, the President lost faith in his Secretary of War; but when Davis was failed by Braxton Bragg, he only placed greater faith in his own friend.

Bragg, like Pemberton, was "regulation" in his approach. He was tactful, deferential, adroit at flattery, and never exposed to Davis his contumacious side. Nor did Davis observe him when action jangled his nerves and he vacillated between exuberance and depression until he lacked the force to sustain the action to its conclusion. Davis knew him as loyal and hard-working, which none of his officers denied. They said he simply could not fight, and gave the evidence to support it—as if the record itself were not enough.

When the fall of Vicksburg settled affairs in the West, the Union armies turned their attention to the center, at Chattanooga. Since summer Rosecrans had consistently outmaneuvered Bragg and had kept him retreating until Bragg went beyond Chattanooga without ever feeling in a position to defend it. The prize fell without a shot being fired.

Then Rosecrans, flushed with victory, pursued Bragg southward in the mountains. There, in his confidence, he dispersed his troops so widely that Bragg was nearer Rosecrans's separate units than they were to one another. Bragg could understand such a military situation as that and turned to attack.

He was to be helped by two divisions of Lee's army, under Longstreet in person. As Virginia seemed safe for the moment, the Confederates also concentrated at the center. With the addition of these experienced troops, and his own men spoiling for a fight, Bragg was offered one of the great opportunities of the war.

His unbalance at the moment of commitment made him dilatory. By the time he had gathered his own men, poised to strike, Rosecrans was gathered too. The initiative, however, still lay with Bragg, and

Longstreet was there. So, having lost strategical advantages, he let the soldiers slug it out.

They charged as ferociously as any Confederate troops who ever fought. They beat back, they broke through, they ripped apart. They defeated the Union troops so decisively that only unshakable Thomas saved them from rout and complete disaster. The stout Virginian that day won the name of "The Rock of Chickamauga," while below Richmond his sisters prayed for a Southern victory. They got the victory, in spite of Thomas—but not the fruits.

Bragg was spent when the immediate action was over. He allowed the beaten army to stagger back to Chattanooga, and all his officers echoed Forrest, who said, "Why does the man fight battles?"

This time his officers did not limit their disgust to a vote of no confidence; they had an uprising against him. While Seddon was shelved in his war office, for backing Johnston, the President hurried out by train in October to see what he could do for Bragg.

He talked to all the officers. All agreed that nothing could be hoped for with Bragg in command. These attacks on his friend aroused Davis—not to the needs of the army—but to the support of Bragg. Unconsciously reducing the movement to himself, the President was motivated by need of vindication and refused to accept the opinions of officers in the field over his personal judgment. To restore harmony, Davis left Bragg in command and removed the chief pests.

The most outspoken was D. H. Hill, lieutenant general, so Davis sent him back to North Carolina. Bishop Polk was sent elsewhere and Forrest back to Mississippi, to "raise" a new mounted army of his own. Longstreet, "jealous of his own rights" and too big for Bragg, offered a solution for his case. As he yearned for independent command, Longstreet was sent northward with his men to besiege Knoxville.

Davis, having quelled the uprising and enjoying the moral satisfaction of supporting his friend, took his second trip through the South.

On his way out he had stopped in Georgia, where he and Governor Brown appeared publicly together, and Davis made a speech complimenting the magnificent work of Georgia troops in the field. He swung back through Alabama, stopping at Selma, where the new ordnance works were producing, and at Montgomery, where he had first gone with his misgivings and idealistic hopes.

Since those early days, so far away from guns, he had surmounted countless obstacles and carried alone, not without success, multiple problems, revealing himself a leader of many capacities. But as a man he had known no growth throughout the experience. Instead, the division, between his concepts and the emergency demands, had widened.

As the merging of those two types of needs produced in Lincoln effectual action, the widening in Davis produced psychic disorders. The strain of the disparity, becoming unendurable, demanded escape. Davis's escape was into a private world from where decisions affecting the outside would be based upon personal considerations unrelated to the movement.

When he returned to Richmond he was undisturbed by public reaction to his support of Bragg, as evidenced by the Chattanooga *Rebel*. An editorial referred to a Davis speech in which he claimed "shafts of malice" had been hurled at General Bragg, "a military commander of the first order."

The newspaper made no objection to Davis's praising Bragg,

... but he has no right to descend to the undignified game of stigmatizing those who cannot agree with him. . . . By going out of his way to inveigh against the thousands of patriotic citizens whose homes and fortunes and families have been, in common with the interest of the whole country, sacrificed to the blundering lunacy of this man, the President offers a gratuitous insult. . . . Bragg is . . . the most dangerous centre of power in the Confederacy.

By November these critics were proven bitterly right.

2

Now that Grant had accomplished his purpose on the Mississippi, he was given command of the West. Immediately he took personal charge of Chattanooga, where Rosecrans was huddling beneath the surrounding hills occupied by Bragg.

In November, Grant, with Sherman and Thomas, came swarming out of the city and at those hills. It takes nothing from the heroic courage of the Union attack that the Confederates, as an entity, were demoralized. Some of their units fought well, a few as well as they ever had; some fought poorly, worse than they ever had. Others simply scattered.

The men were through with Bragg. They had fought for him three soldier's fights—stand-up, slug it out. Two had been draws (in one of which they had not unreasonably thought they won), and the last, Chickamauga, they had won on their own fury—and nothing had happened. Nothing ever happened to the army under Bragg. They marched and retreated and fought, they had been from Mississippi almost to the Ohio River and back into Tennessee, and now they were headed for Georgia.

While Longstreet, off at Knoxville, clumsily slaughtered some men of his own in his independent foray, the thoroughly demoralized army of Braxton Bragg stumbled into northern Georgia, the roadway to Atlanta and the division of what was left of the Confederacy.

That time Bragg was demoralized too. He asked for no votes. He just resigned.

Davis wanted to put Lee in his place. The general understood what the President missed—that he and the Army of Northern Virginia were one. Any improvement Lee could bring to the Army of the West would be at the cost of the one dependable army in the South—and that sadly depleted of general officers.

Davis, unable to order Lee, was forced to appoint the inevitable choice, Joe Johnston.

For taking those bitter dregs, Davis had a chaser. He appointed Braxton Bragg his military adviser, in Richmond.

That was the job that Lee had held and which was now being held, in effect, by Seddon—whose influence was over because he believed in Johnston.

With that act, Jefferson Davis completed his psychotic retreat into his own private world. Dislike of Bragg by then was so general that Mrs. Chesnut commented, "He has a winning way of earning everybody's detestation." One of Jeb Stuart's engineer staff paraphrased Davis's Thanksgiving Proclamation:

> For Bragg did well Ah! who could tell
> What merely human mind could augur,
> That they would run from Lookout Mount,
> Who fought so well at Chickamauga!

Not only was Bragg's appointment certain to antagonize much of the military establishment, not only did it provide weapons for the growing body of Davis's enemies, but it could alienate the people. Whether the President was blind to this last possibility or indifferent to it, in either case it removed him finally from contact with the heart of the movement.

While he had never inspired real affection, the people had thought him great: they admired and trusted him as a leader.

Their belief had been shaken by some of the defeats. There had been resentment at some of his wholly necessary war measures, and bitterness at the unnecessary inequities and favoritism in some of them—especially in the wretchedly run commissary of his favorite, Northrop. Other administration men, like Memminger, were blamed for deficiencies not entirely of their own making. But the people had missed personal contact with Jefferson Davis while exposed to the mounting charges his enemies made from these hardships.

Now the people turned against him. In the winter of 1863–64 the experiment broke into its separate parts—loyal, disloyal, indifferent— and across all elements a weariness of the war was expressed in willingness to return to the Union.

The effort against this weariness and inertia was carried by individuals and groups and the majority of the women. These faithfuls represented every type of prewar sentiment, from Unionist to Secessionist, with a solid block of those of "no opinion." The imponderable of their common fight on their common land against a common enemy had hardened them into unyielding cores of resistance to the end.

Their opinions of the President, as varying as their prewar sentiments, were ultimately of no consequence to their actions.

But the turning against him by the masses of the people struck at the heart of the movement.

A simple and violent people, they responded more from the emotions than the mind. As their loyalties were in narrow and personal geographic areas, towns and counties, Davis was to them the symbol of the whole beyond their conception. When they rejected him they rejected the whole—the Confederacy. They believed it was *his* war, not theirs.

For the majority who turned against the government represented by Davis, there was no violence in the feeling. He was too impersonal and they were too tired. The shift of feelings was gradual, imperceptible, in an individual, a family, a section, until the loyal people in certain areas were exceptions.

In the West the momentum grew more rapidly than in the East because of the loss of battles and of land, and because the disparity between the powerful planter class and the poor whites lacked the gradations of the middle classes in the older and more settled sections. These ignorant provincials in isolated fastnesses were the first women to lose heart and to put pressure on their men to come home.

Where these regions were untouched by the occupation of either army, a woman could write to her husband, "You said you hadn't

[315]

anything to eat. I wish you was here to get some beans for dinner. I have plenty to eat as yet. . . . The people is generally well hereat. The people is all turning to Union here since the Yankees has got Vicksburg. I want you to come home as soon as you can after you git this letter. . . ."

This lady's "turning to the Union," like the conscript evaders she hid, meant nothing political. Her people had fought—under the guidance of planter-leaders and the community kinship of sectionalism —for what they believed to be personal liberty. The sectional unity began to fall apart under the impact of war when the leadership ceased to bind them with personal appeal. Tiring of war where they saw no good to them, they listened to their more articulate neighbors who hated Davis.

Many of these haters were original Secessionists who believed the Administration was heading them toward inevitable disaster. Not all of them despaired of independence. Some wanted a dictator, and the Lynchburg paper came out for Lee. But the hopeless knew the appeal to the masses—they used the old slogan from the exemption of planters with twenty slaves, "A rich man's war and a poor man's fight."

Now the poor man believed the slogan, because nobody paid any attention to him—except to keep him hungry and fighting. They also believed, because of Stephens's delusions, that peace meant simply the cessation of war—they would return to the Union as if nothing had ever happened.

The slogan that effected the collapse of the South, unlike the North's slogan of "Fighting for freedom," failed to carry into history. The dissolution of the South beginning in the winter of 1863–64 was obscured, as were all facts of the South, by the legend.

Jefferson Davis, ignoring the people, saw in Richmond only those who lived the legend. That this handful (symbolic of similar handfuls scattered over the South) could sustain the legend in warfare with their country disintegrating around them, that they could perpetuate it into the third generation after them, against all the statistics, was the triumph of the magic of the myth to those who believed.

3

The social life of the loyalists in the capital became accelerated as the underprivileged began drifting away. There was almost a frenzy of dining out. Parties and dances were given somewhere every night, and burgundy and sauterne, sherry and madeira flowed freely despite

Connie Cary's "starvation parties." Charades and all sorts of parlor games and amateur theatricals became suddenly fashionable.

The famous production of *The Rivals* at the elegant Iveses' (featuring Connie Cary and Mrs. Clay) ranked with Gettysburg as a high point to the glamour set. Virtually all of official Richmond, including the Davises, turned out, along with a number of generals.

The Semmeses gave a charade party which the Davises attended to see their little girl, Maggie, perform, as well as the President's secretary, Burton Harrison, who shaved off his mustache in order to play the part of an Indian.

A group of literary-minded men and women met in one another's parlors, called themselves the Mosaic Club, and played the "forfeit essay." Two hats were passed around, and everyone drew a question from one and a word from the other. At the next meeting the word and question were connected in a song or essay, story or poem. John Esten Cooke and John Thompson were among the professional writers who went, and Colonel Bledsoe, once the scourge of war clerk Jones, came down from Charlottesville, where he had returned to teach when his efforts went wasted in the war office.

There was also a lot of musical entertainment at the Mosaic, led by Mattie Paul, a fine pianist, and Madame Ruhl, the soprano and teacher in St. Paul's Choir. The music lovers developed a strictly musical club of their own, which met at the Barton Haxalls'.

Chiefly fluid groups gathered at a few houses, talked and flirted and danced, and made life pleasant for the uniformed heroes—with names. Completely different from the men about town, with their stylized wit, the new favorites were men of action whose humor was often unconscious.

General Edward Johnston, called "Allegheny," carrying a huge staff as a crutch while recovering from a leg wound, reacted very forthrightly to the young ladies who made him the center of parties. With an uncontrollable winking in one eye, he made extravagant love in a loud voice, and he seems to have won popularity by a certain piquance of character.

Another new lion, whose basic appeal appears to be the amusement he provided, was John Hood, the blond-bearded giant who first won fame leading the Texas brigade. Now a fiercely fighting division commander, of magnificent physique and an almost primitive naïveté, he was something of an outsize pet. Hood also improved his time by riding out with the President—forming an attachment that was to be as deadly to the South as Davis's favoritism for Bragg.

Even bigger than Hood and more unique was Heros von Borcke, the Prussian volunteer staff officer of Jeb Stuart. His compliments were heavy-handed and his stories exaggerated, but his Old World courtliness and Germanic accent made him charming to many women. In his way, as one of the most deeply loyal Confederates, Von Borcke symbolized in the capital the volunteer foreigners throughout the Southern armies.

Many Germans were field and line officers, and others were in special services, like bands and medical corps. Germans were second in number only to the Irish, whose contingent was topped by Major General Cleburne of County Cork. Another foreign major general was Prince de Polignac, who won the admiration of the Texans he led, though they called him Prince Polecat.

Among brigadiers there were four Irishmen and seven other foreign-born. There were thirty foreign-born colonels, including Swedes and Hungarians, Mexicans and Canadians, and several Poles headed by Colonel Oladowskis, Bragg's miserly ordnance officer. Three hundred foreign-born officers were below the rank of colonel, and these included a Greek, a Dane, and a Spaniard. There were Irish priests and English doctors.

Men in the ranks of foreign birth or foreign descent were so numerous that over a hundred companies were composed either partly or almost entirely of them. There were the Spanish Guards of Mobile and the Savannah Steuben Jägers, the Garde Lafayette and the Garibaldi Legion, Emmett and Shamrock and Emerald Guards were scattered everywhere, floating banners with harps and "Erin-go-Bragh." Two Irish boys in the Army were the sons of John Mitchel, the Irish patriot, who made many friends in Richmond.

Confederate heroes from other parts of the South always provided reason for entertaining. Parties were given all over town during the visit of John Morgan, the great raider, just after he escaped from the penitentiary in Columbus, Ohio. All the Kentuckians gathered then, and Morgan's sister came with her husband, General A. P. Hill.

Powell Hill, with his pleasant, courteous manner, was well liked in Richmond, though he took the social life quietly. Ending his third year of fighting and now handling a corps, he was suffering the strain of war and responsibility and was frequently unwell.

A fellow corps commander, Dick Ewell, with one leg amputated, was also failing physically, and to some extent he was suffering the strain of following Stonewall Jackson in the old Second Corps.

From Longstreet's First Corps, George Pickett had not recovered from the terrible afternoon of his charge. Before going in at Gettysburg he had written his fiancée that the waiting was "almost unbearable. . . . My brave Virginians are to attack in front. Oh, God in mercy help me as He never helped before."

Now married to the young brown-eyed girl, Pickett was still haunted by those hours of slaughter. He had been a very colorful personality. Jeb Stuart admired his dash, and Longstreet was devoted to him. Now detached from the main Army, and vaguely guarding Southside Virginia, he came in to Richmond with his wife, trying to find escape from the memory.

Even the Old Man of the army, Lee, showed the effects of the fighting. He came to Richmond to be with his wife and daughters, and he appeared publicly only at St. Paul's Church. Aged and whitened, he suffered paroxysms of pain in his left side.

Mrs. Lee, herself crippled with arthritis and deeply wounded by personal tragedy, was desperate about the general's health. When they first married, she had preferred the familiar comforts of her home to the bleak life of barracks and frequently stayed away from her husband for long intervals. As the years passed she grew closer and more dependent and felt his necessary absences very keenly.

When she settled in Richmond, Mrs. Lee needed all her unselfpitying courage. Her twenty-three-year-old daughter had died, her son Rooney had been captured while wounded, and his wife had died while he was in prison. Her youngest son, Bob, had left college to serve in the artillery. And she was in need of unprocurable medicines. In her way the same rocklike character that her husband was, Mrs. Lee, like him, found solace in church. At St. Paul's she was deeply moved at the tribute the congregation paid her husband by remaining in their pews as he moved slowly down the aisle to leave the church.

Mrs. Lee figured in another drama at St. Paul's which significantly revealed a strong feeling of a different character. St. Paul's was primarily a Virginian's church, though the Davises and other Confederates worshiped there. In the Cabinet, Mallory was a Catholic, and Benjamin, when he attended church at all, went to Beth Ahabah synagogue. At St. Paul's Mrs. Lee was as familiar as any native, and when she appeared alone she was ushered to the honored pew in front of the chancel.

She was plainly dressed and probably sat ungracefully with the crippling from her arthritis. As she waited for the service to begin, two beautifully dressed young women appeared at the pew. It was their family's pew the old woman was occupying, and they waited arrogantly outside for her to vacate. As Mrs. Lee moved painfully out, every pew was thrown open to her and hisses were audible. One of the young ladies was Margaret Howell, Mrs. Davis's sister, who had observed only that the occupant of her pew was an old woman.

While no one could blame the President's wife for her sister's conduct, it was the sort of story that enemies used against the family. It served to bear out the charges of arrogance and imperiousness. It was true that Mrs. Davis, aside from her friends, the government people, and the gay set she met at her levees or at friends' parties, was removed from the people of the Confederacy as far as was her husband.

It was not because she was uninformed about the Confederacy. Her husband took her into his confidence as he always had. Before Davis had private secretaries in Richmond, Varina had helped him with research, taken notes for his speeches, and taken letters in longhand to spare him eyestrain. Now in his tortured hours he talked over the problems of their experiment, and his wife concentrated on the subjects that absorbed him. In her memories she was vividly aware of all the campaigns, the battles, and the leaders of the armies.

But who was in those armies? Who was back home, waiting? What were they thinking down in the canebrake, up in the Smokies, in the hot Gulf country and the red foothills? Or what were they thinking a few blocks away, in the small houses below Capitol Square, where the hungry people had turned rioters and thieves, and were hunting through the alleys, like stray animals, for something to burn for warmth, with wood at fifty dollars a cord? There is nothing to indicate that she knew or even thought.

She was aware that they were paying the same prices for food as she was—$300 for a barrel of flour, $80 for a bushel of meal, $75 for a bushel of white beans, $60 for a turkey, $35 for a pair of chickens, and $15 for a pound of butter. Even the common stand-by, turnip greens, cost $4.00 a peck. "Relief must come soon from some quarter, else many in this community will famish. . . ."

At the same time she gave a luncheon for her ladies and served gumbo, ducks, chickens in jelly, oysters, lettuce salad, chocolate cream, jelly cake, claret and champagne. Except for the drinks there was nothing expensive, no meat, but—though she used no perquisites—she was aware that families less fortunately placed could not approach such a feast. For them, "What a change a decisive victory—or defeat—would make."

That was the way her husband thought, and Varina Davis never turned her woman's intelligence to the end of *making* a difference for the people. She had not changed in her adoration from the starry-eyed girl who first fell in love with Jefferson Davis. To her, he could do no wrong.

The fury of the attacks on him, after his appointment of Bragg, only made her more proudly aggressive in her defense of him. As he was the leader, she grew more bitter at the people who made his dream unrealizable. Seeing him wasted from trying to carry *their* burden, Varina often wept when she was alone in the big bedroom in the southwest corner.

All the warm pleasure she had experienced in arranging the new home, all the care she had given her flowers, returned to break her heart now. She could draw no more comfort than could her husband from the certainty of being right.

To those beyond the narrowing circle of people around the high house on the hill, she could give no more comfort than he.

CHAPTER TWENTY-EIGHT

The Laughing Boys

IKE Judah Benjamin in the war office, Braxton Bragg had been misplaced in field command. With all the clamor caused by his appointment to a position approximating chief of staff, Bragg, again like Benjamin, was not unfitted for his new job. He has been harshly treated by history because he was sustained as a favorite after failure in the field, and he could be unpleasant, but his record is not all black. He had been a superb organizer before his unhappy battle experiences, and he brought the same talent and considerable drive to the new job—along with his spitefulness and desire to remain a favorite.

By the nature of his assignment, to some extent Bragg came between Seddon and the President. His work made Seddon's ill-defined position even less clear. Duplication immediately occurred when Bragg endorsed Seddon's recommendations on specific items and then sent them on for the President's endorsement. On several minor matters Davis supported Bragg over Seddon, and in one that was to be significant.

Lee wanted some idle cavalry from South Carolina for the coming spring campaign against Richmond, and, as Beauregard feared destruction if he lost even a drummer boy, his chief of staff sent on a petition signed by South Carolinians protesting against the transfer. Seddon endorsed the petition by mentioning that the citizens were "influential." Bragg was opposed to any dispersal and strongly recommended that Lee get the troopers. He did.

If Seddon felt some natural jealousy of Bragg, it did not affect his relationship with Davis. In fact Senator Wigfall acted on Seddon's friendship with Davis in trying to induce him to appeal to the President in his handling of Congress. Because the worst of Davis's opponents, like Foote, were against him in everything, Davis was hostile to all opposition on anything. But Seddon felt this was out of his province. In any case his frail health was failing under the strain, he was losing faith in their victory, and he limited his efforts to that which was indicated.

At that time Seddon grew closer to Senator Hunter, also deeply pessimistic. During the week Hunter acted as the president of the Senate, but every Sunday morning he visited the Secretary when the office was quiet and they could enjoy privacy. Frequently the two Virginia planter-politicians strolled together through the Square in that mild and pleasant winter, and it was the belief of Seddon's war clerk that Senator Hunter persuaded the Secretary not to resign.

If Seddon considered resigning, it was probably because he felt ineffectual with the end of his larger plans, and, with Bragg to work on military affairs, the office details seemed too burdensome. He lacked Benjamin's facility in running an office and blandness in dealing with people. He was under constant pressure from favor seekers, and nothing in his background equipped him with the technique of giving the pleasant brush-off, of which the visitor remembers a genial personality and not the speed with which he went in and out of the office. Seddon's courtliness required time. When he lacked the time he could well give the impression of haughtiness. Falling behind in work, he refused to see claimants—and they were hurt, in a land accustomed to personal dealing.

By the time ugly-visaged Bragg came along, Seddon was too worn to make a fresh adaptation. Otherwise he could have shifted greater attention to office details and to the bumbling commissary, where the irate and stern-mannered Northrop, under Davis's protection, reigned like a half-cracked potentate. Clearly Bragg was capable of handling troop movements in a way to get results.

Toward the end of winter, army units engaged in diversionary attacks on occupied North Carolina points inland from the coast. The forces were too weak to present any real threat, but as soon as Bragg took over they achieved a success on an immediate objective which at least raised the people's hopes from the pall left at the end of the year. Bragg got the troops concentrated for the storming of Plymouth and insured success by a unique version of the amphibious war which had hitherto been practiced against the South.

As the flank of Plymouth was the river emptying into Albemarle Sound, the Union gunboats there not only made it safe but offered a threat to the Confederates. Here again another of the Confederate Navy's ingenuities entered to bring consternation to one and all.

This home-style "ironclad" was improvised more wildly than even the fabled *Arkansas*. Commander Cooke, of Portsmouth, Virginia— who had served in the Confederate Navy since he resigned from the old navy on Virginia's secession—was put in charge of building the

[323]

ship on Roanoke River. With the aid of two civilians he collected work-men "as inexperienced as their material was incongruous." A cornfield, with a nearby blacksmith shop, was the shipyard. The timbers were unseasoned wood, and the iron was the refuse of scrap heaps they scoured throughout the countryside.

Despite Cooke's herculean efforts the *Albemarle* was not ready to operate with the Army when the day came. Not to go back on his word, he started the ship on her maiden voyage at dawn, with ten portable forges burning and sledge hammers banging, while the newly arrived crew exercised at the guns. Late in the afternoon the boat landed the forges and workmen, cleared the decks and moved ahead toward the Federal fort.

Before dawn, less than twenty-four hours after her launching, this makeshift assemblage of junk bore into the enemy gunboats, rammed and sank one, dispersed the others, and opened fire on the vulnerable flank of the fort. The Union second-in-command stated in his report that, without Cooke's contraption on his flank, the fort would have held indefinitely.

The adventurous John Taylor Wood performed the liaison between the land forces and the ram—a type of work he had perfected, along with piracy on the Chesapeake Bay and in the Sound country which diverted some U. S. Navy attention as well as gathered supplies.

The *Albemarle,* after her Plymouth triumph, soon went the way of all the Confederacy's originalities. To rid the river of the menace the Unions sent two forays of gunboats—the second time eight—and the "ironclad" stood her ground, though badly battered and with only one gun firing. Worn then by his labors, the redoubtable commander fell sick, and Cooke's creation went into unexplained retirement.

Carelessly resting at Plymouth, in command of a new captain, the *Albemarle* was destroyed by the device so often used by the Confeder-ates—a torpedo. The bold night attack of the Unions was led by a young officer who, in 1861, had studied under Lieutenant Parker, the present commandant of the Confederate Naval Academy.

2

The Naval Academy at Richmond was one of Mallory's pet inter-ests, and he had passed the bill for it in early 1861. Lieutenant William Parker, its commandant, had graduated head of his class at Annapolis, where he was serving as an instructor when Virginia seceded. Resign-ing two days later, he was seen off by his fellow officers. He then served actively in the Confederate Navy and, in his middle thirties, was well qualified for the post he assumed in 1863.

Under Lieutenant Parker there were a dozen instructors in astronomy, navigation, surveying, mathematics, seamanship, gunnery, physics, infantry tactics, French, and German. The school had about fifty students between the ages of fourteen and eighteen. Though many of them were sons of famous Confederates, their training was no escape from combat.

The entire Academy consisted of one ship, the *Patrick Henry,* which served as barracks and classrooms and for all other features except actual fighting. The side-wheel steamer had a mast fully rigged with square yards stepped in her for practice.

The morning gun sounded at seven, and the boys breakfasted off hardtack and sweet-potato coffee. Their dinner at two of salt junk and corn meal was sometimes varied with a vegetable. Tattoo was at nine-thirty and taps at ten.

The classes were held regularly on hurricane decks and regularly interrupted by calls to action. The students helped man the guns at Drewry's Bluff, which, as spring came, they fired more than they practiced on their own. They also scouted in small-boat expeditions. One of the students recollected that they went from schoolbooks to carbines and cutlasses.

Secretary Mallory always brought friends to attend the examinations, for he was acutely aware of the Navy's need for junior officers. Lieutenant Parker said of their volunteer officers, "These gentlemen were officers of the Navy without being naval officers. . . ."

The training ship comprised part of the James River fleet, all built or converted into warships at the Richmond navy yards. The main ships, the *Richmond* and the *Virginia,* were ironclads on the general order of the *Merrimac,* though smaller, and the ends were not submerged. They were not very menacing to the Unions, but they patrolled the river below the city and contributed to keeping the enemy at a distance and from springing any surprises.

Far more dangerous to the enemy were the torpedoes. Though probably thousands of them were picked up in Southern rivers and inlets, they destroyed thirty ships, damaged nine, and provided a very definite check on enemy gunboats making free in inland waters. Of all varieties of make and action, these torpedoes achieved fair production with no uniformity of parts.

A basic frame torpedo—sunk in the river at a 45-degree angle—consisted of three pieces of timber meeting at a point to which was attached a cylinder containing a shell. The cylinder was on a spring; when the cylinder touched the spring, the spring pressed a percussion cap and the shell was launched.

There was a raft torpedo and a keg torpedo, made from lager-beer barrels, which were just what they sound like; a drift torpedo attached to driftwood and floated downstream, and an electric torpedo fired from the shore.

In Charleston Harbor, when the Union monitors and ironclad frigates began attacking in earnest that spectacularly beautiful city, the defenders went from torpedoes to torpedo ships. The admiral of the Confederate fleet there did not hold with what he called "new-fangled notions," and the first attempts against the Union fleets were made in rowboats. Then the *David* was built by private citizens. Fifty feet long and seven feet wide at the center, this boat had a cubbyhole for the captain, engineer, pilot, and fireman, and the torpedo was attached to a projecting spar. In a night attack this strange craft damaged the great frigate, *New Ironsides*.

Another invention, called the "fish ship," dived under a warship, dragging a torpedo that would hit the victim after the "fish ship" rose on the other side. The only weakness revealed in four trials was that the fish ship did not rise. Thirty men were drowned in the experiments, but six more volunteered for the fifth attempt—in action against an enemy. Her deadliness was complete. She sank the Union ship *Housatanic* and stayed down herself, this time for good.

Of the ironclads at Charleston, the *Palmetto State* was a marvel of the Confederacy. Her engines always worked.

Finally at Charleston, as everywhere, it was the shore batteries that stopped the Union attacking fleet, and infantry that fought off landing attempts. However, the Confederate Navy and the private citizens, who turned ship inventors and builders, demonstrated that they could have made very real accomplishments if, as Matthew Fontaine Maury proposed, they had concentrated on original ships for their own immediate protection instead of adapting to the political policy regarding the blockade.

The great destruction of the commerce raiders, the *Alabama,* the *Florida,* and the *Shenandoah* in the Pacific, failed to draw off the Union blockading fleet to protect the commercial ships—though over seven hundred ships were transferred to British ownership. While ships of war were engaged in chasing the raiders, and the *Alabama* destroyed one, the effect on the blockade was negligible.

The other great scheme on the blockade direct, ironclads built abroad, failed when diplomacy failed—when the armed forces failed. When the toughening United States bore down on evasive Napoleon, the frightened Emperor ordered the French shipbuilders to dispose at once of the ships designed for the Confederacy. Trying then to appease the United States, Napoleon assumed a righteous rage as if he had just discovered the whole thing. This fooled nobody, but it brought a futile end to three years of Bulloch's energetic and resourceful efforts.

At home men, for the most part of lesser gifts than those wasted abroad, and many without previous experience, had developed naval resources all over the South. At Petersburg ropewalks were made from cotton manufactured with tar as a substitute for hemp cordage. At Augusta there was a plant for shells and gun carriages; at Columbia, powder mills; at Selma, heavy guns to be used against ironclads in the batteries at Mobile, Charleston, and Wilmington. At Charlotte there was a large ordnance works and laboratory. These had been developed by an agrarian people who formerly depended on purchases and had started cold while under invasion.

Observing the disparity between even their makeshift accomplishments and the wastefulness of the naval policy, the people turned against Mallory. Captain Wilkinson, of the *R. E. Lee,* thought him a fool. Their attacks did not disturb the phlegmatic Floridian. He had done, extremely well, what the Administration asked. If the total policy nullified his efforts, well . . . he had never believed in secession in the first place.

In the quiet neighborhood near the President's the first warmth of spring brought green out in Mallory's front yard. The red-brick and gray-brick houses, with their white-columned porches, were pleasant to look at as he walked home to dinner and to practice his skill on his renowned mint juleps. Genial guests still crowded the table over which his beautiful wife presided and they all found his little girls charming when they said grace.

3

The jokes about Mallory's friend Benjamin having nothing to do in the State Department were coming true as far as diplomacy went. War clerk Jones mentioned with sour humor that Benjamin, desperate for occupation, visited Seddon to enlist his aid in getting Northern newspapers for the State Office—though the Richmond *Examiner* thought Benjamin had so many papers already that his office should be called the "Confederate Reading Room."

But Benjamin found plenty to do. He was concocting schemes of physical sabotage in the Union states, and he was arranging cotton credit to finance some rather desperate secret agents in the North. Naturally he did not confide in anyone the missions of these gentlemen quietly leaving his office and not seen again in Richmond.

He was handling the explosive question of arming slaves—to be freed if they fought. The Irish General Cleburne suggested emancipation as a means both of using man power and undercutting the United States' slogan. Joe Johnston, non-committal, forwarded Cleburne's letter to Davis. The President gave him a courteous but complete dismissal. "While recognizing the patriotic motives of the distinguished author, I deem it inexpedient at this time to give publicity to this paper, and request that it be suppressed."

Benjamin, on the other hand, naturally took a more realistic view. While he also realized that the time was inopportune, he did not discourage discussion that might hasten to bring the expedience into the open. As his objections were purely practical, he saw no point in causing patriots to "suppress" their ideas. To him the idea was to win.

More directly with Davis, he helped the President draft messages to Congress and contrived to get newspaper notices favorable to the Administration. On the chief purpose of his department, however, Benjamin could give the President no help. When Davis reviewed a bedraggled group of exchanged Confederate prisoners in Capitol Square, the President exhorted them to new efforts by telling the men that it all depended on the Army now. He said, "We have no friends abroad."

Benjamin, for all his efforts, could only agree. From England, Mason was writing his wife that the social life was very agreeable in a "large circle of Confederates," and English ladies and gentlemen were giving a bazaar in Liverpool for the benefit of sick and wounded Confederates and relief of Confederate prisoners in the North.

In France, Slidell had lost even the social life once provided by the devious Emperor. When the threatening attitude of the United States forced him to renounce his sympathies toward the South, Napoleon had just sent Maximilian to his propped-up job in Mexico. The throne was held for him by Bazaine, hard-bitten professional soldier and ex-sergeant in the Foreign Legion, and Napoleon assured the archduke that, "whatever events may occur in Europe, the assistance of France will never fail the new empire."

As the Emperor abandoned hope of an independent Confederacy for the Mexican neighbor, he tried to gain United States favor by

VIEW FROM LIBBY PRISON

Looking west. Winder's Castle Thunder on the right. Richmond docks on the left. Tallest building on the left was Gallego Flour Mill. At the extreme upper left was Belle Isle, prison for enlisted men. Wood engraving from a sketch by Harry E. Wrigley. Courtesy of Valentine Museum, Richmond, Virginia.

VIEW FROM HOLLYWOOD CEMETERY

Showing Kanawha Canal and James River. In the upper left background can be seen the manner in which the ⋯ William MacLeod. Courtesy of Valentine Museum, Richmond,

cutting his former Confederate friends in Paris. For Slidell there were no more invitations to Vichy, and no more receptions at Eugénie's for his wife and adored daughters.

The cut that wounded Slidell the deepest came from Maximilian. The wispy archduke had been very eager for Confederate friendship before his boss shifted his loyalties. Once in Paris, Maximilian refused to grant Slidell an interview and even left his notes unanswered. The archduke was busy drawing up the regulations for his court. Official etiquette provided for all types of functions which might be given, all gradations of invitations, how to hold the Emperor's sword and hat and how to hold public mourning on his death.

Slidell, the old politician who had gone soft with a cause, had nothing to do in Paris any more. He wrote his old friend, "I find it very difficult to keep my temper amidst all this double dealing. . . . This is a rascally world and it is most hard to say who can be trusted."

Slidell passed the time dining with his friends, playing pinochle and hating the Emperor. No Yankee enemy was so despised as this vulgar schemer, this postcard Napoleon blowing his smoke dreams of empire. With the bond of the Mexican bubble burst, Napoleon needed new friends in Europe. With the rumble coming from across the Rhine, he needed the Hapsburgs in Austria. Soon he would pull Bazaine's soldiers out of Mexico, betraying his stooge there.

Maximilian, who had no time for courtesies to John Slidell while arranging his court regulations, was not long away from the desertion of the French troops who protected his reign—and from the Mexican firing squad who were not to bother to read the regulations covering the public mourning after his death.

When Bazaine chased Juarez out of Mexico City, Juarez sought sanctuary in the north, where the Confederates' Quintero had operated the border to obtain Confederate supplies. In handling Governor Vidaurri, Juarez's enemy, Quintero had dealt with highhanded cupidity. Juarez was a different proposition. Not only could he close the border to supplies, but he could deliver Confederate agents in Mexico to the United States.

If Robert Hunter, when he was Secretary of State, had not been interested in the distant Cuban, Benjamin definitely was. He was very relieved to receive his young friend's dispatch stating that Juarez was still persuaded by the same power that the United States' Corwin had used on him—money. When Juarez learned that the $11,000,000 for interest on his European debts was not forthcoming, as Corwin had promised him, his practical support went to the government which gave him revenue for cotton shipments across the border and supplies in. Business went on as usual.

From the practical details with Quintero, Benjamin went into the spiritual realms of the Catholic Church. The United States, in addition to its own man power, enlisted men in Ireland under the pretense of hiring laborers. The United States agents had sold the emotional Irishmen on the slavery angle until, in effect, every Irish soldier believed every Rebel was a wicked slaveholder.

Back at Gettysburg an Irish Virginian was captured, and, in his temporary prison pen, he heard two of his guards talking in Gaelic. To their surprise, he entered the conversation in Gaelic. They were very saddened to discover a fellow Irishman among the Rebels and explained to him how he was on the wrong side to be fighting for his slaves.

" 'Tis you who are on the wrong side," he said, and explained that he had seen more Negroes in the Union Army than ever in the Shenandoah Valley. He owned his little farm which he had developed among friendly people, since coming from Galway, and now *they* were coming down on him like a British landlord to deprive him of the fruit of his honest labors. That night he was permitted to escape.

To set the Irish people right in a similar way, Benjamin had Robert Dowling working in Dublin, and sent over Father Bannon and Captain Lalor, who reported to Hotze. They were to move about Ireland, "to enlighten the population as to the true nature" of the war with an end to defeating recruiting. They pointed out that the Know-Nothing Party of anti-Catholics had existed in the North, and that when Meagher's Brigade was sacrificed at Fredericksburg a New York paper stated that the North could afford to lose a few thousand scum of the Irish.

Benjamin also had his hand in the co-ordination of credit for purchasing and delivering supplies. Early in '64, over the attacks of pressure groups, the Administration passed the law confining to the government cotton purchased for credit and supplies shipped in from abroad. In this the administration forces had made the concession to states of allowing them to continue with their own commercial contracts.

The states—still unsatisfied, as the government was a tougher competitor than unorganized speculators—carried their rivalry into the fields where cotton was purchased. Here, of course, the Confederacy had to go through its usual period of conflicting agents and cross-purposes, with their cotton now in inaccessible places.

With all of that, Benjamin could provide Davis with figures to prove that the government was making a hundred bales go as far as six hundred went when they had paid high prices in cotton at twelve cents a pound, with cotton actually quoted at forty-eight.

4

With everything else, probably the most satisfying event to Benjamin was in the nature of revenge. With England, it would seem that the lion's roar at the Confederacy increased in proportion to its tail being twisted by the United States.

English industry—munitions and shipbuilding—had a very good thing out of the war, and her merchant marine was given a tremendous boost in superiority as United States ships were driven from the seas by the high insurance rates caused by the Confederate raiders. Despite the vocal anti-slavery sentiment, the money men had good reason for wishing the war to continue; and the government, as if to save face at being imposed on by the United States, went out of its way to make petty trouble for the Confederacy.

As early as the fall of 1862 Benjamin had written Mason that "it is lamentable that . . . a nation so enlightened as Great Britain should have failed yet to discover that a principal cause of the dislike and hatred toward England . . . is the offensive arrogance of some of her public men." In the South this arrogance was reflected by the British consuls, especially in their manner of demanding that British subjects be free from military service.

The Confederacy had clearly stated to the consuls that an alien was to be considered domiciled if he showed clear intent of establishing his home and future within its borders. A British citizen representing an English firm, if he had remained in the South for twenty years, would not be considered domiciled. But if a man bought a home and land with the obvious intention of developing it for permanent use, he was a Confederate.

During the period when Benjamin hoped for recognition he was very lenient with all the English-born residents of the Confederacy who suddenly became passionately British. They were required only to sign an exemption oath with one creditable witness. The Southern people, whose fathers and grandfathers had fought the British, and never held with making friends by accepting insults, had long opposed the Confederate tolerance of the consuls' demands. When hope of recognition faded and the need of man power grew acute, Benjamin felt that he could gratify his people's resentment without cost to the cause.

Consul Moore in Richmond was selected as the victim. As he had protested a conscription law in Mississippi, Benjamin pointed out to him that his *United States* exequatur gave him authority only in Virginia and asked him to submit his commission to the State Department.

Ignoring this, Moore wrote the War Department concerning two Irishmen he was trying to exempt from Greenbrier County. These men were landowners and farmers who had voted. When their lawyer received a letter from Moore condemning the Confederacy, that was too much even for him, and he turned the letter over to the authorities. It reached Benjamin. Immediately Benjamin had Davis revoke Moore's exequatur.

Following that, in Savannah, Consul Fullerton challenged Governor Brown's draft proclamation. In paraphrasing Lord Russell's instructions, Fullerton had said that Britishers, if captured, would not be treated as prisoners of war but "as rebels and traitors."

Governor Brown, with amazing calm, answered that while England refused to recognize the existence of the C.S.A., "You, as her representative, are permitted to represent her interests here and to be heard for the protection of her subjects and their property." As those subjects were protected by the C.S.A., and all they were asked to do in turn was to help protect their state, their actual locality, against invasion, they had the choice of leaving the state if they did not wish to render this service.

Fullerton rudely replied that England, against any fighting by British subjects, could not admit that a foreigner, residing peacefully in a state "formerly part of a federal union, should be compelled by that state to take part in hostilities against other states which when he became a resident were members of one and the same confederacy." He even threatened European intervention.

Brown answered with a simple provincial's viewpoint. If the consul's pretensions were right, that the U.S. was not a foreign power and Georgia was still a part of its government, "your appeal for the protection of British subjects resident within this state should have been made to the Government at Washington and not to me."

After a couple of more such exchanges, Fullerton appealed to the Confederate authorities. Brown, whose business it was to know the people's sentiments, made the correspondence public. The newspapers rallied and clamored for the expulsion of all the consuls, who had not even shown the courtesy of applying for a Confederate exequatur. This offered Benjamin his big moment.

For the first time in the history of the United States, a cabinet member called a cabinet meeting. (It was when Davis was in Chattanooga, saving Bragg's skin.) The Cabinet agreed to expel the consuls. This small gratification was not really Benjamin's game, but it must have done him good after all the indignities his commissioners had suffered. Also, calling that cabinet meeting showed where he stood with the President.

Davis's enemies could use that assumption of power in their attacks on him, and he, more than Memminger or Mallory, was their target. They slurred at his race until even Hitler's bully boys would have felt tolerance in reaction. He called them "croakers," knowing they could not affect his position and knowing that whatever chance his now desperate cause held could not be furthered by either their favor or hatred.

If the Confederacy won, Stephens and his crowd would be dead ducks in a peacetime government. If they lost, he could be sunk no deeper by the enmity of fools.

For now, it was pleasant, at the socialite Haxall house, to enjoy such attention that Mrs. Chesnut would say, "Everything Mr. Benjamin said we listened to, bore in mind, and gave heed to it diligently. He is a Delphic oracle, of the innermost shrine, and is supposed to enjoy the honor of Mr. Davis' unreserved confidence."

As a confidant, Benjamin's danger to his own cause lay in his desire to soothe rather than direct the sick man racked by frustration. As a Northern observer found the Secretary, he had "not the stamina to originate, or even execute, any great good, or any great wickedness."

Perhaps that is why, in a city of high-running passions, he made more friends in high places than any other Confederate.

CHAPTER TWENTY-NINE

"Not Mine, O Lord"

OVER on Church Hill, in the dramatic house set deep in the hillside garden, Elizabeth Van Lew had her dream come true: she acted as a secret agent for the Federals.

This Richmond-born daughter of Northern parents, educated in Philadelphia, was the reverse of most Virginians in that she loved her state but the Union more. For all the nervous little woman's self-dramatizing, she possessed the ardor of the genuine abolitionist.

Different from her Northern allies, she did not regard Negroes as her equal. Those she owned (some of whom she had bought to reunite families) were treated very strictly. She permitted no presumptions and did not allow them to be seated in her presence.

Because of her utterances and air of mystery more than her acts, Miss Van Lew was surrounded by legends of secret tunnels and hidden panels and desperate Yankees appearing in dark passages. Probably she did help some Negroes and escaped prisoners on their flights and conferred with Union spies, but on the record her first work with the Unions prior to the spring of 1864 was a collaboration with Beast Butler during that winter.

General Butler, commanding the troops at Fortress Monroe on the Peninsula, occupied himself with long-distance legal arguments with Judge Ould in Richmond over prisoner exchange and dreamed of striking a spectacular blow where few of the armed enemy would be involved. As he toyed with the notion of delivering the prisoners in Richmond, he received a bouquet and letter from Miss Van Lew, stressing her Unionist sympathies and willingness to help.

Butler sent her a return message by a spy. The innocuous-sounding family letter was addressed to "My dear aunt" and signed James Ap. Jones. By applying acid the real letter came through:

MY DEAR MISS:
The doctor who came through and spoke to me of the bouquet said that you would be willing to aid the Union cause by furnishing me with information if I could devise a means. You can write me through Flag

of Truce, directed to James Ap. Jones, Norfolk, the letter being written as this is and with the means furnished by the messenger who brings this. I cannot refrain from saying to you, although personally unknown, how much I am rejoiced to hear of the strong feeling for the Union which exists in your own breast and among some of the ladies of Richmond. I have the honor to be,

Very Respectfully, Your Obedient Servant . . .

Through spies and Unionists in Richmond, and her own free run of Libby, Crazy Betsy collected information about a contemplated movement of prisoners and wrote him at once:

DEAR SIR:

It is intended to remove to Georgia all the Federal prisoners. Butchers and bakers to go at once. They are already notified and selected. Quaker (?) knows this to be true. Beware of new and rash counsel, beware! This I send you by direction of all your friends. No attempt should be made with less than 30,000 cavalry, from ten to fifteen thousand infantry to support them, amounting in all to 40 or 45,000 troops. Do not underrate their strength and desperation. Forces could probably be called to action in from five to ten days, mostly artillery. Hoke's and Kemper's brigade gone to North Carolina. Pickett's in or about Petersburg. Three regiments of cavalry disbanded by General Lee for want of horses. Morgan is applying for 1000 choice men for a raid.

Butler's letter to Elizabeth Van Lew would not indicate that she had acted previously as a Union secret agent, and hers to him was both naïve and uninformed. She asked for more cavalry than the Unions had in Virginia, or probably in the United States at that time.

Miss Van Lew showed the excitement of a novice by ignoring Butler's suggestion for communication and employed the more adventuresome methods of delivering her message through a Union spy, who in turn paid an intermediary a thousand dollars to escort a boy into the Federal lines at Williamsburg. When the boy delivered his message he added that, from his observation, "I don't think there are many men on the Chickahominy, or only a few cavalry."

This was Butler's moment. Acting immediately, he assembled six thousand men for the dash into Richmond, around which only a few Confederate units were scattered. The movement was superbly planned and executed and got the advantage of a rainy night. At three o'clock in the morning the troops reached Bottom's Bridge on the road to Richmond and gathered for the dash that would brush aside the sleepy pickets.

They dashed into a blinding fire of Confederate infantry. The Union troops recoiled and waited for daylight. Then they saw the planks removed from the bridge, the opposite banks lined with infantry under cover, and artillery in position.

Without any adventures or the payment of a cent, the Rebels had been warned by a Union deserter who walked into their lines. Private William Boyle, of the New York Mounted Rifles, had escaped from the Union army which held him prisoner for having killed a lieutenant. This fugitive killer undid Miss Van Lew's first recorded operation as a secret agent.

This only spurred her to greater efforts, again involving the release of prisoners. On the first of March, a dark and rainy morning, the city was startled to hear gunfire and artillery close to town. There being no military units in Richmond, a boys' company and companies formed of department clerks rushed to the fortifications that engirdled the city.

The action amounted to little, but the repercussions were tremendous. While Lee and Meade faced each other in northern Virginia, waiting firm roads for spring action, the Union general sent General Kilpatrick toward Richmond with a strong raiding party. At some distance from the city Kilpatrick sent a segment of his force under young Colonel Ulric Dahlgren off on an angle to come to the city from the west and south. Kilpatrick's main force hit straight down from the north and was easily discouraged at the breastworks, slipping eastward to the safety of the Williamsburg lines.

Colonel Dahlgren led his few hundred down the River Road through rolling Goochland County, to where Mrs. Allan, the spy, had retired after her trial. Apparently to make up for the oversights she complained of in Stoneman's earlier raid, Dahlgren engaged in some piddling destruction and burning along the way, allowed his men their diversion of pilfering goblets, and descended personally on the fine plantation house of Secretary Seddon.

Alas for Mrs. Allan's designs on her neighbor's property, Mrs. Seddon had gone to school with young Dahlgren's mother and been courted by his father. Mrs. Seddon and her old friends' son drank a few glasses of wine together, while some of the men drank a good deal more, and Dahlgren went on about his business of turning loose the prisoners in Richmond.

It was the last fun he had. The ford across the river to the south side was unfordable, and he came on straight from the west. Liaison with Kilpatrick failed, and Dahlgren's command broke under the fire from the boys and the department clerks. Wandering vaguely north of

Richmond toward safety, he ran afoul of a small detachment of regular cavalry searching for him and was killed.

The aftermath of this fiasco of a raid was the appearance of orders purportedly found on the body of Ulric Dahlgren:

We hope to release the prisoners from Belle Isle first, and having seen them fairly started, we will cross James River into Richmond, destroying the bridges after us, and exhorting the released prisoners to destroy and burn the hateful city; and do not allow the rebel leader, Davis, and his traitorous crew to escape. . . . Do not allow any personal gain to lead you off. . . . The men must be kept together and well in hand, and once in the city, it must be destroyed and Jeff Davis and his cabinet killed. . . .

General Meade denied knowledge of these orders, and unquestionably that gentleman would never have given permission to such. Union authorities claimed the papers to be forgeries, and maybe they were. True or fake, these orders served the purpose of inflaming the city against the enemy and hardening the spirit of resistance with a unity impossible in the remote regions.

Miss Van Lew's contribution to the mysterious nature of the whole thing was rather macabre. She was credited with having had Dahlgren's body stolen from the grave and, amid dark-of-the-night hocus-pocus, the corpse vanished to realms unknown. When Colonel Dahlgren's father asked for the body, the Confederate authorities were unable to produce it, and Miss Van Lew's achievement could have gratified only her drama-loving soul.

Though she sent other messages to Butler, the spinster was largely neglected by the United States and rewarded only by her sinister reputation in Richmond and the attention of scared little boys who, at a discreet distance, called her "witch."

2

The President was put in a bad humor at hearing those guns at the city's gates, and the pleasant warm spring did nothing to lift it. Trees were budding by March 12, and the grass was bright green in the walled garden of the Executive Mansion. But Jefferson Davis and his wife no longer found sanctuary there on Sunday afternoons, with Varina embroidering and Banny drinking tea and the children playing on the terraces. Now spring meant the coming of the crucial campaigns with Grant.

Assuming command of all Union armies, Grant was to bring his personal attention to Virginia and a general plan for breaking the last of the Confederacy into pieces by weight of numbers.

The President could not sleep. There was insecurity in his home since arsonists had set fire to the wood stacked in the basement during the last levee. His body servant, Jim, had run away. Another servant had run away and was captured with stolen money and chicken and ham.

He forgot to eat, and his body grew wasted and his stomach went off. A doctor's visit cost thirty dollars. Mrs. Davis sold her horses and the fine carriage that Pollard had found too regal. Some anonymous friend returned them, but they still could not afford to feed the horses. The President sold his own horses, except those, his wife said, needed "for his duties with the army."

Those "duties" were all that kept him going. Every afternoon he rode outside the city to the breastworks and to the little scattered camps of the few soldiers under General Ransom, protecting the city since the raids. Frequently the President rode alone, overruling the protests of his staff. Once a young soldier insisted in accompanying him on a lonely road because he knew enemy skirmishers were near.

On those rides Davis learned the topography of the Richmond environs like an engineer. General Ransom was vastly impressed with his knowledge of every detail. But what about the details to meet the master plan of Grant the hammerer?

The plan was very simple: to hammer the South into submission by hitting its two main armies and driving to its two main areas. The North now possessed tremendous superiority in man power, equipment, and artillery. Recruits were gathering to flow in as replacements, holding up the size, while any man the Confederates lost was gone. There was no one to take his place. They were losing even the horses which supported Confederate superiority in cavalry, while the North had built up that branch of arms proportionately to overwhelm by numbers, by quality of mounts, and repeating carbines against muzzle-loaders.

Grant in Virginia would keep hitting Lee, at whatever cost to the Unions, until the Army of Northern Virginia ceased arithmetically. The area protected by Lee was Richmond, a collateral objective.

Sherman, now in command of the West, would keep hitting Joe Johnston, with his objective the rail junction of Atlanta and the doorway to the Atlantic—which would divide the remaining half of the Confederacy.

To distract Lee and destroy his source of supplies, Grant would send an army under Sigel into the bread basket of the Valley before the spring wheat was in; great cavalry raids to Richmond of which Kilpatrick's was a weak forerunner; and the army under Butler at Fortress Monroe would drive from the East, either directly at Richmond or to cut its railroads from the South—"and scoop Richmond out of the Confederacy."

In the West, Sherman was in a more vulnerable position with his long railroad line of supplies back to Nashville. His diversionary maneuvers would be for the purpose of protecting his communications. To that end he would send harrying raids into the Deep South and start Banks, who had succeeded Butler at New Orleans, eastward toward Mobile.

The Mobile expedition failed to come off because Dick Taylor's foreign legion caught Banks up in the Red River country above Shreveport and took any offensive out of him.

As for Sherman's plan of protecting his communications by sending down raiding expeditions, Bedford Forrest, the uncouth native genius, immediately penetrated that design. Figuring that no raiding party could destroy more in Mississippi than Sherman already had, Forrest wanted to let Sherman's diversions do their worst and hit the main enemy where it would disrupt his major plan. He wrote Joe Johnston that he wanted to strike into middle Tennessee and cut off Sherman's supplies.

This move was so feared by Sherman that his orders were that the land over which Forrest passed must be "devastated" until the people there realized "he will bring ruin and misery" on them. *"If we do not punish Forrest and his people now, the whole effect of our past conquests will be lost."*

Perceiving the purpose of Sherman's fearful designs, and getting no satisfaction from Joe Johnston—who did favor his plan—Forrest wrote directly to the President. The letter was referred to Bragg. Though he concentrated on organization problems, Bragg endorsed the projected move into middle Tennessee as of vital importance. Joe Johnston also stressed to Davis the importance of this operation of Forrest. Even civilians suggested it. But . . .

John Hood, recovered from his wound and with Joe Johnston, found that army in fine shape and suggested offense by Johnston. From Hood's days of lying around on Richmond sofas wrapped in a rug, paying awkward compliments to Mrs. Chesnut about her husband (who was close to Davis), the President respected the word of his fiery friend who had suggested that Davis himself take command. "I would follow you anywhere," the simple young giant declared.

Davis desperately wanted an offense. Knowing that Lee could only defend, the President knew the offense had to be in the West. Anything but a despot in the decisions crowding him, he hungered for advice from everybody.

Bragg, having failed on the field and now turned grandstand quarterback, pressed for an offensive in the West—by Joe Johnston and the communications raid of Forrest. Defense-minded Johnston naturally wanted only Forrest to take the offensive. Davis, missing the size of Forrest, wanted only Johnston to take the offense.

The self-conscious aristocrat never appreciated the power he had in Bedford Forrest. Neither a West Pointer nor a gentleman, Forrest ran his "critter company" so that Davis's inspectors found it lacking in organization, and infantry generals complained that their deserters joined his cavalry for booty. A district judge in Mississippi had just written Davis that deserters and women were "at work to weaken our army" and "cavalry sent after them are a nuisance on the Country: they spend their time in gaming parties, drunkenness, marrying, horse-racing and stealing."

Such an irregular command violated Davis's sense of organization, and in this outrage he was sustained by Bragg. Beyond that, Bragg could still conceive of the use of Forrest in a larger strategy; Davis could not. Never thinking flexibly and originally of strategy, under the strain he depended more heavily on organization.

Strategy in Virginia was Lee's; in the West there was no one Davis trusted. Bragg occupied the place of influence held by Seddon the year before, but his plans involved Johnston and the wild man, Forrest. Davis probably feared that Johnston would never do anything, and Forrest's cause-and-effect maneuver was outside Davis's understanding.

Campaigns were not won by doing something in Nashville, Tennessee, to effect a move in Dalton, Georgia. They were won as at Buena Vista by a gallant charge. That is what Joe Johnston should do—the way he himself had done it, the way he would do it.

He could see the upraised sword shining through the smoke, see the thin gray line magnetized by his own fearlessness. *Charge, men! Charge* . . .

3

Inside the Capitol, which Davis passed on his way to the office, Henry Foote's clique yammered like the plotters gathering around a Shakespearean king. They wanted peace. Who didn't? The North also wanted peace. The country was sick of carnage. But the North wanted it on their terms of union, and these jackals here had weakened on the dream of independence—or else, like Stephens, they thought they could return like lovers making up after a quarrel.

Even passionate rebels, like Seddon, were losing heart. After the Dahlgren raid, Mrs. Seddon sent in twelve demijohns of wine and sold them at five hundred dollars a piece. Davis knew his own wife was deeply depressed, and feared the fall of Richmond.

The President climbed the steps to his office, overlooking downtown Richmond, the straight, hilly streets, the prisons and the hospitals, the river and the Basin, the vast government warehouses and the stores stuffed with auction goods from private homes. He had seen that view nearly every day for three years, and it had become synonymous with the stability of their country.

For its defense he turned to plans suited to his gifts—troop disposition. Lee not only could spare no men but, suffering intermittent illness, needed his undivided attention against Grant's massive forces. To protect Richmond against raids and the armies of Butler or Burnside or whoever might come, Beauregard was ordered up from Charleston.

Defensive troops in that area, which had always seemed insufficient to Old Bory when he commanded there, he now thought could be spared for his new department. Of course the immediate area south of Richmond had to become a department, and the original Hero beat Davis to the punch and named it first. It became the Department of North Carolina and Southern Virginia.

The gorgeous Creole had lost none of his vainglory since he had left Virginia nearly two years before, when Lee was a humble work horse without an army. He wrote the war office in his usual purple prose that he would serve with pleasure under General Lee, "aiding him to crush our enemies. . . ."

For all his theatrics, Beauregard had proven a faithful patriot, and Davis set a bad example for the war office in sneering at Old Bory's inappropriate eloquence rather than accepting him on his spirit.

He endorsed Beauregard's letter, "I do not doubt the readiness of General Beauregard to serve under any general who ranks him. The right of General Lee would be derived from his superior rank."

Even in these desperate preparations rank and right remained the inflexible man's guides. Supported by these preoccupations, he worked so steadily at appointments that Mrs. Davis had to bring him his lunch on a tray.

She pushed the papers aside on his desk and uncovered the dishes. Davis was trying to ease his locked nerves when a servant rushed in.

The oldest boy, Joe, had fallen from the balcony to the brick walk below, and they thought he was dying.

The stricken man and woman staggered in their hurry up the winding paths, along the shaded streets to their own house. It was the last day of April, and all the windows were up, but no sound came from inside. When the couple reached the child's side, he was already dying. They were there in time only to witness his death.

"Gentle and affectionate," called "the good child of the family" by Mrs. Chesnut, Joe was, Mrs. Davis said, her husband's "greatest joy in life!" Every night, wherever his father was, the boy would run in to say his prayers at his father's knee.

He had been playing on the balcony that ran around two sides of the house—south and east. To the south, steps led down to the garden. To the east, the balcony rose higher above a brick walk between it and the out-buildings. Joe had been walking along the balustrade along the edge, and in climbing over one of the protruding connecting posts he had slipped and plunged down.

When the Davises had learned the details, a courier arrived with a message for the President. He stared at the paper and then turned with a fixed expression to Mrs. Davis. "Did you tell me what was in it?"

She saw that "his mind was momentarily paralyzed by the blow," but finally he tried to write an answer. Then he cried out, "I must have this day with my little child," and moved blindly to the stairs.

The news spread, and at dark General and Mrs. Chesnut came. The windows were still open, and the wind was flapping the curtains. All the gaslights were burning over the whole house. Mrs. Barksdale and Mrs. Semmes were there, and Mrs. Semmes told them that Jeff, the brother, told her, "I have said all the prayers I know how, but God will not wake Joe."

The Chesnuts went up to see the child laid out. He looked "white and beautiful as an angel, covered with flowers." Beside the boy, his Irish nurse was weeping. It was the only sound in the house except the footsteps of Mr. Davis, pacing the floor of his room.

"Not mine, O Lord," he said, "but thine."

As Mrs. Chesnut left, John Reagan and Wade Hampton came, beginning the line of callers that was to move steadily in and out of the house until the funeral. Thousands of children followed the procession to Hollywood, "where it wound among those tall white monuments, up that hillside, the James River tumbling about below over rocks and around islands."

Then Mrs. Davis stood back "in her heavy black wrappings, and her tall figure drooped."

Jefferson Davis stood alone, straight and lean beside the open grave, and his dark hair showed the gray in the bright sunshine.

CHAPTER THIRTY

A Study in Competence

THREE days after Davis buried his son, Beast Butler moved up from east of Richmond to the defenseless south side of the city. Even the guard at Camp Lee had gone to Lee's army, being replaced by the boys and old men. Through Miss Van Lew, Butler knew the area was bare of troops, and he came on confidently with approximately twenty-five thousand effective troops, strong in artillery and cavalry, and a fleet of transports and gunboats that established a great supply base at City Point, southeast of Richmond.

While the guns from his troops advancing from their base echoed in Davis's office, the President received the news that Grant had struck in Virginia, northwest of Fredericksburg. Lee lured Grant into the Wilderness, where the superior Union cannon was nullified and, as Union General Meade wrote his wife, Grant discovered "Virginia and Lee's army was not Tennessee and Bragg's army." Grant was repulsed with eighteen thousand casualties, though at the moment where his complete check could have been turned into decisive defeat, Longstreet was wounded—by his own men, just as Jackson had been the year before in the same neighborhood.

As the war office pored over these dispatches, wild cries for help from south of the river went virtually ignored. Butler was driving toward the railroad between Petersburg and Richmond, or he could swerve toward either city. Poor, shattered Pickett, no longer a favorite of anyone's, wired desperately from Petersburg as he tried to cover all angles with no troops.

If Petersburg fell, the capital was finished—for the smaller city, twenty-two miles to the South, was the railroad junction that connected Richmond with the South. Even if the connecting railroad between the cities was captured, Richmond and Lee's army would be hard put for supplies.

Finally, between Richmond and Petersburg, seven miles from Richmond on the south bank of the James, Drewry's Bluff was the only fort that protected Richmond from gunboats. If that fell the enemy would be in a position to strike at the city from the south, with the aid of his river fleet.

Butler could be aiming at any one or all three of the objectives. Of organized Confederate units in that area, there was not one. Of unorganized and scattered, there were not enough men to form one unit. Even from the river the Beast was safe.

While Butler was landing his army a gunboat was blown up by a torpedo, set off by men on the shore. Two Rebels were captured, and of one of them Butler said, "If you can use him, do so; if not, hang him." They used the captured man by lashing him to the cutwater of a boat and forcing him to reveal the location of the torpedoes in the river.

With that menace removed, the supporting Union fleet was safe, for the gunners from the little Confederate river fleet were manning the guns on Drewry's Bluff against the land advance. The sixty midshipmen under eighteen years old, with ten officers (instructors), landed to act as skirmishers against Butler's infantry.

There was virtually nothing else between Butler and Richmond by way of Drewry's Bluff. It was the greatest opportunity of the war.

In Richmond the war office awoke from its paralysis into a confusion caused by the divisions of its departments. Everybody was wiring everybody else to do something. Ransom had a little force called two brigades north of Richmond. Pickett had a staff at Petersburg, where he was commander of that department within the newly created larger department of Beauregard.

Beauregard fell sick at Weldon, North Carolina, south of Petersburg, and wired Bragg. Seddon wired Beauregard. D. H. Hill, deposed for criticizing Bragg, came along as a volunteer for the remnants of troops coming up from South Carolina.

These were the units only recently ordered north, coming on the rickety railroads whose tracks Butler's men were attacking to tear up. *Two hundred* men got past. They stopped Butler's army for part of an afternoon. Two hundred more. Ransom's two small brigades hurried to support from north of Richmond. Together the less than one thousand men held Butler until nightfall.

Pickett got sick from all the worry and excitement, and the tracks were torn up south of Petersburg. Butler was hitting everywhere—south of Petersburg, south of Richmond, between the two cities. Beauregard wired he was coming. Two hundred more troops came, walking through the gully where the bridge had been destroyed. Another bridge was destroyed.

Seddon sickened with neuralgia. Bragg sent orders hourly. Then a wire came to Davis from north of Richmond. With the defenses there stripped bare, the full force of Sheridan's cavalry was at the breastworks.

Davis hurried home and went upstairs to his room. There he buckled on two pistols, one heavy navy Colt, and pulled the flaps of his long gray coat over them. He strode erectly down the white marble steps and turned to the stable.

From the house, where Mrs. Davis gathered the children to pray, little Jeff (whose faith had been shaken since Joe did not wake up) said, "You had better let me have my pony saddled, and let me go out and help Father; we can pray afterward."

His mother held the children to her as Davis galloped up wide Clay Street, where other families came out on the porches of the great houses. They could hear the firing clearly. . . .

The fight had started in open rolling farm country, near where a road passed a little hostelry called Yellow Tavern. Sheridan's big cavalry force, superbly mounted and well gunned, armed with Spencer repeating carbines, had started the drive to draw Stuart's worn troopers off from Lee.

Stuart's men had not perceived the force of the blow at once. A brigade went after Sheridan, called back for help, and then a division followed. Soon Stuart had the bulk of his men pressing hard on their poor horses. The two forces converged on the road to Richmond, less than ten miles out.

The Rebels were behind when they went into the fight, and they never caught up. They charged, they retreated, they dismounted and fired. They checked the Yankees here, bent them back there, but they could not contain those hard-bitten blue men.

Shaken down by three years of bitter and humiliating experience at Jeb Stuart's hands, the Yankees knew the ropes now. They had the weapons and the horses, the condition and the will.

The fight swirled over miles, on both sides of the little road and across the farm land. Stuart was fighting in the thick, rallying a sag. The point steadied, catching dismounted Yankees who had overrun the position. One of them, running back, turned and fired at the big red-bearded man shouting commands. The bullet caught him in the side.

Stuart held his saddle. His aides got him down, into an ambulance. He was in terrible pain and gravely wounded. The Yankees came swarming back, and Stuart's friends had to cut their way through for the ambulance.

The Rebels could not get organized again. Sheridan's troopers won the way to Richmond and came on toward dusk. The local defense troops—the old men and boys, the department clerks and workers in the Tredegar Battalion—had reached the high earthen breastworks.

The solid masses of the blue horsemen brushed them off. The armed civilians scattered back to the inner lines. Some guns came up. Ransom's little brigades, which had just rushed over to hold Butler, rushed back. President Davis was with Ransom. The general found his coolness an inspiration and felt that the President stood ready to assume command if the emergency came.

With Sheridan between the outer and inner lines, the Confederate cavalry, re-formed and as vicious as a wounded tiger, came at him for more.

Sheridan boasted that he could have gone on into the city then, only he knew he couldn't hold it. Probably he could have, but he would have had a hard time getting out. His men were anxious to get out of the spot they were in right then. The aroused hornets were buzzing.

On what is now the edge of the suburbs, where Route 1 for Washington begins, Sheridan turned his troopers east. With all their condition, they were very tired too. They fumbled through the night parallel to the city, past good farms and misleading byways. Impressed guides misled them and were killed. Sheridan kept the units steady and moving.

In the morning they got across the Chickahominy and crossed the road where Stonewall Jackson had come down from the Valley in the early days of his fame. They followed the periphery of the Seven Days around Richmond, and Sheridan kept his hand in by burning a farmer's mill that had survived the two armies before. Finally the Union cavalry reached the safety of the gunboats on the James River, where McClellan had established his base in the old soft days of the war.

There Sheridan could swagger while his men and horses rested. He was a hard, coarse, vain man, and he was an able leader of the mounted might that had won its first big victory over the weakening cavalry of the Army of Northern Virginia.

But the thirty-two-year-old man who lay dying in Richmond had brought his own vanity and flamboyance to war. There was a plume for the repeating carbines, Sweeney's banjo for the rifled artillery guns, and some romance in the color and the laughter of that archaic Rebel leader that will ever stir hearts responsive to physical action.

With Stuart, with young Pelham and big Von Borcke, with all who rode when their horses were festooned with roses on West Franklin and were gone now—with them something was lost in the grim days at hand when their war was reduced to fighting off the implacable machine closing in on them.

2

Jefferson Davis left the stricken house on West Grace Street, where the little crowds waiting in the drizzle heard the dread words that Jeb Stuart was no more. The President rode home where his own dead was still close and fell on his bed.

The next morning General Ransom ate breakfast with him, and for the guest Mrs. Davis brought out "a very small plate of butter" which a friend had donated. For the rest, they had a dish of fat bacon, cut thin and fried crisp, cold bought bread and hot corncakes. The coffee was thin. Then, while Ransom went off to watch for Sheridan, Davis rode south of Richmond, to where the scurrying forces had gathered to push Butler back.

The Beast had proven to be a miserable soldier, thwarted from his opportunity by the few little panting bands. Now they were going to defeat *him* anyway.

Beauregard was there, with his large staff. The President, with some of his staff and his friend John Reagan, hovered behind in the foggy morning when the battle began. They aimed to drive Butler back from the railroad where he had made lodgments and from sectors in the outer defenses of Drewry's Bluff. As he fell back another force was to drive up from Petersburg and catch him in flank.

The battle started well. Butler drove. Then confusion came in the Confederate ranks, the units unfamiliar with one another and no support coming from the flank movement. The little cluster of men with the President grew anxious.

A light shower fell, and then a gun boomed from the south. Davis smiled and said with relief, "Oh." Then silence from the distant flank. It was never broken.

Butler escaped back to his fortifications. They were in a curious geographic position. Flowing southeastward, the James River makes a series of vast loops. Paralleling one of the southerly loops, the Appomattox River flows northeastward into the James, making the land between in effect a peninsula. At the open land end Beauregard stationed his troops and Butler was trapped inside, as Grant said, as if Beauregard had put a cork in a bottle.

But that was only Butler and Sheridan. From the Valley came news that Sigel's drive had been checked by a small Confederate force under Breckinridge, supported by the corps of the Virginia Military Institute, whose boy cadets won on that field (New Market) the only battle flag of any college in the United States.

Then there was Grant. Stopped in two more battles since the Wilderness, he used his superior numbers to sidle around Lee's flank to get between him and Richmond. He missed, but he was getting nearer. He was taking a heavy toll from Lee's grizzled veterans, and he kept coming on.

Back in his office, Davis read the reports, then read a grandiose scheme of Beauregard's. Lee should retreat to the breastworks of Richmond, while sending some of his men with whom Beauregard would annihilate Butler. Then Lee's men would return, and, with Beauregard's men, they would annihilate Grant. Lee answered, in effect, if Old Bory could spare any men to send them on now.

It was a grim note from Lee. Beauregard missed the urgency, spinning his dreams of *la gloire*. Bragg wired him that it was an order. Bragg got more results than Seddon with troop movements. He understood orders better, and he was less polite. Those South Carolina troopers he had ordered to Virginia had given invaluable aid in support of the weakening cavalry against Sheridan. Now Bragg got a division from Beauregard when Grant—drawing on Butler's bottled-up forces —had sidled and fought to the outskirts of Richmond, where McClellan had come two years before.

With Grant's guns audible in Richmond, reports poured in from the South, about Sherman's drive down into Georgia, where Joe Johnston retreated before him. Although Sherman had been allowed to gather his supplies without molestation, Joe Johnston still believed a raid by Forrest on his supply line in middle Tennessee would check the advance. Davis's old West Point bishop friend, General Polk, just before he was killed urged the President to send Forrest. Johnston's most reliable corps commander, Hardee, seconded the appeal.

But from Alabama, Stephen D. Lee, commander of the Department of Alabama and Mississippi, wired Richmond he had ordered Forrest to stay there to protect the country against a Union raid of destruction gathering at Memphis. Though the expedition was being sent by Sherman for the purpose of immobilizing Forrest, Davis did not overrule Stephen Lee. Forrest would contain a local raid while Sherman, unimpeded, marched on toward Atlanta.

Never thinking in terms of such long-range countermeasures, Davis could not be reached by the strategical urgency with the pressure of attacks outside his door. He could only think that it was Joe Johnston who should attack Sherman. That was an army as Lee's was an army.

Bragg constantly urged the President to force Johnston to fight or he would never stop retreating. Hood, on the ground, believed attack was the weapon.

Hood was young, impetuous, and ambitious. Bragg had left Joe Johnston a demoralized army which had taken months to rebuild. But what Davis thought was that Joe Johnston was a retreater and secretive. As he distrusted the commander, the commander was withholding confidences from him.

While the voices clamored and Davis tried to think, his windowpanes rattled when Lee and Grant collided at Cold Harbor, in the battle area where Lee had first emerged.

The Old Man had been sick in this campaign against Grant. He was aging, and he was exhausted from the strain and the hard physical life. He missed the brilliant savagery of Jackson and the stubborn dependability of Longstreet, lost with his wounds. Even old Bald Dick Ewell was fading too far to remain in active command. Powell Hill was not the leader of a corps that he had been of a division, and he fell sick during the campaign. Prolonged combat was exercising its own attrition.

But where the old white tavern had nestled in the shade at the little summer place of Cold Harbor, Lee got the co-ordination he needed. With Richmond at their backs, his ragged veterans beat the hell out of Grant's army. Nearly ten thousand fell in fifteen minutes. Even Grant, who was not too generous, admitted it was one fight he would like to have missed.

Since Grant had started his spring campaign, he had lost as many men as Lee had in his army. But he had them to lose. Recruits came in.

As Lee's hungry legions rested in the heat that rises in smothering waves outside Richmond, Grant side-slipped again. The only place he could go was south of the river, but that might be a feint. Lee could not uncover Richmond, nor could his battered cavalry make contact in the wooded country to discover the Unions' purpose.

To the Richmond war offices the anxiety of Lee was brought by his telegrams to Beauregard, to Davis, to his cavalry: "Endeavor to ascertain . . ."—"as soon as you can ascertain . . ."—"until I can get some definite information . . ."

Davis hurried to the war office. Bragg hurried to Davis. Nobody knew where the blow would fall. Beauregard said it would fall on his handful at Petersburg and screamed for reinforcements. But he always hollered for reinforcements.

This time he was right. Half the weight of Grant's army fell on his few thousand in the earthworks outside the little hilly city on the Appomattox River.

With all his spinning of fancy strategy and his theatrical rhetoric, Old Bory saved Petersburg with a few thousand men, against fifty thousand, by skillful and determined defense. In that, his greatest moment, he was a good soldier, as well as a good likeness of one—but it was too late for any favor with the war office. Disliked from Davis down for his vainglorious manner, he was brushed off—into uselessness —after he saved the capital for them.

He was leaving the stage of Heroes for good when Lee, certain Grant's main blow was aimed at Petersburg, hurried his own weary ragamuffins through the dusty June heat. They had to fight off Yankees near the turnpike to get there. Then the two armies met again and Grant failed again—and the Old Man took over.

By then Grant's blue men were physically and morally shattered. Under the steady, baking sun Grant settled down to the one thing he had started out to avoid—a siege of a city.

That was also what Lee wanted to avoid. After Cold Harbor he wanted to maneuver, to try to defeat Grant in the field. He realized they could no longer hold Richmond and win. Forced to a static defense of the capital, he said it was "then only a question of time."

But for the President no change of concept was possible. The events immobilized his reason. He was capable only of reflex actions on the level of mental habits.

When, in the beginning, Davis had the chip of honor knocked off his shoulder, he had the courage to fight—but not the desire. He was like a smaller boy with a bully, determined to put up as good a fight as possible until spectators separated them. He had put up the good fight, but everyone watched with indifference while the bully turned out to be bent on killing him.

He could only quit in order to save his life or pick up a rock. With his honor he could no more quit than he could have avoided the fight; he would die first. If he picked up the rock and lost, the end would come fast. In his heart he was always afraid that he could not actually beat his enemy. Afraid to try to defeat the enemy, and unable to quit, he could only hold on—bloody and weakening—and hope for he knew not what. He just hoped. . . .

3

Grant was fighting not only Lee's army but Davis, just as Lee in 1862 fought not only McClellan's army but Lincoln. Since then Lincoln had learned his limitations as a commander in chief and turned that function over to Grant. Davis, not learning, was still to himself the man who had met the hour.

Yancey had been unwittingly right in that introduction down in Montgomery. Davis was the man to meet an hour that was passing. He was the true representative of the South's unique and anachronistic culture. His self-awareness only molded him into the unadaptiveness of the culture, creating in him the unusual type who is defeated by the commonplace. Grant was that commonplace.

Grant was the man whom fortune brought to every hour with precisely the qualities needed in that time and place. He could not have been a successful Confederate general because he was too wasteful of life and too dependent on numerical and material superiority. As his side possessed the physical supremacy, he brought the talents best fitted to use those resources at each time and place; and each success developed the confidence which was a necessary ingredient in his methods.

At all times he brought a single-minded aggressiveness and bulldog determination. In the early going, at Donelson, those qualities were best suited to the divided Confederate command fixed by their own indecision.

At Shiloh, when Sidney Johnston got the jump on him and won the first day, Grant got the reinforcements under Buell while the Confederates' commander was killed and their reinforcements lurked futilely west of the Mississippi. Grant had no part in either getting his reinforcements or the Rebels' not getting theirs; but victory fed his self-assurance.

Then, during the Confederate resurgence and the Union lull, Buell received the wretched assignment of scattering his troops and building railroads, while Grant was inactive. In his next action, the drive on Vicksburg, again came the divided command that separated the Confederate forces (and a Confederate deserter turned spy delivered to Grant these facts) and the indecision of Pemberton that divided his own command.

Flushed with confidence in his single-purposed hard hitting, he went to Chattanooga *after* Bragg's army had suffered demoralization from failure to follow battles, and Davis had turned the command into clay pigeons by sustaining Bragg while removing the able men who complained of him.

Following that, when Grant came to Virginia as commander in chief, he possessed the vast assurance and power drive of success, of prestige, of presidential support—and he inherited a superb army.

If Grant had come to Virginia the year before, he would have met the Army of Northern Virginia at the peak of its morale and man power; the cavalry equal and possibly holding an edge through Stuart; Stonewall Jackson at the height of his genius and his Second Corps capable of the most audacious and involved maneuvers; the general officers not yet worn by the strain, and Lee still physically vigorous.

As it was, he could not defeat them. He faced no indecision, no divided command, no demoralization. The survivors of Lee's army had lived and fought together for so long they had become like a separate people, a nation within a nation. As all ideologies had gone from the Northern armies, and they were fighting only to conquer, so the classless cross-section of Southerners with Lee, bound of blood loyalties, were fighting only that they personally should never be conquered.

The deserters refused to fight Jeff Davis's war; Lee's men fought their own war. In Virginia they fought for Bacon's Castle and Purkins Corner; Bent Creek and Old Point Comfort; Mobjack and Martin's Store; Paint Bank and Fancy Gap; Cabin Point and Providence Forge; Columbia Furnace and Burnt Ordinary; Disputanta and Drakes' Branch; Elk's Garden and Forks of Buffalo; Green Spring Depot and Bowling Green; Tobaccoville and Ware's Wharf; Iron Gate and Lebanon Church; Stuart's Draft and Shady Lane; Old Sweet Springs and Sweet Chalybeate; Jamestown Island and Yorktown.

The golden laughter that was lost with Stuart was never theirs. Their laughter was of the earth, bawdy and rowdy, of physical things of long associations, rabbits and catfish, horses and mules, molasses and corn pones. It derived from their stealing and lying, whoring and drinking and gambling. It spun into fabulous tales and macabre incongruity, born of their undisciplined self-assertion and the hunger and the danger in which they lived. Their poorest makeshifts provided a joke as they huddled from Grant's sharpshooters in the stinking trenches around Petersburg and boasted to the Yankees of their superior prowess at cards and horse racing.

Grant could not beat them. Nothing in the mechanics of confidently applied power was enough. But they could not beat him either.

At the Wilderness, at the moment of turning the battle against him, Longstreet was lost. Crossing the North Anna, when Lee caught Grant with his army divided by the river, Lee was ill and sent Powell Hill to do what Jackson's Second Corps once did. When Hill failed, Lee could only bitterly upbraid the ailing subordinate for not doing what Jackson would have done.

At Cold Harbor, when Grant's army was staggered back, Lee's men were too thinned in numbers and too worn in bodies to try a counter-maneuver—and there was no general officer capable of executing it. The army could only wait while Grant pigheadedly refused to request a truce to bury his dead and gather his wounded—wait with their terrifying humor that said of Grant, "He's trying to stink us out."

Against even this indestructible line, by coming at the time he did, Grant was still safe. His army—organized by McClellan and turned over to him with high morale by Meade—had suffered as no Union army ever sent against Lee, and their morale was gone. The Northern people, sickened at his casualties, lost confidence in him and grew discouraged of ever defeating the South. For the first time in two years the Confederate dollar was checked in its slow fall and gained two points.

But Lincoln supported him. Lincoln believed that Grant's insensibility to losses, imperviousness to setbacks, while he doggedly hammered away in the certainty of arithmetic, were the only qualities needed in the summer he came to Virginia. For all the shattered morale of his exhausted men, they could rest while the gaps were refilled by recruits, secure in the knowledge that Lee was too weak to hit back.

Only one element could defeat Grant's competence—and that outside his control. If Johnston performed as well against Sherman as Lee against Grant, the political forces of the North might move for peace with a people over whom victory came at too high a cost. The fall elections were near, a peace party was formed, and the people were tired of war.

By battles Virginia had proven too tough a nut to crack. If the Union force at the other end of the line failed, there might not be enough heart to support Grant's arithmetical grinding in Virginia.

CHAPTER THIRTY-ONE

No Villain Need Be

I N LATE June, in the big upstairs bedroom, Mrs. Davis gave birth
to a girl, Winnie ("the Daughter of the Confederacy"), but her
husband had no more time for new life than for death.

Joe Johnston had retreated all the way to Atlanta, and the
clamors reaching Davis followed him everywhere, every hour of the
day and night. *Send Forrest on Sherman's communications,* they cried
from the South. *Make Joe Johnston attack,* said Bragg in his ear.
"Concentrate all the cavalry . . . on Sherman's communications,"
Lee advised. *We should take the offensive,* wrote Hood from Johnston's
army.

Over at Petersburg, Grant blew up a segment of the Confederate
line with a mine tunneled under them, and the city hung by a thread.
Using his superior numbers, Grant had first made a threat at Richmond from north of the river, drawing off part of Lee's force, then
used the Crater (an underground V-2) against the weakened line.
To add fury to his attack, he sent in Negro troops. Instead, they added
fury to the Rebels' defense, and the tricky attack boomeranged with
heavy losses to Grant.

But the strain took its toll from the anxious men in those hot city
offices. Sweating in his high stiff opened-fronted collar, Davis read a
wire asking for co-operation in Georgia from, of all people, Governor
Brown. With an army finally at his gates, Brown suggested that Forrest
could "do more now for our cause in Sherman's rear than anywhere
else."

Now it was *our cause.* By Howell Cobb's estimate Brown had
exempted from the army three thousand militia officers of military
age, five thousand civil officers, and God knows how many unlisted
exempts—in addition to his home guard and "details"—all of whom
had joined with the cracker vote to give Brown the 1863 election over
the aristocratic candidate. His militia, grabbing arms intended for
the armies, had disported themselves for three years at home against

the invasion threatened by Brown. Well, here was the invasion. Let the militia defend Atlanta.

Davis wired Brown that Forrest was needed for the Alabama-Mississippi Department, where the proportion of Yankees against the Rebels was even greater than Sherman's against Johnston's.

Governor Brown was a foolish obstructionist of the whole when hot for power in his own state, but when Georgia became endangered he was as shrewd in understanding its defense as he was in defending himself politically. He wired back that the country expected "points of less importance should be for a time overrun," and Forrest's operation in those peripheral sectors had no effect on the major issue of Atlanta.

As to the relative strength of the Alabama and Georgia armies against the Unions, he suggested that the President's information came from unreliable sources. "If your mistake should result in the loss of Atlanta . . . the blow may be fatal to our cause and remote posterity may have reason to mourn over the error."

Every nerve in Davis's body twitched. Now it was military lessons from this bumptious clown who had done more than any other man in the Confederacy, even Vance, to force dispersal of man power and matériel on the country. From the open window to the east came that incessant rattle of guns down along the north side of the river where Grant kept pressing to weaken Lee's main army at Petersburg. Clerks had been down there weeks now, their department heads complaining and Tredegar slowing down production with its men away. Even Pemberton, victim of Vicksburg and unwanted by any army, striving to serve where he could, was down there as lieutenant colonel of artillery.

Davis, his voice articulated with cold precision, dictated a message for Brown. "Most men in your position would not assume to decide on the value of the service to be rendered by troops in distant positions. When you give me your reliable statement of the comparative strength of the armies, I will be glad also to know the source of your information as to what the whole country expects, and posterity will judge."

That's putting him in his place. Right here in Virginia, Lee's army was showing them how to handle an invader. Grant, still trying to divert forces in order to get the setups he enjoyed in the West, arranged more raids to western Virginia.

When the V.M.I. cadets and Breckinridge's two thousand drove off Sigel, Grant ordered another and bigger force under Hunter to operate in the Valley. To make certain the destruction of that source of supply, and the Virginia Central Railroad which brought the food to Richmond, Sheridan was sent out to make a juncture from the east.

The Confederate cavalry understood Sheridan's methods now, and the whole force started after him. Under Wade Hampton, the Rebel troops cut Sheridan off, fought him to a standstill, and caused his withdrawal to Richmond.

At the same time Lee detached Jubal Early's used-up corps to rid the Valley of Hunter. Enraged at being interrupted in his despoiling, Hunter burned the V.M.I. buildings in Lexington before he fled to the safety of the West Virginia hills. Equally enraged, Early turned north on an "invasion" of his own, crossed the Potomac, and instigated the first organized retaliation in destruction.

Grant found himself sending troops of his own for the protection of Washington, though Old Jube had less than ten thousand men, and then Sheridan was detached to go after Early.

Why didn't Joe Johnston do something like that down at Atlanta— instead of trying to interfere with the only department that had sur vived the shrinkage of the country?

But Joe Johnston was not saying what he proposed. The general wrote Mrs. Chesnut personally, "Joe Johnston does not say exactly that Jeff Davis betrays his plans to the enemy, but he says he dares not let the President know his plans, as there is a spy in the War Office who invariably warns the Yankees in time."

Though Davis had never heard his commander in the West so express himself, his actions clearly indicated that attitude. And in his manner of secretiveness Johnston further showed that, as Mrs. Chesnut said, "His hatred of Jefferson Davis amounts to a religion. With him it colors all his days."

Johnston was "magnetic, advancing or retreating, and draws good will," but the President only got the back of the general's hand per sonally. Militarily "Retreating Joe" gave up territory with an abandon that agonized Davis, obsessed as he was with holding ground.

Johnston's retreat had been masterly before a numerically superior enemy. Though he was flanked out of position after position by Sher man's equally skillful advance, he kept his army intact, the men had the morale lifter of defeating Sherman (Kenesaw Mountain) in his only direct attack, and they were still between the Yankees and Atlanta—though backed up into its breastworks.

But with all Johnston's ability in avoiding casualties, he might be only repeating what he had done in Virginia, when they almost had to tie him outside Richmond to make him fight. Now the joke from Atlanta was that Johnston was preparing a fleet of transports to continue the retreat by water to the Bahamas. And Joe Johnston, as at Richmond, refused to tell anything!

In the haze of the hot, dry month of July, Davis had to know. The only man he could trust to discover the facts was Bragg. He believed in the offensive too. The rough-bearded man in his middle forties was dispatched to Atlanta. At last they would learn Johnston's intentions.

With his new favorite gone, the President lost an old faithful from the floor below him. Memminger resigned. The dour, cold little man probably demonstrated more clearly than any cabinet member that the methods of American democracy with inferior resources against a strong and ruthless enemy are impractical.

War clerk Jones commented sadly that if they ever fought for independence again, the permanent government should be established *after* success.

By any normal American standard Memminger was at least as capable as the average government economist. His failure to think in terms of a rebellion that his country, unaided, must win by its own ingenuity indicated both an attachment to democratic principles and an expectancy of foreign help shared by many world statesmen before and since. An inability to handle Congress was certainly not unique in American history, and the Secretary's forbidding personality merely made the struggle more unlovely.

His climax with them came over something called the Funding Act. Depressed by the treasury notes flying about like leaves in the fall, Memminger wanted to draw off some by the purchase of government bonds (which sale he would stimulate by making them forever tax-free) and refund the rest with a new $200,000,000 issue which would comprise a modified repudiation. Congress jumped on this with changes so complicated that OPA verbiage would be simple in comparison and, in effect, tried to make one in the hand out of two in the bush.

Notes under $100 would be exchanged at three old for two new, and those over $100 were to be taxed 33⅓ per cent, and then 10 per cent monthly until taxed out of existence. This virtual repudiation chiefly increased the fears of the populace, and, though great numbers of the notes were refunded, the old bills continued to circulate in defiance of the government and to the confusion of one and all.

On viewing the chaos it had wrought, Congress turned on Memminger. Because he had offered the original plan the Secretary was blamed for what Congress had made of it. To the hard-working, systematic man of figures this was too much. He had wanted to resign when Congress put through the Funding Act, and now Davis could not dissuade him. His tight-lipped insistence on the rights of his department had gotten him into arguments with all the other cabinet members, and he yearned to escape to the quietude of the countryside.

For Davis, yearning for action for Johnston, everything he heard was depressing. From overseas Napoleon, the master betrayer of both sections, practically sent the great raider *Alabama* to her death, ordering her out from Cherbourg, where the iron-protected *Kearsage* waited. In the fight the marksmanship of the *Alabama's* unpracticed crew was indifferent, the ammunition was defective from two years of storage in all climates, and two eleven-inch pivot guns on the *Kearsage* were too much for her.

Admiral Semmes struck colors, and the *Alabama* was fired into five times more at four hundred yards. No boats were put out for her crew until the ship went down, but Semmes and a number of drowning men were rescued by the British yacht *Deerhound*.

Another saga ended abroad, and at home even red-faced Mallory showed temper under the successive disasters. Pessimistic Hunter came out of the war office looking as red as Mallory, and the clerk suspected him of sampling a bottle of good bourbon in the disburser's desk.

Below the river Grant tried striking farther south at the railroads. He was beaten again in the grim monotony with which he whittled away at Lee's forces.

But Mallory's friends went on exchanging new stories and laughed as if nothing were wrong at all. Even Benjamin went off with the Navy Secretary on some little outing of their own down the river, for which they borrowed an army ambulance. For the crowds packing the new Richmond Theater, a newspaper notice announced:

The manager, ever ready to contribute to the comfort of the patrons of this establishment, has procured a magnificent silver water cooler from which

ICE WATER

Will nightly be dispensed to the patrons of the Dress Circle free of charge.

How could people play and laugh now?

Peace movement in the North, not only among Democrats and disloyalists, was very active. Horace Greeley was corresponding with

Benjamin's Confederate agents in Canada and trying to obtain Lincoln's permission to publish the correspondence.

Lincoln gave permission, without any authority, for a Methodist minister and lecturer to come to Richmond for an interview with Benjamin. Nothing came of that, but the visitors felt the South should be willing to negotiate, with Grant at Richmond and Sherman before Atlanta.

But somebody had been at Richmond during the whole life of the Confederacy. If they drove Sherman away from Atlanta, the North would be convinced there was no reason for the South to negotiate. Then peace movers would recognize that the Union must admit that the seceded states had won their right to independence.

But if Atlanta fell—— Then from Atlanta came Bragg's wire, "I find but little to encourage." It seemed that Johnston would abandon Atlanta, but, "I cannot learn that he has any more plans in the future than he had in the past."

It was Richmond all over again. Angrily Jefferson Davis sent Johnston a wire asking specifically *what was his plan.*

Johnston refused him a direct answer. That was the end.

Atlanta must not be sacrificed as Vicksburg had been. Somebody was going there who would fight Sherman and who would keep the war office informed. But who?

Thirty-three-year-old Hood, the fierce fighter and respectful admirer —he believed in offense and he would work with the President. Yet he was young and untried in major command.

Seddon, racked with neuralgia, worrying about his office, could be of no help. But Lee—Hood had fought under him. Davis wrote the Old Man.

Lee, the gentleman, the kind and generous, answered as a man and not as a Rebel. Saying nothing outright against the ambitious and loyal Hood, his tactful pussyfooting clearly implied that he thought the choice unwise. Hood was devoted and brave, but Lee was "doubtful of other qualifications . . ."—"a bad time to change . . ."—"why not Hardee? . . ." But even Lee felt Atlanta should not be given up. . . .

Finally, as always, Davis must decide. The steps paced in the upper floor as on the night of his child's death. In the bedroom where he paced then, his wife lay with her newborn baby. Upstairs young Jeff and Maggie were asleep, and handsome young Burton Harrison waited for any call. The cabinet room, long and narrow, with a window on the south for any vagrant breeze in that hazy heat, held the ghosts of the cabinet members who had met to make other decisions.

O Lord, help me, I pray. . . .

Could it be that he was being influenced by his dislike of Joe Johnston? Of that Georgia pack led by Governor Brown? Other Georgians, Ben Hill and Howell Cobb, loathing Brown, still had suggested the employment of Forrest. But Bragg, on the scene, believed it should be Johnston.

Davis went into the bedroom, where his wife suffered through the motionless heat. He tried to tell her his problem, and then he cried, "If I could take one wing and Lee the other, I think between us we could wrest a victory from these people."

2

The next morning he decided to stake the decision on Bragg. Though Bragg too had been a victim of spite and jealousy, he had the cause at heart and he was outspoken. From him Davis could get a yes or a no— and he was on the scene. Davis wired his adviser and asked point-blank if, after all, he thought Johnston should remain in command.

Bragg justified his faith. Without equivocation he wired back, "I am decidedly opposed, as it would perpetuate the past and present policy which he has advised and now sustains."

Davis called a cabinet meeting and, with its approval, sent through Adjutant General Cooper the telegram relieving Joe Johnston of his command. The charge was of having "failed to arrest the advance of the enemy to the vicinity of Atlanta."

The guns crackled down on James River. The unrelieved heat smothered the city. Davis was weak with the decision behind him.

At home his wife was downstairs again, her hair turning gray. In the corner parlor, where she could catch any faint breeze that stirred, she stood in front of the huge gilt-bordered mirror over the fireplace and saw the heaviness, the droop in her full figure. In her late thirties, Varina did look middle-aged, as the country editor had said. Each year must have been like five to her.

She suffered with her husband the violent newspaper reaction to Johnston's removal. But then Joe Johnston put the President back on sure ground. In the general's testy telegram of acceptance he included an ungenerous and gratuitous comparison with Lee's army:

"I assert that Sherman's army is much stronger, compared with that of Tennessee, than Grant's compared with that of Northern Virginia.

Yet the enemy has been compelled to advance much more slowly to the vicinity of Atlanta than to that of Richmond and Petersburg, and penetrated much deeper into Virginia than into Georgia. . . ."

When Davis read that, its perversion of facts must have hardened him in the fateful decision he had made. In Virginia and in Georgia each Confederate commander had retreated to the city which he must defend, and in Georgia the retreat had actually been farther in mileage. In Virginia, Lee had contended with two armies coming from different directions, completely supplied by water, over which he had no control. Johnston had only one army to contend with, and that supported by one long thin railroad.

At Richmond and Petersburg—two separate places—Grant's and Butler's armies were through for the season. Their fighting had been taken out of them. No large-scale attack was possible. When Sherman reached Atlanta he was coming on, up to the point of the big attack. That Johnston would twist these facts and derogate Lee for his own defense certainly buttressed Davis's reasons for distrusting and disliking him.

Atlanta, supporting the other end of the line from Richmond in what remained of the Confederacy, was as vital politically—to both sections—as it was physically. If the two cities held, the whole East would prove as impregnable as Virginia, and McClellan's candidacy for President on a Democratic peace platform would have a real chance.

What Joe Johnston missed was that Lee, at his end, had taken the fight out of his enemy and to some extent out of the enemy country. Because Johnston had not accomplished the same, his enemy was the hope of the North. Johnston's enemy must be defeated, at least approximately as Lee's had been. At worst, Atlanta could not fall.

But Atlanta became merely the bone of contention between the two honorable gentlemen—one born, one made. Refusing to give an inch to the other, Davis and Johnston collaborated and gave the state of Georgia to Sherman.

Hood's offensive was an anti-climax to the personal battle between the general and the President. Hood fought impetuously as always and not badly. His co-ordination was faulty; Sherman was sharp and overwhelmingly superior numerically. Their losses were equal, but five from one hundred thousand is much less than five from forty thousand, when the men were already edgy from facing heavier numbers for three months.

In the office on the second floor of the Treasury Building, Davis

[362]

read reports of Sherman's "retreating"—right into Atlanta. Hood had fought, as he promised, leaving his intrenchments to do so, and Atlanta had fallen—as Governor Brown had prophesied.

When the battle of personalities was over, the supporting end of the line from Richmond was gone.

Hood, out in the open, would threaten Sherman's communications to force a retreat, but that was to be ineffectual.

With the fall of Atlanta—as a city and as the doorway to the sea— the will to war cut like a two-edged sword. In the South the people as a whole began to lose heart, while in the North the spirits revived to support the final conquest of individuals—chiefly that group clustered around Lee.

Though General Lee symbolized those men of individuality, and not the feudal South typified by Davis, they were equally archaic. Against them Grant was the man of the machine, of the new age waiting impatiently to cover the land with uniformity.

CHAPTER THIRTY-TWO

"Eat, Drink, and Be Merry . . ."

WHEN the individuals, in the Army and in the population, entered the last phase, the leaders no longer represented a people. Where, the year before, war fatigue and loss of faith in the Administration and loss of interest in the reasons for fighting had started an undermining of the movement and a peripheral falling away, by the end of the summer of 1864 a more general hopelessness started the collapse of the Confederacy as a nation. The leaders were a group of desperate men, holding out because they knew nothing else to do, like fugitives living from day to day as their hour ran out.

In Richmond the little cabinet group welcomed a new member for the last-ditch stand—George Trenholm. Succeeding flustered little Memminger in the Treasury Department, Trenholm was the big-time, American-style businessman, and one of the richest men in the East.

A Charlestonian, he had left school at an early age, started at sixteen to work for John Frazer & Company and, in Alger fashion, gone on to own the big shipping company. Besides steamships and wharves, he owned hotels and cotton presses, plantations and slaves, was director of a bank and of railroads. Devoting all his resources to the Confederacy, he operated fifty blockade runners, brought in the first forty thousand Enfield rifles, regularly coal and iron, arms and ammunition, and salt. He shipped out cotton, tobacco, and turpentine.

With all his financial accomplishments, George Trenholm, in his late fifties when he brought his family to Richmond, was a cultured and charming gentleman of distinguished appearance and an easy ability to handle people. Davis hoped to use his affability in expediting Memminger's basic principles through Congress. Though the new Secretary did get along fine with the members, who, as Lee said, were busy "eating peanuts and chewing tobacco," Trenholm enjoyed no more success than had Memminger in passing his measures.

Trenholm perceived at once that the partial repudiation of currency

[364]

had aroused distrust in the people and "apprehension of ultimate repudiation crept like an all-pervading poison into the minds of the people." To restore faith he advocated a discontinuance of the tax on old notes; a drastic raise in taxes for the purposes of revenue and for redeeming the outstanding notes—both to decrease the amount of currency and stabilize its value.

Congress debated long, on both sides of the great marble hall where the life-size statue of Washington loomed above them, and the two houses came up with a plan of their own. They issued $80,000,000 in new notes to pay the arrears to the Army.

After that, Trenholm did not even bother to have stationery printed. He just scratched out Memminger's name and wrote in his own. The dollar was at 23 to 1 by the end of summer and, reflecting the fall of hope in general and of faith in the Confederate bill, was dropping fast. The newspapers stated that the money began its serious dip when the harlots from New York and Baltimore applied for their passports home.

If Trenholm could do nothing for the plummeting currency, he did much for the palates of the gourmets. The madeira he brought by the cask rivaled Mallory's mint juleps in popularity, and his fifty blockade runners did not neglect luxuries for the Trenholm table. Mrs. Trenholm's Saturday-night suppers became the big event of the week. With Mallory and Benjamin and Trenholm, all amusing men, the conversation suggested anything except their country collapsing around them and an armed enemy closing in on the city where they laughed through the mellow Indian-summer evenings.

Mallory's navy was drifting back toward the size of the early days. As the country shrank, few places remained for the building of any of his ingenuities. In Mobile Bay the last of the ironclads, the *New Tennessee*, lumbered out to certain death by a desperate attack on Farragut's fleet.

Even the raiders went as fast as new ones were commissioned. The *Shenandoah*, purchased by Bulloch to replace the *Alabama*, sailed for the Pacific, knocking off prizes on the way. The *Tallahassee* was commissioned, operating for a while under John Taylor Wood, but then the *Florida* followed the *Alabama* to the bottom.

This ship had left England before the *Alabama*, but, because of yellow fever, it had to run the blockade to get into Mobile, badly battered. Starting out from there in January 1863, the *Florida* ran down thirty-seven ships by October '64. Then, resting at anchor in Bahia, Brazil, with the captain and half the crew in town and the guns unloaded, she was rammed at night by the U.S.S. *Wachusett*, which opened fire at pistol range. Some of the crew jumped overboard, the rest surrendered, and the ship was brought into Hampton Roads.

Brazil petitioned for the return of the ship and the prisoners, in violation of neutrality. The United States, coming up toughly in those days and not then fat, allowed the ship first to suffer an "accidental collision" and then in a secluded spot allowed her accidentally to sink.

Since the first United States policy on Confederate privateers, sea raiders had always been regarded in a different light from the land raiders of the Union armies. Prisoners from such ships and from the little launching ships of torpedoes were frequently treated as felons, and the prisoners from the *Florida* were among those who received brutal treatment.

But Mallory still had his social obligations to return, and he invited Trenholm and Seddon to his house for "pea soup." Clerk Jones, seeing the invitation, commented that "his 'pea soup' will be oysters and champagne. . . . They may feast possibly while the very pillars of the government are crumbling under the blows of the enemy."

Seddon's socializing, however, usually took place in his office, where Hunter and other friends gathered in lugubrious conversation. Indeed plump Hunter had cause for gloom. The Yankees had recently destroyed his plantation, and if the Confederacy failed he would have no slaves with which to rebuild it. Worse, there would be no country for him to be President of. Political life would be over and his accumulations of a lifetime wiped out.

In those whispered conversations in Seddon's private office the men must have talked of peace. With the end inevitable it was natural they should have considered what terms they could get.

Hunter's Virginia friend Mason, in London, had just inadvertently produced the acme of futility. He had busied himself shopping about London for the artist worthy to make the great seal of the Confederacy. In July he announced that he was ready to send a solid-silver seal with an ivory handle, in a box with a spring lock. It was to be accompanied by a press to make the raised impressions, with 1,000 seal papers, 1,000 strips of parchment, wafers, 100 brass boxes and 100 silver cords. This was paid for in gold.

In the fall everything arrived—except the press. This never got out of Bermuda, where it may still be. Thus the seal remained a beautiful ornament that, alas, was of no use.

Henry Hotze, with a pleasure in the game for its own sake, continued circulating accurate news colored favorably to the Confederacy. In '64 he published records from agents to show that five hundred ships had gotten through the blockade in the past fifteen months, and listed sixteen ships that had run the blockade more than ten times. Now that it no longer mattered, he even handled the news for France too.

The Davis pet, DeLeon, whom Hunter had sent to France with $25,000 a year expenses, had spent the money bribing the venal French press. When he discovered that he had been duped, he wrote Davis berating the French as mercenary and criticized old Slidell. When the dispatch was captured and appeared in the New York *Tribune,* Benjamin fired DeLeon.

Hotze, perceiving that the French journalists were without conviction, gave his military news to Havas, telegraph and correspondence agency. Through it he represented his country well at little cost—but his efforts were only of academic interest by then.

The valuable accomplishments of Hotze and the agents were in the field of purchases and shipping. Some while after McRae took charge of credit abroad and co-ordinated purchasing, the Confederacy got around to a central authority for buying cotton, shipping it, and establishing the credit used by McRae. With Thomas Bayne entering the field late but working well with the purchasers abroad, the agents realized the potentialities that had always existed in the South for obtaining supplies without being gouged by speculators and involved in Erlanger deals.

Once the political failure of cotton was admitted, the government discouraged its growth and urged planters to turn their crops into foodstuffs. Of course individuals such as Bob Toombs, the rebel against the Rebels, refused to comply and defied the tyrants who would interfere with a man's freedom of initiative. On the whole very little cotton was grown—though not always because the government urged the measure. With the coming of autumn the individuals within the geographic boundaries of the Confederacy acted pretty much according to their natures.

In Richmond even John Reagan, since the death of his wife, developed a bent toward socializing in a rough-and-ready fashion with other men.

Colonel Lubbock, former governor of Texas and now on Davis's staff, lived with the Postmaster, and Reagan showed pretty strong feeling about drawing the full beef ration from the government for his guest. Serving plain food, he depended on quantity, and urbane Benjamin was enticed there by the good fellowship.

The night Benjamin came Reagan was serving ham among other dishes. At the last moment the host hesitated, fearing to offend Benjamin's religious customs. The plump little cosmopolite instantly exclaimed how glad he was to see some ham, as a thief had stolen his from the smokehouse.

From ham and eggs to oysters and champagne, Benjamin went the rounds, while the desperate stratagems he had set in motion in the spring came to their wild fruition in the fall.

2

To Canada, Benjamin had sent Jacob Thompson (former Secretary of the Interior, under Buchanan) and Clement Clay, the Alabama senator whose wife had been the famous hostess of the two capitals. Their purpose was to make contact with the disaffected elements in Indiana, Illinois, and Ohio and promote political meetings with the purpose of affecting the Republicans in the fall election.

In July, Jacob Thompson had written Benjamin that the disaffected elements could be useful only for war purposes, as a peace party would have no chance without Confederate victories—specifically, Lee holding Richmond and Johnston defeating Sherman. To use the disloyal Sons of Liberty as Thompson suggested, Benjamin placed a scheme for freeing Confederate prisoners under Captain Thomas Hines—one of Morgan's raiders who had escaped from the penitentiary with Morgan.

Captain Hines went from Richmond, crossing the lines in the West, and organized sixty other Confederate fugitives. In late August, for the Democratic Convention, they filtered into Chicago. There, with the help of the Sons of Liberty, during the confusion of the politicking, the Rebels were to spring five thousand prisoners from Camp Douglas and seven thousand from Springfield.

When the day came, hope was gone for Atlanta; the usual betrayal in such movements (on both sides) alerted the garrison; the Sons of Liberty grew timid at action, and the Confederates wandered aimlessly about, looking at the sights.

As the Rebels were there and eager for action, they decided to make another attempt without depending on Yankees. The leaders of this expedition were Captain Cole, formerly with Forrest, and young John Beall, one of those free-enterprisers who had captured supplies from Yankee boats in Chesapeake Bay. Captured himself, he was put in irons as a pirate, and only prompt Confederate retaliation had caused him to be exchanged in May.

The scheme of Cole and Beall was to free the prisoners on Johnson's

Island, where many generals were held. For this they were to capture the gunboat *Michigan,* patrolling that part of Lake Erie, and use her fourteen guns on the prison garrison. Following the familiar pattern, Cole was betrayed and captured on the *Michigan.* Beall's party successfully captured the steamer *Philo Parsons,* from Detroit, but when no signal came from the *Michigan,* Beall's men mutinied, robbed the ship, and then ran her into Canada and burned her.

Thwarted in all their efforts with any purpose at all, the restless Rebels decided on a foray for action's sake. Led by Lieutenant Young, from Kentucky, twenty Confederates attempted to visit on New England some of Sherman's and Sheridan's measures.

Raiding down into St. Albans, Vermont, they herded the citizens in a public square and robbed the bank. The citizens started to attack the soldiers. The Rebels fired, set fire to a number of houses, and escaped on stolen horses. Some were captured, including Young, who was beaten with sticks and swords. He was rescued by the British and confined in Canada with other prisoners, where a long trial for extradition went on. . . .

With everything failing, Benjamin instigated a final fantastic adventure out of the realm of derring-do, and probably motivated at least in part by a personal urge to retaliation. He sent cavalry Lieutenant John Headley directly from Richmond, up through the Western route. From Canada, with Lieutenant Colonel Robert Martin and seven others, Headley came down to New York City, where a peace movement was definitely strong. It was reported that twenty thousand were ready for an uprising as election approached.

The Confederates made contact with leaders of the disloyalists and very cautiously used their homes and stores as meeting places. While waiting for events to develop, the young men had a pleasant visit in the great Northern city.

Headley and Martin stopped at the St. Denis Hotel (Broadway and Eleventh), the Fifth Avenue, and the Hoffman; visited theaters and "places of interest"; heard a lecture of Artemus Ward, a sermon by Henry Ward Beecher, and attended meetings of Tammany Hall. They saw torchlight parades for McClellan, with caricatures of and hisses for Lincoln, and listened to speeches against the war. Their conduct was so innocent that detectives, set to watch them by the inevitable betrayer, were convinced the lead was a fake.

In early November, just before election, General Butler arrived with ten thousand troops. In his element among civilians, the Beast issued a proclamation on his proposal to deal with disorder, and the New York

Times approved his choice as the hero who "scattered the howling rabble of New Orleans like chaff."

As usual, the disloyalists quit before action, and the leaders tried to dissuade the Rebels from going through with their plot of burning the business section of the city. But these young men had read in the New York papers approving stories of Sherman's burning of Atlanta, had heard jubilant speeches on the street over the destruction, and they determined on action this time, traitor or no traitor.

Each took a room in several hotels. They entered with an ordinary small valise, containing a Greek fire manufactured for them by New York chemists. Around eight o'clock in the evening each was to set a fire in his own room of each hotel he was in—nineteen hotels all together. Most of the fires did not take a good hold because, the men suspected, the New York chemist had given them inferior Greek fire and the Fire Department was very alert.

The one good blaze they got was in Barnum's Museum, where Captain Kennedy, waiting after he had fired his hotels, saw a good opportunity and threw a bottle of Greek fire apparently just for luck. The whole city was aroused, and the young men, mingling with the crowds, heard that they were going to be strung up on lampposts. They also read in the next morning's paper that their presence was known and detectives were hunting them down.

This was borne out when they discovered the arrest of Mr. McDonald in his store, one of their meeting places, just as they were going there. A later newspaper mentioned how they had been trailed and abandoned on information given by an informer, and all their movements were revealed. That night they left town on a sleeper and safely reached Toronto.

Completing their international adventure, the Confederates furnished money and testimony to clear Henry McDonald and traced down their betrayer—Godfrey Hyams, of Arkansas. He fled Toronto, where the Rebels rendezvoused. With this, Thompson wrote Benjamin that they had failed.

Jacob Thompson stayed on, supporting the defense of the various Confederates who had been captured and were standing trial. Young Beall was sentenced to be hanged as a spy, over the protests of many prominent Northerners. At Governor's Island his words did not pass into legend. He said, "I protest against the execution of this sentence. It is murder. There is nothing more to say—except I die in the service and defense of my country."

Though none of their projects had been in themselves successful and the little damage and the alarums they caused had no more than a nuisance value, Grant said that the threat of releasing Confederate prisoners and of the Copperheads caused many U.S. troops to be detached for that duty, like Butler's ten thousand.

With such petty maneuvers Benjamin used the agile brain that two years before had worked on recognition from England and France. But they kept him cheerful. Strolling up Main Street in the hazy twilight, he puffed his mild Havana and twirled his gold-headed cane like any carefree dandy. To assure his comforts, he leased his pleasant redbrick house for another year.

CHAPTER THIRTY-THREE

"... For Tomorrow You Die"

THE leader of the little band, the President, lacked wild stratagems or the escape of elegant socializing. His home was made very cheerful by the young people whose company he liked. The Trenholm girls ran in and out, and "Little" Morgan, a young blockade runner, courted one of them in the Davis parlor. But Little Morgan felt the President was very lonely after one day when he interrupted the lovers and talked to them at great length, describing the merits of a particular kind of bridle bit.

Jefferson Davis was lonely in the deepest sense: he lived in a world whose realities were different from his own. His concepts, to which he clung, belonged in a lost land of romance where, even four years before, imagination had triumphed over reality. Now that the myth had lost its puissance and the pattern of the physical life was shattered forever, Davis still conceived of the Confederacy as the South had been in his imagination.

When Atlanta fell, following his own fateful decision on Joe Johnston, Davis turned to a wishful thinking that produced no more than fantasies, daydreams in which his choice would be vindicated and the South of his imagination would rise and vanquish all its enemies.

In Georgia, Sherman, a man loyal to his government, understood Governor Brown and Vice-President Stephens to be disloyal to theirs, and made overtures for a separate peace. Demagogue Brown was by no means disloyal according to his lights; he just wanted votes in Georgia. He would have nothing to do with Sherman's offer of a soft treatment of Georgia civilians. But Stephens was a different proposition. Bob Toombs, instinctually loyal to his region with all his rebelling against constituted authority, went to work on him.

In Richmond, Davis could understand that kind of danger. On a Monday in late September he left for Macon. His hurried trip was unscheduled, and, finding no arrangements for him, he appeared at a rally for the aid of Atlanta refugees.

In that speech he revealed he was living in his own private retreat, cut off from the world of the Confederacy. He exhorted the men absent from the army to fill the ranks and, as a reward to the disheartened crackers, promised that "the limping soldier" would be "our aristocracy." He compared Atlanta (in the Deep South) to Moscow and predicted for Sherman's Northerners a Napoleonic retreat across the South's Russia. To indicate his assurance of the "destruction" awaiting Sherman, he shouted to the crowd the battle plans of Hood—to attack Sherman's communications.

Then he reviewed the dispirited army, and they shouted, "Give us General Johnston."

Though Hood offered to resign, Davis was less able to admit this mistake than he was his mistake of the autumn before, with Bragg. Besides, now he nurtured plans to prove that the change to Hood was not a mistake.

In the Alabama-Mississippi Department, Stephen D. Lee had been replaced by Dick Taylor, the highly accomplished gentleman and natural soldier who was Davis's brother-in-law by his first wife. As soon as Taylor took over, he ordered Forrest on the middle-Tennessee raid to cut Sherman's communications. Taylor said defending his territory was of only "local interest," while the Georgia campaign was of general importance.

Now that Sherman was occupying Atlanta, Davis grasped at the policy he had previously rejected when it could have helped. To insure its success he sent Hood's whole army on the same objective for which a few months before he had refused even Forrest's cavalry.

Forrest raided as always, and Hood used a whole army to capture some supply depots. This wreckage to Sherman's communications would have been critical when he was back in the mountain country in the spring. Now having been provided with full knowledge of the Confederate plans by Davis's speech, with the flats opening ahead and no army in front of him, Sherman decided he could subsist off the civil population. The Confederate policy to grow food instead of cotton was, despite Toombs, just providing a fattish countryside.

First burning the city of Atlanta, for practice, Sherman started his famous plundering expedition and, as Lincoln said of the Mississippi, moved unvexed to the sea. There was no one to oppose him.

Back in Richmond, indifferent to the cause and effect of military on politics, and vice versa, Davis was unmoved by the overwhelming majority that swept Lincoln back into office. That was the United States' affair.

[373]

For his country there were military appointments to make. Bragg, the military adviser, was sent down to Wilmington to try to aid in its defense, then to Georgia to supervise conscription, and then back to Wilmington.

Beauregard, with no place in Lee's army, was given a paper department even greater than the old Department of the West and unconnected with any function except fitting into the President's tables of organization.

With Joe Johnston idling around Richmond, being admired by old friends, and Pemberton serving with the local defense east of Richmond, two of the first Heroes (Beauregard and Johnston) and the whole Department of the West a little more than a year before (Johnston and Pemberton and Bragg) were without armies.

Down in Georgia solid, long-suffering Hardee, who had been passed over when Hood went in, gathered such of Georgia's militia and oddments as he could to offer an illusion of something in front of Sherman. Hood, after Sherman ignored him on the Union communications, prepared to strike into Tennessee in a farfetched counterinvasion of Sherman's Georgia drive.

Outside Richmond, Lee's army was suffering for experienced generals. Old Bald Dick Ewell had been forced to give up active command and took charge of Richmond defenses, providing much entertainment by his eccentricities. Longstreet had not recovered from his Wilderness wound, and Powell Hill was slipping from illnesses that came partly from the mental strain. The division and brigade commanders were being killed off as soon as they showed promise.

But—in the cozy little study where the fire burned in the white marble fireplace—when Lee visited to talk over affairs of the army, Davis captured the illusion of his world still steady.

2

With an intimate like General Lee, Davis could lie on the black horsehair sofa, easing his aches, smoking a cigar, and even the closing in on the citadel provided discussions on solid, familiar ground.

The threat from Early's ten thousand, which had drawn off Sheridan and infantry, was ending with the collapse of Early's little command. Backing up the Valley, away from Sheridan's superior forces, Old Jube's starving veterans suddenly turned (at Cedar Creek), ripped the Yankee lines apart, and reached their bulging wagons. Then, like a ravening animal on its kill, they forgot everything except gorging themselves.

Sheridan inspired a poem on his ride from Winchester, forty miles away, though (in a rare burst of generosity, according to one of his officers) he admitted the fight would have gone the same way if he had been there and ended the same if he had never come. The Yankees reformed during the Rebels' confusion and pressed back. They captured prisoners in droves—men with their mouths and hands full of food, men dormant and sick from stuffing. Some Confederates, missed in the melee, found the liquor, and one of those reported waking up three days later in West Virginia.

The Rebels who fell back had little organization. Guns were abandoned. Officers failed to rally men. The will to fight had momentarily ceased. Later the remnants collected farther south in the Valley, but Sheridan was free to spread such waste that Lee's army would never again be fed from there. Then Sheridan could send back forces to build up the odds around Richmond.

Things were bad enough with him away. Grant was operating on a simple method of wearing out the army he could not beat, striving to weaken Lee sufficiently at some point so he could make a push through.

Holding superior forces at the center of his line in front of Petersburg, Grant sent attacks in force to his left (to the railroad south of Petersburg) and to his right (directly at Richmond from north of the James River). Lee would race his tired men to stop a thrust in front of Richmond, and then back they would hurry south of Petersburg to check another thrust by another fresh force.

They could not keep open the Weldon Railroad to the south, but the South Side Railroad was safe. In front of Richmond one surprise attack captured Fort Harrison, a key section in the line of fortifications. Before this could be exploited, the still ferocious remnants of the famed Texas Brigade hurried to the rescue of the clerks and old men holding the breach.

Nothing worked, but each smallest skirmish whittled away at Lee's forces, and in the President's informal little study General Lee proposed plan after plan to build up man power. He wanted stricter measures against deserters, a roundup of conscript evaders and exempts, and to arm Negroes while promising them freedom.

Not even Lee could shake Davis from his rights in pardoning deserters, and, for the rest, the governors were fighting their last-ditch stand on states' rights as the Administration fought for the life of the experiment.

The Alabama governor threatened civil war if conscription officers did not let his state troops alone, and Mississippi's governor said he would protect his state officers with force if necessary. In Virginia the new governor, Extra Billy Smith, less pugnaciously exempted favorites by appointing them to the state administration. Sometimes he exempted as many as fifty a day.

Congress convened and finally brought into the open the ticklish subject of arming slaves, but all the states were opposed even to furnishing slaves to work on fortifications. North Carolina's Vance objected when, with coastal railroads in danger, it was vital to protect the interior lines supplying Lee's army. The point of the politicians was that slaves sometimes escaped or were hurt from exposure, and payment by the government was slow. The fact that defeat would remove all the slaves permanently seemed preferable to helping the government whose armies were maintaining the institution for them.

In all phases the governors became more opposed to any nationalism at all, and, as the danger increased, political unity decreased. On food impressment, which Seddon tried hard to enforce, the legislatures offered no suggestions, but constantly passed resolutions which encouraged opposition and erected all manner of obstacles. The farmers had valid reason to object to impressment of their produce, as the government was months behind in pay and frequently the soldiers on impressment details acted harshly in appropriating foodstuffs. But all recalcitrants were supported by the governors, who were determined to go down fighting—not the Yankees, but Davis.

Where the two gentlemen talked in the fall afternoons, these matters were less pressing to Davis than the movement of Lee's troops back and forth. Grant had tried another one-two punch—attacking with one force south of Petersburg and sending Butler straight at Richmond from the east.

There was such clear purpose in the drive to Richmond, while Grant pinned the main army down around Petersburg, that Lee shifted north of the river. With the help of the battalions from the ordnance works and the Tredegar, the attack was driven back—but the workers began to desert when they had to fight. Also the basic matériel of war stopped flowing with the workmen in the lines.

Lee seemed unable to impress Davis with the point that failure to maintain production of the Richmond arsenal nullified the military reason for holding the city. The Tredegar, in producing over twelve hundred field guns and over three hundred heavy guns (some of which were refitted captures), was still the mainstay for the armies in the field, though the works at Selma were extremely important for heavy guns. Also Tredegar was a self-sustaining unit which delivered its matériel with no drain on the government.

When food became scarce in Richmond, Tredegar sent missions into unfought-over sections and built up stores of corn, rice, and bacon; when the Confederate money began to lose value for purchases, the missions bartered with nails and spikes. When cloth became unobtainable, the Tredegar refitted a government blockade runner, shipped out cotton, and, while bringing in the required half of cargo in arms, brought in cloth for its people. When leather shoes vanished from the market, Tredegar started its own tannery.

The government-made shoes, according to a wearer, "were approved by all except those who wore them. The soldiers exchanged them with the first prostrate enemy who" no longer needed shoes.

In small arms, ammunition, and equipment, Gorgas accomplished comparatively as much as Tredegar and showed an inventiveness of his own. For gun carriages Lee's men cut timber to be used in the spring while charcoal, gathered from the south side of the river, ran forges for the iron. The armory constantly experimented in efforts to make cartridges for the captured Spencer repeaters and tried howitzers, with a jointed trail, to be fired at a high angle as a substitute for mortars.

For making caps they invented a machine requiring only two men helped by six girls or boys, and when their copper grew scarce they sent missions for the coils from turpentine and applejack stills. For the fulminate of mercury in caps they finally achieved the manufacture of sulphuric acid in North Carolina. For niter the earth from caves was worked around Richmond, and dead horses and animals were used. From the sulphuric acid and niter, nitric acid was made on the banks of the James River. When the bureau ran out of the mercury which had been brought in early from Mexico, they used chloride of potash and sulphuret of antimony from around Richmond.

The major portion of rifles had formerly come in through the blockade and from the harvest of battlefields. At the peak of the armies' strength in 1863, their 300,000 rifles came from these sources: 25,000 originally on hand; 40,000 manufactured; 185,000 through the blockade; 150,000 from the enemy, reworked in the armory, against 100,000 lost on the fields. By late 1864 only 30,000 more had been imported, 20,000 manufactured (less than one half the anticipated figure because of the absence of workmen), and the amount obtained from the enemy was only 15,000 more than those lost.

[377]

In addition to his rifles, artillery ammunition, and every form of equipment, Gorgas, starting with an abandoned armory, the buildings of tobacco factories, and equipment from little iron manufacturers, had turned out over seventy million cartridges and twice that many caps.

In October he had said that this ammunition production would decline, as rifle production already had, if he did not get back the men lost to the army; and if additional men were lost, little more could be hoped for from his ordnance plant. Materials were then so short that on lead he barely kept abreast of current expenditures by scouring the battlefields.

Lee had previously ordered Gorgas's workmen and the Tredegar Battalion out of the lines. To the War Department he made it plain that sufficient man power must be supplied his army from other sources so that production could be maintained, or Richmond would have to be abandoned. In the latter event some equipment and workmen could be shipped to plants that Gorgas had scattered through the South, and the other men could be put in the army for its bid through open maneuver.

In either case General Lee preferred a chance for strategical warfare to supplant the foredoomed assignment of protecting a lengthening line of over thirty miles, with railroads and two key cities.

But to Davis the win-or-lose gamble on a maneuvering campaign held no appeal. Though the army around Richmond and the people in it were being slowly choked to death, the capital had become the rock on which he stood.

Armies had become like toy soldiers which he moved on maps, with no awareness of the individual lives composing those armies or the populations of the areas over which the symbols moved.

Lee, for his part, always limiting his attention to his own army, retained the habits of a lifetime in the Regular Army and did not presume to act outside his prescribed sphere in relation to the constituted authority. With Bragg away, Lee held informally, in addition to his command, his old position of military adviser; but he only advised —and that advice was offered with more tact than fire in the respectful atmosphere of the established relationship.

When Lee visited the President during the rainy season of late fall, he apologized for stepping on the white rug with his muddy boots; and when Mrs. Davis entered to speak to him, he admired her silver saucepan on the hearth. Observing the fatigue on the friend whom she so deeply admired, Varina heated some *café au lait* and gave him some in a Sèvres cup. The general said, "My cups in camp are thicker, but this is thinner than the coffee."

Lee's reassuring presence did not lift Mrs. Davis's depression as it did her husband's. She looked at the two men, so aged by the past four years, gratefully sipping the hot coffee in this moment of respite, and she knew the city was doomed to fall.

But she, no more than General Lee or Benjamin, intruded in the President's private world.

3

Grant's hammering tactics took a heavy toll of his own people in ways other than battle casualties. Among the victims were the prisoners in the Confederacy. In the summer of 1864 Grant officially ended the exchange of prisoners, though in effect exchange had virtually ceased before this. With the actual end of exchange the static prison population in the South entered the phase of acute suffering.

Prisoners shifted to the South, especially Andersonville, Georgia, were kept in open stockades with inadequate shelter, sanitation, and food and suffered for lack of medicines which, being contraband, the South never obtained in sufficient quantities. Many prisoners wasted away, many grew ill, and many died. The North grew outraged at the pitiable plight of these men, and the prison officials were accused of villainy. When Sherman saw the holes in the ground dug by Union prisoners for shelter, he added the theme of vengeance officially to his long-established policy of despoliation: "Let it be more devilish than can be dreamed of."

Later Northern investigation established the lack of willful intent in the majority of the prison officials and guards, and admitted that the men had striven for humane conditions with the inadequate resources at their command. These investigators understood that their blockade and armies had contributed no small part to these inadequate resources. In early autumn in the Valley of Virginia, Sheridan reported to Grant:

In moving back to this point, the whole country from the Blue Ridge to the North Mountains has been made untenable for a rebel army. I have destroyed over 2,000 barns filled with wheat, hay and farming implements; over seventy mills filled with flour and wheat; have driven in front of the army over 4,000 head of stock, and have killed and issued to the troops not less than 3,000 sheep. A large number of horses have been obtained, a proper estimate of which I cannot now make. Lieutenant John R. Meigs, my engineer officer, was murdered beyond Harrisonburg, near Dayton. For this atrocious act all the houses within an area of five miles were burned.

That Sheridan was able to accomplish this unhampered was at least partly attributable to the starved condition of the Confederate soldiers, who had lost at Cedar Creek when they glimpsed the food in his wagons. For Mosby's Rangers, trying to harass his expedition, Sheridan reported, "Mosby has annoyed me and captured a few wagons. We hung one and shot six of his men yesterday."

From the deeper South, where he was avowedly bent on ruin, Sherman reported that he had carried away more than ten thousand horses and mules as well as a countless number of slaves. Beyond that, "I estimate the damages done to the state of Georgia and its military resources at $100,000,000, at least $20,000,000 of which has inured to our advantage, and the remainder is simple waste and destruction."

However, that the Union prisoners were forced to share the privations brought upon the Southern people was never a wish of the Confederacy. Grant's willingness to let the Northern soldiers suffer rather than release Confederates in exchange for Unions was a vital part of his policy of using supremacy of numbers to crush out resistance.

As the Confederates released from prisons usually returned to their armies, they reduced the odds against the South. Fifty thousand men against one hundred thousand made a closer contest than twenty-five thousand against seventy-five thousand. Grant said, "At this particular time to release all Rebel prisoners in the North would insure Sherman's defeat, and would compromise our safety here."

So that Sherman would be safe to devastate the South, the Northern prisoners would have to starve with the other occupants of the land.

Beast Butler, down on the Peninsula, wished to continue the exchange and was anxious to exculpate himself from any guilt over Northern suffering. His heart bleeding for the prisoners and their loved ones, he said:

Those lives were spent as part of the system of attack upon the rebellion, devised by the wisdom of the general-in-chief of the armies, to destroy it by depletion, depending upon our superior numbers to win the victory at last. The loyal mourners will doubtless derive solace from this fact, and appreciate all the more highly the genius which conceived the plan, and the success won at so great a cost.

What the South was losing at even greater cost from the same treatment was of no consequence. In Northern prisons Confederate soldiers died in the same numbers and at the same percentage.

In a bountiful unoccupied land they were placed in prison camps where in the damp cold and with insufficient clothing they froze to death and contracted every form of respiratory disease. Camp Douglas, near Chicago, had the country's highest mortality rate over any given period—10 per cent in one month. At Elmira, New York, by the statement of Northern officials, prisoners suffered acute want through inefficiency, venality, and divided authority.

Also, as the Union armies so destroyed crops that it was impossible for anybody in the South, including prisoners, to be properly fed, some Northern prisons retaliated by reducing Confederate rations.

However, below Richmond, Butler got his personal revenge. In a night raid he arrested the impoverished family of Luther Libby, whose offense was having his business taken away from him so fast that his sign remained up as a name for the prison.

4

For the people in Richmond the fighting around the city became so steady that when, in the middle of October, there was no firing for a day, the silence was commented upon. When the attacks grew heavier again, friends of the war office climbed up on the roof to watch the flashes where the fortifications stretched across the flat farm lands. In November cannons were heard rumbling through the rainy darkness.

When the weather turned cold, with ice and frost everywhere, girls working at the arsenal struck. Speeches to them availed nothing. One of the officers had to draw directly on a new cargo from the blockade and distribute bacon and sirup and clothing. Later an ordnance store was established, selling at a quarter of the prevailing prices.

The bills issued in their own communities, which the people had handled so gaily—Richmond and the County, Southern Exchange, and Southern Rights Bank—were now pathetic little white slips on the backs of worthless bonds. As it took thirty dollars of those slips to equal one dollar, potatoes went to thirty dollars a bushel, and soup associations were formed to give potato soup to the needy. The City Council appropriated $30,000 for food for the suffering.

At the same time one of Winder's detectives kept a mistress in a house that rented for more than his month's salary. Former Secretary of War Randolph, who could not earn money defending exempts as fast as he lost the fortune of his beautiful wife, sailed with his family for Europe.

Ads for runaways grew fewer as the chances of recapturing them dwindled along with the money. Indicating a hopelessness about the institution that depended on the Confederacy, $500 was offered for a slave and $1,000 for a sorrel mare.

Negroes constantly figured in the news. Slaves were charged with stealing cash from a Locust Alley proprietor, a sheet from the Confederacy, four hundred pounds of bacon, bedclothes, and brass casings from the Virginia Central Railroad. A white man was charged with stealing $300 from a female slave, and another man with shooting a free mulatto woman who was reputed to be his mistress. A group of Negroes, runaways and some stolen by the Union armies and captured by the Confederates, were imprisoned awaiting identification papers of the owners.

The street fights that had become frequent during the war were now commonplace. Faro banks continued despite a law abolishing gambling, but "The circle admitted to the game is small and select . . . embracing officials and military men. . . ."

Cafés on Main Street stopped serving meals and tried to refund the "bales" of Confederate notes they had accumulated. The new Richmond Theater continued packing the house to its dramas, while down near Locust Alley the Varieties offered quartets and dancers and "comicalities."

A Dutchman in town, entering into the gaiety in his own way, was arrested for beating his new wife when the pleasures didn't turn out as he expected. "I vants a vife vat can drink whisky," he said.

With illness prevalent, doctors few, and the scarce medicine prohibitive, leechers advertised their wares and services. "I have on hand a supply of fine leeches and . . . can be found at all times at the BARBER SHOP opposite the American Hotel." On the front page of the dwindling newspaper a rival proclaimed simply, "LEECHES! LEECHES!"

John Morgan, who only a short time before had been feted in Richmond after his escape from the penitentiary, was returned as a corpse. Worn out by his raids, a psychic casualty useless to the Confederacy, he was killed in a messy little fight. When Bald Dick Ewell was leading the military escort toward Hollywood Cemetery, he received a dispatch announcing another of the attacks east of Richmond, and the soldiers had to hurry away from the procession. Morgan's brother-in-law, A. P. Hill, fighting a few miles away, was not many months from his own death.

The newspapers announced the presence of a celebrated visitor at the Ballard House, Belle Boyd, who was never as glamorous to Richmond as she was to herself. She had completed a tour of the South after her imprisonment in Washington and was on her way to Wilmington to take a blockade runner for Europe. On the same ship was Edward Pollard, needing a change after his unremitting newspaper warfare on the Davises. Both were captured along with the captain of the blockade runner, former U.S. naval officer Bier.

Belle Boyd seemed at her best in captivating susceptible young Yankees. She soon drew Ensign Hardinge under her spell, and her friend Bier escaped into Canada. Pollard was sent to prison, Belle Boyd banished from the country, and young Hardinge dismissed from the Navy. He followed her to London, where they married. He died soon after, and she lived on into a legend of her own making.

All such doings were remote to the hungry people of Richmond, huddling apprehensively against the coming of another winter. Even the fall of Savannah to Sherman was distant and unrelated, as was the final disaster to which Hood led the long-suffering Army of Tennessee back in Tennessee. Only remnants of that army, betrayed by leadership, escaped through the bitter cold to wander vaguely southward.

Later John Hood returned to Richmond, the scene where he had been a lion the year before, but he did not ride out in the afternoon with the President. There was no place for the shattered fighter, haunted—like Pickett—by the memory of the carnage.

Instead of admiring the heroes, civilians—and deserters among them—wondered what they were going to do for food with white beans at $75 a bushel and over $50 for a bushel of corn meal. And their hungers went deeper than for food. They wanted peace—not the arranged peace that politicians on both sides were maneuvering for, but a cessation of fighting.

Banded together in the same desperation that held the leaders, the people did not have the same stakes. They had not made the gamble. The leaders had risked fortunes and political positions in an experiment; the people had risked their lives in what was to them primary independence.

To them the movement—either with the dream of the Confederacy that had filled them with exultance or in the simplest unarticulated definition of personal liberty through their state—had failed. Many did not want to give up. Many did not know how to give up. But all, weakened by privations and anxieties, numbed by the constant hammering at the city, lived from day to day, waiting for the end.

As seen by a young officer in Richmond for a wedding, they "were scantily clad in every kind of makeshift garment, ofttimes in rags.

People without overcoats met one another upon the streets, and talked over the prospects of peace, with their teeth chattering, their thin garments buttoned over their chests, their shoulders drawn up, their gloveless hands sunk deep into their pockets for warmth."

Yet the fashionable weddings went on, though the receptions now showed an acute pinch even among the wealthier. The ingenuities of the ladies' makeshifts went to such bizarre measures as using fish scales in the shape of pearly flowers for necklaces and sprays in the hair. Palmetto, cut into lacelike fibers, was used for pins and necklaces, and palmetto and straw, trimmed with the feathers of domestic fowls, were used for hats. Scarfs were made of colored wool, worn-out shoes were covered with old pieces of satin, and Mrs. Clay appeared in unbleached homespun cotton with gourd-seed buttons dyed crimson.

But, for the wedding, "few girls with any social pretensions in Richmond had failed to wheedle or cajole some admiring blockade-running magnate into fetching them a silk or ribbon or feather from the outside world for this occasion." The dresses were curious variations on a theme, as one dress brought in through the blockade would be copied by all the owner's friends, with changes to adapt to the material at hand.

The visiting officer, younger son of Henry Wise, had come in a borrowed dress-uniform coat so much too large that one of his sister's friends, trying to be tactful, remarked on his "nice new overcoat."

The inventiveness of the social-minded people extended even to their catering. There were no ices or sweets, no ducks or *pâtés,* and even oysters had been cut off by the enemy. But they could still raise hogs and shoot turkeys, and the platters were heavy with sliced turkey and ham and sausage, garnished with stuffed eggs and pickles, and the punch bowls were kept full of hot toddy from homemade apple brandy.

All the members of the Cabinet attended the wedding reception, and the President and his lady. The young officer, observing the thin, careworn, graying man and his buxom wife, remembered the old expression, "The gray mare was the better horse."

But Mr. Davis, among his friends, showed the personality which his wife wished his enemies knew. Young Wise found his smile "winning, and his manner most attractive."

The gaiety of the guests was heightened and the beauty of the women made dramatic by the sense of the transient hour between dangers and the greater danger of the unknown tomorrow.

Before returning to the cold, muddy trenches at Petersburg, young Wise thought, "Eat, drink, and be merry, for tomorrow you die."

CHAPTER THIRTY-FOUR

One against the Gods

AFTER the New Year, 1865, it became clear to many of the leaders that the time had come to negotiate for peace. No workers were returning to the ordnance plants, and no deserters or conscript evaders were returning to the Army; for the trickle of the few privileged noncombatants who were forced into the lines, veterans deserted in streams.

Women's letters asking soldiers to come home were no longer sent mostly from the remote sections, but from all over what remained of the Confederacy. The old soldiers knew the Army well enough to measure its poor chances, and they could see nothing gained by allowing their womenfolk and children to starve. Even worse to the men were the silences from women in the areas where Sherman's hordes had passed. . . .

At the ratio of desertions as the winter bore down, by spring every other man would be gone from Lee's Army of Northern Virginia— the only actual army left in the field. Remnants from Hood's were attempting to re-form with militia in the Carolinas against Sherman's march, turning northward from Savannah. But these defenders under half a dozen generals without defined authority could scarcely be designated an army. The departments—Alabama-Mississippi and Trans-Mississippi and minor spheres—had scarcely any existence outside Davis's tables of organization.

But Davis talked now of putting heart back into the people. The faceless anonymities whom he had never known in his whole life, the indolent background for aristocracy, were somehow to be fired with a dream of independence—that would support the failing experiment. The leaders listened, knowing better, but nobody contradicted him. Nobody wanted to be stigmatized as a quitter. Yet they were open to negotiations. . . .

The fort protecting Wilmington fell, numbering the days of that port, and—as a minor disaster—Beast Butler was removed from command. He had taken a crack at the Wilmington fort, using a fancy scheme of sending ashore a power-laden ship which would explode and stun the garrison. It barely awakened them. When the next expedition under another general was successful, the political general was returned to the bosom of his constituents—and the Confederate defenders lost an enemy leader they could depend on to blunder.

Henry Foote, the loud-mouthed vituperator in Congress, was arrested trying to enter the enemy lines in an attempt to open private negotiations for peace. His fellow members were offered a variety in their harangues by debating on whether or not he should be expelled.

Nobody else made an overt move, but Vice-President Stephens had been in town since early December, paying thirty dollars a day for his room, with light and fuel extra. He actually presided over the Senate, though he was writing his brother that he had a good mind to resign, as he had never approved of the principles in the first place.

By staying on in the Senate he could cast the deciding vote which at last restored habeas corpus. With that tyrannical act gone, if they could just get rid of food impressment and conscription, recruits (seeing liberty triumphant) would flow back into the armies, which would avoid battles and fixed positions—and exist apparently in the ether as a menace to the enemy. But Stephens did not feel the Union would be an enemy much longer. Now that his friends were beginning to clip the wings of the despot Davis, the Constitutional South would soon find the ways to peace and restoration of the Union.

Then a negotiator came down from the North. Secretary Seddon raised his head from between his knees, the manner in which his clerk found him sitting before the fire. Robert Hunter, his fat cheeks flat and pallid, moved with new alacrity. General Lee looked brighter when he came to town.

At the White House, Mrs. Davis put another leaf in her round rosewood table and ransacked her cellar for punch ingredients to fill the huge pink china punch bowl. Francis Blair, Sr., was an old friend of Varina's, and she made it seem like old times.

Blair entered into the spirit, for he was not there officially but out of the goodness of his heart. Lincoln had given him permission to come to try his own method of opening a basis for negotiation. After Blair had dined with the Davises he retired to the President's study and made his proposition.

As a means of ending the bloodshed he suggested that the sections unite to act against the French in Mexico, in execution of the Monroe Doctrine. Presumably, once they were peaceably reunited, their differences could be ironed out.

Davis felt no hope for any such scheme. The North was committed to union and the South to independence. However, the peace sentiment among his own leaders demanded a conference. While the Stephenses forced Davis to show he was willing to negotiate, he not only rigged the conditions of negotiation to make any compromise impossible, but he gave the job of negotiating to Stephens.

The Vice-President did not want this assignment, but to avoid it would admit a disbelief in a negotiated peace. His fellows were Robert Hunter and Judge Campbell, Assistant Secretary of War.

Though it meant the end of his life's dream, Hunter was sickened of the people's suffering, repelled by the killing of boys under seventeen, and willing to discuss peace terms. Campbell, anti-Secessionist who had acted as intermediary between the Lincoln administration and Confederate commissioners four years before, over Fort Sumter, wanted to try to end the war he had failed to prevent.

Benjamin, of course, was selected to write the instructions, and his circuitous original draft showed a subtle realism about the whole conference.

Lincoln had written that he would be happy to receive commissioners "with a view of securing peace to the people of our common country." Benjamin's instructions made no reference either to common country or separate countries, but, he said, "my idea was to make them [instructions] as vague and general as possible, so as to get at the views and sentiments of Mr. Lincoln and to test the reality of the peace intentions represented by Mr. Blair. . . ."

But Davis changed the instructions to read, "for the purpose of securing peace *to our two countries.*" Benjamin said his own "purposely vague language" caused Davis to feel that assent might be implied to Lincoln's "one country," thus making Davis's motives suspect in a way to derogate his personal honor. While Benjamin was "anxious to keep out of view any topic that might defeat the object of the proposed conference," he wrote Davis, "*not* at the risk of any assault on your character or honor."

Benjamin was the "brains *in* the Confederacy" well enough—but not *of* it. Personal honor was the brains of the Confederacy.

Davis, the embodiment of personal honor, had no object in the conference except to prove that negotiated peace was impossible. Realistic Benjamin wanted to find out what was possible. What were the Yankees getting at? What went on? But, out of deference to Davis's honor, he at once withdrew his vague language.

With this bad start the three commissioners went to the Union supply depot of City Point, down on the James River, and waited for instructions from Washington. They were courteously received by General and Mrs. Grant and met many of their old acquaintances. General Meade and other officers obviously wanted peace without rancor, and Grant wrote Lincoln that he felt the Confederate commissioners desired peace.

After a wait Lincoln advised the commissioners to proceed to Fortress Monroe, and there he and Seward met them in the saloon of a steamboat, *River Queen,* in what was called the Hampton Roads Conference.

Stephens opened the conversation brightly and then came to the point of means of restoring the Union.

Lincoln's flat answer was unexpected. He said the only way was "for those who were resisting the laws of the Union to cease that resistance."

But, Stephens replied, what about the joint action in Mexico?

Oh, that proposition of Blair's? "Whatever he said was of his own accord and without the least authority from me."

Judge Campbell saw the same old shell game of four years before, when Seward spoke apparently with authority and it was then proved it was his own opinion. He was not surprised at Lincoln's attitude.

Stephens was more than surprised; he was incredulous. After four years of behind-the-scenes power on the basis of abstractions, the pale little fantasist was trapped with reality in a steamboat saloon.

He listened, appalled, as Lincoln went on in a kindly manner pointing out that, once the sections were reunited without slavery, he believed the people of the North would be willing to pay an indemnity for the slaves. Lincoln said he knew some who believed $400,000,000 should be appropriated for indemnity. Seward got up and paced the floor and added that he didn't see why the North should not be willing to pay indemnity instead of supporting the war.

This was all very well, but what they were saying, as cheerfully as possible, was that complete submission was required of the South. Hunter believed both men were afraid of the extremists in their own party, and he asked on what terms could negotiations be opened.

Lincoln replied simply that the South be unarmed.

There was nothing the commissioners could say. This was not negotiation; this was demand for surrender. They were asked to submit helplessly to any terms the victor might impose, without even the assurance that Lincoln could carry through his personal preferences. They were not even asked to return to the Union but, like any conquered peoples, to lay down their arms first—and take the consequences of having borne them.

The three commissioners returned to Richmond in what Judge Campbell called great "chagrin." After they reported to Davis—who at least enjoyed the satisfaction of being proven right—Hunter came up with one definite idea.

He offered to make a resolution himself, proposing a peace overture on the basis of one country but not on the basis of the complete submission proposed by Lincoln. As Hunter felt defeat was inevitable and independence not possible, he was concerned with obtaining peace on less harsh terms. He believed his overture would either cause Lincoln to retreat from his extreme position or go on record to the world as bringing submission through the force of arms.

But Davis was far from conceding defeat. Hunter's proposal only brought about his split with Davis, for the President saw Lincoln's unyielding stand as the means he needed to put heart back into the movement.

When the people were disenchanted of the fantasies that led them to believe they could return to the Union, when they recognized that only a degraded subjugation awaited them if they failed to establish their independence, they would be aroused to fight for the freedom that *he* had realized all along was the only issue.

Davis personally was truly aroused. The Union had denied that "the individual states could be recognized as having power to enter into any agreement prescribing the conditions of peace," though these same states had entered into agreement with Great Britain regarding their freedom and, as free states, had entered agreements with the other states now composing a separate union.

Fired by his logical rightness and outrage at the enemy who denied it, the President addressed a rally two nights after the commissioners reported. He was impassioned as he rarely was before a crowd, and even Stephens said his speech "had that loftiness of sentiment and rare form of expression, as well as magnetic influence in its delivery, by which the passions of the masses" are stirred.

The passions of Stephens, however, were not among those stirred. Davis had asked him to speak to the rally too, but Stephens was still shocked at his discovery of what the war was about. He was preparing to go back to Georgia—this time for good. Holed up in his home, Liberty Hall, he waited for the inevitable end.

2

Robert Hunter was not deceived by the volatile emotions of a crowd, nor was Lee. The general had received too many promises from the politicians, and at last he knew that no more men were coming to his army, no more food or shoes or warm clothes for those now starving in their rags. Hearing of Hunter's willingness to make an overture for peace, he came to visit the senator at his home in Richmond.

Lee said he believed any negotiated peace was preferable to surrender and suggested that Hunter make his resolution in the Senate.

But Hunter believed that Davis had betrayed his earlier conversation, for now he was regarded as a submissionist. He suggested that Lee make the resolution.

Lee replied that, from him, such a suggestion would be equivalent to surrender.

Then Hunter suggested that if Lee thought their chance of success was slight, he tell the President.

To this Lee made no reply.

Nobody wanted to be the one to tell Jefferson Davis.

But another suggestion for a negotiated peace came to Hunter from a peculiar source—the new Secretary of War.

James Seddon had given up. He was blamed for all the military disasters of the Confederacy, though his influence was long past, and he got the opprobrium for something he did not do and no credit for the details of the war office which he did run. Now his frail health was failing under the strain and the sacrifice was useless. Judge Campbell could run the office well enough for the time left the Confederacy, and the only loss by Seddon's resignation would be to the opposition. They would have one less target.

His successor, like Trenholm in the Treasury, was a man of great reputation and dynamic personality—John Breckinridge. In his middle forties, he had been a U. S. Vice-President, Southern Democratic presidential candidate in 1860, U.S. senator from Kentucky at the beginning of the war, and a Confederate general since. Big-bodied and powerful, he was vastly admired for the prodigious quantities of whisky he could consume, and all manner of observers commented awesomely on the aroma of bourbon that preceded him wherever he went.

Once Breckinridge took over the job, he rarely went to the office and evinced no interest in policy. Having come to the civil post from the

Army, he was concerned only with what resources the departments possessed for maintaining the armies in the field. To this end he had hard-minded Campbell get detailed reports from each department head.

Northrop sent him a long apologia full of suggestions to the Treasury Department on how to get funds, to the Quartermaster Department on how to handle wagons, to the railroads on how to deliver supplies, and to the impressment officers on how to get food from farmers. Indicating Davis's desperation, the President allowed Breckinridge to fire Northrop and replace him—after four years—with an able man.

The commissary showed in Richmond, in the supply depot of Greensboro, North Carolina, and en route from Georgia and Charleston, existing rations that totaled about six pounds of meat per man; seven hundred thousand rations of wheat and flour, and eight million rations of other foodstuffs "purchased" in Georgia. As material below Greensboro was by no means certain of arrival, an officer was sent to Georgia to expedite grain. He reported the stuff seemed "swallowed up" between there and Richmond.

When the railroads reported, they claimed the skilled men were pulled away to the Army and they lacked replacement of equipment. Checking with field transportation, Breckinridge got the same story— no men, no money. Transportation needed over ten thousand horses and mules. Quartermaster Department needed money. Engineers needed men. Surgeon general demanded that men working on substitute medicines be exempt and let alone. Even over at Chimborazo Hospital, with all their communal efforts, they had to pay $25 cash for a shin of beef, $30 for a chicken, $20 for a dozen eggs in March.

In Richmond warehouses, where quantities were known, there were thirty thousand pounds of coffee—less than one pound per man in Lee's army—and forty-two thousand pounds of sugar.

For buying material, gold was now needed, and market reports showed the state of their money. For two and a half years, up to Gettysburg, their dollar had held at 1 to 7; in the next fourteen months, up to the fall of Atlanta, it had dropped at the rate of about one point a month, and, even in September, it was still 1 to 23. Then, in the next five months, it dropped thirty-five points, and when Breckinridge took over, the Confederate dollar stood at 1 to 58.

For any material the South could hope to import from abroad, Wilmington fell and then Charleston was evacuated as Sherman drove up north. The last ports on the Atlantic were closed.

Thomas Bayne, in charge of obtaining cotton to be sent abroad for purchases, could only suggest opening new ports and fixing railroads from them—while keeping open the contraband trade with the enemy. New York had imported eight hundred thousand bales of cotton during the war, Boston one hundred thousand, and not much over half of it came from sources other than the Confederacy. With the dwindling surface of the Confederacy, even smuggling would offer less now.

With these facts, the well-liked Secretary of War turned his energy toward peace—through Hunter—and to means of getting his fellow Kentuckians home when the end came.

But Hunter, at last an enemy of the Administration, spent his time in Congress. Both houses were on the rampage. Finally the opposition had the majority to appoint a commander in chief of the armies. By then the opposition contained many supporters of Davis's administration in general who sincerely believed that he was not qualified to command the armies.

In the President's house Mrs. Davis regarded the whole business as an affront to her husband. He was suffering from neuralgia at the time, and she wanted to keep the big rooms warm for him. Even buying at government prices from the arsenal, they had to pay $245 which they could ill afford for seven cords of wood. For all the depreciation of currency, the Confederate bills were still all they had.

Seeing her husband broken, Varina bitterly blamed his enemies. As for their appointment of a military commander superior to him, she said, "I think I am the person to advise Mr. Davis, and if I were he, I would die or be hung before I would submit to the humiliation."

Perhaps Davis realized that the appointment of Lee as the general in chief would not be a humiliation. The President made the appointment of his friend graciously enough, and the general did not let him down. Ignoring Congress, Lee stated that the honor came to him through the supreme authority.

Though the general could not have been unmindful of the clamors for him to assume the full powers of a dictator, such a role was antithetical to his character and beyond the scope of his limited mental interests. In Lee's Anglo-Saxon line only one military hero—Cromwell—ever assumed dictatorship, and his immediate hero, Washington, needed as direly as did Lee a central power under his control.

General Lee held his own concept. At its center was a largeness of character compounded of virtues long honored by Christian people. In relation to his environment, Lee was of the essence of the *status quo* of his country—which in his time and place was Virginia. The men

JEFFERSON DAVIS

After two years as President, at the age of fifty-five. From a painting by John Robertson. Courtesy of Confederate Museum, Richmond, Virginia.

GENERAL WEITZEL'S WHITE AND NEGRO TROOPS ENTERING RICHMOND

Monday, April 3, 1865, following the evacuation of the last Confederate troops at 7 A.M. Wood engraving from a sketch by Joseph Becker. Courtesy of Valentine Museum, Richmond, Virginia.

in his army and the last-ditchers among the civilians instinctively yielded him leadership because by the expression of his nature he fought for the direct, unrationalized personal liberty of his own land, as did the least of them.

With Davis that was never true. His tragedy was that he actually represented the articulated experiment, and the spiritual leader became the soldier who evinced no interest in the experiment. Lee personified to his followers the one quality that made the people fight: loosely, love of the home place strong enough to die for it. Davis, appealing to the head, never realized why the people fought and, consequently, why they stopped. The home places were gone, and going, and the existence of the whole was presupposed on its parts. For the whole was never more than the sum of its parts, not even as much.

When Lee was appointed general in chief, the whole was scarcely more than a name to the people. The soldiers knew it. They said quite casually, "The Confederacy's gone up the spout," and they kept on fighting. Lee was the symbol of that element, and he never would or could have been more to the Confederacy. When he took over he went on with the President as he had before. They exchanged rather formal letters and talked in the warm little study off the hall in the White House—and Lee gave his final confidences to other soldiers.

The foolish body of men in Congress must have known that was the way it would be. Their act (at least for the majority) was chiefly a slap at Davis. The opposition was in the driver's seat, and they were out to have one hell of a time. Their frantic irresponsibility indicated at least elements of mass hysteria.

First they passed, over Davis's consistent veto, the bill authorizing free postage on letters and packages mailed to soldiers. Nothing of course was done to assure the arrival of the packages, as Confederates suffered equally with Yankee prisoners from having food boxes rifled.

Then Congress collaborated with the states'-rights bloc and revoked the shipping restrictions imposed by the government. Davis, in proving to Congress the value of government-operated shipping, gave figures which the newspapers were permitted freely to publish, making this information available to the enemy.

Apparently with no sense of admitting how he also proved his own foreign policy wrong for three years, he showed that the co-ordinated system of Bayne and McRae netted over $2,000,000 on the same amount of cotton on which the old haphazard system netted only $500,000. Ninety per cent of the cotton shipped had gotten through before the fall of the Atlantic ports, and shipping was now booming on the Gulf. With this cotton the government paid for purchases at the market price of 48 cents a pound instead of being robbed by contractors.

The bemused man did not seem to realize he was saying that now, with all hope of foreign intervention lost and a supply shortage resulting from the ruinous system, he was using with intelligence and vigor the assets they possessed from the first. To convince Congress, he listed (for publication) the amounts of every item received. He made no mention of the huge discrepancy between invoices at the dock and actual material to the fighting forces and the starving people of Richmond.

As far as Congress was concerned, nothing he said would have made any difference. They killed the law because it was his, and then busied themselves rigging a vote of no confidence on Benjamin. The Secretary of State offered to resign, but Davis would not hear of that.

By then Benjamin had nothing to do except his personal work with Davis. His last gesture had been to send Duncan Kenner, Louisiana congressman, abroad to discover if the abolition of slavery would effect foreign recognition. It would not.

Finally Congress reached a decision on the arming of slaves. In the early voting, even Hunter was so swayed by the property he owned as of that minute that he went against the measure—though Lee had stressed its passage was vital. By then slaves were at one tenth their prewar value. Finally Hunter realized that his slaves were gone anyway, and he voted on the measure which passed in the middle of March —though, obstinate to the end, Congress did not include emancipation in the bill to arm slaves.

By then it was of no consequence to anyone except themselves what they did. Union General Ord, speaking for brother officers, told Longstreet they thought he should suggest to General Lee a conference with Grant, with a view to peace. Lee, more than willing, immediately tried to feel out Grant. But Grant, under strict instructions from Lincoln to enter no negotiations of any kind, wrote Lee that any such conferences must be conducted by the governments. That ended the soldiers' bid.

3

The government was one deluded man, and Lee and his generals— as dutiful to the shadow form of their government as were the Union generals to their established order—could only fight on, knowing their best did not even approach being enough.

The spiritual collapse which started with Atlanta was finished by winter's physical attrition. In the nine months since Lee had stopped Grant at Petersburg and Johnston's army against Sherman's held the future in their hands, Lee's once fearsome units had dwindled to no more than a collection of half-starved tatterdemalions clinging to their battle flags, and what had been Johnston's army at Atlanta were scattered survivors of Hood's debacle, garrison troops from evacuated ports and militia—again under Joe Johnston.

Reinstating Joe Johnston was one act Lee committed as general of the armies. As Johnston's subordinate, there was again Beauregard. The two Heroes of four years before, who had rivaled each other for glory in the days when decisions concerned invading the North from Virginia, now, as then, reported their men insufficient—this time for checking a conquering horde marching northward from *south* of Virginia.

Militarily they dickered with Lee over some desperate means of uniting the two forces to defeat Sherman. Lee would have to slip away from Grant, uncovering Richmond. The Unions would occupy the city, but by the time Grant moved his army with its necessary supply bases to North Carolina, Lee and Johnston, having disposed of Sherman, would be ready to take him on.

With the sorry state of every one of the physical departments of an 1865 army—horses and wagons for transportation, horses and ammunition for guns, ammunition and food and shoes for men—the only basis for these dreams of action was the aura of invincibility that clung to the still unconquered Lee—and the hope that, in the event Sherman was forced to retreat, he would be destroyed by the people.

The devastations of Sherman's "bummers" had long since exceeded any military necessity. Grant believed in living off the enemy population to cut off the source of supplies to its armies and to reduce the will to resist in the people. These harsh measures to him expressed a definite military policy which extended to his own people, in his permitting Union prisoners to suffer want and in his sacrifice of life. But wanton destruction beyond military advantages was not his policy.

Individuals in his army certainly stole—Wilson's cavalry raiders were mounted burglars—and many men exercised extreme brutality on helpless civilians in their pillaging. Grant also had in Sheridan and Custer a couple of bully boys in whom the circumstances brought out a cold-blooded viciousness. Grant did not discourage his cavalry in their personal indulgences—it was good for their morale—but bring·

ing suffering to civilians never expressed anything in Grant's character. With Sherman apparently it did.

What Sherman started got out of hand, though past experience in the West, by his own orders, showed him it would. Individuals incited one another, until the most decent man competed in pillage with the most depraved, and the acts inflamed the group to create the uncontrolled hoodlumism of a mob. As in any mob of hate turned loose on unprotected people, destruction goaded them to more destruction, greed and rapacities fed upon themselves. When these terrorists struck up through South Carolina, their body seemed formed of pyromaniacs and sadists, assaulters and rapists, thieves and foulers of homes.

Whitelaw Reid, in writing of Sherman in South Carolina, said:

The last morsel of food was taken from hundreds of destitute families that his soldiers might feast in needless and riotous abundance. Before his eyes rose, day after day, the mournful clouds of smoke on every hand, that told of old people and their grandchildren driven, in midwinter, from the only roofs there were to shelter them, by the flames which the wantonness of his soldiers had kindled. With his full knowledge and tacit approval, too great a portion of his advance resolved itself into bands of jewelry thieves and plate-closet burglars.

Major General O. O. Howard, of Sherman's command, wrote to Major General F. P. Blair, Jr., on "the most outrageous robberies of watches and jewelry, etc.":

A case has come to my notice where a watch and several articles of jewelry were stolen by a foraging party under the eye of the commissioned officer in charge. Another where a brute had violently assaulted a lady by striking her, and had then robbed her of a valuable gold watch. In one instance . . . an officer with a foraging party had allowed his men to take rings from the fingers of ladies in his presence.

And a lieutenant from Boston, writing to his wife, said, "We have had a glorious time in this State. Unrestricted license to burn and plunder was the order of the day. . . . I have at least a quart of jewelry for you and all the girls—and some No. 1 diamond rings and pins among them. . . ."

However much Southerners would have welcomed a day of reckoning, the measurable known of the devastation was the hardship it would bring upon the defeated people when peace came. The sooner the peace came, the more suffering would be spared the population.

But Davis, though extremely sensitive about the suffering of his

[396]

fellows, dreamed not of peace but of independence. The details were lost in his dream of a Confederacy which—as he was it and it was he —could not die while life lasted.

In late March, with the weather bright though still sharp, new green in his terraced garden presaged the end of the terrible winter. From the dining-room window overlooking the gallery where his son had fallen to his death, Davis could see the magnificent sweep of Shockoe Valley where Broad Street dipped past the Virginia Central Railroad Depot and rose toward old St. John's white steeple on Church Hill.

Then Davis climbed, very slowly, those steep curving stairs to his office where all the great men of the Confederacy had come and where, working late into the night, he had made so many appointments to the armies.

Those appointments provided the one detail left that came through clear and whole. Turning the gaslight up, arranging his tired body in the cushioned chair, he took up a pencil and prepared papers to be sent over to the war office—where the new Secretary did not even bother to tarry.

CHAPTER THIRTY-FIVE

Not with a Whimper but a Bang

AT METROPOLITAN HALL there was a benefit performance for a Memphis refugee, recently widowed when her
husband was killed in action. Smith's redoubtable band
played for a singer and danseuse, a Child Prima Donna,
and the Terpsichorean Sisters. Up on Broad Street at the fashionable
Richmond Theater the new play was a dramatization of Mrs. Brad-
don's novel, *Aurora Floyd*, while at the Opera House in the bright-
light section of lower Franklin Street, Budd & Buckley's Minstrels,
along with "their Side-splitting Jokes," gave a repeat performance of
the burlesque on "Recruiting Unbleached Virginians in the Confederate Army."

The back sheets of the thin newspapers were nearly covered with ads
for Auction Sales, mostly of household goods from private homes,
though right behind the Governor's Mansion a dealer in blockade
goods advertised sugar and coffee, rice and flour and pickled beef, soap
and candles and writing paper. The speculators had held on too long.
Even the market quotations of 1 to 60 failed to express the worthless-
ness of the Confederate dollar. It could never be refunded for gold—
even one dollar for one hundred—and pocketfuls were just paper,
"shinplasters."

The people stopped going out, and the streets seemed deserted. A
few curious spectators ventured to Capitol Square to observe the two
uniformed Negro companies, but this extremity only deepened their
depression. The city still had its die-hards who could not conceive of
the fall of Richmond—but President Davis was no longer among them.

As far removed as he was from reality, by late March the facts
pressed too close to home to be ignored. The remnants of Jubal Early's
little army out in the Valley, considered at least enough of a force to
cause some diversion from the Union Army, were scattered by Sheridan
and disintegrated as a unit. Sheridan's tough troopers rode back to
Grant, to operate on Lee's last railroad and overextended flank. And
Lee, trying to contract Grant's expanding pincers by a blow at the

[398]

Union center, failed with heavy losses. He reported that his grim prophecy had come true: unreinforced, his lines had stretched too thin to hold.

All other fixed points presented the same picture. The small force in southwest Virginia could only retire before Stoneman's cavalry, driving out of Tennessee. From the east coast, a new army under Schofield struck west, aiming for juncture with Sherman, blazing up into North Carolina. Down in Alabama, where Dick Taylor had a paper force and Forrest's once dread horsemen had thinned to exhausted skeletal units, Wilson led an awesome command of mounted infantry toward the final dismemberment of that territory. From the gulf, Mobile was folding under the siege.

Exclusive of the distant Trans-Mississippi Department—a separate empire under Kirby Smith in Texas—the practical theater-of-war area was bounded by the Atlantic and the Alleghenies, the James River and mid-North Carolina. In this little square, about the size of a state, Davis could visualize a concentration of forces to operate against the enemies in the field. Galling as was the abandonment of cities, this inevitable was finally forced upon him. He could still dream of the recapture of the cities when the enemies were defeated in the field, but —for now—he had to admit that Richmond was no longer safe for his wife and children.

When he came home from the office, walking very erectly, Mrs. Davis knew there was trouble from his ashen color. She came to him, and his arms shook when he held her. Then he got out the words—that she and the children must leave him.

Varina instantly protested and argued that her place was by his side. He soothed his wife and told her she could comfort and help him best "by going yourself and taking our children to a place of safety."

When she still hesitated he told her that they would be together when the struggle was ended, but, "I do not expect to survive the end of constitutional liberty."

Seeing, then, there was no more to say, Mrs. Davis turned to the duties of a housewife at which she was so efficient. She arranged her large collection of silver plate, but it could not be moved with the limited traveling space, and her husband feared friends might be "exposed to inconvenience or outrage" if they kept the silver. Then came her bric-a-brac which, she said, sentimental people call their "household goods," but her husband called it "trumpery." That too was not to go. So Mrs. Davis sold her cherished possessions to an auction dealer, but in the rush of packing forgot to cash the check.

Even several barrels of flour were forbidden her, as Mr. Davis said the hungry people of Richmond needed it.

Finally the distracted woman had no more than clothing for herself and four children—the oldest nine and the youngest barely out of arms. When she was ready for her unwilling leave-taking, Jefferson Davis gave her a pistol and carefully showed her how to use it. He hoped she could avoid the enemy, leaving wherever she was at their approach, but, "You can at least force your assailant to kill you."

He gave her all his small store of gold, leaving only a five-dollar piece for himself. Then the President helped his family into carriages, with Maggie Howell (Mrs. Davis's sister), Ellen, a mulatto maid, James Jones, a mulatto coachman, and Burton Harrison, Davis's private secretary who had lived with them.

At the station they met the lovely daughters of Secretary Trenholm, and "Little" Morgan, the young naval officer who was engaged to one of the girls. In the dilapidated car the President saw them all arranged on the "threadbare, brownish red plush seats." Then, as he turned to go, his daughter Maggie clung convulsively to him. It looked as if her father would finally lose his control. From his expression Mrs. Davis saw that "he thought he was looking his last upon us." Then, as the train threatened to start, Davis hurriedly left his family. The train puffed without moving, and Burton Harrison joined the President on the platform.

It was full night when the train finally started, and young Harrison jumped on as it lurched forward. He saw the thin man standing erect in the gloom of the depot, and then the secretary re-entered the dingy car. They were passing over the James River, and the little party stared silently at the dark waters below them, their "hearts bowed down by despair" as the train headed south.

2

Off the North Carolina coast Captain Wilkinson prepared to make his run in through the blockade to Wilmington. Since he had commanded the famous *R. E. Lee* both he and his old ship had fared badly. He had been sent to Canada to participate in some of the wild schemes to release prisoners, while the new captain of the *R. E. Lee* had allowed her to be captured.

Now the able captain was operating a blockade runner again. He had taken the wounded Von Borcke on it to Bermuda, from where the big Prussian volunteer aide of Jeb Stuart was going back to Europe to try his hand in the Confederacy's behalf. Wilkinson brought his ship in carefully, for the fort protecting Wilmington had been under heavy fire when he went out.

He was ready for his run in before he discovered Wilmington was no longer a Confederate port. With heavy spirits he turned his ship southward to try Charleston. The Yankees held it too. With his cargo of arms for Lee's army the captain put back to Nassau—for his last run.

He recorded, "As we turned away from the land, our hearts sank within us, while the conviction forced itself upon us that the cause for which so much blood had been shed, so many miseries bravely endured, and so many sacrifices cheerfully made, was about to perish at last."

3

The first Sunday in April was a beautiful spring day. Recent rains had brought out the yellow and pale green flowers, and the trees were bright and young. Going to church across from Capitol Square, the President did not share the feelings of Captain Wilkinson. The fall of places was not the end of the cause. The cause was rendered more desperate, but freedom from behaving like an established country gave them the chance to fight more directly, more naturally. Yesterday Mallory was seen with a pistol in his yard, presumably practicing.

When, in the middle of the service at St. Paul's, the messenger brought the fateful words from Lee, the President was not unprepared. As the death of a loved one long ill still comes with a shock, Lee's message that he must retreat from Petersburg and Richmond be evacuated "came sooner than was expected." But Davis was aware of posterity.

In all his life of living by concepts he never acted more consciously of his role. "I quietly left the church," he said. "The occurrence probably attracted attention, but . . . the people had known me too often to receive notice of threatened attacks, and the congregation at St. Paul's was too refined, to make a scene at anticipated danger. . . ."

Down Ninth Street hill was less than a block, past the war office where the Secretaries had come and gone, and into short Bank Street along the southern border of Capitol Square. Up on the hill, where the pillared Capitol stood, his enemies in Congress had adjourned, so there would be no politicians to contend with.

He turned into the quiet Treasury Building and mounted the steps that for four years had led him to the scene of his power and anguish.

Even on Sunday clerks and aides were there, and he dispatched these after the members of the Cabinet and Adjutant General Cooper.

The men gathered without excitement. They too had been long prepared, and they adapted themselves to the President's manner of calm decisiveness. Again as with the death of a loved one who has suffered long, the group of men felt, with their shock and sorrow, a certain sense of relief. It was over now—the long watch—and anything new was better because it was new.

With the blind hope that caused Davis to procrastinate before any decision involving a retreat, preparations for the evacuation were sketchy. Government archives had been shipped south in only small quantities, and government monies not at all. The supplies that Lee needed for his break into the open were stored in warehouses.

Each department head would supervise a hurried packing of the records considered most valuable and have them delivered to the Richmond & Danville Depot. The cabinet members dispersed. Secretary Trenholm was ill, and a Treasury Department teller and a wounded veteran acting as navy paymaster took over the packing of the bullion in the Treasury's vaults.

It was not much, less than half a million dollars, but it represented the whole wealth of the nation. There were silver bricks and gold nuggets, Mexican silver coins and gold double eagles. Clerks got the bullion packed into boxes and crates and canvas sacks, along with boxes of books and records. Micajah Clark, chief clerk of the executive office, collected the President's papers. When he and the Treasury clerks carted the packages to the depot, there was no one to guard the valuables.

Mallory's James River fleet was being prepared for destruction—the last of his efforts to be destroyed by a retreating army. The crews from those ships and the gunners from Drewry's Bluff were forming somewhere under Admiral Semmes, who had taken over their command when he returned after the sinking of the *Alabama*.

The remnants of the Marine Corps were somewhere around too. They had numbered nearly a thousand officers and enlisted men at one time, including former officers of the U. S. Marines and with a band of twenty-two musicians. Now they seemed incorporated into Ewell's conglomerate Richmond defense units east of the city. Apparently those units would pass through the city, covering the evacuation before joining Lee wherever his army went.

General Kemper, wounded in leading one of Pickett's brigades up Cemetery Ridge, now commanding some of the local defense units, was trying to find someone to get orders from. Assistant Secretary of War Campbell was roaming outside his office, clutching two books and talking to himself. The Secretary, Breckinridge, was mounted and preparing to ride toward Lee's army for definite information. The war clerks packed records and wondered what provision was made for them and their families.

Captain William Parker had perfect discipline in his naval cadet corps of sixty. *They* could guard the government's money. In fine order, and very serious, they packed it in the cars outside the depot on Fourteenth Street near the river.

Down there train dispatchers were sending and countermanding orders. *Hold all Richmond trains. . . .* Then, *Come to Richmond with all engines and empty passenger cars and boxcars you can pick up. . . . Too late, Richmond is being evacuated. Arrange for all track possible in Danville.*

With no official reports, the news passed by word of mouth. Lee's thin line had finally broken, and the men were stumbling westward in retreat. They might reach Joe Johnston in North Carolina, but here— here the government was fleeing. Could it be that their city was to fall at last? How did a city fall? What would happen?

The President had completed arrangements at his office and was walking through Capitol Square on the familiar way to his home, to pack his personal belongings. There were more people on the streets then, more than for days.

Some of them asked him if it was true—was Richmond to be abandoned? With grave though confident voice he told the people the government was leaving now—to return under happier auspices. He recorded that they answered "with generous sympathy . . . 'If the success of the cause requires you to give up Richmond, we are content.' "

That was his memory of the words of the few who spoke. But the other thousands—standing aimlessly, watching the government wagons roll through the streets, each group faster than the one before—they showed no contentment, only wonder and apprehension. Negroes looked as bewildered as the whites. The local defense units started drifting in, taking positions around the government warehouses. Lee's army would never get those rations.

Other troops from the defenses east of the city came shuffling up Main Street hill. As they passed the American Hotel several ladies watched from the iron-grille balcony. One of them limply waved her handkerchief in the old familiar gesture. Not one soldier recognized her compliment. The girl's arm fell to her side, and she looked pale and hurt.

Wagons crowded past the soldiers. Nondescript vehicles jostled with the army wagons, and they were racing now, careening around corners. The civil workers watched them leave. There was no provision for the clerks' families.

In the war office Jones recorded in his diary, "I remain here, broken in health and bankrupt in fortune, awaiting my fate, whatever it may be. I can do no more. . . ."

In the White House the President gave directions to the housekeeper for closing up his home. Aides helped him pack—coats and trousers and waistcoats, linen shirts, a silk tie, dressing robes—a roll of court-plaster and a pair of gaiters, underclothing, extra shoelaces—a small dressing case, a razor strop, a comb and brush, two towels and two toothbrushes—eyeglasses, envelopes and note paper, six boxes of cigars—and last, a nine-shooter pistol and a double-barreled revolver, two holstered pistols, a pistol case, a case of ammunition, and two packages of metallic cartridges—a picture of his wife and himself and one of General Lee.

He was dressed carefully, in Confederate gray waistcoat and breeches, a Prince Albert coat. His whitening beard and hair were brushed, his wide-brimmed felt hat squarely placed. He was ready.

It was dusk when he reached the depot by the wide street slanting toward the bridge over the river and out of the city. They were all there. Sick Trenholm had come in an ambulance, but his spirits were good. Benjamin, smiling through his curly black beard, was as jaunty as ever, and red-faced Mallory observed this with reassurance. Attorney-General George Davis appeared as poised as ever, and John Reagan chewed ruminatively while he whittled a stick.

Breckinridge was not going with them. He was mounted on a large horse that observers noticed for some while before they discovered why he looked strange: the animal was *fat*. Breckinridge was talking with the President, both trying to obtain some news of Lee's army before the train left.

The confusion mounted in the depot and in the neighboring streets. Individuals, families, and groups fought to get on the overcrowded trains. Some were allowed without baggage into boxcars. Gorgas brought some of his ordnance workers. A dozen wounded veterans who had been acting as the President's sentries had to be gotten out.

The engine had steam up and was puffing to move. Davis was holding up the train. Farewell parties and curiosity seekers milled among the crowd. They could find no depression on the members of Cabinet, and President Davis presented a picture of calm, resolute dignity.

Four years before, in another spring, he had faced a crowd at a depot by the James River. He was as aware of his historic moment now as he had been then. He was the leader going out to carry on the fight as long as life lasted. He was the unvanquished living out his immortal destiny.

He climbed on the creaky car. The whistle blew. The train jerked out onto the bridge, the faint lights glimmered over the river and then vanished in the darkness beyond.

The citadel had returned to the Virginians, for them to surrender.

4

Around the Court End of town, where the Confederates had enjoyed the fevered gaiety of the big houses, shutters were closed on windows and doors were barred. From Chimborazo Hospital at the tip of Church Hill to Camp Lee on the old Fair Grounds the city was darkened.

Near the depot, around the government warehouses along Fourteenth and Thirteenth and Cary, the crowd was larger than when the trains were leaving. The word spread that rations were to be issued and the buildings destroyed.

Near morning the first explosions came. Gorgas's ordnance works were going up. Soldiers pushed west along the canal to burn the Tredegar next. The Tredegar Battalion barred the way. That was private property of Anderson's, and he refused to have it destroyed.

The soldiers circled ·back toward the bridges and started burning those west from Fourteenth Street. That bridge remained open for the troops still moving in from the defenses, shuffling between the mobs that were spilling out of their dives. They threw garbage at the troops and shouted obscenities.

Then the tobacco warehouses were fired, and the government warehouses. The crowd surged toward the buildings to salvage what they could from the flames. Officers broke open the whisky barrels, and the gutters ran with bourbon. Men and women sprawled flat to drink up the whisky and scraped it up in broken cups or anything else available.

The crowd, swelling and changing into a mob, grew frustrated in their fight against the flames. Some of them must have remembered the newspaper ads of a few days before—of Leffew's, on Thirteenth Street, with six barrels of bourbon and a couple of apple brandy, and Roberts's, on Thirteenth and Cary, with four barrels of apple brandy and a little of everything else. And there were those blockade-supplied stores right up the hill.

The mob began to spread the fire. There was no one to stop them. Flames were jumping buildings, and whole streets became ablaze. At daylight the Confederate rear guard, passing through the city, was ordered to disperse the mob.

Only shooting would accomplish that. What was the use? The last Rebel soldiers pushed through the smoke and on to the Fourteenth Street bridge. They burned that behind them. It was seven o'clock in the morning.

There was no law in the burning city.

Mayor Mayo and a couple of old friends rode east in a buggy, past the vicious groups around the wharf section and up the hill to a country road. Near a farm the old gentleman discovered they possessed nothing white to serve as a flag of truce. Decorously they retired to a clump of bushes, where they tore off the tail of the whitest shirt in the group.

With the shirttail fluttering on a stick they advanced toward General Weitzel's troops, marching steadily toward the blazing capital. On this country road, a few miles outside the city, the old men formally surrendered Richmond and asked General Weitzel to bring order. Thus was born the catch phrase, "Like Grant took Richmond."

General Weitzel's troops, white and Negro, entered the city by the short, direct route, straight up Main Street. The buildings on either side were gutted by then, though still burning. Negroes followed the line of march, but few whites appeared on the street.

The Yankees turned up into Capitol Square, where Davis had walked so many times from his office to his home, and they grew excited when they saw the Capitol Building with the red stars and bars still flying.

Homeless women and children and old men were huddled in the Square, some lying down on pieces of furniture they had saved from their burned homes. The soldiers ran past them, racing up the broad stone steps of the Capitol toward the goal of hauling down the Rebel flag and raising their own.

5

When Lincoln came to the city his carriage was followed by Negroes —slave and free, native Richmonders, fugitives from the country and some abandoned by families themselves now fugitives.

The United States President wore a tall black hat and had a very reassuring presence as he was driven toward the White House, which General Weitzel had taken over.

Legends abound as to his actions inside the high-ceilinged rooms where the Davises had lived, but clearly he was interested in the details of the house and of their life. Some of the officers commemorated the occasion by taking souvenirs in the form of silver and china, and an ivory seal with "J.D." on it.

CHAPTER THIRTY-SIX

"Let the Long, Long Procession Go"

AFTER Richmond, Danville seemed quiet and tranquil. In the tobacco and farming country of Southside Virginia, virtually on the North Carolina border, the pleasant small city was southwest of Richmond and seemed an ideal temporary capital. Government supplies were stored there, and the officials brought some crowds in, but no guns rumbled and no rifles crackled, no wagons of wounded and dead groaned through the streets, and those anonymous masses that had jammed Richmond were happily absent.

Major Sutherlin offered President Davis the use of a fine house, and visitors flocked to see him, expressing their pride and pleasure in having the government at Danville. Not worn down as had been the Richmond population, these gracious people brought a freshness in their welcome and some of the excitement the officials had found long ago in Richmond.

As soon as Davis was settled he issued a confident proclamation. Admitting the injury of the abandonment of Richmond, he stressed the advantages resulting from it—chiefly that "the largest and finest army of the Confederacy" would no longer be handicapped by guarding the capital:

We have now entered a new phase of the struggle. Relieved from the necessity of guarding particular points, our army will be free . . . to strike the enemy in detail far from his base. . . . Animated by that confidence in your spirit and fortitude which has never yet failed *me, I* announce to you, fellow countrymen, that it is *my* purpose to maintain your cause with *my* whole heart and soul. . . . [Italics inserted]

The only trouble at the moment was that the President could learn nothing of the movements of Lee's army, which he presumed was retreating toward Danville. He wrote his wife, who was safe in Charlotte with the children, that he was still waiting to hear any news of

[408]

General Lee. The penciled handwriting on lined foolscap paper looked tired. Across the middle of the second sheet of note paper the words seemed to fade off . . . "your ever affectionate Husband."

Mrs. Davis wrote him that "our little ones are all well, but very unruly. . . . Jeff is very much exercised about his pony, Maggie about her saddle . . . and I about my precious Old Ban, whom I left behind me with so keen a heartache. . . . Believe me as ever your devoted wife . . ."

By Saturday night, a week since the President had received the news in Richmond of Lee's retreat, there was still no word from the general. By now anxiety was mounting, and that night the Cabinet met around a large dining-room table in the Sutherlin house. About eight o'clock a tired-looking young lieutenant was admitted to the room. He was General Wise's son John, and he bore a message from General Lee which simply stated that Lieutenant Wise was authorized to make an oral communication.

Standing at the opposite end of the table from Mr. Davis, young Wise explained that the army had retreated west beyond the railroad to Danville and could not turn south to come here.

Under the jolt of this the President and his associates threw questions at the lieutenant, who answered the details as best he could while giving the impression that the army was falling apart. Just before he had left General Lee young Wise heard his father excitedly advise the general to surrender. General Wise told Lee that his duty was to the men, because *he* was the country to them and it was his responsibility to spare them further bloodshed and hardship.

Now, when the President asked directly if the lieutenant thought the army could reach a place of safety, Wise answered with a flat no. "From what I saw and heard, I am satisfied that General Lee must surrender . . . if I may be permitted to add a word, I think the sooner the better . . . to spare the useless effusion of . . . blood."

These were the words that no one before had said plainly to Davis. Almost a shudder went around the table. Not one of them agreed with Lieutenant Wise that it was wrong to continue "the useless effusion of blood." Whatever the individual members might have thought privately, they supported Davis's determination to carry on the hopeless struggle.

All day Sunday they waited for further news. All the archives and quartermaster stores, which had been rushed down from Richmond, were still in Danville. Only the Treasury's bullion, under the naval cadets, had been sent on to Charlotte. Admiral Semmes, formal and austere, commanded the defense composed of some naval units from

Richmond and a little infantry. Even a strong cavalry raid could take the temporary capital.

Then, on Monday, came the word that Lee had surrendered the day before. Less than ten thousand Confederates reached Appomattox Court House with guns in their hands.

If, as Davis said, this was "the largest and finest army of the Confederacy," its surrender removed the last legitimate prop to his delusions. As General Wise said, Lee was the country to his army. Even if he were less to the rest of the people, certainly there could be no country without his army. Had Davis been realistically representing a people, here was the moment to recognize that their country had exhausted its capacities to defend.

Any armed resistance from here on could not rationally be regarded as a part of the original experiment.

But Davis was living in a historic drama, of which he was the central character, and the needless killing of human beings had no more reality to him than off-stage sound effects of battles. His factual problem was to find a safer "capital."

Lee had retreated on a line parallel to the Virginia-Carolina border, and the point he reached was not as far west as Danville, on the border. Also east of Danville, in North Carolina, Sherman was almost as close to the border from the south as was Grant from the north. The point farthest away from the two Yankee armies was Charlotte, almost at the southern border of North Carolina and well west of Sherman's path. They would start for there, by way of Greensboro.

When the government officials and property were again jammed into a southbound train, the element of flight was apparent in the confusion. The evacuation of Richmond had involved a plan, however farfetched and desperate. Actions had some reason. Without Lee's army there could be no reasonable plan. In Danville the rush to the depot was a stampede to escape.

Instead of troop units preparing a military evacuation, groups of individual soldiers fought and pushed to leave with the officials. All during the rainy night troops drifted into the city. There were some organized remnants from little forces about the state and some stragglers from Lee who had not stayed on for the kill. Some honestly wanted to join Joe Johnston and carry on the fight, and others vaguely wanted to reach Kirby Smith's faraway forces in Texas. But those bringing disorder to the crowded depot just wanted to get out of Danville.

Others joined the mob that started looting the government stores. Pushing through the lawless crowds, every kind of official petitioned

Davis and the Cabinet for places on the overloaded cars. More cars were added over the protests of the trainmen.

Burton Harrison, having placed Mrs. Davis in Charlotte, had returned to help the other member of the family off. Over his objections a general in charge of torpedoes got in the President's car along with his daughters and piled his torpedo equipment in another car.

Through the torpedoes Harrison got rid of the famous Spencer, a roguish Negro who had attached himself to the President during the war and had taken to calling him "Marse Jeff," which of course no one else did. "Inefficient, unsightly and unclean," he loved to answer the doorbell and tell visitors Mr. Davis was not at home. Even to friends he would insist, "The President 'clines to see you." Harrison put him in the car with the torpedoes, and, when Spencer discovered that, he mournfully announced that "Marse Jeff" would have to get along without him.

Even without Spencer more cars were added on until the distracted trainmen said the train would never move. Near midnight, when it finally left, the engine promptly broke down. Frantic trainmen started moving up another.

In the President's car there was none of the calm resolution with which they left Richmond. The calmness was of gloom, as the men sat, silent and depressed, waiting for the train to start. There was only one sound in the dusty stillness. One of the torpedo general's daughters, seizing her moment to be charming to the President, chattered steadily in a high, gay voice.

Finally the train lurched ahead. The few members of the Confederate government, jerked across the dark countryside, left, without knowing when, the soil of the battleground of Virginia. . . .

2

As the train rattled toward Greensboro a trestle over which it passed was burned right behind them. Stoneman's Union cavalry had closed in from the west.

When rumors of the cavalry reached Charlotte, Mrs. Davis moved her family farther south—into western South Carolina, the line beyond and untouched by Sherman's march. She was accompanied by the sixty naval cadets under Captain Parker. They had stored the Treasury's money in the Charlotte mint. Now they moved it and drew rations of flour and meat from the Charlotte navy yard. Some of the naval workers joined them.

At Chester, South Carolina, Mrs. Davis visited her old friend, Mrs Chesnut, but she was afraid to tarry. There was no railroad ahead, and the party pushed along the muddy road in wagons. At night, when Mrs. Davis's ambulance stuck in a boggy stretch, she got out and walked five miles with the baby in her arms and mud over her shoetops. They camped at night, and the ladies slept in a church—Captain Parker in the pulpit.

When they reached Abbeville, Mrs. Davis and her children and two servants were guests in the handsome home of Major Burt. Untouched physically by the war, the people of the little town "lived in great comfort," and the homes were strung with wistaria and honeysuckle and yellow jasmine. Varina received her warmest welcome among those South Carolinians.

There her escort of naval cadets left, taking the government bullion on to Washington, Georgia, just south of the South Carolina border. Captain Parker was becoming very anxious about this responsibility and was trying to find someone to turn the money over to.

He had left over $70,000 back in Greensboro for the government, but when he tried to wire there for directions, he discovered that Stoneman's cavalry had raided Salisbury, between where he and the Cabinet were. Furthermore the raid had just missed his treasure train. The naval officer hardly knew which way to turn and could find no one to advise him.

In her comfortable retreat Mrs. Davis heard the rumors of Lee's surrender confirmed, and she wrote her husband it "fills me with horror." Her letter was jerky, full of oddments of news about the children, about old enemy Wigfall and broken hero Hood leaving together, bound for Texas. She said, "May God in His mercy keep you safe and raise up defenders for our bleeding country. . . ."

3

In Greensboro, North Carolina, the President's party encountered no welcome like that at Danville. Far from feeling honored at the presence of the Confederate government, the people felt uneasy and wished them gone. Greensboro was the center of a Union stronghold; the Confederates in the section realized the war was over when Lee surrendered, and the citizens in general were afraid of their homes being burned if they sheltered the government.

John Taylor Wood, the naval adventurer, had engaged a house for his wife, and, over the protests of his landlord, he arranged a room there for the President. Wood was a nephew of Davis's first wife. While engaged in his coastal raiding, Wood had been officially a colonel on the President's staff. Now Wood acted as an aide, along with Colonel Johnston, the son of Albert Sidney Johnston, and Colonel Lubbock, Reagan's house guest from Texas.

For Johnston and Lubbock and the cabinet members there was no house. They crowded into a leaky boxcar and ate their meals out of tin cups, using pocketknives for utensils. Under such physical circumstances their attention became centered on the immediate adjustment, and they all rallied. Benjamin started with humorous observations, and Mallory and Lubbock followed with stories. Without straining, they made of their poor shelter a little world of cheerfulness and charm.

By nightfall of the second day they settled down to the grave business at hand when they went to Davis's room on the second floor in Wood's house, there to meet Joe Johnston and Beauregard. The matter of continued armed resistance had to be put before the men in charge of it—two of Davis's bitterest enemies, both of whom he had humiliated by removing them from command.

The small room contained only a bed and a few chairs, with writing materials on a table, and John Reagan never found a cabinet meeting so funereal. The President tried to brighten it, as was his habit at the opening of meetings, with general conversation "introducing some anecdote or interesting episode."

The pleasantries were not entered into by Joe Johnston, tart and aloof, or Beauregard, the picture soldier, his dark face set as he stared at the President with brooding eyes.

Soon Davis got to the point of their situation. He thought the disasters were not "fatal." He said, "I think we can whip the enemy yet, if our people will turn out." But fast action was necessary. "We have not a day to lose."

Neither Johnston nor Beauregard answered. No one in the room spoke. The President then said, "We should like to hear your views, General Johnston."

There was no equivocation from the old enemy now. His voice terse, Johnston said, "My views are, sir, that our people are tired of war, feel themselves whipped, and will not fight. Our country is overrun. . . ."

As Johnston went on, he warmed to the subject, and his tone and manner became almost spiteful as he jerked out his words. "My men are daily deserting in large numbers, and are taking my artillery teams to aid their escape to their homes. Since Lee's defeat they regard the war as at an end. . . ."

[413]

Davis sat motionless, staring at a piece of paper which he folded and unfolded. The general whom he had so often put in his place was letting him have it now. . . .

"If I march out of North Carolina, her people will all leave my ranks. It will be the same . . ." in other states . . . "and I shall expect to retain no man beyond the byroad or cowpath that leads to his home. . . ."

Then the peppery, high-bred little man completed the thrust. "We may, perhaps, obtain terms which we ought to accept."

There was a pause, and then Davis, still without moving, said in a low voice, "What do you say, General Beauregard?"

"I concur in all General Johnston has said."

There was a longer pause, while Davis stared at the piece of paper in his hand. Then, in the same low voice, he asked Johnston how did he propose to obtain any terms with the Union.

Johnston replied confidently that Sherman would treat with him. Davis was skeptical of that, but he said, "We can try it."

There in the house where they were unwelcome, in the little town where they were unwanted, the Confederate Cabinet gave Joe Johnston the authority to treat with Sherman on terms of peace based upon the surrender of all armed forces in the South.

When Johnston and Beauregard left, to ride east to meet Sherman, the President and his followers turned to their only remaining function —keeping safe.

In leaving Salisbury the party had to take to the roads. Some tired cavalry had joined them at Greensboro, and these would act as escort. Quartermaster stores and records were packed in wagons, and the troopers had to protect these from mobs from Greensboro. The people had already stolen horses and food, and they were after the money that was supposed to be somewhere around. Of the money the naval cadets had left at Greensboro, only $35,000 remained with the Cabinet. The sum of $39,000 was set aside to pay Johnston's army.

Davis's chief clerk, Micajah Clark, finally arranged a train of wagons and ambulances. Dibrell's cavalry took another road, a Kentucky cavalry company went ahead as scouts and guides, and the President's party headed south over roads turned into mires by recent rains.

Breckinridge had joined the Cabinet, catching up with them after leaving Lee's army shortly before its surrender. Only he and Mallory and Reagan rode. Jefferson Davis felt sick and went in an ambulance, as did the ailing Secretary Trenholm.

In another ambulance was a gay party of non-riders—Benjamin

and his suave brother-in-law, the handsome Attorney-General George Davis, and old Adjutant General Cooper. It was a sorry ambulance they drew, and a sorrier team—old dirty gray horses with spots like fly bites. But Benjamin had never been more cheerful.

The horses heaved and staggered. The ambulance sank deep, then lurched ahead. Its spasmodic movements became fewer and fewer. Finally Burton Harrison rode back to investigate and found it bogged down in a mudhole.

George Davis and Benjamin's brother-in-law were shoving fence rails under the wheels to give it a perch when the driver laid the whip across the horses. From inside the ambulance came the glow of Benjamin's cigar and his dauntless voice rolled through the night:

> "Lead out the pageant: sad and slow,
>   As fits an universal woe,
>   Let the long, long procession go . . ."

Harassed Harrison went back and found a bivouacked artillery unit and persuaded them to come and help the ambulance out of the ditch. The soldiers lent their teams, and the ambulance pitched through the mud. . . .

> ". . . and let the mournful martial music blow;
>   The last great Englishman is low. . . ."

4

In Charlotte the people were not so unfriendly as in Greensboro, but the welcome mat was not exactly out either. For quarters, the President and his staff had to accept the hospitality of a gayish bachelor named Bates, an agent for the Southern Express Company, the chief distinction of whose home was its well-stocked sideboard. The President's secretary thought the raffish atmosphere unsuited to Mr. Davis.

Harrison himself went off with Benjamin and his brother-in-law, Jules de St. Martin. They were being beautifully entertained by a fellow Jew, Weil, who had been extremely gracious to Mrs. Davis.

Davis was curiously cheerful while they waited for word from the Sherman-Johnston conference. On the way from Greensboro they had received a wire from Joe Johnston, who, on second thought, had decided it would be a good idea to have some of the Cabinet along for his peace conference with Sherman. Reagan and Breckinridge went. While Sherman might refuse to treat with Reagan, Breckinridge could confer (as he did) in his capacity as a general.

While they waited, the cheer of everyone else was dispersed by the worst news since Lee's surrender—Lincoln's assassination. The Confederates were not then certain they would be blamed, but they did know that Lincoln's humanity and moderation would have provided a check on the radicals. Now not only was he lost but the vengeance-minded in the North were given a theme, and Andrew Johnson, the anti-bourbon Southerner, particularly hated Jefferson Davis and all the concepts he embodied.

Then Reagan and Breckinridge returned, bringing the peace terms from Sherman and Johnston. Though changes had been made, Sherman—once the war was over—offered surprisingly generous terms. Benjamin, who thought they were the best terms that could be hoped for, summarized them as:

. . . an agreement that if the Confederate states will cease to wage war for the purpose of establishing a separate government, the United States will receive the several states back into the Union with their state governments unimpaired, with all their constitutional rights recognized, with protection for the persons and property of the people and with a general amnesty.

Once an offer came, the Cabinet showed clearly they wanted to accept. Davis could not continue armed resistance against the will of the generals and the Cabinet, but he still kept his eye on posterity. Calling a meeting in the directors' room of a bank, he asked each of the members to put his opinion in writing. Judge Reagan stated his the most frankly and fully.

He gave a résumé of their hopeless situation—the loss of ordnance and munitions and military stores, the end of "our naval establishment," the fall of workshops and depots at Columbus and Macon in Georgia, at Selma and Montgomery in Alabama (during their flight), the inadequacy of the little army west of the Mississippi, the closing of the ports to outside help and the loss of the purchasing power of the currency, the hostility to impressment at home and their inability to prevent armies from melting away in the field. Means were lacking even to continue the functions of the governmental departments.

"The country is worn down by a brilliant and heroic, but exhausting and bloody struggle of four years." He did not trust the enemy, "who will now add the consciousness of power to their love of dominion and greed of gain," but, considering "the general welfare of the people," it would be better for Davis to assume the responsibility to end the struggle without referring the matter to the separate states.

The other members agreed that Davis should act as commander in chief and personally effect the end of the Confederacy by acceptance of the Johnston-Sherman agreement.

The decision he dreaded more than death was in Davis's hands only a moment. Then came the word that the Andrew Johnson government in Washington repudiated Sherman's peace. Joe Johnston must surrender his army on the same terms as Lee—the men to be paroled, officers to retain their side arms and the cavalry their mounts, which were personal property.

This rejection of terms removed the last hope from the members of the Cabinet. Now they knew they were literally fugitives from the law, and a law of vengeance. They could only surrender like the soldiers, but without the soldiers' parole. Northern newspapers made it all too plain they were regarded as criminals.

The Confederacy ceased for them when they signed the agreement to the Sherman-Johnston terms. From then on, their decisions revolved around their personal fates. They could try to escape, or surrender, or remain with the President with his forlorn hope of reaching Kirby Smith's band in Texas—though, in advocating surrender, Breckinridge had said if the fighting continued it would lose "the dignity of regular warfare . . . degenerate into an irregular and secondary stage out of which greater evils flow to the South than to the enemy."

Attorney-General George Davis made his decision first. He left them at Charlotte to look after his motherless children and his property in Wilmington. Maybe he could join them later. (Later he escaped to the Florida coast, where he decided to surrender and, before he did, was arrested.)

The others decided to stay with Davis through the next move, farther south. The President seemed bright and relieved. He talked of horses and dogs, Byron and Scott, and to his young secretary he said, "I *cannot* feel like a beaten man."

Wholly detached from the composition of the Confederate territory and lost in his personal drama, Davis had attained the ultimate in his concept: he was the old feudal leader hunted across his own land while attended by his loyal followers. From that nucleus he would arise triumphant. For less selfish reasons than Bonnie Prince Charlie, he was equally indifferent to what suffering his hegira would bring upon the people. His heart pure, he ruled by the divine right of personal honor.

Before leaving Charlotte he wrote Joe Johnston to ignore the surrender and, instead, disband his infantry that they might re-form elsewhere and send his cavalry southward to the chieftain. But Johnston, not removed from humanity by a fixation, ignored the order and surrendered. (Among the paroled was "Brigadier General" Raphael Semmes, the old sea raider. He was hunted out later and arrested for his "crimes.")

For this surrender Johnston, the ancient enemy, was listed in Davis's books as a traitor. But the lack of Johnston's troops did not materially affect his plans. On his southward flight he was bearing westward. Eventually he would turn west and make for the Confederate forces in Texas, there to carry on the dream.

He wrote his wife:

> . . . this is not the fate to which I invited you when the future was rose-colored to us both; but I know that you will bear it even better than myself, and that of us two, I alone will ever look back reproachfully on my past career. . . . There may be better things in store for us than are now in view, but my love is all I have to offer, and that has the value of a thing long possessed and sure not to be lost. . . .

5

Her husband's letter heartened Mrs. Davis, in Abbeville, as she prepared to continue her journey. On cheap, black-bordered paper, Varina wrote him that she was going on, hoping to reach the Florida coast and a boat out. Major and Mrs. Burt, her hosts and friends, begged her to stay, but she was afraid the Yankees would burn their home. "I can think of no better use for it," Major Burt replied.

However, Varina had been made fearful by the rumors of Yankee troops' carryings-on, and she was determined to escape the country. Burton Harrison had been sent back by Davis to look after his family, and he had to borrow a horse and wagon to get Mrs. Davis south of the Savannah River, to Washington, Georgia.

In the little town of Washington the party met two officers, from Mississippi and Louisiana, returning to the army from furloughs. One of them lent Mrs. Davis his light covered wagon, and both joined the party. There were three Kentuckians also acting as escort, and the teamsters of the four wagons were soldiers.

They got good wagons from the quartermasters in Washington, and in those the men piled Mrs. Davis's luggage, two light tents for the ladies and children, cooking utensils, food and forage, and muskets and ammunition. Before they left town young Harrison drew some gold for Mrs. Davis and $110 for himself.

Bob Toombs, their old friend and later enemy, came out to see them off. He wore an ill-fitting black Websterian coat, a shabby broad-brimmed hat, and looked more rebellious than ever. Toombs knew it was all over, but he had no notion of surrendering himself.

They left him there in the public square of the little town where he lived, and the cavalcade moved southward over the country road, heading for Florida.

6

When the Presidential party left Charlotte, with a train of wagons, the cavalry escort numbered about three thousand from assorted commands—virtually the last organized troops east of the Mississippi, as Dick Taylor and Forrest were only days away from surrender in Alabama. The largest force was under Dibrell, an old Forrest commander; there was a brigade under South Carolinian Ferguson; and from the small force from southwestern Virginia, Vaughan's and Duke's brigades were under the department commander, gigantic General Echols.

Echols's troops, infantry and cavalry, had been moving for a juncture with Lee when they received the news of Appomattox. The troops were offered an option of going on or disbanding. The infantry and half the cavalry gave up. Echols brought the two cavalry brigades, less than a thousand men without artillery and some mounted on mules, to Charlotte. They had to evade Stoneman's Yankee cavalry to get there. Minor skirmishes showed the men to be of low morale, and the mules were poor animals to fight from.

When these troops left Charlotte with Dibrell's and Ferguson's cavalry, the horsemen were soon depressed by the slowness of the wagon trains. The troopers were mostly raiders, accustomed to mobility, and an "impedimental procession of ambulances with dressing cases on wheels" was not their idea of the way to move from one point to the other with any resolution. The men knew the war was over, and they were continuing mainly to secure the President's safety against the raiding Yankees who were reported everywhere—but this way seemed asking for trouble.

Almost as bad as the raiders were their own unorganized soldiers. Some deserters, some parolees, some going home without parole, they swarmed the countryside, plagued the quartermaster and commissary trains, and brought confusion to the otherwise orderly if slow movement.

Once in South Carolina, in the fat, unharmed countryside west of Sherman's torch, the President's party encountered warm and hospitable people, and the flight assumed the appearance of a triumphal march. Invitations flowed in. Ladies wanted to meet the notables, especially President Davis, and the flower-strewn path was like Richmond four years before.

Jefferson Davis, in his best mood, was gracious to all, and the soldiers found him a pleasant and noble-spirited gentleman. As in Richmond, Benjamin was the belle of the ball. Even the tough-bitten troopers were fascinated by him—though the officers felt that nobody in the President's group, except Breckinridge, knew what it was all about.

Secretary Trenholm, his illness increasing, dropped out en route. He joined his family, was arrested and sent to the Charleston city jail. Because of his ill-health he was released by a Union officer under oath to remain in town, then rearrested by the radicals and imprisoned.

John Reagan was Acting Secretary of the Treasury when the party reached charming Abbeville, almost on the Georgia border, a week later. Davis was put in the big, columned home of Major Burt, where his wife had stayed, and in its flowered garden, in the mellow heat of early May, the illusion was sustained.

He called a meeting of his Cabinet and his military leaders to plan for the dash across the Lower South to Texas. From the old, great days, only ugly, dyspeptic Bragg was on hand—a recent joiner of the party. For the Secretaries of War who had enjoyed their hour, there was now General Breckinridge, heavy in alcohol, who, on being questioned for advice by a soldier, had answered, "My young friend, I advise you to return to your home in Richmond by the nearest available route."

For the Lees and the Stonewall Jacksons, the Longstreets and Joe Johnstons, there were a handful of tired cavalry raiders, previously unknown to the Executive—Dibrell and Ferguson and Vaughan, young Colonel Breckinridge and young Basil Duke.

In the late afternoon they gathered in a big downstairs room, with a window opening west over the garden. Davis, in his euphoria, was at his social best—affable, graceful, humorous. After he saw that everyone was at his ease, the President turned to the subject of continuing their struggle. Now living the role of the hunted patriot—Alfred the Briton, Bruce the Scot, O'Neill the Celt—he said, "I feel that I ought to do nothing now without the advice of my military chiefs," and he gave an arch smile.

The few tired horse soldiers were amazed at this address to themselves. They gaped at one another as the thin, aged man went on, enrapt, comparing their situation to the Revolutionary heroes. "Even if the troops with me be all that I can for the present rely on, three thousand brave men are enough for a nucleus around which the whole people will rally when the panic which now afflicts them has passed away."

It was a bad moment for the cavalrymen. They had to tell the truth, and nobody wanted to be the first. Unlike his Cabinet or the traditional followers in Richmond, someone was the first. Somebody among the five blurted it out, and then they all came in.

This was no panic among the people. They were worn out. It would be the cruelest injustice to the people to ask them to struggle on with no means to support warfare. Their devastated country would be further injured if guerrillas operated from it. Even for the soldiers, the officers felt it wrong to ask them to go on when they would be no more than brigands and lose what chance they had of returning to their homes.

Under this fervent but friendly tirade Davis showed none of the control he had used against Joe Johnston's spitefulness. He asked the men abruptly why they went on fighting if they were without hope.

"To see to your safety, sir," they said.

Davis turned very pale and sat in silence. The poetic drama was being stricken from him by these strange, unshaven men in gray. There were no followers for the Confederate Washington. There was to be no Valley Forge.

"Then," he said bitterly, "all is indeed lost."

He arose, but he was so weak that he staggered, and Breckinridge took hold of his arm. Bragg, the old favorite, had said nothing. He said nothing now, nor did Breckinridge.

In the heavy silence Davis straightened and walked out alone. The delusion was over. What was left?

He found Mallory and talked with him. Mallory had plans for boats on the Florida coast in which he could escape. Davis answered him coldly that he would never leave Confederate soil as long as a regiment remained on it. . . .

Those regiments were fast dispersing. Mainly their minds were on the Confederate gold.

Poor Captain Parker and his naval cadets, after wandering around Georgia with the responsibility of the Confederate Treasury, returned to Abbeville. There, after storing it in a public warehouse, Captain Parker at last turned his burden over to the government.

Mallory had previously given orders to disband the naval cadet corps. Captain Parker now gave each his orders which read: ". . . You are hereby detached from the Naval School and leave is granted you to visit your home. . . ." From Reagan, Acting Secretary of the

Treasury, Captain Parker drew $40 for each boy from the gold they had saved. They never surrendered and were never paroled.

They started their walk back to Richmond, some with their Negro servants behind them. It was a long walk for those boys. Any wagons were going the other way. Families sometimes gave them a meal. Sometimes in town they would buy food and cook it at campfires. Some soldiers fell in with them, dropped off. The band dwindled as the boys turned off to their homes.

When one boy alone reached the south side of the James River, there was only a pontoon bridge across. Where all the warehouses had loomed along the river and canal Basin, there were only blackened walls of buildings against the sky. Crossing the bridge, he was checked by a Yankee guard. Turning up Main Street hill, he walked between the charred debris of what had been banks and stores and commission houses; and farther up, near the Capitol, he saw the remnants of what had been homes. Men and women were scavenging in the wreckage. The streets had been taken over by strangers and Negroes. Then suddenly he turned into a side street as a Union band came playing toward him.

In the troops behind that band, Abner Small, of Maine, felt particularly triumphant. He could see the barred windows of Libby, where he had been a prisoner. As they passed the street where the young naval cadet hurried away from them, Small said, "Our band crashed gaily midst the ruins."

7

When the President's party was ready to push on south from Abbeville, Davis said to one of the midshipmen who had not left town, "I am *very* sorry Mr. Mallory gave you that order [to disband]." The boy understood the regret when he saw the demoralized cavalry selling and throwing away their arms. He thought they were not there to protect the treasure, but to get it.

Generals Dibrell and Duke defended their men, but the impression among the civilians was that the troopers were after the money. In any event, when the party moved from Abbeville across the Savannah River to Washington, Georgia, General Breckinridge—in command of the armed escort—paid out $108,000 at $26.25 in silver per man. This was $26.25 more than anybody in Lee's army got.

On the way from Abbeville, Davis lost the official mistress. When Benjamin realized the ship was sinking, he decided not to go down with it. That might be required of the captain, but there were other worlds for the cheerful sybarite. He had given everything he had when the President's beclouded irresolution had not affected his personal well-being. Now, seeing that his friend's slowness and indecision could only end in capture, he took a cordial leave after breakfast at a farmhouse.

Unable to ride horseback, Benjamin hired a carriage in which he passed himself off variously as a farmer and a Frenchman. After adventures as hazardous as any on which he had sent his agents, he reached the Florida coast. In his middle fifties, plump and self-indulgent, a stranger to exercise, he took off in an open boat for the Bimini Islands. Eventually he reached England and became as great a barrister in London as he had been a lawyer in Washington. . . .

When an old Confederate acquaintance met him in England some years later, he barely referred to his experiences in the Confederacy. Only two things seemed to have embittered him—the loss of his wine cellar and the Yankees' burning of his law library.

Mallory also suffered the loss of his library burned. He gave up the experiment shortly after Benjamin. Phlegmatically, he left the party at Washington, Georgia. He went off to join his family at La Grange, where he had sent them before the evacuation of Richmond. There he was arrested as if, like his sea raiders, he was prepared to shoot it out to the end. The unwilling Rebel was hurried from his home without a chance even to pack his clothes.

By the time Mallory abandoned hope in the President's personal cause, the conglomerate residue of the Confederacy's supporting services had dwindled away. The ranking quartermasters and commissary officers, Adjutant General Cooper and then ill-favored Bragg, junior officers and clerks, soldiers and teamsters, had dropped off or disintegrated into wagon rats. The highest quartermaster officer was a captain, Watson Van Benthuysen, and his command consisted of two brothers and five Marylanders. Nothing organized was left except the demoralized cavalry.

Then, in the environs of Washington, Georgia—a settlement formed by land grants to Revolutionary veterans—this surviving guard dissolved. When Davis sent word to the cavalry camp for troops to reconnoiter in his front, where Yankee raiders were reported, the cavalry officers were unwilling to order their men to more fighting. General Breckinridge sent back word, "Nothing can be done with the bulk of this command. It has been with difficulty that anything has been kept in shape. . . ." He thought a few hundred men could be depended on to continue southward, for the Trans-Mississippi. . . .

When the five cavalry brigades originally joined Davis, the men did not realize the extent of the Confederate collapse. This was borne upon them as they accompanied the President's party south, when they also realized that such a method of travel would inevitably involve them with Union cavalry and cause more useless fighting.

More of the men would have felt obligated to go on as the loyal band of Davis's concept if he had shown a clear purpose to escape. The men felt he could have escaped. But this dawdling along ten miles a day, with stops to hold conferences, showed a vague and irresolute purpose that completed their demoralization.

If the troops had not assumed charge of the money, their disintegration would probably have been more gradual. But once they had a chance at a little stake, no matter how small, they wanted to preserve life and fortune. With their $26.25, the troops surrendered largely as units, preserving some of the dignity of their commands. They were paroled as soldiers and did not degenerate into armed bands of brigands.

With the last organized troops gone, the officials disposed of the remaining Confederate wealth. Eighty-six thousand dollars was put in a false-bottomed buggy and started on its way to England, to be credited to Fraser, Trenholm & Co.—apparently for the government to draw on when they reached Texas.

Six thousand and forty dollars was divided among Davis's four aides —Lubbock and Sidney Johnston's son, John Taylor Wood and Charles Thorburn, a naval purchasing agent and blockade runner who had joined the staff on the way. Three hundred dollars was divided among the few Marines who had hung onto the party from Richmond, and the same amount among Captain Campbell's Kentucky scouts. Ten picked men from this party of scouts was all that remained as a military escort.

When these details had been arranged, General Breckinridge— Secretary of War and the last military commander—left the party. Taking $1,000 in gold, he rode off with a few hundred cavalry in an effort to mislead the Yankees.

Papers and Confederate notes had been burned along the way, and other papers hidden, and in Washington the President's message books were sewed in blankets and hidden. The last written order in those books was the appointment of the faithful Micajah Clark, who had brought the books from Richmond, as Acting Treasurer.

There was only one cabinet member left, John Reagan. Over his protests, $3,500 in gold was put in his saddlebags.

SPOTSWOOD HOTEL

Corner of Eighth and Main streets, where Mr. and Mrs. Davis first lived in Richmond, and center of early government activities. Lithograph by Simons & Grehen. Courtesy of Valentine Museum, Richmond, Virginia.

GARDEN VIEW OF THE HOME OF ELIZABETH VAN LEW, UNION SPY

The gallery faced directly south, where the garden fell away into a hill only a few blocks from Libby Prison. On the right of the walk, near the house, Miss Van Lew can be seen. Though the picture was taken some years after the war, her hair is still in ringlets and her sharp, alert features are unchanged. Photograph, courtesy of the Valentine Museum, Richmond, Virginia.

The vast train that had annoyed the cavalry was reduced to one wagon and two ambulances, under the charge of Micajah Clark, assisted by quartermaster captain Van Benthuysen and a guard of seven. The wagons contained, in addition to some personal baggage, the two boxes of bullion that had been with the President's party since Greensboro, North Carolina. With expenses paid from it on the way, this amounted then to about $25,000.

Raiding parties of Yankees were reported from all directions, and Davis's dilatory actions in getting started made everybody nervous. Davis's vague plans, to reach Texas by skirting the Lower South, were retarded by his bestowing presidential courtesies on his admirers in the little Georgia town and complicated by a desire to reach his wife.

The younger men in the party, aside from the few committed to guard Davis personally, were driven by a very clear purpose to reach the Florida coast. Armed stragglers were everywhere, excited by the rumors that ballooned the Confederate treasure, as silver was heard jingling in the pockets of the troopers. Even if bands of marauders could be fought off, they would certainly attract the Yankees.

But they all had to wait for Davis to finish his portrayal of the poised leader taking to the hills.

Shortly after the party left Washington, Union troops came in— white and colored. They posted placards offering $100,000 reward for the capture of Jefferson Davis, the assassinator of Lincoln.

The soldiers made a considerable nuisance of themselves in the little town and rushed into Bob Toombs's house while he was sitting in the front room waiting to be called to dinner. Toombs got out the back door and, while his wife stalled the Yankees, mounted a horse and rode away. He showed that escape was possible if one was determined on it. He hid about Georgia for some while and then went to Europe.

8

On the road going south the little wagon train under Micajah Clark branched off to make for Florida, where they would rejoin the President's party later.

This party was now reduced to Reagan and four aides, Captain Campbell and a few soldiers. Moving directly south towards the Florida border, they could have made it if Jefferson Davis had not grown alarmed for his wife.

Her party, under Burton Harrison, had left Washington not long before the President reached there. The country through which she traveled was infested with marauding bands composed of Union strag-glers and Confederates on the way home. Most of the Rebs were after quartermaster stores and mules, but the more vicious bands were look-ing for the "treasure train." Any of them could have overpowered the small group protecting Varina Davis.

At nightfall, after a hard ride, word reached Davis of a specific band ahead, in the direction of his family. Captain Campbell said the horses were too tired to push on, and Davis and his personal party left the last of their armed escort. It was a bright moonlit night, and they found the darkened camp off the road. As Davis and his aides approached it, Burton Harrison's alarmed but determined voice called out, "Who's there?"

It was a welcome sound to the husband, sick with exhaustion and fear. He found the camp arranged for defense—the wagons forming a corral with the animals inside, and the few soldiers sleeping where they could quickly move into action. They had been taking turns at guard, and it happened to be Harrison's turn when Davis arrived.

Mrs. Davis was nearly exhausted from the journey and the alarms, but she did not want her husband to jeopardize his own safety by stay-ing with her. He determined, however, to remain with her party until they were through this worst belt of stragglers. Also, Davis was pretty well done in.

The next day, when the two parties joined, Davis rode in an ambu-lance. The oldest child, Maggie, kept looking at her parents with wor-ried intensity, but the headstrong younger children were very frolic-some. To quiet little Jeff, his father showed him how to shoot derringers at a target.

They stopped on the night of the ninth of May, near the town of Irwinsville, only sixty-five miles from Florida. The party camped in a pinewoods near a creek, and the staff understood that they were to leave Mrs. Davis that night and push on. But Davis had been warned of another marauding band near by, and he decided to stay with his family until that danger had passed.

By now it would appear that the deluded man, worn physically by his flight and confused by the successive psychological disasters, did not know what he was doing. He picketed his saddled horse near by, with holstered pistols on the saddle. He remained fully dressed—in boots and a velvet-collared gray frock coat, and Confederate gray waistcoat and trousers. Then he lay down to sleep in his wife's tent. Probably he and his staff intended an early start, but, with the general fatigue, the whole camp slept through the night—except for Thorburn. He left for the Florida coast, where he had arranged a boat for a passage west.

Before first light, John Taylor Wood and young Colonel Johnston were aroused by James Jones, the free Negro. He heard sounds as of men approaching cautiously. Fearing a marauders' raid, Johnston sent Jim to awaken the President, while he got up to pull on his boots.

Johnston started toward the campfire to ask the cook if he had heard anything. John Taylor Wood, who had been sleeping beside Johnston at the foot of a pine tree, got up more warily. By the time James Jones awakened the President, firing swept towards the camp on a rush of hoofs.

For a moment everyone was startled into confused action. The President looked out of the tent and called to his wife, "They are not marauders but Federal troops!"

Varina urged him to escape. He hesitated, loath to leave her. At that moment there was a sharp crackle of fire down the road, directed at the Yankees in the camp. The Union officer yelled at Burton Harrison, "Have you got any men?"

Harrison, either assuming that the new fire came from his teamster-soldiers or thinking to confuse the Union officer, said, "Certainly."

The Union troops turned to fight off the other party. Then Davis, having reached his decision, ran out of his tent towards his saddled horse.

For the before-dawn chill, he grabbed up a raglan cloak. In the darkness of the tent he took his wife's by mistake. Varina, seeing that he was bareheaded, threw a shawl across his head as he ran out.

One mounted soldier saw him and, raising his carbine, yelled, "Halt!"

Davis swerved towards the trooper, who—again calling "Halt!"—aimed his carbine. Mrs. Davis, suspecting that her husband intended to fight it out with the soldier, ran to Davis and threw her arms about him.

During the excitement John Taylor Wood slipped a couple of his twenty-dollar gold pieces to a guard and quietly walked off into the darkness of the wood. His naval raiding around the Bay country had him listed as a pirate, and they all feared his capture.

Colonel Lubbock was struggling with two soldiers who were trying to grab his saddlebags. They threatened to shoot him if he didn't turn them loose, and he shouted, "Shoot and be damned, but you'll not rob me while I'm alive and looking on!"

By then the Yankees had discovered that the shooting had come from another party of their own and the camp was filling with the soldiers. An officer took Reagan's cocked pistol from him and his saddlebags with the new $3,500 in gold in them. Lubbock, freed of his assailants, strolled over to where Davis was sitting on a log beside a campfire.

Already soldiers were pushing past, brushing Mrs. Davis aside as they burrowed into the tents to break open the trunks.

"This is a bad business," Lubbock said.

"I would have heaved the scoundrel off his horse as he came up," Davis said, "but she stopped me."

"It would have been useless."

Then Colonel Pritchard, commanding the Federal party, came towards them.

"Well, old Jeff," he said, "we've got you at last."

Jefferson Davis lost his temper and shouted, "The worst of all is that I should be captured by a band of thieves and scoundrels . . ." and he denounced the conduct of the soldiers to his wife.

Pritchard stiffened and said, "You're a prisoner and can afford to talk that way."

Then he informed Davis that his party was under arrest and should prepare to start moving.

The grinning soldiers took over as the little party was herded together for the journey back north. "Get a move on, Jeff," they said.

9

Less than forty miles away, Breckinridge, with his few hundred cavalrymen, heard the news. He disbanded the troops and, in adventures more hair-raising even than Benjamin's, made his way to the coast. There he met John Taylor Wood. With ingenuity, Herculean endurance, and unflagging will they reached Cuba in an open boat—avoiding Union boats and practicing piracy to make it. After being vastly feted in Cuba, Breckinridge went on to London.

Also to London came the last great Confederate raider, the *Shenandoah*. In the Pacific, Captain Waddell had not lowered his flag until summer, when the sad tidings reached him. Sailing his ship as an ordinary freighter, Waddell made for Liverpool and there surrendered to the British. They turned the ship over to the United States but would not assist in efforts to capture Captain Waddell.

Five thousand miles away, thirty-nine-year-old Kirby Smith surrendered the Army of the Trans-Mississippi and his own dictatorship, which—controlling cotton—had sustained his army in the field longer than any other.

Back in Florida the little group under Micajah Clark realized that no presidential party would ever come for the contents of their wagon and two ambulances. On a plantation near Gainesville, Florida, they buried two chests and a trunk in a cow stable and divided the $25,000 amongst themselves.

Chief clerk Clark wanted to pay the party only a reasonable amount for their risk and effort in handling it, and to send the rest to the Confederacy's credit in England. He was overruled by Watson Van Benthuysen, the quartermaster officer, who claimed there was no Confederate government and it was their privilege to divide the money between them.

What gave strength to his argument was the presence of his two brothers and the five Marylanders who had accompanied the train as guards. They all agreed with Van Benthuysen. Clark, the three Van Benthuysen brothers, and the five Maryland soldiers took about $2,000 each. Several hundred dollars more was distributed among cooks and Negro servants.

Clark did get the promise of the Van Benthuysens to hold for Mrs. Davis and her children 1,400 gold sovereigns, worth nearly $7,000. (Later, when Davis asked for the money for his trial defense, he was sent $1,500 of it.)

But the Van Benthuysen brothers, with their ten thousand in gold, were still not the big winners. Colonel John Pickett, the Kentucky revolutionary whose mission to Mexico had ended in farcical failure, proved more adept at handling his own fortunes than the Confederacy's.

During the evacuation of Richmond the wife of a State Department clerk took the diplomatic correspondence for safekeeping. Some years later Pickett appeared on the scene as agent for the sale of these papers to the United States and sold them for $75,000—in addition to being immortalized by the Library of Congress, which lists the Confederate diplomatic correspondence as the Pickett Papers.

The final gainer, rather petty, was Thomas Selfridge, rear admiral in the U. S. Navy. He had acted as agent for the United States in purchasing the papers, and, in appreciation of the $75,000, Colonel Pickett secretly gave him the great seal of the Confederacy—which the admiral secretly kept. When the silver seal (which, for want of a press, had been only an ornament) was traced to the admiral, he relinquished it to the city of Richmond for the consideration of $3,000—raised by private citizens who placed the handsome symbol of futility in the Confederate White House, where it still remains.

Down in Florida the Union troops who dogged the Clark-Van Benthuysen party fared much less well. After the Confederate guard disbanded, leaving the chests and trunk in the cow stable, Yankees grew hot on the scent of the "treasure," which by then U. S. Secretary of War Stanton evaluated at $13,000,000. Finally a determined searching party ran down the trunk and chests, and the officer in charge had his Negro troops carry them in triumph to Jacksonville for the officials to open.

There the officials beheld a collection of letters from various Confederates and some of the belongings which Mr. Davis had packed in Richmond for his flight—including the picture of himself and wife and one of General Lee.

10

Of the time when the captured presidential party started from the camp in the piny woods at dawn until finally they were on a boat that was to take President Davis to a Virginia prison, Mrs. Davis said, "The insults they heaped upon us were hard to bear. Of the horrors and sufferings of that journey it is difficult to speak."

With the passing of Lincoln and his concept of union, the spoilers took over the conquered; and the hatred—which had always motivated one segment—was allowed full expression. To make Jefferson Davis and his cause appear ridiculous, the avengers spread the story that he was captured in women's clothes. This passed into legend, despite the written denials of the soldiers who participated in the capture.

If Davis had lost his poise in the outrage of his capture, he regained it when he understood the nature of the "peace." Dignified and calm, he showed less strain than he had for years. Perhaps with him, as with an officer in his last cavalry escort, "the long agony was over."

His feudal dream had failed, but he had never faltered in his personal concept. Deluded as he had been by a sense of honor, with honor and with courage he entered his martyrdom.

Relatively short prison terms were served by the other captured Confederate leaders—including Vice-President Stephens, and Seddon and Hunter, who were first imprisoned in Libby in Richmond. Poor Walker was not bothered, nor was Memminger, whose Treasury Department the Unions probably considered no enemy.

But Davis was kept in irons in solitary confinement under the most brutal possible treatment in Fortress Monroe. He grew so ill and wasted that for a time he could not rise from his cell bunk. When a sympathetic doctor wanted to ameliorate his suffering, the doctor was removed. In his loneliness the broken man tamed a mouse.

After two years he was released on bail in Richmond, of U. S. Military District Number One. In the city, rebuilding from its ashes, under a Reconstruction government, Mr. and Mrs. Davis went to the same rooms in the Spotswood Hotel which they had occupied six years before.

The crowds lined his path again. The people did not dare cheer. Men uncovered their heads as he passed.

In that other lost spring, with sweet wistaria then as now in its brief, dramatic bloom, when he stood slender and erect, his brown hair brushed back from his fine forehead, Davis had personified the ideals in their experiment when it was young and lordly. Now, attenuated and white, his filmed eyes peering out from a mass of wrinkles, he embodied the failure of their legend.

During his imprisonment qualities of character emerged that had grown blurred and almost forgotten during the days of fury when he was forced to the hourly decisions of a task beyond him—perhaps beyond anyone. Certainly the task was beyond the powers of anyone committed to democratic methods in inflexible interpretations of honor and constitutionality.

Of them all, on both sides, the tortured dreamer most steadfastly held to the concept by which he offered himself to history. He took his pose on a page already fading, and only heroism in action could stand out against the shadowy background of defeat. It was his tragedy that he wanted that kind of action himself. . . .

While waiting for his trial, Davis visited the Confederate colony in Canada, which centered around the home of James Mason. Mason's fellow commissioner, Slidell, had written him that he would never return.

"I am sick, sick at heart." To make ends meet, the old political intriguer and manipulator of fortunes moved to a cheaper apartment and sold his library. "I little thought when I left the Confederacy that the time could arrive when I should be compelled to make these calculations."

When general amnesty was declared for Confederates in 1868, the little Canadian colony dwindled away. James Mason had no desire to come back to where his house had been destroyed and "the graves of my parents desecrated," but as he weakened with age he did not want to leave his family in a foreign land. "I feel that I ought to take you

[431]

back to your own people." In the twilight of his life he passed the time quietly in the companionship of his brother-in-law, Adjutant General Cooper.

Davis, who was never brought to trial, was freed in the general amnesty. Against all the urging of his friends, he would never ask for pardon. He could never have explained why as simply as did Bob Toombs.

That old Rebel returned to the United States and insisted on remaining unreconstructed. When asked why he did not seek pardon, he bellowed, with his waning passion, "Pardon for what? I have not pardoned you all yet."

Bibliography: How It Happened

IN LISTING a bibliography, a writer does not necessarily explain his emphasis or original compulsion, or whatever response caused his particular use of available material. As reference books, John Esten Cooke's could scarcely be listed, yet reading in childhood his *Lee* and *Jackson, Surry of Eagle's Nest,* and *Wearing of the Gray* stimulated a reading interest in a subject which had been in my consciousness as long as I can remember.

As I lived near the house of Miss Van Lew, the Union spy, who had then only recently died, my first bogeymen were conjured out of the sinister secrets still locked within its walls. The first school I attended was in a building formerly used as a Confederate hospital (Bellevue), and on the park where I played, construction work on the site of the Chimborazo Hospital sent us digging for bones and buttons and belt buckles. The first shotgun I fired was aimed by a former scout of Jeb Stuart who, when directing my eye to a stump, said, "Imagine that's a Yankee."

Bedtime stories of my grandmother and Negro nurse were of the plantation between Richmond and Petersburg, where they had lived as young girls before and during the war; from where four brothers had gone to the armies and one of whom, a chemist, in Richmond's Company F, experimented on meat substitutes for the Confederate Army and later for the people of Richmond.

A counterpoint to these impressions received without selectivity came in later years when, in living in New York City, I met the professional Southerner who always seems at his egregious worst away from home. Yet, even at home, I discovered he lived in a pride-bound ignorance of the nature of his region's past.

My first conscious effort, begun over ten years ago and not for this specific book, was to evaluate this past as objectively as is possible for a citizen of a geographic area which, as a result of a violent dislocation to its civilization, suffered a regional psychosis.

In the study, beginning with a physical city, my first guide remained my best—my father, now dead. In the changes of the expanding city he knew every old section and site, what each had been used for, when and how each changed, and which remained unchanged. Even today, in modern Richmond, the general geography of downtown is the same and, though obscured by the gas stations and movie houses and characterless buildings of a new era, the old places can still be found.

Along with a city went the study of the general background of the country, funneling down into the Confederacy. The bulk of that reading was done prior to work directly for this book and left, as did childhood experiences, a total impression.

For this book I am not listing general material which formed that impression—like the books of Adams, the Beards, Bowers, Commager, Sandburg, and the like—but only those that were referred to during this specific work. In that way I list Schlesinger and Randall, because they happened to appear during this period of work and were fresh for any reference required. While Dixon Wecter's *Hero in America* could not be listed in this bibliography, its basic idea was provocative, as perhaps with other books that do not come to mind.

Similarly, on military material nothing is listed that was not used definitely for this book—except the books on Richmond troops, which I think fair to list, as each contributed to the total picture of Richmond under the impact of war, to the composite story of the men in the Army of Northern Virginia and their reaction to the changing fortunes. Of the military books listed, each either treated of the relation between a general and the government or was used as a basis for the military campaigns which affected the government.

On the Navy, I read everything I could find on the Confederate side, and listed only those from which material was used. I do not list Soley, for the U. S. Navy, because, after checking him for facts, little from his work was actually used in this book. Scharf was the main source on the Confederate Navy.

For the books listed, it is inevitable that those must be included which contributed only a stray paragraph, an oddment of a fact, or contributed to some particular background. However, it is at least possible to point out the material most depended upon in the larger phases of the book.

For life in Richmond, the most constant references were the women's diaries, especially Mrs. Chesnut's and Mrs. Putnam's; Jones's *War Clerk's Diary* and to a much less extent De Leon's frivolous recollections; the newspapers and the Valentine Museum, where Mrs. Catterall offered every courtesy.

For Jefferson Davis, the most rewarding were Mrs. Davis's memoirs, McElroy and Winston, Dunbar Rowland and Eron Rowland on Mr. and Mrs. Davis. Davis's own book merely indicates the type of man he was, and is largely a defense. For the White House, nothing compares with the White House as it is today as the Confederate Museum, every facility of which was made available by Miss India Thomas.

For Benjamin, Robert Douthat Meade was the best source and most personal books on the period contain references. For Benjamin's work in the State Department, and for all Confederate diplomacy, I am heavily indebted to Professor Owsley.

For finance, I depended largely on Schwab, and for the physical Confederate currency . . . well, I have some, and a friend had a lot more.

August Dietz, Sr., was the only source on the post office, aside from Reagan, and Hendricks for Brown and Vance. Volume One, *Official Records,* was the chief source for Seddon; and he provides a case in point for the one-paragraph-reference book: Bruce's *Recollections* contains nothing of interest except about a page and a half on the personal life of Seddon—and yet it was a valuable page and a half.

For the war in the West, besides *Official Records* and the Davis references, I used mainly Horn's *Army of Tennessee,* Henry's *Story of the Confederacy* and *Forrest,* with some details from *Battles and Leaders.*

Much material on all phases was drawn from the *Southern Historical Society Papers*—especially on ordnance manufacture and the flight of the Confederate cabinet and its treasury—but these items have not been listed separately. The material on the Tredegar, and other Richmond manufacturing, was based almost entirely on a research study done for this book by Mrs. Dolores Lescure.

For the military in the East, I used *R. E. Lee* and *Lee's Lieutenants,* and Dr. Freeman personally gave invaluable information in general, and particularly on the spies in Richmond.

The Honorable Alexander Weddell offered suggestions on Richmond's manufacturing background, and the Virginia Historical Society, situated in General Lee's wartime residence, made all their facilities available—as did the Richmond Public Library and the Virginia State Library, where Miss Elizabeth Thomas was unfailingly helpful.

Bibliography

Adams, Henry. *The Education of Henry Adams*. Boston, 1918.

Agar, Herbert. *The People's Choice, From Washington to Harding: A Study in Democracy*. New York, 1933.

Alexander, E. P. *Military Memoirs of a Confederate*. New York, 1907.

Alfriend, Frank H. *The Life of Jefferson Davis*. Cincinnati, 1868.

Andrews, Eliza Frances. *War-Time Journal of a Georgia Girl*. New York, 1908.

Avary, Myrta Lockett, ed. *Recollections of Alexander H. Stephens*. New York, 1910.

Basso, Hamilton. *Beauregard, the Great Creole*. New York, 1933.

Battles and Leaders of the Civil War. 4 vols. New York, 1887.

Blackford, William Willis. *War Years with Jeb Stuart*. New York, 1945.

Blanton, Wyndham B. *Medicine in Virginia in the Nineteenth Century*. Richmond, 1933.

Boykin, E. M. *The Falling Flag: Evacuation of Richmond, Retreat and Surrender at Appomattox*. New York, 1874.

Bradbeer, William West. *Confederate and Southern State Currency*. Mount Vernon, N.Y., 1915.

Bradford, Gamaliel. *Confederate Portraits*. Boston, 1914.

　Wives. New York, 1925.

Bruce, Kathleen. *Virginia Iron Manufacture in the Slave Era*. New York, 1930.

Bruce, William Cabell. *Recollections*. Baltimore, 1931.

Bulloch, James D. *Secret Service of the Confederate States in Europe*. 2 vols. London, 1883.

Butler, Pierce. *Judah P. Benjamin*. Philadelphia, 1906.

Campbell, John A. *Reminiscences and Documents Relating to the Civil War during the Year 1865*. Baltimore, 1887.

Capers, Henry D. *Life and Times of C. G. Memminger*. Richmond, 1893.

Cash, W. J. *The Mind of the South*. New York, 1941.

Cavada, Frederick F. *Libby Life: Experiences of a Prisoner of War in Richmond, Va., 1863–64*. Philadelphia, 1865.

Chamberlayne, C. G., ed. *Ham Chamberlayne—Virginian*. Richmond, 1933.

BIBLIOGRAPHY

Chase, P. H. *Confederate States of America Paper Money*. Bala-Cynwyd, Pa., 1936.

Chesnut, Mary Boykin. *A Diary from Dixie*. New York, 1929.

Chimborazo General Hospital, C.S.A., Map of. *Virginia Medical Monthly*, March 1944.

Christian, W. Asbury. *Richmond, Her Past and Present*. Richmond, 1912.

Clay, Mrs. Clement C. *A Belle of the Fifties*. New York, 1905.

Corbin, Diana Fontaine Maury. *Life of Matthew Fontaine Maury*. London, 1888.

Craven, Avery Odelle. *The Coming of the Civil War*. New York, 1942.
Edmund Ruffin, Southerner: A Study in Secession. New York, 1932.

Curry, J. L. M. *Civil History of the Government of the Confederate States*. Richmond, 1901.

Daniel, Frederick S. *Richmond Howitzers in the War*. Richmond, 1891.

Davis, Jefferson. *The Rise and Fall of the Confederate Government*. 2 vols. New York, 1881.

Davis, Varina Howell. *Jefferson Davis, ex-President of the Confederacy: A Memoir by His Wife*. 2 vols. New York, 1890.

DeLeon, Thomas Cooper. *Belles, Beaux, and Brains of the Sixties*. New York, 1907.
Four Years in Rebel Capitals. Mobile, 1892.

Dictionary of American Biography. New York, 1928—

Dietz, August. *The Postal Service of the Confederate States of America*. Richmond, 1929.

Dixon, Thomas. *The Victim: A Romance of the Real Jefferson Davis*. New York, 1914.

Dodd, William E. *Jefferson Davis*. Philadelphia, 1907.

Douglas, Henry Kyd. *I Rode with Stonewall*. Chapel Hill, 1940.

Eckenrode, H. J. *Jefferson Davis, President of the South*. New York, 1923.

Eggleston, George Cary. *A Rebel's Recollections*. New York, 1875.

Foote, Henry Stuart. *Casket of Reminiscences*. Washington, 1874.
War of the Rebellion. New York, 1866.

Freeman, Douglas Southall. *Lee's Lieutenants*. 3 vols. New York, 1942–44.
R. E. Lee. 4 vols. New York, 1934–35.

Fuller, Claud E. and Richard D. Steuart. *Firearms of the Confederacy*. Huntington, W.Va., 1944.

Gildersleeve, John R. "History of Chimborazo Hospital, Richmond, Va., and Its Medical Officers during 1861–1865." *Virginia Medical Semi-Monthly*, July 8, 1904.

Grant, Ulysses S. *Personal Memoirs*. New York, 1885–86.

Grimes, Absalom C. *Absalom Grimes, Confederate Mail Runner*. New Haven, 1926.

Guedalla, Philip. *The Second Empire*. London, 1922.
The Two Marshals: Bazaine, Pétain. New York, 1943.

[437]

Hanna, A. J. *Flight into Oblivion*. Richmond, 1938.

Harris, William C. *Prison-Life in the Tobacco Warehouse at Richmond*. Philadelphia, 1862.

Harrison, Burton H. "The Capture of Jefferson Davis." *Century Magazine*, November 1883.

Harrison, Mrs. Burton H. *Recollections Grave and Gay*. New York, 1912.

Headley, John W. *Confederate Operations in Canada and New York*. New York, 1906.

Helper, Hinton Rowan. *The Impending Crisis of the South: How to Meet It*. New York, 1857.

Henderson, George F. R. *Stonewall Jackson and the American Civil War*. London, 1900.

Hendrick, Burton J. *Statesmen of the Lost Cause: Jefferson Davis and His Cabinet*. Boston, 1939.

Henry, Robert Selph. *"First With the Most" Forrest*. Indianapolis, 1944. *The Story of the Confederacy*. Indianapolis, 1931.

Hergesheimer, Joseph. *Swords and Roses*. New York, 1929.

Hesseltine, William Best. *Civil War Prisons: A Study in War Psychosis*. Columbus, O., 1930.

Hopley, Catherine C. *Life in the South: From the Commencement of the War*. London, 1863.

Horn, Stanley F. *The Army of Tennessee: A Military History*. Indianapolis, 1941.

Hume, Major Edgar Erskine. "Chimborazo Hospital, Confederate States Army, America's Largest Military Hospital." *Virginia Medical Monthly*, July 1934.

Huse, Caleb. *The Supplies for the Confederate Army*. Boston, 1904.

Jeffrey, William H. *Richmond Prisons 1861-2*. St. Johnsbury, Vt., 1893.

Jones, John B. *A Rebel War Clerk's Diary at the Confederate States Capital*. 2 vols. New York, 1935.

Journal of the Congress of the Confederate States of America. 7 vols. Washington, 1904-5.

Kern, M. Ethel Kelley. *The Trail of the Three-Notched Road*. Richmond, 1929.

Leech, Margaret. *Reveille in Washington, 1860-1865*. New York, 1941.

Little, John P. *History of Richmond*. Richmond, 1933.

Loehr, Charles T. *History of the First Virginia Regiment*. Richmond, 1884.

Lonn, Ella. *Desertion During the Civil War*. New York, 1928. *Foreigners in the Confederacy*. Chapel Hill, 1940. *Salt as a Factor in the Confederacy*. New York, 1933.

Lutz, Earle. *A Richmond Album*. Richmond, 1937.

MacDonald, Rose M. E. *Mrs. Robert E. Lee*. Boston, 1939.

Macon, T. J. *Reminiscences of the First Company of Richmond Howitzers.* Richmond.

Mason, Virginia. *The Public Life and the Diplomatic Correspondence of James M. Mason.* New York, 1906.

Maurice, Sir Frederick. *Statesmen and Soldiers of the Civil War: A Study of the Conduct of War.* Boston, 1926.

McCarthy, Carlton. *Detailed Minutiae of Soldier Life in the Army of Northern Virginia, 1861–1865.* Richmond, 1899.

McElroy, Robert. *Jefferson Davis: The Unreal and the Real.* 2 vols. New York, 1937.

McGuire, Judith W. *Diary of a Southern Refugee During the War.* Richmond, 1889.

Meade, Robert Douthat. *Judah P. Benjamin: Confederate Statesman.* New York, 1943.

Milton, George Fort. *Conflict: The American Civil War.* New York, 1941.

Moore, Albert Burton. *Conscription and Conflict in the Confederacy.* New York, 1924.

Moore, Mrs. M. B. *The Geographical Reader for the Dixie Children.* Raleigh, 1863.

Moran, Frank. "Colonel Rose's Tunnel at Libby." *Century Magazine,* March 1888.

Morgan, James Morris. *Recollections of a Rebel Reefer.* Boston, 1917.

Munford, Beverley B. *Virginia's Attitude Toward Slavery and Secession.* New York, 1911.

Munford, Robert Beverley. *Richmond Homes and Memories.* Richmond, 1936.

Official Records of the Union and Confederate Armies. Washington, 1880–1901.

Olmsted, Frederick Law. *Journey in the Back Country.* New York, 1860.

Owsley, Frank L. *King Cotton Diplomacy.* Chicago, 1931.

   States' Rights in the Confederacy. Chicago, 1925.

Parker, William Harwar. *Recollections of a Naval Officer, 1841–1865.* New York, 1883.

Patrick, Rembert W. *Jefferson Davis and His Cabinet.* Baton Rouge, 1944.

Pember, Phoebe Yates. *A Southern Woman's Story.* New York, 1879.

Pemberton, John C. *Pemberton, Defender of Vicksburg.* Chapel Hill, 1942.

Pendleton, Louis. *Alexander Stephens.* Philadelphia, 1908.

Phillips, Ulrich Bonnell. *Life and Labor in the Old South.* Boston, 1929.

Photographic History of the Civil War. 10 vols. New York, 1911.

Pickett, George E. *Soldier of the South . . . Pickett's War Letters to His Wife.* Boston, 1928.

Pickett, LaSalle Corbell. *Pickett and His Men.* Atlanta, 1899.

Pinkerton, Allan. *The Spy of the Rebellion.* New York, 1885.

Pollard, Edward A. *A Life of Jefferson Davis. With a Secret History of the Southern Confederacy.* Chicago, 1869.

 The Lost Cause: A New Southern History of the War of the Confederates. New York, 1866.

Potts, Frank. *The Death of the Confederacy.* Richmond, 1928.

Pryor, Mrs. Roger A. *Reminiscences of Peace and War.* New York, 1904.

Putnam, Sallie A. Brock. *Richmond during the War.* New York, 1867.

Randall, J. G. *Lincoln, the President.* 2 vols. New York, 1945.

Reagan, John H. *Memoirs, with Special Reference to Secession and the Civil War.* New York, 1906.

Richardson, James D., ed. *Messages and Papers of the Confederacy.* 2 vols. Nashville, 1906.

Richmond Directories.

Robinson, William Morrison, Jr. *The Confederate Privateers.* New Haven, 1928.

Roman, Alfred. *Military Operations of General Beauregard in the War between the States.* 2 vols. New York, 1884.

Rowland, Dunbar, ed. *Jefferson Davis, Constitutionalist, His Letters, Papers and Speeches.* 10 vols. Jackson, Miss., 1923.

Rowland, Eron. *Varina Howell: Wife of Jefferson Davis.* 2 vols. New York, 1931.

Russell, William Howard. *My Diary North and South.* 2 vols. London, 1863.

Scharf, J. T. *History of the Confederate States Navy.* New York, 1887.

Schlesinger, Arthur, Jr. *The Age of Jackson.* Boston, 1945.

Schwab, John C. *The Confederate States of America.* New York, 1901.

Scott, Mary Wingfield. *Houses of Old Richmond.* Richmond, 1941.

Sears, Louis Martin. *John Slidell.* Durham, N.C., 1925.

Seitz, Don. *Braxton Bragg, General of the Confederacy.* Columbia, S.C., 1924.

Semmes, Raphael. *Memoirs of Service Afloat during the War Between the States.* Baltimore, 1869.

Shanks, Henry T. *The Secession Movement in Virginia.* Richmond, 1934.

Sigaud, Louis A. *Belle Boyd, Confederate Spy.* Richmond, 1944.

Simkins, Francis Butler and James Welch Patton. *The Women of the Confederacy.* Richmond, 1936.

Simms, Henry H. *A Decade of Sectional Controversy 1851–1861.* Chapel Hill, 1942.

 Life of Robert M. T. Hunter. Richmond, 1935.

Small, Abner R. *The Road to Richmond.* Berkeley, Calif., 1939.

Southern Historical Society Papers. 49 vols. Richmond, 1876–1943.

Stanard, Mary Newton. *Richmond, Its People and Its Story.* Philadelphia, 1923.

Steele, Matthew F. *American Campaigns.* Washington, 1909.

Stephens, Alexander H. *A Constitutional View of the Late War Between the States.* Philadelphia, 1868–1870.

Stephenson, Nathaniel W. *The Day of the Confederacy.* New Haven, 1919.

Stovall, Pleasant A. *Robert Toombs, Statesman, Speaker, Soldier, Sage.* New York, 1892.

The Stranger's Guide and Official Directory of the City of Richmond. Richmond, 1863.

Stuart, J. E. B. *Letters of General J. E. B. Stuart to His Wife. 1861.* Atlanta, 1943.

Sturgis, Thomas. *Prisoners of War 1861–5.* New York, 1912.

Tate, Allen. *Jefferson Davis: His Rise and Fall.* New York, 1929.

Tatum, Georgia Lee. *Disloyalty in the Confederacy.* Chapel Hill, 1934.

Taylor, Richard. *Destruction and Reconstruction: Personal Experiences of the Late War.* New York, 1879.

Thomason, John W., Jr. *Jeb Stuart.* New York, 1934.

Thompson, Samuel B. *Confederate Purchasing Operations Abroad.* Chapel Hill, 1935.

Tilghman, Tench Francis. *The Confederate Baggage and Treasure Train Ends Its Flight in Florida.* Rollins College, Winter Park, Fla., 1939.

Trexler, Harrison A. *The Confederate Ironclad "Virginia" ("Merrimac")* Chicago, 1938.

Turner, Robert. *Recollections of the Secession Convention in Virginia.* Unpublished manuscript in the Virginia Historical Society, Richmond, Virginia.

Von Borcke, Heros. *My Memoirs of the Confederate War for Independence.* London, 1866.

Walthall, Ernest Taylor. *Hidden Things Brought to Light.* Richmond, 1933.

Weddell, Alexander Wilbourne. *Richmond, Virginia, in Old Prints. (1737–1887)* Richmond, 1932.

Weddell, Elizabeth Wright. *St. Paul's Church, Richmond, Virginia: Its Historic Years and Memorials.* 2 vols. Richmond, 1931.

White, E. V. *The First Iron-Clad Naval Engagement in the World . . .* Portsmouth, Va., 1906.

Wiley, B. I. *The Life of Johnny Reb.* Indianapolis, 1943.

Wilkinson, John. *The Narrative of a Blockade-Runner.* New York, 1877.

Willson, Beccles. *John Slidell and the Confederates in Paris.* New York, 1932.

Winston, Robert Watson. *High Stakes and Hair Trigger: The Life of Jefferson Davis.* New York, 1930.

Wise, John S. *The End of an Era.* Boston, 1927.

Worsham, John H. *One of Jackson's Foot Cavalry . . .* New York, 1912.

BIBLIOGRAPHY

Wright, Mrs. D. Giraud. *A Southern Girl in '61: War-Time Memories of a Confederate Senator's Daughter*. New York, 1905.

PERIODICALS

Harper's Illustrated Weekly. Richmond.
The *Magnolia Weekly*. Richmond.
The *Record*. Richmond.
The Richmond *Dispatch*.
The Richmond *Enquirer*.
The Richmond *Examiner*.
The Richmond *News Leader*. Bicentennial Supplement. September 8, 1937.
The *Southern Illustrated News*. Richmond.
The *Southern Literary Messenger*. Richmond.

Index

(Index by John Askling)

The
White House of the
Confederacy

LOUISVILLE

MISSOURI

KENTUC

Belmont

Columbus

Paducah

Mill Spring

Ft Henry

Ft Donelson

Nashville

Murfreesboro

TENNESSEE

ARKANSAS

Cha.

Little Rock

Memphis

Holly Springs   Corinth

Tupelo

MISSISSIPPI

Shreveport

Vicksburg

ALABAMA

Jackson

Montgomery

TEXAS

Natchez

Baton Rouge

Mobile   Pensacola

LOUISIANA

New Orleans

Galveston

GULF OF